"For decades, I have been responding to these 'seven core issues'
parent by adoption, as a poet. Now I imagine myself as a therapist trying to help someone
in the adoption constellation. I would definitely want this book close at hand."

—*Penny Callan Partridge, Co-founder in 1973,*
*Adoption Forum of Philadelphia*

"Even a cursory glance at the Table of Contents makes clear what we're in for: a beautifully-organized handbook, full of both strong, conceptual understandings and practical recommendations for living, surviving and thriving in this world of adoption.

The section on Mastery and Control is, all by itself, worth the price of admission. The many losses of control experienced by each and every member of the constellation are enumerated, but the authors don't stop there. We are then led, in plain language, to understanding not only the underlying reasons why such losses are profound, but what behaviors (the child attempting to over-control, for example) can then be expected and accepted.

The experience and maturity of the authors is revealed in chapter after chapter. The reader can FEEL it: these authors have walked this walk. They tell us what they've seen. I, for one, felt grateful.

What courage and clarity-of-purpose it must have taken for the authors to virtually begin this tome with a definitive—if not exhaustive—discussion of Loss. No punches are pulled. Without an acknowledgement that loss DOES lie right there, at the beginning of whatever process has led those in the constellation to wherever they are, now, we would be without understanding of all that then happens, and is going to continue happening, in one form or another, for decades to come. And then, page after page, the astounding varieties of the possible losses are actually spelled out. Absolutely marvelous."

—*Michael Trout, Director of The Infant-Parent Institute*

"As an adopted person, I'm very familiar with the seven core issues, both comprehensively and experientially. Yet even with my prior knowledge, there was a deeper understanding to be attained through the pages of this book. Having had the pleasure to work with and consider both Sharon and Allison my friends, I've seen first-hand the passion they have for adoption and helping children find permanence. Their collective expertise, contained here, is, in my opinion, the gold standard for understanding and working towards permanence in adoption."

—*Keith Silverstein, Voice Actor and Adoption Advocate*

"What do you get when two highly experienced, talented, thoughtful and respected adoption experts write a book together? The answer is this exceptional piece of work, which falls into the rare 'must-have', must-read and must-use' category of literature relating to all sorts of 'nontraditional' families. From my perspective as both an adoption professional and an adoptive parent, I couldn't recommend it more strongly."

—*Adam Pertman, President of the National Center on Adoption*
*and Permanency and author of* Adoption Nation

"This is a book that has been itching to be written for a very long time, as the framework of the Seven Core Issues has shaped thinking on adoption for the last three decades. Yet the benefit that this book was not written until now is that it is even more expansive. Rarely if ever have I read a book that covers so much ground so effectively. I have immense respect for the authors and their work. Roszia and Davis Maxon are critical thought leaders."

—*Betsie Norris, adoptee, Executive Director Adoption Network Cleveland: The Ohio Family Connection*

"This is a very comprehensive, inclusive, updated version of the *Seven Core Issues in Adoption and Permanency*, which is an amazing resource for families, agency professionals, clinicians, academics, consultants and many others impacted by adoption. The excellent contributing authors have had a variety of professional and personal experiences related to child welfare (i.e. as adoptees, foster youth, kinship care providers, and adoptive and foster parents), as well as having professional training and expertise in working with diverse population groups impacted by the child welfare system.

Not only does this book highlight the core issues of adoption and permanency, it is unique, as it includes specific chapters which focus on these issues for ethnically diverse families including Latinos, African Americans, Tribal communities, Asian and multi-racial families. The book includes content on the implications of the core issues in work with adoptive, kinship families, birth/first families, foster families, and LGBTQ families. It provides very real and practical examples of the impact of losses, vicarious trauma experienced by children and parents, while including content on strategies for coping and gaining resilience. I would highly recommend this book for use in courses on 'Contemporary Issues in Adoption and Foster Care', 'Child Welfare' and others which are designed to prepare professionals for work in this very important area."

—*Ruth G. McRoy, Ph.D Professor Emeritus Boston College School of Social Work*

# Seven Core Issues
# in Adoption and Permanency

*of related interest*

**The Science of Parenting Adopted Children**
A Brain-Based, Trauma-Informed Approach to Cultivating Your
Child's Social, Emotional and Moral Development
*Arleta James, LPCC*
ISBN 978 1 78592 753 9
eISBN 978 1 78450 572 1

**The A–Z of Therapeutic Parenting**
Strategies and Solutions
*Sarah Naish*
ISBN 978 1 78592 376 0
eISBN 978 1 78450 732 9

**Parenting in the Eye of the Storm**
The Adoptive Parent's Guide to Navigating the Teen Years
*Katie Naftzger*
*Foreword by Adam Pertman*
ISBN 978 1 78592 701 0
eISBN 978 1 78450 244 7

**Games and Activities for Attaching With Your Child**
*Deborah D. Gray and Megan Clarke*
ISBN 978 1 84905 795 0
eISBN 978 1 78450 152 5

**Keeping Your Adoptive Family Strong**
Strategies for Success
*Gregory C. Keck and L. Gianforte*
ISBN 978 1 84905 784 4
eISBN 978 1 78450 028 3

**Attachment, Trauma, and Healing**
Understanding and Treating Attachment Disorder in Children, Families and Adults
*Terry M. Levy and Michael Orlans*
ISBN 978 1 84905 888 9
eISBN 978 0 85700 597 7

# Seven Core Issues in Adoption and Permanency

A Comprehensive Guide to Promoting Understanding
and Healing in Adoption, Foster Care, Kinship
Families and Third Party Reproduction

**Sharon Kaplan Roszia** and **Allison Davis Maxon**

Foreword by Deborah N. Silverstein, MSW

Jessica Kingsley *Publishers*
Jessica Kingsley *Publishers*
London and Philadelphia

First published in 2019
by Jessica Kingsley Publishers
73 Collier Street
London N1 9BE, UK
and
400 Market Street, Suite 400
Philadelphia, PA 19106, USA

*www.jkp.com*

**Library of Congress Cataloging in Publication Data**
A CIP catalog record for this book is available from the Library of Congress

**British Library Cataloguing in Publication Data**
A CIP catalogue record for this book is available from the British Library

ISBN 978 1 78592 823 9
eISBN 978 1 78450 930 9

Printed and bound in the United States

# Contents

# Foreword
## Deborah N. Silverstein, MSW

Sometimes, maybe only once in a lifetime, we are lucky enough to meet someone who changes our world for the better. I call this a miracle, and it happened for me in 1978 when I heard Sharon (Kaplan) Roszia speak at an adoptive parent meeting. She said all the things I had been experiencing as a parent to three "special needs" children. At the same time, my husband, Stan, and I had been approached about adopting a 14-year-old boy. No social worker would consider that possibility since he would be older than all of our children. I approached Sharon. She would not only consider us, she was enthusiastic. That was it! The rest, as they say, really is history. As we learned to parent a troubled teen, Sharon and I developed a friendship, then camaraderie, and finally a partnership. What a ride it has been!

We began to advance our ideas about the core issues in 1980, giving voice to both our personal and professional experiences. I remember so well our first joint presentation at the North American Conference on Adoptable Children (NACAC) in Texas. I spoke in the role of the adoptive parent, and Sharon, the social worker. The audience response was immediate. We had struck a chord. Then, we sat at her dining table many days and nights honing the concept. Suddenly, we came to understand that what adoptive parents experienced, so did birth parents (and their families), adopted persons (young and old), and all others touched by adoption. Thus was born the concept of the Seven Core Issues in Adoption.

Sharon and I worked together in the subsequent years, discussing, refining, presenting our concept. We had some wild adventures traveling the country, meeting wonderful members of the constellation who shared their experiences, wisdom and courage. In the late 1990s, we were joined in our work by Allison Davis Maxon, who had been working in a nearby residential treatment facility. She brought a new perspective and her valuable experience. We taught families and professionals separately and together. We joined forces to work with a cadre of highly skilled clinicians to open a mental health center, utilizing the core issues as the framework for clinical interventions. Allison is a brilliant teacher who can make complex material accessible. She also knows how to have a really good time.

Regrettably, Sharon and I never sat down to engage in the toil of writing out the material. I retired, but Sharon and Allison have taken up the task and produced this glorious book, encapsulating almost 40 years of work. It has been my great joy to read their materials, to smile as I recognize some of the people in the vignettes, and to remember again why I loved this work so much.

# Acknowledgments

We are deeply indebted to Deborah Silverstein for her years of contribution to the field of social work and her co-authoring of the original *Seven Core Issues in Adoption*. We honor Deborah's wisdom, wit and compassion that is elucidated in her writing, practice and teaching.

For those individuals who are no longer with us, but have influenced us and the field greatly, we thank you for your life's work: Gayle Ward, Marri Rillera, Betty Jean Lifton, Annette Baran, Reuben Pannor, Barbara Tremitier.

*From Sharon Kaplan Roszia:* To my loving family and "framily" whose support in life keeps me realistic, hopeful, anchored, safe, balanced and joyful. I am truly blessed by each one of you!

Thank you to the clients who still seek me out and allow me to continue to serve in a field I love. It has been one of the true gifts of this career to have met so many wonderful people all over the world.

Thank you to my daughter Lori. Her travels through the world of adoption started in her childhood and continue today in her marriage and reunion with her sister Lisa. Lori's work ethic, enormous creativity, brilliant mind that questions, learns and shares insights, and her sense of humor are all treasured. Thank you for bringing such a bright and talented musician to the family; love you, John!

To Michelle, John, Larry, Amanda, Kevin, Toni and Ezra, I love you all so very much and am so proud to be part of a wonderful and growing family. To all my cousins who spent such precious time with me growing up in Cleveland and who continue to remain close, I am grateful.

Thank you to Mark, Jeff, Josh, Noah, Aliya, Chase, Aaron and Sarah who claimed me as an aunt. What a bonus in my life you have been. Thank you to Ben and Noreen for making me Mommy 1.5!

*From Allison Davis Maxon:* To my loving husband, children, family and friends, thank you for being my deepest source of nurturance, love and inspiration.

To the children and families whose lives I have been blessed to touch.

To my mentors who have so generously shared their love and wisdom: Dan McQuaid, Denise Daugherty, Deborah Silverstein, Sharon Kaplan Roszia, Carol Biddle and Carol Bishop.

To my many brain-crushes: Joseph Campbell, Virginia Satir, Carl Jung, Thich Nhat Hanh, John Bowlby, Robert Karen, Vera Fahlberg, Louis Cozolino, Bessel van der Kolk, Michael Trout, Dan Siegel, Brene Brown, Andrew Solomon, Sean Anders and Nadine Burke Harris.

*From Sharon and Allison:* To John Crye and Michelle Gardner of Beacon Street Collective for bringing the Seven Core Issues to YouTube—your generosity is immense.

To Janet and Erik Horwitz, whose generosity, love and support over the years have been beyond measure.

To Melissa, Tut, Alan, Barbara, Stan, Deborah, Lori and Penny Partridge, who were readers of the manuscript as it unfolded. Your feedback has been crucial.

To Kinship Center, which brought us together and captured the Seven Core Issues of Adoption in the curriculum of the ACT and Pathways to Permanence.

To Stephen Jones and the team at Jessica Kingsley Publishers, who welcomed us into the fold and guided us on the path to publication.

Allison and Sharon want to acknowledge Sharon's antique oak table on which the original Seven Core Issues in Adoption was written and on which the expanded Seven Core Issues in Adoption and Permanency was conceived and brought to fruition. This oak table (below) was the foundation for creativity, deep thought and partnership.

Sharon and Allison congratulate each other for dedicating a year of their lives to a collaboration that enriched their minds, creativity, love of the field and each other.

# Disclaimers

The authors acknowledge the following in relation to the content of the book:

- Constellation members have strong opinions about the language, words and phrases used to describe their role in adoption and permanency. It is impossible to use all the specific words that would please every individual.

- In the pursuit of acknowledging racial, ethnic and cultural communities we asked other contributors representing those communities to speak about the Seven Core Issues in Adoption and Permanency from those unique perspectives.

- Every individual's experience with adoption and permanency carries with it their own specific point of view. The authors have depended on their years of experience in working with thousands of constellation members to determine the most often expressed themes, challenges and deeply held thoughts and feelings. It is impossible to encompass every individual's unique perspective.

# Preface

It is crisis and/or trauma that create the circumstances that lead to adoption and permanency. For a long time, there has been an undoing and redoing of family systems and family trees. The crises of an unplanned pregnancy, rape, incest, poverty, addiction, divorce, mental illness, war or a country's crisis that results in refugees, natural disasters, epidemics and cultural biases leads to the displacement of children.

The Seven Core Issues in Adoption and Permanency, which include loss, rejection, shame/guilt, grief, identity, intimacy and mastery/control, are created through the disassembling and recreating of new families. Until humanity has addressed the larger issues generated by the oppression of poverty, prejudice towards the mentally ill, the impact of war and its creation of refugees, human trafficking and the diseases of addiction, these core issues will be experienced by the individuals touched by adoption and permanency. This book underscores that all alternative forms of family building begin with a crisis. In almost all cases, the individual in distress did not create the circumstances under which new families were formed. The addressing of these crisis issues and the impact they have on the lives of individuals and families intergenerationally begins with an examination of societal biases about what constitutes a family. The language in adoption and permanency has often been divisive, separating and shaming. Adoption and permanency language can be both negative and positive and has evolved. Language has the power to wound, separate, connect, label, define, shame and heal.

The authors propose that any time a person is parenting a child not genetically related to them or to whom they did not give birth, the Seven Core Issues in Adoption and Permanency are present. Adoption and some forms of permanency, such as guardianship, are both legal terms and descriptions of relationships. These connections may be formalized by law or through chosen, informal commitments. This would include kinship or guardianship parents who may not legally adopt; foster parents who are an arm of the child welfare system or others who are informally caring for a youth; placement of an infant or older child where parental ties have been severed and a legal connection to a new family is then put into place by the courts; step-parent adoption;

and third-party reproduction such as donor insemination, egg donation and surrogacy. These are all different forms of permanency.

The professional and community response to the disassembling and re-assembling of families may create additional problems. The building of families related to people's desire to parent because of infertility and/or some moral imperative, as well as a child's need for a family, has led to a practice that focuses on solving an immediate problem and often ignores the long-term impact on the individuals involved. No matter how the public may view adoption, foster care, kinship care, families of divorce, step-parenting or third-party reproduction, some type of crisis triggered the formation of the new family system. The long-term issues generated by these crises have been poorly understood and addressed. Historically, the professionals and other "helpers" have proceeded to assist with solutions without drawing on the wisdom of the people they were serving or the wisdom from those who were served in the past. An inclusive term for all of those individuals touched by adoption and permanency is "constellation member." Constellation members' experiences underscore how often their input about major life decisions was not solicited or was given and ignored. The lesson is: when you do something *for* me, *without* me, you're doing something *to* me.

The original framework of the Seven Core Issues in Adoption was created in the 1980s by Deborah Silverstein and Sharon Kaplan Roszia out of a shared concern about children forced to lose family connections in order to gain permanency. An additional concern was that constellation members were being viewed as having distinctly different emotional issues from one another. There was little acknowledgment of similar emotional experiences among adoptive families, birth/first families and adopted individuals. If Deborah and Sharon wanted constellation members to see each other as more alike and less distinct, they had to confront the destructive myths, biases, stereotypes and practices that supported those views.

Deborah and Sharon studied the literature, theorized, and interviewed hundreds of people impacted by adoption. They discovered that there was a set of specific emotions and tasks that all members of the adoption community experienced, regardless of their role. The framework of the Seven Core Issues, they postulated, starts with the fact that everyone touched by adoption must lose something significant before gaining anything. Loss begins the adoption journey. Loss triggers the core issues of rejection, shame/guilt, grief, identity, intimacy and mastery/control. The identification of the core issues became a normalizing and unifying concept for members of the adoption constellation. Birth/first parents and adoptive parents spoke about their experiences with similar words and phrases. Adopted people shared feelings of physical distress when thinking about their adoption experience. Sometimes the constellation members seemed to have the same emotional expressions on their faces, and many physically carried themselves in a self-protective posture, often with arms crossed over their mid-sections. In fact, if you did not know the specific role that a constellation member fulfilled, the emotional lives of adopted individuals, birth/first parents and adoptive parents were much more alike than different. This was an astounding and life-changing revelation.

The Seven Core Issues in Adoption concept has been used nationally and internationally as an educational tool for constellation members and professionals and as a therapeutic framework for understanding and normalizing the lifelong impact of adoption, as well as in assessment and treatment planning. It shifts the view of the adoption constellation members' emotional responses and behaviors away from pathology towards an adaptive and normative reaction to an abnormal life experience.

A colleague of ours heard about the Seven Core Issues in Adoption and Permanency and commented on what a negative concept it seemed. Our response was that we did not see them as negative; the acknowledgment of the core issues was necessary to address in order for individuals to become the hero or heroine of their own story. Our colleague thought about it and related it to the concept of "the shadow" written about by Carl Jung, the early 19th-century Swiss psychoanalyst. Jung described our conscious ego as being the surface part of our psychological being, the tip of the iceberg. A much larger part of the iceberg, or psyche, remains unconscious, filled with emotions resulting from one's life experiences which have had an unrecognized or repressed impact. "The shadow" has the power to strongly and unintentionally influence both our behavior and our relationships simply because it is unconscious. It is critical for the healthy development of the adult to process the shadow material by bringing it into consciousness and thereby allowing for an enriched life of self-knowledge. The next time we spoke to our colleague, she had shifted her opinion and realized the benefits of the hard work of exploring the core issues.

*Seven Core Issues in Adoption and Permanency* expands the use of the original framework which was focused exclusively on the adoption community. The authors of this book have experienced the seven core issues as impacting a broader community as family-building options have expanded.

In an effort to be more inclusive and to elucidate the specific points of view of the varied communities touched by the Seven Core Issues in Adoption and Permanency, the authors invited the expertise of additional professionals who wrote many of the chapters in Part 2. Each of these chapters will examine the Seven Core Issues in Adoption and Permanency through a specific lens. A new norm in defining what it means to be a family has occurred, with increased numbers of kinship families, adoption-built families, guardianship families, step-families, foster families, blended families, lesbian, gay, bisexual, transgender or queer (LGBTQ) families, multiracial families and single-parent families. The redefinition of family is underscored in the groundbreaking book *Adoption Nation*, where Adam Pertman makes the case that "America is forever changing adoption even as adoption is forever changing America" (Pertman 2011, p.5).

In order to expand the Seven Core Issues in Adoption and Permanency, the authors integrate information drawn from other professional fields such as the study of attachment and neuroscience, pre- and peri-natal psychology, child development, social work and research on developmental trauma.

In an effort to shift people's perspectives, the authors offer a new image that more accurately reflects permanency in today's world. When considering adoption in the past, a representation of a triangle, known as the "adoption triad," was common (see Figure P.1). This was a limited consideration of who was impacted by adoption. The authors propose the image of a triangle that places the Seven Core Issues in Adoption and Permanency, attachment and trauma as the three sides of the triangle, with constellation members in the interior (see Figure P.2). This image more accurately acknowledges the complex interplay between those three issues as well as the lifelong impact that they have on constellation members.

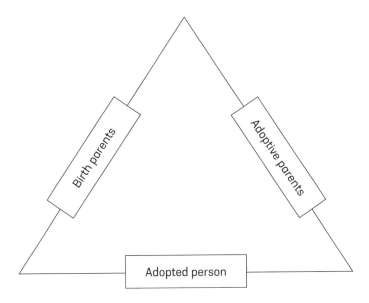

*Figure P.1: Adoption triad/triangle*

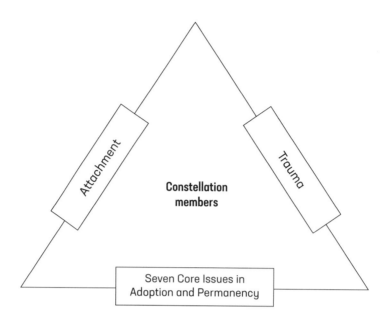

*Figure P.2: The impact of the Seven Core Issues in Adoption and Permanency, attachment and trauma on constellation members (Maxon and Roszia)*

The Seven Core Issues in Adoption and Permanency is the foundation of the triangle; for constellation members, adoption/permanency creates lifelong intergenerational tasks, opportunities and challenges.

Attachment is the second side of the triangle. Humans are social, emotional beings that are wired to attach in order to get their most basic needs met through human connectedness. Infants enter the world ready to attach to their caregivers in order to get all of their primary biological and dependency needs met through human interaction and stimulation. Early bonding and attachment experiences result in a cascade of biochemical processes that stimulate and enhance the growth and connectivity of neural networks throughout the brain (Schore 1994). Babies are touched, kissed, held, fed, comforted and rocked to sleep by their parents. They learn the touch, sights, smells, sounds and rhythms of their parents and are comforted by their proximity and distressed by separation. These early attachment experiences set the stage for future interpersonal skills and relationships.

Attachment theory teaches that every single attachment behavior must be learned; parents and caregivers must actively teach children how to attach. The primary parent–child attachment relationship helps the child maximize their physiological, emotional, social, cognitive and conscience development. Before the child has a separate identity, they are in a "we" state with their attachment caregivers and do not see themselves as being separate. Children become securely attached as they seek proximity to caregivers who remove their distress and increase their pleasure states. Childhood attachment experiences become encoded in sensory memory as children develop a *pattern of attaching* in order to get their most primary biological and emotional needs met. Parents have an *attachment pattern and style* that was experienced, learned and subsequently internalized from their caregivers, which is what the parents will be intuitively passing along to the child. Most of these attachment behaviors and patterns function outside conscious awareness. It is similar to learning how to dance with a partner. Once the dance is learned, people tend to move to a certain emotional rhythm in their interpersonal relationships.

To understand your own attachment dance, explore the following questions: What was the dance and the rhythm of your family? Was it a dance of love and connection? Was it a dance of pain and isolation? Do you welcome a dance partner? How close will you let them get to you? How do you invite others to dance? Do you move slowly, hearing a waltz, or quickly, hearing a swing? Is your dance complex or fairly basic? How comfortable are you with touch and movement? Can you take turns leading and following? Can you communicate your emotional needs? Can you adapt and learn new dance steps to meet the needs of another? Can you apologize for any missteps?

Exploring the above questions and acknowledging the learned attachment pattern will enhance and strengthen emotional intimacy. For the adults to provide a secure attachment relationship for each unique child, the adult must be emotionally available in order to attune to the needs of the child. No matter the risks or legal circumstances, it is imperative that children be claimed by caregivers the day the child arrives in a family to allow a child to feel safe, valued and connected.

Every constellation member has experienced the loss of a significant attachment. All attachment experiences have the potential for loss. All children who are being moved to a new family system have already suffered the loss of their original primary attachment relationships, even if placed at birth. Children who had a lonely experience in utero because their birth/first mother had trouble acknowledging their existence can be more prone to failure to thrive, distress and depression. Their new caregivers will have to work harder to engage, pleasure, soothe and comfort them. Birth/first mothers have had a nine-month relationship with the baby that grew inside them. For most, this was a deeply intimate and bonding experience that is broken when the baby leaves. This broken attachment is felt physically and emotionally for the baby and the mother. For birth/first mothers who were unable to emotionally attach to their child in utero for a variety of reasons, their denial, avoidance or trauma reactions may keep them from building healthy attachment relationships in the future.

Birth/first fathers have not had a biological experience with their child but may have had an emotional experience of growing attachment to their child during the pregnancy. The loss of the potential attachment relationship with the father's genetic offspring has often been minimized or not acknowledged.

Trauma is the third side of the triangle. Trauma is a deeply distressing or disturbing experience. All members of the constellation have experienced some kind of emotional trauma, and some will have experienced physical trauma as well, such as rape, abuse, domestic violence, incest or witnessing violence. As a result of trauma, many individuals experience toxic stress, which occurs when one lives in a chronically stressful environment. Toxic stress is when the body releases cortisol and other stress hormones which raise the heart rate and blood pressure and triggers a fight, flight or freeze response. Toxic stress has a negative impact on one's ability to physically grow, maintain positive physical health, learn and retain information, continue to emotionally develop, and create and sustain emotional attachments.

Although all constellation members may have experienced trauma, the most vulnerable constellation member is the displaced baby, child, teen and eventual adult. These individuals are the most significantly impacted as their early attachment experiences were disrupted. The separations may have occurred at a pre-verbal stage of development when the child had no way of understanding or giving language to the overwhelming feelings associated with losing their primary caregivers. The neuroscience research has shifted the focus to the vulnerable and malleable brain of the infant/child, who is often moved several times before permanency is gained. This creates toxic stress that impacts brain development. Separating a newborn baby, who has spent nine months in utero with their birth/first mother, creates trauma in their sensory system. Children enter foster care due to neglect, physical abuse, sexual abuse, domestic violence and in-utero drug exposure, and many of these children will suffer the effects of complex developmental trauma. The child brings this trauma into the kinship, foster or adoptive family. The way in which these families are prepared, trained and supported must reflect both the particular needs of each child/youth, as well as the uniqueness of each family receiving a child.

Our society has become more aware of the lingering effects of childhood trauma and toxic stress through a series of studies conducted by the Centers for Disease Control and Prevention and Kaiser Permanente (Felitti and Anda 1998). The studies concluded that adverse childhood experiences, such as physical abuse, sexual abuse, emotional abuse, physical neglect, emotional neglect, family violence, substance abuse, mental illness, parental separation, divorce or death, or an incarcerated parent, can disrupt a child's neurodevelopment and lead to the child or adolescent developing negative coping strategies such as substance abuse or self-harm. In addition, the cumulative and ongoing effects of chronic early exposure to toxic stress and trauma often lead to significant physiological, emotional, learning and behavioral problems. If the caregivers, or other children in the family, had previous trauma, it may resurface with the addition of a child with a trauma history.

The traumas of losing a child, infertility and adverse childhood experiences are intergenerational issues. Trauma can change one's genetic code. This change has been proven by following African Americans, Native Americans and Holocaust survivors intergenerationally and is referenced as "historical trauma." Trauma leaves its mark on cultures, world views and physical well-being.

It is imperative that everyone be trauma sensitive and informed when working with, or being a part of, a complex family system. All parties should be sensitive to the trauma being created for the child. At times, it may be crucial to engage the guidance of an adoption and permanency competent, trauma-informed and attachment family systems professional. Constellation members' lives have been impacted by some type of trauma related to adoption and permanency, which may subsequently create challenges in attachment and relationship building that are connected to the Seven Core Issues in Adoption and Permanency.

The authors of this book are anchored in a set of core values that guide their practice and teaching. These core values are the foundation on which the book was created. Chapter 9, "The Authors' Foundational Values and Beliefs," elaborates on these core values.

We feel strongly about the importance of using language that is respectful of all constellation members; we apologize to readers who find the term "adoptee" offensive or limiting. We have chosen the term "adoptee" for its brevity. We also acknowledge that being adopted is only a part of a person's story. We have chosen to use the descriptive term "birth/first parent" to remind people that birth/first parents are connected to the beginning of a child's life and never lose their role as the birth/first parents. Parents who did raise their children for a period of time, and the children who remember their lives in those families, refer to the term "first parents." When most people hear the term "birth parent" they assume the parent placed the child at birth or lost the child at birth. The expanded term "birth/first parent" includes those parents who did raise their children for a period of time and allows for a more flexible, accurate and descriptive term to be used by members of the constellation and the professionals who serve them. All constellation members are more than the labels assigned to them in adoption and permanency. Parents are parents: parents by adoption, parents by foster care, parents by birth, parents by kinship care. They are all equally real in a child's life. Children are children first and may also be children who were adopted, children who were/are in foster care or children in kinship care. When we use the terms "foster child" or "foster youth," that becomes a defining aspect of the child at the time they are developing their self-concept. Every time an adoptee introduces themselves as an adopted child, even when they're 60 years old, they are diminishing all of the other aspects of themselves.

The focus of the book expands the seven core issues to include all forms of permanency family building; addresses the emotional journey of all those individuals who have experienced the reformation of their family; underscores the importance of constellation members' voices and the similarities of their experiences; and offers practical tools to address and ameliorate the core issues in order to create a stronger and more empathetic community.

The Seven Core Issues diagram can be downloaded at www.jkp.com/catalogue/book/9781785928239

# ◉ Part 1 ◉

# Conceptual Framework

# Chapter 1

# Introduction to the Seven Core Issues

The Seven Core Issues in Adoption and Permanency—loss, rejection, shame/guilt, grief, identity, intimacy and mastery/control—are lifelong and intergenerational in scope. The concept addresses the truth in adoption and permanency, both the pain and the gain. It is used to normalize issues and feelings and give words to emotions that are experienced as bittersweet. The core issues are present in all forms of permanency, including infant adoptions, older child adoptions, kinship or guardianship families, foster families, step-families, third-party reproduction and in both open and closed adoptions. The presence of these issues does not indicate, however, that either the individual or the institution of adoption/permanency is pathological. Rather, these are additional and expected issues that evolve logically out of the nature of adoption and permanency. These issues create dynamics in people's and family's lives that must be acknowledged and addressed in order for healthy authentic relationships to unfold.

Clearly, the specific experiences of people tied to these forms of family building vary, but there is a commonality of affective experiences which persist throughout the individual's or family's lifecycle development. The intensity of the reactions of constellation members depends on many variables. These variables might include temperament, level of resilience, gender, age, cognitive and language ability, mental, intellectual or physical disabilities or other challenges. They also may include genetic factors that impact personality type, which might include one's motivational system, level of curiosity and sensory sensitivity. Other variables include: trauma—the duration, intensity and developmental stage when the trauma or neglect occurred; the types of trauma which can impact cognitive, verbal and emotional development and skills; multiple primary attachment disruptions, whether the trauma was experienced in isolation or with others such as siblings, family or friends; acknowledgment of the crisis or trauma by the individual's familial and community supports; the ability to seek and make use of supportive services; and the emotional availability of the people supporting the individual in crisis or trauma over time.

---

The following story shows the impact and interplay of attachment, trauma and the core issues on constellation members whose lives were intertwined and affected each other. A mother struggling with alcoholism and poverty had her two young children, aged 3 and 1, removed by the court. The children were placed with a couple who had struggled with infertility and had never parented previously and whose goal was to adopt. They received training, education and support, which they also shared with their extended family and close friends. The children arrived into the foster/adopted family after experiencing neglect and abuse. For several months, the children suffered with night terrors, feeding issues and physical ailments and were exhibiting violent outbursts with each other and their new parents. After six months, the children began to feel safe and secure as their new parents met their needs and their attachments to their new family deepened. The extended family became an integral part of the children's lives. Visitation was occurring with their mother as they were "dropped off" at a social worker's office for a one-hour visit twice a month. Each time the foster parents were asked to wait in their car. The children returned after each visit very distressed and upset.

A year into the foster placement, the birth mother became pregnant and enrolled in a rehabilitation program. The foster parents, in an effort to support the mother who might possibly be parenting three children soon, reached out to her, thinking they could be helpful since they had been parenting two of her children for over a year. The mother declined their offer, thinking that she did not need their help. As the foster placement entered the second year and the mother gave birth to her third child, the courts extended the time to allow the mother to continue to work towards reunification. She moved into a special program where she could live with all three of her children while getting the support she needed to maintain her sobriety. Because neither the judge, the attorneys, the rehabilitation staff, the mother nor social workers had an understanding of the impact of trauma, broken attachments and the core issues, the children were removed abruptly from the foster family after two-and-a-half years. The mother was discouraged from accepting a photo album, toys and favorite stuffed animals from the foster family. The foster family was told that this was "in the best interests" of the children and that they would have no further contact. The extended family never had the opportunity to say goodbye to the children. Two weeks later, the foster family's social worker shared with the parents that the oldest of the two children had reported to the mother's social worker that she and her younger sibling were again being abused. The staff at the rehabilitation center dismissed the claims as a child's attempt to return to the foster family.

If all the professionals involved with this actual case had had the proper understanding of the core issues, attachment and trauma presented in this book, several outcomes would change. The mother of the children could have had ongoing support from the foster parents, the children's trauma would be diminished as they would have retained all of their connections, the foster family's attachment to the children would have continued while they supported reunification, and the agency would have retained the foster family, who ultimately were devastated by the experience.

It has been a part of our culture's narrative to put a positive spin on adoption and permanency in order to emphasize the gains. First and foremost, society came to view adoption and permanency as a single, simple, problem-solving event, where people benefited. Parents who are unable to parent the children they bring into the world, prospective parents who are challenged with infertility or those who choose to make room in their families for additional children, and children who lack permanency, all have additional needs to address as a result of adoption and permanency. Many people see these placements as a single event that affects one generation. The examination of deep emotions is often avoided in our current culture and people are encouraged to just "move on" and "get over it." Pop psychology teaches individuals to "live in the present" and "stay positive." Adoption and permanency leads to emotions and tasks most would prefer to avoid. It takes time, resilience and support to be able to address the losses and attendant core issues that follow. In the authors' experience, if individuals do not take the time to address these issues, they may become detached and walled-off from aspects of themselves, limiting emotional, intellectual, developmental and spiritual growth.

The majority of people were not raised in a family where adoption, foster care or kinship care were the norm. Few people imagine that they will be infertile, lose a child, or grow up in another family. People generally have a vision for how they want their lives to unfold over time and come to believe that is the way it is supposed to be. This does not occur for members of the constellation.

Individuals have normative developmental tasks to address as children, adolescents, adults, parents and grandparents. Being a part of the adoption and permanency community adds additional complex tasks as an overlay to each of these stages of development. For some people touched by adoption and permanency, the number of tasks gets larger if they occupy more than one role simultaneously; for instance, an adoptive parent who is also an adopted person; a birth parent who is also an adoptive parent; a grandparent who is both a parent and a grandparent to the same child; a foster parent who becomes the child's adoptive parent; and/or an adoptee who becomes an adoptive parent.

The Seven Core Issues in Adoption and Permanency describes both a *structure* and a *process* through which a person can more fully understand a path through adoption and permanency. The seven core issues *structure* is that of a wagon wheel which moves individuals along in their life. The hub of the wheel is the center and represents the core issue of loss. Loss begins the journey. It requires an acknowledgment that everyone lost something significant as a part of adoption and permanency. The sequential core issues are like the spokes of the wagon wheel and include in this order: rejection, shame/guilt, grief, identity, intimacy, mastery/control. Each spoke leads to the next. The spokes connect to the outer wheel, which connotes forward movement. Occasionally, the wheel hits a rut, gets stuck or breaks, and forward motion stops.

The Seven Core Issues in Adoption and Permanency is also a *process*. Identifying the original and subsequent losses in one's life allows an individual to bring the core issues into consciousness. The losses in adoption and permanency are profound. They include original losses, secondary losses, ambiguous losses and vicarious losses. Some are losses that all constellation members share, while others are experienced by individual constellation members depending on their roles.

Loss creates feelings or fear of rejection. It is the first spoke in the wheel. When a person has suffered a life-altering loss, they tend to personalize the loss as a way to understand what happened and how to stop it from occurring again. It sets up the dynamic of fearing rejection or feeling personally rejected.

Feelings of rejection lead to the second spoke on the wheel, shame and guilt. If a person has felt rejected by another person, a whole country, a culture, a race, a family, God and their body, shame and guilt impact on their core beliefs about themselves. Shame and guilt are different. Shame can begin before birth, can embed in the body in early childhood and may continue to impact a person for the rest of their life. Shame may not have words; it goes to the heart of *who* you are, to your very being. Guilt is a behavior, something you did. It requires the development of a conscience, which is based on attachment and learned empathy. Rejection, shame and guilt impact on self-esteem.

If an individual has acknowledged their losses, experienced rejection, shame and guilt, they then can move into the hard work of grief, the third spoke of the wheel. Grief is the gateway to healing. It takes time, emotion and support and is physical, spiritual and emotional. It encompasses a variety of emotions such as numbness, depression, sadness, relief, anxiety, anger and exhaustion. Over the developmental life of a child, loss and grief will be revisited as a deeper understanding of what happened to them unfolds.

When an individual has acknowledged and processed their grief, they are able to move onto the last three core issues. The fourth spoke in the wheel is identity. For all members of the constellation the key question becomes "Who am I?" or "Who am I really?" Identity is both who we are and who we are not. Self-identity is the sum of our knowledge and understanding of ourselves, a collection of beliefs about ourselves. Identity is about where we come from, how we are presently seen by others, what we believe about ourselves and what we think we can become. Where information about one's genetic, early life and/or familial history is missing, this task becomes more complex. By changing roles on a family tree or by changing family trees, major identity shifts have occurred.

A strong self-identity allows people to enter into healthy relationships with others. Intimacy is the fifth spoke of the wheel. It allows for attachment, trust and joy to come together in deep, meaningful, sustainable relationships. Intimacy requires both a knowing of oneself and the ability to read and respond to the needs and cues of the other. Without a strong self-identity, intimate relationships may feel unsatisfying, chaotic or superficial. Without the ability to understand, articulate and value their own needs, a person may feel disconnected, isolated and depressed.

When constellation members acknowledge their losses, their feelings or fear of rejection and their feelings of shame and guilt, process their grief and explore self-identity which allows for strengthened emotional intimacy, they can then address the last core issue of mastery and control. Mastery and control is the sixth and final spoke of the wheel and represents the gains in adoption and permanency. If an individual does not do the work of addressing the core issues, the result can be lifelong themes of fighting for power and control. An ongoing sense of victimization can permeate one's life and decision making, leading to self-destructive behaviors, helplessness and ongoing anger and depression. If a person masters the core issues, the gains include a strong sense of self, deep joyful relationships and increased self-awareness. For many, a deep spiritual connection and a sense of inner peace, calm and satisfaction can also be found.

Subsequent losses, that may or may not have anything to do with the core losses in adoption and permanency, can spin a person back on the wheel of the core issues again. If one gains mastery, the cycle through the Seven Core Issues wheel allows for an understanding of the new loss, what triggered it and how best to regain power and strengthen resiliency.

Part 1 will explore the core issues in depth and offer techniques and tools to address them. Part 2 explores the core issues through the eyes of very specific members of the adoption and permanency community.

# Chapter 2

# Loss

Loss begins the lifelong, intergenerational
journey in adoption and permanency.

Loss begins the lifelong, intergenerational journey in adoption and permanency.

Adoptive, foster and kinship families are created through loss. All adoption and permanency constellation members share in having experienced at least one major, life-altering loss. Loss is the beginning out of which the additional core issues flow.

This core/original loss is experienced as a traumatic event that strikes at the center of a person's being. It alters their experience of themselves and their world. It transposes people from one location in the human mosaic to a totally new place. It changes the trajectory of their life, and the long-term ramifications cannot be fully understood at the time the loss occurs.

Full understanding and acknowledgment of the core loss unfolds through different developmental phases in life. These life-altering core losses affect every developmental stage of the individual and their family's systems over time. Some losses are concrete, such as the loss of things, people, relationships or roles. Others are abstract, such as fantasy parents, fantasy children or a fantasy family. Subsequent sub-losses that may retrigger the original traumatic experience are more subtle and gradual and tend to surprise people. These are the losses that are highlighted in day-to-day interactions as people are living their lives. They can be triggered by a question, a picture, an event, a dream, a nightmare, an anniversary, a birthday, a season, an item, a movie, a commercial or even a look. They can include events that trigger a sensory memory such as a smell, a touch, a sound or a feeling. The feelings triggered might include sadness, fear, anxiety, confusion, anger, disorientation, rejection, abandonment or helplessness.

> Sharon and her family were at a pizza parlor when she noticed that her son was looking around the room, staring at the wallpaper with a very sad look on his face. When asked what he was looking at, he started to sob and said it was the same wallpaper that was on his grandmother's dining room walls and how much he missed her. He asked to never go back to the restaurant.

The original core loss can change people's perspectives, attitudes, beliefs and values through which they navigate their world and relationships. It can affect the choices they make around career, partnership, child bearing, parenting and friends. The core losses that are attached to adoption and permanency are in addition to the normative losses that occur for all individuals; everyone experiences losses as they move from one developmental phase to another, and as they age and become more self-aware or more fragile and vulnerable.

The losses in adoption and permanency and the role that they play have largely been ignored. The initial core loss also creates subsequent losses that have a cumulative effect on the individual constellation member. Loss in adoption and permanency is not a single occurrence.

## Ambiguous loss

So much of what happens in adoption and permanency is ambiguous. Ambiguous loss is an injury that occurs without closure. This type of loss leaves a person searching for answers and thus complicates and delays the process of grieving. It is akin to a person missing in war or kidnapped, where the family is uncertain about what happened to that individual. For instance, adoptees have lost a whole family, but there are no bodies to bury, no grave to visit, no rituals to commemorate the loss. In addition, what makes this difficult is that this loss is not recognized by the larger society.

For the birth/first parent who lost a child to another family, ambiguous loss is the ongoing hope that the child is alive, well and happy, along with the ongoing experience of the loss of the parenting role.

For the foster/adoptive parent, the ambiguous loss is connected to celebrating the child that you are parenting, but missing the child you would have birthed. For parents who are loving and caring for a child in foster care but missed the opportunity of parenting a non-traumatized child, or the chance to intervene earlier in the child's life, ambiguous loss is present. An ambiguous loss for an adoptee could be loving their adoptive family and the life they provide, but missing the family of origin and a chance to grow up with them. If a person who is adopted does not know if their first/birth parents are dead or alive, they typically struggle with ambiguous loss around birthdays, Mother's Day, Father's Day and other holidays. Even in an open adoption, all parties are mourning the loss of the role but not the loss of a person, which creates ambiguity.

> "I remember feeling angry all the time when I was a teenager. I had all of these questions in my mind about what happened, why it happened, where they were now and did they think about me, but I didn't have anyone that I could talk to. It was clear that talking about adoption or my birth family was upsetting to my parents. I felt like it was my right to know, it happened to me! Looking back, I think my adoption losses hit me the hardest when I was a teenager. I know now that I was feeling the loss and pain pretty deeply, but for some strange reason, I felt guilty, like this was a long time ago, why am I feeling this way now?" (Adult adoptee)

Ambiguous loss often drives individuals to create an internal narrative in order to understand and cope with their fantasies or fears. This internal narrative may contain "ghost relationships" created from remnants of information or experiences. Ambiguous losses are difficult for individuals to identify and address. It is important to note that children and teens may be creating an internal narrative based on their core and ambiguous losses and not grounded in the facts of their story. The amount of time an individual is consumed with their fantasy or internal narrative, and their constant vigilance in scanning their environment, yearning for a match to their fantasy, may create social anxiety, boundary issues and anxious attachments.

## Vicarious loss

Vicarious losses are traumatic memories and experiences that are embedded into one's senses and are outside explicit, conscious memory. This causes them to be easily retriggered in times of distress. Children who arrive with these traumatic sensory memories from their history "unpack" their trauma into their new family. As the new family is attaching and claiming the new child, the child's distress may be easily "caught" by family members, because emotions are contagious. As new parents absorb the pain of the child, they "catch" the trauma, and a healthy environment can turn into a stressful place. Other children in the home can "catch it" as well. The entire family may feel stressed, frustrated and angry without understanding why.

For example, a child moves into a new home, with new smells, sounds, tastes and routines. This new environment triggers what seem to be illogical behaviors such as screaming, not sleeping, physical aggression, hoarding, lying, stealing, and an inability to receive affection. The new family, struggling to understand these behaviors, becomes triggered themselves and, in response, may react with escalated behaviors such as screaming, punishing, rejecting and isolating. The parents are now experiencing vicarious trauma brought into the family by the child.

Another example of vicarious trauma occurs when a man or woman who previously lost a child to adoption is now parenting another child and becomes easily triggered or emotionally reactive. Their traumatic loss may cause them to be overprotective, fearful, rejecting and/or punishing to the child. They may transfer the unacknowledged or unresolved emotions from those losses to a subsequent child.

Many parents are already carrying losses from their own childhood that may be outside their conscious awareness, such as previous trauma, having a mentally ill parent, a parent who was addicted to alcohol or drugs, or having experienced physical abuse, neglect, abandonment, sexual abuse or emotional abuse. These can become indirect trauma triggers that are not evident until a person finds themselves within the emotional intimacy and demands of the parent–child attachment relationship.

Adoptive parents who have lost children through infertility; foster parents who are firmly attached to a child who is returned to the family of origin; and kinship parents whose extended family were impacted by addiction and mental illness have suffered traumatic loss that may be encoded and stored outside of conscious awareness and may be easily triggered by the new emotional demands placed on them by their trauma-reactive child. All of these vicarious traumas are intergenerational patterns that are inherited without conscious intent or awareness and can impact every aspect of one's interpersonal skills and relationships.

## Secondary loss

Secondary losses spring from the original core losses. They are the losses that are rooted in our day-to-day lives that bring back the original memory of the traumatic loss. Secondary losses often catch us unaware as they can be triggered by sensory memories. A birth/first mother who sees a 5-year-old child in the park may find herself grieving the lack of contact with her now 5-year-old child. A birth/first father may wish he had his son with him on Father's Day. Every time an adoptive parent is filling out a medical history at the pediatrician's office, they are reminded that they cannot provide complete information. An adoptee who is asked why they were adopted may be taken back to their original core loss. When a child who spent his first few years with his birth/first mother is walking through a department store and smells the perfume his birth/first mother wore, his original core loss may resurface. The effect of never knowing when a secondary loss will occur, and the fact that they never end, creates a lifelong challenge. An acknowledgment of the original loss and an accumulation of insights about how and when secondary losses surface may diminish the negative effects of secondary loss. Over time, people gain resilience as they develop coping strategies that they can use when secondary losses surface.

> "I get so tired of everyone asking me questions about why I was adopted. I told one of my friends at school that I was adopted, not thinking that it was a big deal, but then once everyone found out, all the questions started. Where are your real parents? Why didn't they want you? Do you wish you lived with them? Is that your real brother? Sometimes I just don't want to think about it. So now I just tell them I don't wanna talk about it." (Teen adoptee)

Denial of losses, and of other constellation members' losses, is at the root of many problems associated with adoption and permanency. If society views adoption and permanency as problem-solving events, with no ongoing impact on constellation members' lives, the pain of these unaddressed losses grows. Losses need to be brought into conscious awareness and acknowledged and validated by others. The cultural mythology and expectations for gratitude and joy that are put on all members of the constellation may inhibit the true expression of these losses. If there is no recognition of the losses, people remain in pain and susceptible to limiting their potential and their relationships. In order to live with the unaddressed losses, people may become emotionally numb to avoid the painful feelings and could even resort to self-medicating or other self-destructive behaviors. Healing requires both acknowledging and confronting these core life-altering losses.

Loss is experienced as a negative, and the current adoption and permanency narrative strives to focus on positive outcomes. However, adoption and permanency is full of paradoxes in that while adoption and permanency addresses real needs it also creates real losses. The losses are not only experienced by the individuals that are a party to the adoption but extend to their families, friends, neighbors and whole community.

Many of the losses reverberate across the constellation because family is typically defined by genetic links or a "blood bond." Our traditional view of family is based on two parents creating a child, each sharing 50 percent of the genetic make-up. Other forms of family building (step, single, adoptive, gay/lesbian, kin, foster, guardianship) may be viewed as "less real" or "less valid" when society mandates genetics as what defines a real family. This leaves adoptive and permanency built families, children and adults having to justify their legitimacy. For instance, the word "parent" is powerful in all cultures. All parents are "real" if they are in the act of parenting, whether they are biological, birth/first/original, guardianship/kin, foster, step-parents or adoptive parents. It is possible to have several different parents, some of whom are connected genetically, some through the law, some by the daily care that those parents provide. Parenting roles can be described as genetic parents, legal parents and "parenting parents," all of whom play a significant role in a child's life. Until society validates all these forms of parenting, we diminish people's significance in other people's lives.

Loss is always a part of constellation members' lives; the losses are never totally forgotten and continue to accumulate. They remain in either conscious awareness or are pushed into the unconscious, only to be reawakened by another loss, or at a later stage of development.

The symptoms of loss manifest within our bodies, minds and hearts. They are experienced physiologically, emotionally, spiritually and psychologically. Symptoms of loss include:

- feeling stuck, weighted down, or shut down emotionally

- ongoing anxiety

- depression, sadness and tears

- being fearful

- feeling emotionally numb, flat, with little interest in anything pleasurable

- physical exhaustion

- feeling emotionally reactive; angry, agitated, short-fused

- using poor self-care

- feeling isolated

- misplacing or losing items

- engaging in extremes of behavior, such as not eating or overeating and not sleeping or sleeping too much

- perseverating over the same issues again and again; telling the same stories over and over

- slowing of development; physically, emotionally, intellectually and socially

- confusion and emotional distress for children who have experienced overwhelming or chronic losses at early stages of development

- distress and behavioral acting out for adolescents. This may surface as self-destructive behaviors such as self-medicating with drugs or alcohol, acting out sexually, depression and isolative behaviors, complaining of physical ailments, inability to complete tasks, engaging in high-risk behaviors such as speeding, stealing, assaulting, bullying or cutting, early pregnancy, running away, dropping out of school, not allowing themselves to succeed at any task or putting themselves in harm's way with a poor choice of peers.

## Impact of loss on all constellation members

Loss began the journey for all members of the constellation and is the unifying issue that binds them together. Men and women come to adoption and permanency with the life-altering losses of a crisis pregnancy, an inability to parent the children they brought into the world, a failure of a family member to parent, societal needs in response to war, oppression or poverty, and genetic risk. A healthy response to the shared losses would be the ability to come together and help support each other's healing. Instead, the tendency is to discuss whose losses are greater than others'. This is destructive and hurtful.

The following material includes several pages of bulleted losses that may feel overwhelming or perhaps validating. Since the public at large tends to dismiss or minimize the losses of constellation members, it became imperative to include the voices of all of the parties who have shared their stories of loss with the authors. It is difficult to ignore the enormity of the list. In the process of accumulating the collective experiences of constellation members, the authors acknowledge in advance that there may be some losses that are not included, not because they are not important, but because there are an infinite number of personal losses that each individual constellation member has experienced.

All constellation members may be at risk of losing:

- a family member

- their original role—perhaps a child would have been the oldest and is now the youngest or the only child; a person who was a parent is now not; a person who was infertile is now a parent; a person who was a grandparent is now a parent

- power—control is in the hands of the court system as judges, social workers, police officers and lawyers are in charge of the outcomes of constellation members' lives

- experiences and relationships with others from whom they are separated

- certainty that life will unfold in a predictable manner. The image of their life trajectory was undermined, changed and/or thwarted

- naivety, as bad things do happen to people

Sharon's daughter by birth was 6 when Sharon and her husband decided to expand their family through the adoption of a set of toddlers. They were preparing their daughter for the toddlers' first visit. Her daughter asked why the children needed a new family. She was a safe and loved child, claimed by a large extended family that included all four great-grandparents, two sets of grandparents and aunts and uncles, with whom she was close. When Sharon and her husband explained that the toddlers' mother had died and their father was not in their lives, she asked where their grandparents, aunts and uncles were. With each question her voice rose to a higher pitch and she became more upset. The news had rocked her world. She couldn't believe that no one from their family would come forward to parent them, and she never thought that could happen to children. She was robbed of her naivety.

- time—emotional and mental energy is diverted to addressing the crisis, then the losses, then the additional core issues
- the right to live their own truth, as all members of the constellation are asked to pretend or act "as if." Adoptive parents act "as if" their child came to them by birth, birth/first parents must act "as if" their child does not exist, adoptees must act "as if" the birth/first family is not important to them
- space in their mind as they daydream, worry and fantasize about the lost connection to relatives
- pleasant holidays and happy birthdays that can be fraught with emotional landmines. These special occasions may become associated with who or what is missing
- cultural standing when we cannot "be fruitful and multiply"; when we cannot achieve our cultural expectation of baring and parenting children
- vital physical, mental health, genetic and historical information
- societal status and being a part of the norm
- the opportunity to make mistakes like all other humans—they may feel judged by family members, the courts, social workers and community members for the choices that they made
- the opportunity to be seen as who they really are when the stereotypes from culture and media label them with certain words or phrases. For example, birth/first parents may be labeled losers and addicts; foster parents may be seen as "in it for the money" and child stealers; adoptive parents may be viewed as infertile and needy; adoptees may

be labeled as being lucky or ungrateful; children in foster care may be labeled as damaged and unattached

- the person they would or could have been—taking "the road less traveled"

- certainty when changes in law, public opinion and allocation of resources affect them as individuals and family members

- their basic belief system, religious underpinning, faith or acceptance in their faith or another's faith. Religious ideology and spiritual beliefs can have a dramatic impact as children are moved from and between family trees. For instance, when a child in foster care has parents who are deeply religious and are practicing their faith and the child subsequently moves into an adoptive family that is secular or of a different faith, the child experiences loss

- privacy. This major loss of privacy leaves constellation members wondering who knows what about them. All parties suffer the loss of privacy as the many documents that are generated—for family assessments (home studies), court reports, prospective family/child matches, birth/first parent histories, police reports, progress notes, child development screenings, medical records, child histories in foster care and school records—are read by a large number of individuals. For children, the recognition that so many outsiders know the intimate details of their personal life experiences, like physical or sexual abuse, before they know those details, can feel intrusive and demeaning

- internal power. At the time of the crisis, others may have intervened and taken the power of choice from the person in crisis. Children have no real choice in the matter as they are moved from one family tree or branch to another.

The recognition and naming of these similar affective experiences of loss encourages dialogue among the adoption and permanency constellation. It diminishes people's sense of isolation and normalizes the reaction to the core losses. Clearly, the specific experiences of the constellation members vary, but there is a commonality of loss that unifies the constellation experience.

## Birth/first parent loss

There may be no greater loss than the loss of a child. The biological bond between mother and child is a unique and powerful connection that cannot be replicated. The attachment between a birth/first father and his child is unique in that he will always be the only genetic father; this father contributed 50 percent of the genetic make-up of his child. No one grows up imagining that they will conceive and give birth to a child that they will not be able to raise.

The initial loss for many birth/first parents is access to a well-informed, caring, non-biased advocate who is not connected to the outcome of their decision. All birth/first mothers and birth/first fathers who are either considering relinquishment of a child or involved with the child welfare system would benefit from having an unbiased advocate to assist them in knowing their rights and exploring their best options. Voluntary relinquishment birth/first mothers are often asked to sign a relinquishment soon after delivery while still sedated or while their decision-making capacity is affected by birthing hormones, pain and the crisis of giving birth. This is another area where an advocate would be useful. All birth/first parents should be offered proper unbiased counseling and ongoing post-placement support.

The birth/first mother may lose:

- the chance to make a "true" choice for placing or parenting a child if not given unbiased counseling and support

- the future with her offspring as a baby, a toddler, a young child, a teenager and an adult

- trust in herself and others

- the joyous experiences of pregnancy, labor and birth—these are now associated with crisis, pain, shame, loss and sadness

- the mother she fantasized she would always become

- the comfort of the baby in her belly—she may experience empty arms and full breasts

- the smells and sounds of her baby

- their status, as she is seen differently in her family and community

- the recognition from the world and her own family that she is the mother, even if she is not raising the child

- access to her emotions as she experiences a numbness to protect herself; she becomes numb as she is encouraged to return to her life as if nothing occurred

- her belief system and/or faith

- time out of her life because of the crisis

- the title and role as the only "mother" when there is an adoptive mother or multiple foster mothers as well

- her body image—as she knew how her body looked, felt and responded before the pregnancy

- self-esteem—what kind of mother "gives her baby up" or "loses her baby because of addiction/poverty/abuse/mental illness"?

- the opportunity to name her child. Naming is a claiming behavior and identifies the child as a part of a family or clan

- all the "firsts"—first step, first word, first tooth, first day of school, first date and so on

- power—due to incest, rape and/or coercion

- her children being raised together

- her child growing up and knowing her "family tree"; there will be no relationships built with grandparents, aunts, uncles, cousins or siblings. The child will have no experience of her family culture, history, rituals, values, religion, ethnicity or race

- support from peers, family and the larger community

- her opportunity as a guide, protector and educator, as well as the ability to give and receive love directly to and from her child

- the opportunity to be seen by her family and community as a mature, healthy adult who has moved beyond her indiscretions and poor choices

- her self-respect. If her children are removed by the courts, her view of herself is as an irredeemable mother who may not be able to mother anyone

- peace of mind as she worries about her child and increased emotional pain every year on the anniversary of the loss and her child's birthday. It is common for birth/first mothers to become fearful when natural disasters or other accidents make the news and they wonder if their child was involved

- ongoing knowledge that her child is alive, well, safe and loved

The birth/first father may lose:

- a chance to make a "true" decision about placing or parenting his child if he is not included in the process and given unbiased counseling and support

- a baby, a toddler, a child, a teenager and an adult—a future with his child

- trust in himself and others

- self-esteem

- recognition of his role in the child's life since he did not carry or birth the child

- the joyous experiences with a significant other of pregnancy, labor and birth; these events are now associated with crisis, pain, shame, loss and sadness

- the father he fantasized he would always become

- a positive image in the eyes of his child

- a reflection of a "birth father experience"—there are no role models for a man who has lost his child to adoption and permanency

- the title and role as the only "father" because there is an adoptive father or multiple foster fathers known to his child. Birth/first fathers remain hidden and are a marginalized population

- his social fatherhood role—being seen by the larger society as doing the job of being the father (although he will not lose the role of being the genetic father)

- awareness that a conception occurred, if he was never told of the pregnancy or was never told that his children were removed by the court

- his family lineage; losing a piece of himself. His child will have no relationships built with grandparents, aunts, uncles, cousins or siblings. There will be no experience of his family culture, history, rituals, values, religion, ethnicity or race

- his equal portion of the birth/first parent narrative. The majority of the focus during the crisis is placed on the birth/first mother

- his connection to the mother and the baby, if he knew about the pregnancy and had begun claiming the child. His experience is of a dismantled plan, thwarted wishes, interrupted fatherhood and a loss of an important relationship with the mother of his baby

- a connection to his child when the court determines that the child must be temporarily or permanently raised in another family

- support from peer, family and the larger community, as others do not reach out to give him emotional support. He may experience fear, shame, anger and confusion connected to child support, statutory rape, a possible forced marriage, and the interruption of his life plans. This may cause him to become isolated, disappear, flee or engage in self-destructive behaviors

- his role as a "life giver." He may have no idea of how to form a new and useful role in his child's life as he has no role models and his importance to his child is minimized

- access to his child because he is uninformed of the birth or the removal of the child; because of lies and omissions; because of his youth at the time of the placement; or because of professionals who do not reach out to him and engage him in the process

- respect and support in the community because of the existing stereotypes about birth/first fathers

- the ability to fight for his child because he does not have the funds to initiate and support the legal process. If he fights for his child, he may be seen as disagreeable, intimidating, selfish or destructive. Without the funds to fight for his role in his child's life, he may be labeled as deadbeat, uncaring and irresponsible

- the opportunity to move beyond his indiscretions and the poor choices of his youth. None of us would appreciate being frozen in time based on what we did when we were 21 years old

- the relationship with the birth/first mother. The pregnancy, or removal of the child, may create a crisis that stresses the relationship and causes a break between him and the mother. Each party may blame the other for the crisis; without reparation, one party may make a decision that affects the other and could cause him to be absent from participating in his child's life

- the opportunity to father future children with joy and confidence. Trauma and loss of a child become associated with fatherhood

- the opportunity to love and be loved by his child

- self-respect and control if the court is the determining factor in whether or not he gets to parent his child. Being labeled as an irredeemable father may make him doubt his ability to father anyone

- the privilege of his child carrying his name

- all the firsts with his child—first step, first word, first tooth, first day of school, first date and so on

- the opportunity to raise all of his children together

- peace of mind as he worries about his child, and increased emotional pain every year on the anniversary of the loss and his child's birthday. It is common for birth/first fathers to become fearful when natural disasters or other accidents make the news and they wonder if their child was involved

- ongoing knowledge that his child is alive, well, safe and loved.

## Birth/first extended family

The losses that are experienced by the birth/first parents will be similarly experienced by the birth/first extended family. There is deep sadness about the loss of a relative from one's family tree. The child is genetically related, so it feels as if a piece of the birth/first extended family is missing. The family cannot protect, love, nurture or mentor this relative. Some common questions that surface for extended birth/first family members in regards to their losses are as follows: How will this child know who they are if they don't know the people they came from? What has the child been told about their birth/first family? How will this child know that the extended birth/first family members care about them? What if the family that is raising the child doesn't understand the child and their unique needs? Will we be notified if the placement fails? Who do we go to for information and answers? Who knows what about our extended family? Where do we go for support?

Over the years, extended birth/first family members have shared that they experienced a loss of control in regard to the outcome of the crisis that caused the family member to be separated from the family tree; loss of ability to influence their relative's life; the loss of a family connection to a grandchild, niece or nephew; and the ability to pass along the family's treasures, valuables, name, rituals and inheritance.

In an open adoption, the adoptive family has the power to include or exclude the birth/first extended family. The adoptive or permanent parents can dictate how the relationships will unfold.

> The loss inherent in adoption is unlike other losses we have come to expect in a lifetime, such as death or divorce. Adoption loss is more pervasive, less socially recognized, and more profound. (Brodzinsky, Schechter and Henig 1992, p.9)

## Adoptees and individuals raised in kinship/foster families

Infants who have lost a parent have had a life-altering event. The loss of one's parents as a child is a profound life loss that strikes deeply at the child's still developing sense of self and identity. The pain and suffering created by this loss may overwhelm a child's vulnerable emotional system.

This loss will subsequently change every aspect of who this child becomes. It is also a life-altering event for children who are later placed who may have experienced neglect, multiple losses, attachment disruptions and trauma before joining a permanent family. Once permanency is gained, additional life-altering losses accrue through each stage of development as the child begins to understand what happened to them. Both the cognitive awareness and the conceptual understanding of these original life-altering events are now experienced as an additional series of losses.

Adoptees and individuals in kinship or foster care may experience a total loss of power and control at a very young age. Much of what happens to children is by way of adult decisions into which they have little or no input. Even at the age where children can consent to a placement, which varies legally from state to state, their only option is to say "yes" to adoption or guardianship or perhaps emancipate with no family support. It is ironic that children and youth who survive this "loss journey" are referred to as "lucky." The loss of control in having to lose one's original family and perhaps experiencing multiple additional moves would not be labeled as being "lucky" by most people. The lesson that may have been internalized is that "anything that is good that happens to you is outside your control."

Adoptees and individuals raised in kinship/foster families may lose:

- everything that was meaningful and familiar to them—important people and items, if placed beyond infancy. For instance: their parents, caregivers, siblings, extended family, friends, pets, teachers, foster parents, social workers, therapists, extended foster family, religious community, favorite recipes, toys, favorite clothes, a favorite stuffed animal, the smell of the sheets from the detergent used, the first/birth/ foster mother's smell, court-appointed special advocates or guardian ad litems, group home and orphanage staff, the peacefulness or noises of a prior home, music played in the home, routines, rituals, language and culture. All of the above defined, supported and guided the child *before* placement with the new family occurred. From the child's perspective, these people and items may be cherished treasures that cannot be replaced

- the certainty that adults can be relied on, which causes the loss of basic trust in adults, as the child has experienced both being unchosen and chosen. Fear of loving others and being loved is a common result

- all or parts of their family tree—history, culture, relationships, racial identification, information, familiar images. They are then grafted onto a new family tree or limb of a family tree that is unfamiliar. The family that receives the child must work hard to acknowledge the child's past, build trust and attach to the child who has suffered losses. Even if the child was placed as an infant, a profound loss has occurred

- genetic mirroring causing them to consistently search the faces of others for like characteristics. The conscious or unconscious scanning of their environment in search of "their clan" leads to the possibility of distractibility, anxiety, yearning and a longing for biological connectivity

- a sense of feeling "normal." Many individuals who have suffered the loss of their story of conception, birth and early history feel a sense of alienation from their own beginning and may feel a sense of alienation in the world

- a sense of rootedness within their original and familial family trees. The lack of information about their beginnings leads to the sense of not "feeling real" or even born, which may lead to recklessness and high-risk behaviors

- a sense of security because their current family is not the only family to whom they are connected. How they came to be in their current family can be mysterious and frightening. After all, they have lost at least one family and may always be fearing the loss of their current family

- knowledge of their medical or genetic history, or have an outdated version of it which leads to a "mystery history." The individual will not know what their genetic history holds—how tall they might be, when puberty begins, hidden talents or medical issues. Every time the person answers medical questions, it is a reminder of how little is known to them about their own medical and genetic history

- a sense of mental and physical well-being. Many adoptees report physical ailments such as stomach and intestinal problems, heart aches, hyperactivity, headaches, poor eyesight, weak knees, high blood pressure, weight issues, sleep disorders, addictive behaviors, overall increased stress level and a feeling of disorientation

- access to their complete narrative. Adoptees key into the specificity and meaning in words because they are always looking for accurate truths. Having a complete narrative requires access to all of the facts of one's story, starting with conception, pregnancy and birth, as well as information that includes two familial trees, maternal and paternal. With the loss of a coherent life story, individuals are left with an "episodic narrative" that has an incomplete or disrupted stream of events with rotating caregivers and confused timelines. The amended adoption birth certificate when issued creates a break from the beginning of their life story

- an easily consolidated identity. Some share that they feel they have a "dual identity" creating a longing and desire to search for the missing parts of their story and themselves

- ownership of their personal story; their story belongs to them. There are multiple adults who may or may not honestly share the details of an individual's life story. The story is often shared with family, friends, teachers, therapists, neighbors and parents of the child's friends before the child/individual fully owns and understands their story. Children have receptive language before they have expressive language, which means the child is listening and absorbing everything that is being said around them. The child is interpreting the emotions, body language and the tone of another's voice as they hear what is being shared about them and how that person feels about the story

- pride in their beginnings; the story of origin—the child needed to be "rescued" by well-meaning adults, and society expects the child to be grateful for that "rescue," which may lead to a feeling that they are a "charity case" who might have ended up homeless or alone

- access to their rights and their ability to be seen as adults in a society that refers to them as an "adopted child" or "foster child" all their life. They may feel that they are never seen as old enough, trusted enough or mature enough to be "allowed" access to their original birth certificate or other important information

- space on the original family tree, which impacts their descendants. They may not be included in their first/birth parent's family records such as the family's Bible and the family registry, referenced in family obituaries or even included in discussions at birth/first family gatherings

- the opportunity to give and receive love from siblings. They have lost the opportunity to grow up with their siblings. They were denied the ability to share their day-to-day life experiences and may not have similar language, religion, cultural values, belief systems or lifestyles

- privacy, as all of the child's personal information is recorded for legal and court purposes. The child loses control over what they would wish to share, when to share it and with whom to share it. Children who are of a different race from their adoptive or kinship parents, or enter the new family as an older child or as part of a sibling group, are automatically robbed of privacy in that they suddenly appear in a family system

- information or relationships that can never be fully recaptured. Even if facts are later found, those facts may no longer be useful. Time lost with people is not retrievable

- a serene and peaceful pregnancy. The birth of a child and the experience of the first biological bond highlights the loss of the biological connection with the birth/first parents. Additionally, they may feel the pain of not having been born to the parents who raised them. The adopted person may worry about the genetic make-up of their offspring as well, since they have little knowledge of their own DNA

- their original language—many experience linguistic disenfranchisement

- their original culture—many feel a sense of cultural dislocation

- their country of origin. If they are adopted into a family, community or country where the dominant, majority culture looks different, they may experience physical, cultural and racial isolation. Children adopted internationally also lose language, culture, religion, history, music, food, smells, mirror images and caretakers

- the ability to trust their own perceptions and inner wisdom. Some individuals describe feeling "crazy" or disoriented when others discount, deny or correct their thoughts and perceptions. Can they trust what others are saying, when so often information has been withheld or changed?

- naivety and innocence. The individual may lose the certainty that life is safe and adults are dependable and permanent

- the opportunity to be free from the burdens of ongoing loss. As the child matures and understands their story more fully, the newly understood information connects them to more losses

- experiences and clarity of where they fit if they were placed trans-racially, multi-ethnically and internationally

- assurance of how they came to be named. Names are important. We know ourselves by how we are named by six months of age. Our name forms the beginning of self-identity. For the adopted person, they may or may not have received a name from their birth/first parents. If they discover at a later date that they were given a name on their original birth certificate, the adoptee may feel relieved, and more deeply connected to the parents who gave them life. This may also trigger a fantasy about who they might have been if they had grown up with that name. They may have had nicknames they were fond of from foster families or caregivers that have gone by the wayside. Adoptees do have the legal name they were given by their adoptive family. As names change, losses occur. It is less disruptive to one's identity to add a name rather than erase a previous name.

## Societal view of the adoptee

Being a "chosen child" creates unreasonable expectations as it perpetuates a fairytale narrative that everyone will live happily ever after. Losses are created for everyone when fantasies are not met. When children are adopted from the foster care system they may imagine what their new family will be like. A fairytale narrative may hinder attachment to the new family. If their fairytale is a nightmare filled with fear and rejection based on prior experiences, it can equally impede their ability to experience the love and acceptance of the new family.

Alternatively, a fairytale narrative that may be manifested by the adoptive family could impede their ability to attach to the actual child who joined the family. It puts the burden of happiness on the child. The fairytale narrative of adoption that is built on the backs of children helps to alleviate any guilt for moving children from one family to another.

Adoption and permanency is seen as a "trade up" in the world. The hope is that the child will have a better life and better opportunities. This "trade up" is attached to a fairytale that may require gratitude from the child. Adoptees are consistently reminded about how "lucky" they are to be in a "good" family. For many adoptees, the gratitude becomes destructive as there may be no room for the acknowledgment of ongoing loss and grief. Gratitude may impede grieving, anger, questioning, wondering and searching, as there is a debt to be paid for this "step up" in society.

Adoptees frequently hear that they were a "gift" given to their family. This relegates a human as being an object to transfer. This is how adoption can become more about meeting the needs of the adults and only secondarily about meeting the needs of the child.

The language that society uses to frame the adoption and permanency experience such as "chosen," "gift," "step up," "lucky," "trade up," "good adoptee," "saved," "rescued" and "born from my heart" can be experienced by the adoptee as a diminishment of the traumatic events that occurred in their life.

## The "late discovery adoptee"

"Late discovery adoptees" are people who discover later in their lives that they entered their family, not through birth, but through adoption. The confusion and trauma of this suddenly revealed truth can be either a relief or a major crisis. Perhaps the realization that they are not like the rest of the family becomes a validation of something they always suspected. For some, where growing up in their family was not pleasant, the later discovery of being adopted may bring a sense of relief. For most, the realization that your parents have been deceptive all your life is hurtful and destructive. Realizing that your parents have lied to you and withheld critical information that was needed to form a solid identity based on the truth may lead to a deep sense of betrayal, anger, sadness and fear. A person might wonder who else knew the truth and withheld it, leading to a deep sense of mistrust. This crisis could lead to tragedy as the family disassembles around the newly revealed information. The task that is now thrust on the shoulders of the "late discovery adoptee" is to deconstruct and rebuild their identity, as well as to reframe all of their relationships. The challenge for the "late discovery adoptee" is to adjust to this new reality. This is a major life crisis requiring a significant amount of emotional energy, time and therapeutic support. The tragedy in this scenario is that all the additional losses that accumulated due to the withholding of the truth might have been avoided through honesty.

## Adoptee in search and reunion

Search and reunion have the potential for both gains and losses. Steve Nickman, MD, who is an adoptee, states:

> Once the adoptee is made aware of the adoption status, mental construction of the absent progenitors becomes necessary. That internal dialogue between an adoptee and his or her inner representation or construction of the birth parents is as much of a relationship as the connection between the bereaved individual and the dead person. (Klass, Silverman and Nickman 2014, p.257)

In addition, Betty Jean Lifton, also an adoptee, called the people that live in the fantasy world of the adoptee "ghosts" (Lifton 2009). The child's fantasy often includes perfect parents who don't yell or make demands to finish homework, make beds or brush teeth and who love unconditionally. Or, the fantasies may include that the birth/first parent are homeless, sick, mentally ill, dead, dangerous or rejecting because "fantasies flourish where facts flounder." Such internal dialogue may often be tinged with negative feelings about the self for not having been kept, wanted or loved. The individual might also have had a fantasy of what a loving reunion would look like; the adoptee would be an accomplished and beautiful/handsome individual whom the family of origin is proud to know and is sorry they did not raise.

As an individual confronts fantasies about their family of origin and who they are in reality, there may be more loss. This is called retrospective loss and can create a great deal of pain as one is confronted with the reality of deconstructing one's fantasies. Typically, these fantasies about the family of origin have been positive and comforting. When fantasy becomes reality, the possibility of further rejection, finding relatives already deceased or connecting to painful truths exists. The adoptive person may lose the comfortable retreat that their fantasy world provided. The releasing of fantasies changes their understanding of themselves as they adjust to the new reality, facts, people and relationships. Meeting "relative strangers" about whom the adopted person has had fantasies, and accepting them as "real people" with both strengths and deficits, allows for the creation of honest relationships with people who previously resided only in the mind.

## Adoptive/permanent family

Individuals who adopt a child into their family may be driven by: a social consciousness; a faith perspective; wanting to parent a specific gender; wishing for a larger family; filling an empty nest; adopting a child with a particular need with whom they have had personal experience; adopting a child they fostered; choosing to adopt a child whose culture, race or ethnicity mirrors the family; or infertility.

Adoptive/permanency parents may lose:

- power and control over their lives as outsiders make decisions that impact on their family. For infertile couples, they have also lost control over their bodies

- privacy—they must prove their suitability to social workers in order to parent infants, children from the foster care system or other countries. The family's privacy is impacted as the child's needs are addressed through visitation from social workers, therapists, attorneys, birth/first family members, former foster parents and court-appointed special advocates. They are often required to explain their parenting decisions to others and to justify their parenting of a particular child. Everyone in their environment, from family to friends to strangers, may ask intrusive questions about the adoption and their child's history

- confidence—many of them have successfully parented their own offspring and are not prepared for the extra-ordinary needs of the children and the demands of the system

- the ability to affect the trajectory of their children's lives as they have lost time, history and impact with their newly placed child

- the dream of what their family would look like

- the option of raising a child the same way that they believed they would have raised a child who had been born to them. Adoptive parents must assume additional tasks through each stage of their child's development, which include interpreting the child's adoption story appropriately and in an age-appropriate way; addressing adoption issues in the schools; addressing the reactions and questions from others concerning adoption and permanency

- the ability to carry or birth a child due to medical concerns or genetics, or the stillbirth or death of a child—their "love" child, their genetic offspring and the child they held in fantasy

- some joy as they become aware of the birth/first family's grief and the child's loss and trauma

- their sense of entitlement to parent a child. Some adoptive parents worry that they don't have a right to adopt someone else's child because they feel they are gaining from someone else's misfortune. The entitlement that comes from parenting a child not born to them may lay a heavy burden on the shoulders of adoptive parents that they must be exceptional parents

- a reflection of their family's faces in the child they are loving and parenting. They may see the birth/first family's faces in their child's face. This experience extends into their grandparenting as they will still not see their genetic reflection in the ensuing generations

- being the "only parents"

- the status as a "normal or traditional family"; the lack of seeing their family mirrored back to them in their culture/community

- the belief that love is enough to fix the needs of any child

- the facts of their child's history and story

- time, as they go through fertility treatments, as they struggle to make decisions about what comes next and as they work with an agency, an attorney and a mental health professional, or search for a child

- time with the infant after birth and the child that is in foster care or an orphanage

- the certainty that the child is a permanent member of their family. They may worry when the child emancipates, goes to college, gets married, has children, joins the military, does a search or has a reunion. These events may cause them to worry that the child may not choose them as their parents

- several possible children through failed procedures, miscarriages and death, as well as foster placements with the intent of adoption where the children return to the family of origin

- status within their own family; not being able to reproduce for the family tree

- a normal pregnancy, which includes telling your partner that you're pregnant, sharing the news with family and friends, a baby shower, the extra attention given to a pregnant woman, the teasing of an expectant father

- certainty that, at the time of placement, the baby or child will be adopted by them. The expectation of parenting and attaching without the certainty that the child will remain is not typical for other parents

- money and time in their lives as they pursue fertility treatments, explore other avenues to parenthood, are "assessed and trained" for foster or adoptive parenthood, wait for a possible placement of a child, and then live with the uncertainty as to whether this child will remain a permanent member of their family

- the ability to make major decisions for the child before the adoption occurs, concerning aspects such as religious choice, including baptism, circumcision and religious training; school placement; medical decisions such as vaccinations; and even something as basic as a haircut

- the ability to express honest feelings because they are being judged by social workers assessing them, therapists assisting them, the court and its representatives making decisions for them, birth/first families choosing them and perhaps having an ongoing relationship with them

- access to the birth/first family, possibly because of disagreements, miscommunication and/or changes in the birth/first parents' lives

- the ability to provide for the child's racial, cultural and ethnic needs

- the ability to communicate with the family of origin who may speak a different language. Temporarily, they may lose the ability to communicate with the child who speaks a different language

- money, as they pay for medical procedures, lose wages at work for time off and pay for adoption expenses

- marital satisfaction due to the stress of being focused on getting pregnant and the impact of fertility drugs on the woman's body

- control of the woman's body due to medications and procedures that may impact on her mental health

- hope and faith as each succeeding intervention or treatment fails

- investment of emotion with no positive outcome; the loss of potential life each time a fertility procedure is undertaken. Miscarriages may also occur

- friendships—as they lose synchronicity with friends who have conceived and are already parenting. They may lose their friends' support as the friends don't know how to support an infertile couple or understand the adoption process

- a sense of their femininity or masculinity, which may be connected to the medical crisis of infertility

- certainty that they even deserve this *particular* child when there are so many reports of child trafficking, stealing or scams in adoption

- an opportunity to name their child, which is an attachment and claiming experience for parents.

The extended adoptive/permanency family may lose:

- bloodlines; seeing themselves mirrored in the next generation

- the ability to know how to help family members through infertility and/or adoption

- power to control how their family is built

- knowledge of how to convey and provide access to race, culture and heritage

- the opportunity to be a traditional family

- information because relatives are not telling all they would like to know

- intimacy with family members as they go through the crisis of infertility, decision making and the parenting of children with high needs

- children who are returned to their families of origin by the courts

- mirroring of their culture in a subsequent generation

- traditional parenting tools that have been effective but are not with the newly placed child

- communication if the child speaks a different language

Many of the losses experienced by the adoptive/permanent parents may also extend to other family members—for instance, time that is lost with a later placed child.

Adoptive grandparents often have a great deal of power and influence over how the entire family system accepts and integrates the new children. Grandparents may help to set the tone in regards to whether the change in the family legacy is legitimized intergenerationally. Does the extended family see the adoption as a "fix for infertility" or to meet the needs of a child in need but not as an intergenerational change to the family tree?

## Tools for all constellation members to address loss

- List all the losses in your life since you were born. Be very specific, not general—the pain is in the details.

- What has been the greatest loss in your life?

- What emotions and physical symptoms arise in connection to these losses?

- List all the adoption, foster care or kinship care losses you can think of.

- What tools have you used to address the feelings associated with loss? Have they helped?

- What have you learned from your losses? How do you feel about yourself?

- What unacknowledged losses do you hold on to? And what purpose does this serve? Remember that anger is often the result of unresolved or unacknowledged hurt, loss or pain.

- Who or what are you afraid of losing? Is it a real possibility or an irrational fear?

- Gratitude, forgiveness and helping others can reduce feelings of loss.

- Prayer, gratitude and meditation are all techniques that can be used to address loss and achieve forgiveness. Please read Chapter 11, "The Power of Forgiveness to Address Loss and Grief."

- Identify how and when a grudge began to poison your being and life. Not forgiving is like drinking poison so somebody else will die; it does no good and harms only you.

- To break a chain of anger and address a grievance, forgiveness of yourself or of another requires internal exploration and action. Forgiveness is not passive. To begin the process, you must decide if the grievance is against yourself, another or a group of people. Be clear, name the grievance and state how it has affected your life. Ask yourself what would need to happen in order for you to forgive.

- Forgiveness is a practice and a process; the more we exercise it, the healthier we feel.

- To address a grievance, it is best to meet with the person with whom you have a grievance if it is safe or possible. The purpose of the meeting is to share what occurred and how it has continued to impact your life and why you are *choosing* to forgive them. Do not go into this meeting with an agenda of what you want from them, because if you fail to meet that goal you will have formed another grievance. The only thing you are asking of the other person is that they listen to what you have to say. Think carefully about what it is you want to convey through your words, facial expressions, tone of voice and body language. Practice and rehearse. If you are feeling unsafe, bring a trusted companion.

- If it is not safe or possible to meet in person, you can make use of an empty chair, while using a picture or a symbol of the person, to convey and express your grievances. Choose someone trusted to witness the process.

- Write a letter to express your grievances and mail it if you wish to. Some people choose to entrust the letter to a friend or relative, or read the letter aloud to a trusted friend and burn and release the grievance.

- Create rituals of "letting go" and releasing anger and pain, and making "heart space" for joy and happiness.

- Ask yourself when enough is enough; set a time limit on a grievance.

- Ask a trusted companion, spiritual adviser or therapist to walk through the process of forgiveness with you.

- Celebrate the happiness of another. Be open to wonders. Look for the "awesome" in your life and your surroundings.

- Be in service to others. Send love and support out to the world. Be generous. Pay it forward.

- Practice compliments, both giving and receiving them.

- Examine what your spiritual beliefs advise about forgiveness. What does your religious system teach you about anger, strong emotions, revenge and forgiveness?

- Make a gratitude list before bed every night. Be specific about what you are grateful for, such as people, things, food, your home, your health, friends and all your favorites.

- Touch and be touched. Hug and be hugged. Get body work such as massage, yoga, eye movement desensitization and reprocessing (EMDR) and neurofeedback, if needed, to release toxic stress.

- Breathe deeply and often. People who carry toxic stress are not typically taking in enough oxygen to fully oxygenate their prefrontal cortex, which impacts their executive functioning, thinking!

- Use art, music and dance as non-verbal avenues for healing.

- Use therapy; be sure to include forgiveness work in your therapeutic process.

- Be physical; move, yell, throw things, dance hard! People do better when they go ahead and get angry and pound on a pillow, write a profane letter (not to mail) and build up a head of steam. Address those feelings of indignation and despair. The raw emotion needs to be acknowledged, accessed and discharged from your bodily, neurological and sensory systems. Be smart and safe in choosing with whom and where to do this work.

- Listen to another point of view. When we listen from our heart, we will hear the emotion and heart of the other person.

- Practice compassion for both yourself and others.

- Look for people who have forgiven others and learn from their process.

- What does your culture say about forgiveness? What did your family say or do about grievances?

- Does "turn the other cheek" mean you must forgive without acknowledging your feelings?

- Practice mindfulness; live in the present. Returning to the past to relive or revisit our grievances does not allow us to fully experience the richness of the present moment. With each mindful breath you are returning your focus to your body and mind in the present moment.

- Keeping a journal is an expressive outlet. It can include the good, the bad and the ugly. Feelings of distress, grief, loss, anger, joy, love, compassion and gratitude can all be included. You can write about things that make you smile or laugh; private jokes that make you laugh. Enjoy writing in a free-form fashion—let it flow. Pick a journal that reflects your personality; try to write at the same time of day each day; track your feelings; keep it private or choose carefully with whom you share it; and remember to honor your feelings, as they are neither good nor bad.

- Take in wonders; activate all your senses: wear perfume, smell flowers, wear silk, bake, taste the things that give you joy, gaze at the stars, listen to the birds sing or the silence of snow falling, run your fingers through things and put your toes in the sand.

- Be generous. Keep a coin handy and give it away unexpectedly—don't stop to evaluate or judge. Do it for delight.

- Draw pictures of the masks you wear, both inner and outer. Choose the one you most like and identify why.

- Write a letter to yourself from the person with whom you have a grievance to gain insight into their point of view.

- Visualize meeting the person with whom you have a grievance as they are in the present. If their past actions dominate your perceptions, notice how your feelings and emotions change when you wipe the slate clean.

## Notes to professionals

Professionals need to be aware of their own loss history, triggers and biases.

Since loss of power and control is a major issue for constellation members, how does the professional manage their own loss of power and control and will they be able to share power and control with the constellation members they serve?

The information included in the reports submitted to the court or judge can impact on a person's life intergenerationally. Those reports can offer hope or create further losses, stigmatization and labeling that deepen and preserve the original core losses. Make sure reports are evidence informed, factually accurate, free of bias and utilize current best practice standards.

Part of a thorough intake includes questions as to whether someone has a connection to adoption and permanency. This will allow the professional to incorporate the Seven Core Issues in Adoption and Permanency into their assessment and treatment planning.

Being an adoption and permanency competent therapist requires specialized training. This proficiency includes adoption and permanency clinical training and supervision, clinical training in trauma and attachment, reading and attending conferences related to adoption and permanency, and doing a thorough exploration and understanding of one's biases about birth/first fathers, birth/first mothers, open adoptions, trans-racial, trans-cultural and trans-ethnic adoptions, and gay, lesbian and single parent adoptions.

The recognition of the professional's own losses allows them to be proactive. The framework of the Seven Core Issues in Adoption and Permanency offers the professional a tool for understanding, educating, assessing and introducing supportive language and a safe place for clients to process adoption and permanency issues. Therapists who are members of the constellation bring both the possibility of a special relatedness and clarity from a shared perspective with the client or the risk of the projection of unresolved core issues.

Social workers are on the front lines of adoption and permanency practice. Social workers may experience vicarious trauma as they navigate the crisis of these traumatic losses with children and families. Social workers must recognize that their role made them a part of their client's story and their adoption/permanency narrative. Identifying and connecting with a client who is experiencing significant loss and trauma may impact the professional on an emotional level. Since crises continue day to day as children enter the foster care system, professionals often do not have enough time to attend to self-care and to process the trauma. How do you as a professional manage your own distress on the front lines of conflict, crisis and traumatic cases and events?

Therapists and social workers may play an important role in the lives of their clients and may find that they remain in the lives of a client for a period of time, which allows them to be an ongoing part of a family's story, and a holder of the truth.

Many of the following may trigger the core issues for constellation members: be aware of adoption and permanency in the news; changes in the laws regarding adoption and permanency; screen movies, TV shows or books for adoption and permanency themes; and watch for news and online articles highlighting stories related to adoption and permanency. Be mindful that constellation members often feel stigmatized, misunderstood and victimized by the stereotypes that are portrayed by the larger culture.

# Chapter 3

# Rejection

Webster's Dictionary definition of rejection includes: to discard or throw out as worthless, useless or substandard; to rebuff, or fling back.

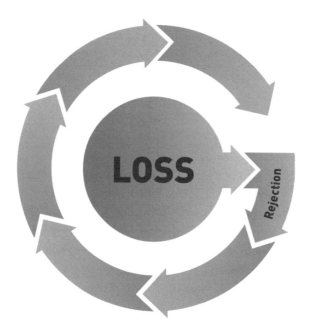

Rejection is the first spoke in the wagon wheel emanating from loss. Constellation members' core losses are most often experienced as a form of social rejection. Rejection is a perceived loss of social acceptance, group inclusion or a sense of belonging. Rejection can be real, imagined or implied. Explicit rejection and exclusion, and, in its extreme, ostracism, are different forms of rejection that can occur within dyads, families or groups. Feelings and/or fear of rejection may also manifest in or between racial, ethnic, tribal, religious, gender, sexual orientation and/or socio-economic groups. Rejection typically creates immediate negative effects. Attempts to regain control might include withdrawal, denial and/or aggression. It may hinder an individual's ability to rein in impulses and make difficult decisions because rejection impairs logic and reasoning abilities. Attempting to "reason" with the individual may not be helpful. The severity of one's experience of rejection will be influenced by any early adverse childhood experiences of trauma, loss and neglect, as well as the individual's present emotional well-being.

The pain of being rejected or excluded is not so different from the pain of physical injury. The depth of the pain is influenced by the closeness of the connection to the individual. Rejection can influence emotion, cognition and physical health. People who routinely feel excluded have poorer sleep quality, and their immune system may be suppressed. Ostracized people can lash out, attempting to externalize the pain of the rejection by becoming angry or aggressive towards others, or they may turn their pain inward and engage in self-harming or self-destructive behaviors. Brain scans show that the very same brain regions get activated when we experience rejection as when we experience physical pain. Therefore, individuals who re-activate a memory of social rejection may feel the physical pain associated with that experience.

Humans have a fundamental need to belong, secondary only to nourishment and safety needs. People get their most basic needs met through human connectedness. Being rejected or ostracized from a person, family or community can leave an individual feeling a deep sense of personal isolation. People describe their feelings as being hurt and experience a general sense of not being of value. Anger and aggression can be triggered by rejection, and even mild rejection can lead an individual to lash out at others, even innocent bystanders.

Humans evolved to live in cooperative groups or communities, and for most of our history we depended on those groups for our survival. Like hunger or thirst, the need for acceptance emerged as a mechanism for survival. A human being in isolation cannot survive or thrive.

Most people can recover quickly from brief episodes of rejection.

## Impact of rejection on constellation members

Constellation members may personalize their core losses in order to gain a deeper understanding about what happened to them and what role they may have played in those events. In an unconscious attempt to avoid future losses and to regain control of their life's journey, the individual may assume the burden of the responsibility of the loss, believing that, if the rejection was their fault, then they can change or act differently and avoid future rejection. Personalization of the losses may trigger feelings of rejection and/or fears of further rejection.

For members of the adoption and permanency constellation it is the core losses, secondary losses, ambiguous losses and vicarious losses that create the various mechanisms through which rejection is experienced. It is the intensity and the cumulative effect of these facets of rejection that can strike at the core of constellation members, increasing their sensitivity to any subsequent "brief episode" of rejection. For example, imagine co-workers are having a dinner party and Bob is the only one who is not invited. Imagine that Bob's life experience is one of perceived rejection by his whole family of origin, so being rejected by his office peers triggers a much deeper pain.

The key questions asked by members of the constellation are "Why me?" and "What did I do or not do to deserve this?" Children, due to their ego-centric thinking, believe that the things that happen to them, including abandonment, abuse, neglect, divorce and death, are a result of something they did; it's their fault. Children may believe that they cried too much; they were ugly; they needed too much; they were bad; or they talked about things they weren't supposed to share, which caused their parents to abuse them, leave them or reject them. Youngsters who are adopted internationally often feel additional rejection from their country and culture of origin and may ask, "You mean nobody from China/Russia/India/South America…wanted me?" As a result of constellation members' experiences of rejection associated with adoption and permanency losses, individuals often share that they feel judged, criticized, unwanted, different, less than, left out, not part of, not good enough and/or disliked.

Members of the constellation may find themselves anticipating rejection from other members of the constellation. "Anticipatory rejection" creates hypervigilant scanning of all social environments as one defends against possible further rejection. In a desire to self-protect, individuals may misread or misperceive situations which cause them to either reject the other or assume they are being rejected. Remembering that rejection is already stored in memory as a sensory experience waiting to be alerted to any new perceived slight or rebuff, many emotional landmines are triggered among and between constellation members at the slightest threat of dismissal. For instance, a birth/first mother calls an adoptive mother at a pre-arranged time, but no one answers the phone. There is no thought that the adoptive mother is sick or has a flat tire and couldn't make it to the phone; the automatic feeling is rejection. The adoptive parents may experience a feeling of rejection when their teenager says, "I don't have to follow your rules, you're not my real parents!" An adoptee could be triggered with feelings of rejection when a birth/first father in an open adoption gets married and announces that his wife is pregnant, leaving the child feeling that he will be replaced by his birth/first father's new child.

Constellation members may also manifest feelings or fear of rejection through self-sabotaging behaviors. If their belief system is that they are unworthy of having anything good happen to them, they may set up scenarios that reinforce their negative beliefs. They may first reject others as a defense against the risk of being rejected. They may provoke by saying things such as "I don't need any friends," "I don't need new parents," "I don't want you to love me," "I don't want your help," "I don't like what you gave me," "You don't really know me" and "You can't really love me because if you really knew me you wouldn't want me." For instance, young adoptees might not turn in homework, might skip school, fail a test intentionally, fall apart at tryouts for sports, choose friends who also see themselves as "rejects," and knowingly break the rules at home, at school and in society. All of these behaviors may be linked to the lingering effects of feelings or fears of rejection.

Additional signs that are manifestations of rejection include self-destructive behaviors such as addictions, domestic violence, poor self-care, isolation, eating disorders, cutting, depression and suicidal ideation. More signs that suggest unresolved rejection include constantly moving and changing jobs, and initiating plans and not completing them.

Some individuals may choose to isolate themselves, risking the pain of loneliness rather than the pain of deep attachments and further rejection.

Remember that the same rejection triggers and sensitivities may be carried by all constellation members into their day-to-day activities and interactions at work, school, extended family functions, religious institutions, neighborhoods and communities. Examples of events that could activate feelings of rejection include: having a friend or a significant partner break up with you; a death in the family; someone ignoring an invitation from you; someone forgetting your birthday; someone forgetting to pick you up at a certain time at school; not being chosen for a position on a sports team; being overlooked for a promotion; and not being invited to a birthday party.

## Impact of rejection on birth/first family

All birth/first family members who experience the loss of a child from the family tree can experience feelings of rejection or fear of further rejection. Birth/first parents may manifest feelings or fear of rejection through either becoming pregnant quickly again and releasing or losing another child; choosing partners who desert them in times of crisis; not pursuing their life goals; and not feeling that they deserve to be a parent. Extended birth/first family members, grandparents, aunts, uncles and siblings may feel rejected by not being a part of the decision that caused a child to be placed outside their family; not being chosen to parent the child, either by the birth/first mother or father, or by the court system; and siblings may feel rejection when they experience the loss of the sibling relationship. All family members might fear rejection from the individual placed outside the family or by the family raising their family member, such as adoptive, foster or kinship caregivers.

> An older woman, who remained anonymous through three lengthy phone calls to a therapist, shared that she was going to kill herself because a daughter whom she relinquished as a newborn had recently contacted her. She had never shared with anyone that she had given birth to a baby at the age of 22 and placed her for adoption. She never shared the details of this event with her husband or her subsequent children or grandchildren. In addition, as a bank manager, she had signed a morals clause and believed that she would be seen as a "liar" and an irresponsible woman if people knew the truth. Her fear of rejection led her to believe that if the truth was revealed she would lose everything that was important to her–her husband, family and career. The impact of her cumulative fear of rejection climaxed at the moment her daughter contacted her. Two years of therapeutic support eventually allowed her to share her deeply hidden secret with her husband and family, and to eventually begin to build a relationship with her daughter. None of her deepest fears of rejection happened.

Birth/first parents may experience rejection:

- from their child. The child disconnected from the family of origin may feel abandoned or angry because of the circumstances that caused them to be separated. Birth/first parents may be concerned that their child will "hate" them for relinquishing them or the circumstances that caused the court to sever their parental rights

- from the children they are raising because of the loss of those sibling connections

- by their parents, who are hurt and angry about losing their grandchild

- by their extended family members for losing nieces, nephews and cousins. Each extended family member may personalize the loss based on their connection to the birth/first parents. These strong feelings can be expressed in an intense and agitated manner towards the birth/first parents

- from society members who discover that the birth/first parents relinquished or lost a child to whom they gave birth. They did not live up to society's standards of taking responsibility for the children they brought into the world

- from themselves, feeling irresponsible for losing a child they brought into the world. They may ask themselves: What kind of mother or father brings a child into the world and is unable to parent that child?

- from people with whom they share that they are involved in an open adoption. People may view the birth/first parents as being selfish for staying connected to the child they are not raising

- from their faith, religion and/or God. Many birth/first parents do not return to their religious community for fear of rejection, or a sense of unworthiness to receive the guidance of their religious family. Some report that they felt unworthy to pray, and others have shared that they were ejected from their religious community for the choices they made

- from the birth/first mother's own body when she is not able to conceive again—"secondary infertility." She may experience the secondary infertility as a form of punishment and feel that she does not deserve to parent

- from family members who do not step forward to help the birth/first parents raise the child themselves and do not offer to parent or adopt the child in order to keep the child in the family

- from social services and the court system that removed the child from their care

- from society for judging the birth/first parents for choosing their own needs and goals over parenting their child. For example: choosing college over raising their child; choosing to parent some of their children and not others; not completing their case plan towards reunification; not entering a program to address their addiction and/or not addressing their mental health needs

- by the other birth/first parent. For instance: birth/first fathers who do not support the mother financially and emotionally through the pregnancy or making a plan for the baby; birth/first fathers who are rejected by the birth/first mothers by not being told about the baby and not being included in making plans for the baby

- from the adoptive family who find a reason to close an open adoption

- from the potential foster and adoptive parents who decide not to parent the child

- from potential spouses/partners who learn about the circumstances of an adoption, and who judge the birth/first parent and end the relationship

- from a potential spouse/partner who threatens to sever the relationship if the partner continues the open adoption relationships. The spouse may have deep feelings about having an ongoing relationship with the offspring of another person's child. They may also have strong feelings about involving their future offspring in the complexities in these open adoption relationships

- from their child when they see them being loving towards the foster, adoptive or kin parents. Feelings of unworthiness, anger or rejection may be triggered when they see their child attaching to the new family, being happy, doing well in school and calling others "mom" and "dad." Rejection may also be felt when they believe the other parents are receiving what belongs to them

- from co-workers, peers and friends who do not agree with the plan of adoption. These same individuals can trigger rejection as they shun or judge the lifestyle that causes the parents to lose the child through the courts to strangers or kin.

## Adoptees and individuals raised in kinship/foster families

Adopted individuals most often view their placement into adoption as a form of rejection. Even if their adoption and permanency experience was positive, the initial separation from their parents may be experienced as rejection. Adopted people, then, may become sensitive to the slightest hint of rejection, disapproval or dismissal, causing them to either avoid situations where they might be rejected or even provoke rejection in order to validate their own negative self-perceptions.

Adopted people can view the placement as a complete personal rejection by the birth/first family, their culture, their race or their country of origin, regardless of the circumstances or the reason for the placement or adoption.

As a way of defending against further rejection, adoptees may work very hard to blend in, not complain, be grateful, not ask for what they need, and please others at the expense of their own needs. They may maintain hurtful or unhealthy connections because they do not feel worthy of having loving and satisfying relationships. At the other extreme, adoptees may be angry, defensive and alone, or act as bullies so they can hurt others before they are hurt. They may exhibit destructive behaviors in order to maintain emotional distance from others or defend against creating dependency to avoid further traumatic loss, rejection and pain. This behavior is a self-protective mechanism to guard against further psychic injury.

> Shawna, a 9-year-old girl, first entered foster care at age 2 due to neglect and abuse. For the next five years, she went through six foster homes. The last two homes were families that she was told were going to adopt her. Shawna's history of trauma, neglect and multiple attachment disruptions left her struggling with chronic distress, developmental challenges and oppositional/defiant behaviors. She trusted no one. She had never experienced any relational permanency. In order to protect herself, she needed to reject others before they rejected her. When a new prospective adoptive family was identified, a therapeutic team was put in place to support the new parents in learning how to parent a child who had intense fear of attaching and depending on caregivers. Shawna's self-protective strategy of rejecting others was developed in response to all of the adults who had previously "rejected" her. Once the parents were able to understand the purpose of the oppositional, defiant and rejecting behaviors, they could empathize with her pain and distress, and refuse to be rejected. Their unconditional commitment to becoming her parents never wavered over the two years it took for Shawna to experience the trust and permanency that attachment offers.

Adoptees and individuals raised in kinship/foster families may experience rejection:

- from their first/birth parents. Adopted children witness poor families, single parents, young parents and even ill parents raising their children. Their conclusion often is that it is something personal about them that created the loss and/or abandonment. They recognize that to have been "chosen" by another family, they had to be "unchosen" or "rejected" by their birth/first parents

- from other first/birth family members who did not come forward to claim them. If adopted as an infant or small child, the realization of these additional losses and subsequent feelings of rejection may not surface until the child has reached a developmental stage that allows them to understand the loss of these connections

- from their adoptive/foster/kinship parents who may minimize their expressions of confusion, fear, sadness and anger. No matter how attached the adoptee may feel to their parents, if these deeper feelings are not acknowledged and validated, the experience of being truly known and accepted by the family is diminished. The child may feel that if the parents cannot acknowledge their deep feelings, a part of them is being rejected

- from society when intense feelings manifest in behavioral outbursts like yelling, cursing, bullying, lying, stealing and hitting. These behaviors may become pathologized and the child may be labeled as "troubled" or "bad." Rejection is triggered for the child as they may be: expelled from school; sent away to a treatment center; hospitalized; and/or sent to a boarding school

- from previous caregivers when they have experienced disruptions in their primary attachment relationships. Children, teens and adults may see these moves and disruptions as a personal rejection. Children in foster care who have changed placements several times and experienced repeated "attachment disruptions" or relational trauma may have an internalized belief that they deserve to be rejected

- from their parents, or they may fear rejection from their parents as they consider the possibility of searching for and having a reunion with their birth/first family. They may wonder if their adoptive parents will reject them if they search, or if they find their birth/first family, they may be rejected (again). In their desire to protect their adoptive parents and their fear of losing their adoptive family, adoptees may reject their very primal need to know the truth of their story

- from family and community when the language and phrases used in adoption and permanency reinforce feelings of rejection, for example "unplanned," "a mistake," "put up," "given up," "unwanted," "illegitimate," "bastard" or "hard-to-place child." The child may feel that they were unlovable, unwanted, unworthy, damaged, ugly, stupid, bad or defective. The child wonders whether if they had been "good," easier, taller, less demanding, cuter, quieter, smarter, sweeter, nicer, less angry, more compliant, more attractive, more "something," they might have been kept, not rejected

- from strangers, friends or family members when they make comments that invalidate the child's place in their family. Commonly asked questions consistently remind them that others may not view their family as "real" or acceptable and that others may see them as not a legitimate member of their family. Examples include: "Are these your real children?" "Do you have any of your own children?" "Why don't you look like your parents?" "Who are your real parents?" An individual may question whether this is their real family and whether they really belong in this family

- when records are sealed from them, even for adults. Adoptees may feel that they are treated as second-class citizens and do not have the same civil rights as all other individuals who can access their original birth certificates and information. Total strangers working for the government can access and read personal information about the adoptee that the adoptee has no right to access

- by the government or state. The creation of a legal document that lists the adoptive parents as the birth/first parents rejects the truth of the adoptee's origins and begins to build a false narrative about the adoptee's life. When the state conspires to seal the original identity, it can feel like a rejection of a person's very being

- from the birth/first parents when the adoption is open. The adoptee may have additional feelings of rejection as they witness the birth/first parents creating subsequent children and raising them. Another experience of rejection may surface when the birth/first parents have chosen to raise the siblings that came before the child who was placed

- from the birth/first parents when they are planning to place or may be losing another child through the courts and that subsequent child is not placed with their adoptive family. The adoptee may wonder if this occurred because their family wasn't good enough or if their adoptive parents didn't want another child "like them"

- when their adoptive parents choose to parent through third-party reproduction rather than adopt another child. The adoptee may feel that their adoption was not "good enough" and, therefore, the parents are not choosing to adopt again. When adoptive parents are willing to go to any length and expense to bring a child genetically connected to them into the family, the adoptee can feel diminished

- when either the adoptive parents or the birth/first parents decide to close an open adoption. It may be experienced as a loss or rejection when those relationships are severed

- when society supports the idea that the "good" adoptee is the one who is not curious and accepts their adoption without question. At the other extreme is the "bad" adoptee who is constantly questioning how their adoption came to be in an effort to understand their story, and is then judged by others as being ungrateful

- when the truth of adoption is withheld from them. They may overhear someone talking about their adoption, discover adoption paperwork after their parents are deceased, or hear that they were adopted from an extended family member. If the parents taught them that honesty was an important value and they then discover that the truth of their origins was withheld from them, they may feel rejected by their family or they may reject the family that raised them for withholding the facts

- when imagining who their birth/first family may be and how their birth/first family feels about them. In a closed adoption without "real" information, children often fill the void with fantasies. Children have active imaginations and have experienced Disney movies, fairytales and books that expose them to wicked witches, kidnapping, mothers dying horrible deaths, babies being left or abandoned, babies being mixed up in the nursery and babies being stolen and sold, and all these stories can build frightening images of birth/first parents. These negative images and fantasies impact a child's feelings of worth—"I came from terrible people." Fantasies flourish where facts flounder

- when the family who is raising them does not accept their true nature and wants the child to be more like them. These differences would include types of humor, interests, skillsets, personality traits and quirks, intellectual and athletic abilities, manner of expression such as speech cadence and speed of thought processes, and artistic or musical abilities. People who are born into their family may experience differences that make them stand out, but being adopted into a family can cause these differences to be less tolerated, creating feelings of being an outsider and unacceptable, a lack of fit. There can be an accumulative effect of these differences that creates a sense of ongoing rejection.

# Adoptive/permanent family

Adoptive/permanency parents may experience feelings of rejection or fears of future rejection due to any losses that brought them to this form of parenting. Grandparents, aunts, uncles, nieces, nephews, cousins and siblings may have fears of rejecting, or not liking, a family member who joins their family tree, and may have fears that the child will reject them since they are not "blood" relations. Relatives may have concerns about diminished feelings in relation to children entering the family who look, act and identify differently from other family members; in cases of open adoptions, the extended family may feel a sense of rejection when roles must be shared with the family of origin. Children already in the family may feel rejection when new children are added to the family with a concern that they were "not enough"; family members may feel rejection when other family members make negative statements or don't fully support their decision to grow their family through adoption/permanency.

Adoptive parents who adopt for the traditional reasons of infertility and/or genetic or health risk have already experienced a rejection of their bodies being able to create a child. They then must enter a system that could also reject them. Adoptive parents may feel that they must prove their worth to social workers, court representatives and birth/first parents, all of whom could reject them. To be approved or chosen also carries the risk of being rejected. The overarching sense for these families is that they must present as perfect. They may manifest their fears of rejection by becoming "super parents." They may over-parent, hover and helicopter, in order to feel deserving of the rights and responsibilities bestowed on them to parent this child. They may feel that they must constantly prove that people were not wrong in their assessment of them. Two additional examples of rejection include never being chosen by social workers or birth/first parents to receive a child, and an ultimate rejection by the child. An additional complexity for families adopting internationally includes the fact that the sending country must also "approve" the prospective adoptive family.

Any system or country that prospective adoptive parents approach to build their family will have a set of built-in preferences and biases that may cause a prospective family to be included or excluded. These vary by agency, public and private, foreign countries that have agreements with the United States to receive children for adoption, attorneys and facilitators who focus on a particular kind of family who fits their service. Opening one's private life to total strangers for examination and approval can lead to feelings of rejection or fear of rejection.

One of the emotional landmines unique to adoptive/permanency parents is the triggering of their feelings of rejection by the children they have been entrusted to raise and love. Children who have not yet attached to their new parents and children at a later stage of development who may be feeling insecure about their place in the family may make hurtful statements to their parents that trigger the parents' feelings of rejection or fear of rejection. Examples include: "You're not my real mom!" "My real parents wouldn't make me do that". "When I'm old enough, I'm leaving you to find my real parents." At that moment, the child is communicating a need or insecurity. These questions and statements from your child stem from their roots of insecurity, loss and feelings of rejection. If parents allow these statements to trigger their feelings and fear of rejection, they will unfortunately respond with statements that will create the very outcome they fear the most—disconnection or detachment. They then can become the rejecters of the child's behaviors, feelings, belief system and place in the family; thus by inadvertently reinforcing the child's insecurities and fears of rejection, the parent may be reinforcing a negative relational pattern.

---

Tyler and Thomas have been married for five years and recently became parents to a boy, aged 8. They are an enthusiastic couple, who have completed a year of assessment, education and participation in an ongoing support group for foster and adoptive parents. They believe that they have what it takes to be excellent parents to their newly arrived child. Initially, the three had a wonderful "honeymoon" as the boy was very excited about his new home. As real life set in and the parents began to set limits, create expectations and enforce discipline, the boy's behavior began to change. He refused to follow directions, lied, did not complete his school work, embarrassed them in public and talked back in a hurtful way. The couple experienced these behaviors as a personal rejection of themselves. Their feelings of confusion, anger and rejection caused them to want to withdraw from the child and their commitment to parenting him. Members of their parent support group who had already experienced similar "rejection behaviors" offered hope, tools and a sense of humor. This empowered Tyler and Thomas to keep going, depersonalize the child's self-protective behaviors, and better understand the child's fears of attaching.

---

Adoptive/permanency parents may experience rejection:

- from society, when they are not viewed as a "real" family, or when society sees adoption as a temporary change for the family, not permanent, lifelong and intergenerational

- from their child, fearing that if their child knew the truth of their adoption/permanency story they would reject them as not being their "real" parents. The lack of honesty and therefore the avoidance of topics

such as pregnancy, birth, sex education and physical differences among
family members may create a larger rejection when the child discovers
the truth about their entry into the family

- when they are marginalized or excluded by family and friends because of
their procreation challenges. Examples include "So sad you couldn't have
one of your own," "We didn't invite you to the baby shower because we
thought it would be too painful," "Too bad you have to share your child
with the birth/first family" and "Sorry your child is not a blood relative"

- from within the family system when one partner is blamed for the
infertility. In some cultures, even if the female is not the infertile partner,
she will carry the burden of the infertility to protect her husband
from the stigma of being infertile. Extended family may continue to
encourage the infertile partner to undergo fertility treatments for a
prolonged period of time or encourage the fertile partner to leave the
infertile partner in order to create offspring with another partner

- from their extended family and friends when they adopt a child of a
different race or ethnicity, or a child who brings trauma and acting-out
behaviors to family gatherings

- from the birth/first family when they make decisions the birth/first
family does not support, including a change of names, religion, a move
to a different community, educational decisions, medical decisions or
a change in the agreement in an open adoption

- from the child because of the attachment impairments or traumatic
behaviors that cause the parent to feel rejected by the child. A child
who has experienced several moves (primary attachment disruptions)
or relational trauma that includes abuse, neglect or violence typically
will work hard to avoid further psychic injury or emotional pain. The
child may self-protect by being avoidant, reactive and provocative. In
order to avoid further pain and rejection, the child may provoke, push
back and deflect against attachment and connection. For the parents,
this can trigger feelings of rejection connected to their core losses as
adoptive parents

- when their child decides to search and pursue a reunion with members
of the birth/first family, triggering feelings of rejection and loss yet
again. Adoptive parents can wonder: "Am I still the parent if there is a
reunion?" "Did I not do a good enough job?" "Does my child still love
me?" "Have I just been a glorified babysitter?"

- from school teachers, neighbors, therapists and extended family who don't believe they're parenting the "right way"; from agencies that might make the decision to not place another child with them

- when the court and social workers are making a determination as to where a child will be permanently placed. They may experience a good deal of ambivalence and rejection as the court and child welfare system determines the best long-term outcome for a child. The rejection may be connected to the court choosing the birth/first family members over foster or adoptive parents

- from other adoptive parents who are raising their children in a closed adoption and don't want their children exposed to a family that is doing an open adoption

- when the parent who was the driving force for the decision to parent through adoption and permanency is blamed by their partner for any problems that surface.

## Tools for all constellation members to address rejection

- List people who you feel have rejected you.

- List people whom you have rejected.

- How does rejecting someone protect you?

- How do you feel when you reject someone else?

- How do you feel when someone rejects you, and why do you think you were rejected?

- What are you doing with those feelings of rejection? Are you repressing or avoiding them? Are you avoiding them through self-medicating? Are you hiding your feelings because of fear of further rejection? Are you turning them into anger? Are you using those feelings to keep others away, believing that you must reject others before they can reject you?

- Who do you go to in order to share your feelings of rejection or fear of rejection and the insights you have gained from self-reflection? You may ask the people you trust and care about to listen to and validate your feelings. Let them know you realize they cannot fix your feelings.

- The cumulative effects of rejection may lead to anger. Anger needs expression in some physical form and vocalization.

- Create a ritual that allows you to identify, express and release feelings of rejection.

- Feelings of rejection may require forgiveness of yourself or another. Refer to Chapter 11, "The Power of Forgiveness to Address Loss and Grief."

- Separate the facts about your experience of adoption/permanency from the feelings of rejection associated with that experience. Were you actually rejected by another? It is helpful to understand the "why" of the rejection if it actually occurred. Understanding the facts may help a person depersonalize the feelings of the rejection and allow them to move to a more accurate interpretation of what happened.

- Feelings of rejection or fear of rejection may not be expressed directly by children. Parents will have to become excellent decoders of their child's emotional and behavioral signals and actions. Children who overreact to perceived slights, such as their brother getting more sweets, may quickly escalate into anger and tears. Parents need to resist the urge to deny those feelings. When the parent shifts to the telling of a happy adoption story, tells the child they are lucky or punishes them by sending them to their room when they are upset, the child feels more rejection. Parents might respond to their child's distressed feelings of rejection by saying "I can see that you are really hurt or angry right now" or "I can understand why you might feel that way."

- In order for children to learn how to express their feelings, try naming, describing, modeling, validating and expressing emotions in a healthy way. Feelings are neither good nor bad, they just are. Children really have no idea why they are feeling what they are feeling or why they are acting the way they are acting.

- Create an "adoption/permanency feelings jar" with your child (one per child), encouraging them to write down all of their feelings, as they surface, connected to adoption/permanency and their birth/first, foster or adoptive family. This helps children learn how to identify, label and express their feelings. Parents can strengthen their child's emotional competency by creating the jar, adding feelings as the child grows, and pulling out feelings to share during quiet moments.

- Parents can help teach the language of emotion most easily through play. Play "feelings" charades, where you act out a feeling without using any words and have others guess what you are feeling. Parents can model how to talk about the more difficult feelings of rejection, fear and anger by sharing their own experiences through play.

- Give your child permission and encourage them to express their feelings of rejection, blame and anger in a safe way. One of children's greatest fears is of further abandonment and rejection. Children will suffer in silence if that is what it takes to avoid being rejected. It may be one of the reasons children do not ask questions or talk about adoption. Tools to help children learn, label and express their feelings of anger, rejection and blame include: throwing wet sponges at the garage door while saying something that makes them angry; providing a punching bag and, with each punch, having the child share something that makes them angry; drawing an angry picture; and having them roll up a magazine and hit a pillow, each time identifying the hurt or angry feelings. Be present physically and emotionally as your child is expressing their hurt and angry feelings. Children can emote and discharge anger through physical exercise, hitting objects or pillows, martial arts, playing hard, laughing and yelling. It is important to note that the expression of anger requires noise and movement.

## Notes to professionals

Clients who have experienced rejection will be more sensitive to perceived slights. In response, they may not keep their appointments, may arrive late, present as agitated, blaming, provocative, angry and silent, may not make eye contact, and may refuse therapeutic assistance.

It is easy for clients experiencing feelings of rejection or a fear of rejection to misinterpret the actions of a therapist or social worker. If the professional has to reschedule or is late for an appointment, does not recall a previous conversation with the client or is required to transfer the case, the client could interpret these actions as rejection. Clients can feel devalued and rejected if a token of appreciation is offered as a way of saying "thank you" and the gift is refused.

One of the ways professionals can understand and build empathy with constellation members is to view rejection through the lens of a particular constellation member by completing the above tools for all constellation members to address rejection. For example, complete the tasks in the tools section through the lens of a birth/first mother.

For professionals who primarily work with adoptees, this exercise will give the professional a window into the experience of the constellation member who is not in the room. In reality, professionals should always be mindful of the entire constellation familial system and its impact on the client they are serving.

As a professional, in order to best serve constellation members, take responsibility for your own reactions to rejection. Members of the constellation may project their feelings of rejection, pain and anger onto the professional who is attempting to assist them. The professional's main task is to move through any feelings of rejection with the goal of creating trust with the client. Being able to create and sustain interpersonal relationships is a learned skill. Professionals are in a position to teach and model these important relational skills; every aspect of this work is relational.

# Chapter 4

# Shame and Guilt

The cave you fear to enter holds the treasure
that you seek. (Joseph Campbell, 1991)

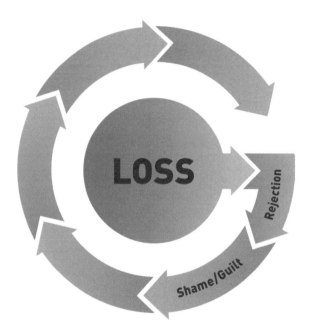

The second spoke in the wheel of the Seven Core Issues in Adoption and
Permanency is shame and guilt, both of which may impact an individual's self-
esteem and self-worth and create anxiety. Everyone, at some point in their life,
experiences shame or guilt. Shame and guilt are both social emotions meant to
keep people from acting in pure self-interest. Shame is a generally maladaptive
emotion, while guilt is generally an adaptive emotion. The same action may
give rise to both feelings, where shame reflects how we feel about ourselves and
guilt involves an awareness that our actions may have injured someone else.
Shame relates to self, guilt to others. Shame is the painful feeling that derives
from the awareness of something dishonorable, disgraceful and/or embarrassing

done by oneself or by another to oneself. Guilt is a feeling of responsibility or remorse for some offense, crime or wrong, whether real or imagined. Shame is about "being," and guilt is about "doing."

There is a difference between the experience of being shamed, stigmatized and stereotyped. Stigmatization is associated with words such as undeserving, unfit, no good, out of place, unmerited, valueless, wretched, evil, bad and unwanted, which can make a person feel ashamed. Stereotyping involves a fixed and oversimplified belief about a particular category of people. Stereotypes create a barrier that leads to prejudice, making one assume that they know someone just based on a stereotype. Examples of stereotypes in adoption and permanency would be that "children raised in foster care are damaged and/or troubled," "good adoptees should be grateful," "birth/first parents are abusive and/or addicts," "adoptive parents are rich, religious professionals who are infertile," "kinship parents are poor and elderly" and "foster parents are in it for the money." These stereotypes rob constellation members of their individual uniqueness and positive attributes and may trigger shame or guilt.

Shame originates as a negative reflection from others. It is an "outside-in" emotion wherein we receive shame from others. All societies use some form of shame as a way to control their population's adherence to their culture's social norms. Shame is experienced when someone: looks at us in disgust; uses an accusatory tone of voice; avoids or denies our needs or existence; doesn't touch us or touches us harshly; will not make eye contact, when culturally acceptable; and uses derogatory words repeatedly that demean a person. When shame is intensely experienced from infancy through the formative years, an inner critic is developed that creates a negative or harsh view of the self, caretakers and the world. Once that perspective is internalized, the individual may look for and/or create reinforcement for that belief system. These shame-based belief systems may be passed from generation to generation through the intimacy of the parent–child attachment relationship.

Shame not only lives in the mind but inhabits the body. Since shame is such an early primal emotion, when triggered, one can feel small, like a child. There is a particular body posture connected to shame and an automatic pattern which is fairly similar to what one would observe when seeing someone else who is traumatized; it is a posture of collapse. The physical response is a lowering of their head, a lowering of their eyes and a rolling of their shoulders in a forward position, similar to a turtle that retreats into its shell. The person's face may elongate as the facial muscles loosen; the face loses color or blushes, and the pupils constrict. Some individuals feel nauseated; their ears may ring, their skin may feel prickly and they may have a limited perspective on themselves, others and the world. Some people may actually faint from feeling and experiencing shame. Shame can impair the prefrontal cortex's ability to regulate what is happening in the mid-brain—the part of the brain that is sensitive to reward or relief. The mid-brain may trigger a person to engage in addictive behavior because those behaviors provide quick relief from the shame.

Trauma breeds shame, and embeds itself in the heart, mind and body.

---

In *The Body Keeps the Score: Brain, Mind, and Body in the Healing of Trauma* (2014), Bessel van der Kolk states that victims of early chronic trauma struggle with making direct eye contact. Making direct eye contact can trigger intense activation deep inside their emotional brains, in primitive areas that generate startle, hypervigilance, cowering and other self-protective behaviors. Van der Kolk found that survivors of chronic early trauma were not utilizing their prefrontal cortex during direct eye contact, which allows for social engagement; their brains simply went into survival mode.

---

Shame greatly impacts self-esteem. Shame leaves a person believing that their core self is "bad" or "less than" others. These beliefs increase anxiety and may lead to defensive behaviors. One way to protect a fragile self is to redirect the pain and blame others. A shamed individual is apt to develop excuses, use denial and even blame others for their own actions and feelings. The tragic result for the individual is a deep sense of isolation as one must not allow anyone to get close to a "bad core." This dynamic may help to explain intimate partner violence, child abuse, gang violence, school shootings and other acts of violence.

Peter Breggin, author of *Guilt, Shame and Anxiety: Understanding and Overcoming Negative Emotions* (2014), says that for a person to flourish emotionally, they need to question and reject any ideas that give them reasons for taking orders from the emotions of shame, guilt and/or anxiety. These negative emotions are imperfect remnants of human evolution and child rearing that impede mature, rational and loving conduct in adults. They are legacy emotions built into our brains and bodies, then triggered and shaped during childhood and adolescence. Adults feel them as emotional baggage. Shame inhibits willfulness and aggression by making people feel intimidated, powerless or too insignificant to assert themselves. Shyness and a tendency to withdraw are common reactions. People feel that it is "them" against "others." Shame can masquerade as confidence or even narcissism, humility, aloofness, sweet and adorable, demure and harmless. Alternatively, shame can be expressed as emotionally reactive, hypervigilant and envious. People with shame avoid, conform and compare themselves to others routinely. The anticipation of shame can infect all of life's experiences, even those that should be experienced as joyous and pleasurable. The deepest shame a person can experience is from not being loved, which is internalized as being "unlovable."

Shame and guilt discourage people from thinking of themselves in a constructive or positive way. This can limit individuals from loving and receiving love as they do not feel worthy. Events are psychologically neutral. It is people's reactions to those events that trigger shame, guilt and anxiety. It is the combination of feelings, thoughts and judgments, both conscious and unconscious, that triggers the emotions of guilt, shame and anxiety. For example, a child who has resiliency based on strong attachments and healthy coping strategies would respond to bullying in school differently from a child who believes they are stupid, unwanted and deserve bad things to happen to them. The event is the bullying, but the emotional response is different based on the child's feelings, thoughts and judgments.

Guilt develops from our earliest parent–child attachment experiences. Guilt is a learned social emotion. Consistent, secure and healthy primary attachment relationships allow the child to experience and internalize the attachment figure's values and beliefs on which a conscience develops. The conscience allows for guilt to be felt and develops as the child internalizes the primary attachment figure's voices, actions and images, which are subsequently carried within an individual for the rest of their lives. Guilt plays an important role in the development of the conscience as the child learns to value not doing harmful things, not hurting others, or bullying, lying, stealing or name calling. Guilt motivates people to seek forgiveness, accept blame for mistakes and correct a wrong. Healthy guilt can change the destructive behavior and attitudes that created the original harm, break in relationship and/or mistake in relation to another.

Maladaptive or unhelpful guilt is defined as a feeling of psychological discomfort against our unrealistically high standards. Much of the time these unrealistically high standards are created in childhood to please an adult. Unhealthy guilt leads people to emphasize self-punishment over behavioral change, trapping them in guilt.

Maladaptive guilt can make individuals question their value as self-criticism and self-blame drive their belief system and decisions. It can be expressed by over-burdening our lives as a form of remorse. This form of guilt can lead one to extreme feelings of remorse. People may take on more and more duties and obligations in reaction to the remorse and be consistently worried that they will never be able to achieve enough to be seen as a "good" person. In addition, the person tries to please others, guess what the other may need, and never asks others to meet their needs. These behaviors may lead to martyrdom and sacrifice. This experience can emotionally immobilize people and lead to feelings of anger, anxiety and resentment. The outcome may be depression, exhaustion and a sense of helplessness.

Maladaptive guilt, along with anxiety, leads to feelings of fright, confusion and being overwhelmed. Anxiety is a place of fear that destroys rational thought and enforces emotional stupidity. It disperses our anger and leaves it with no direction. It undermines our assertiveness. Anxiety encourages people to be helpless. The self-critic uses phrases such as "You can't handle that" and "Don't even think about trying that." Anxiety rarely signals a "real threat" and is a raw and primitive emotion. Physical responses to anxiety include tremors, headaches, stomach problems, sleep problems, paleness and sweaty palms, hyperventilating and an increased heart rate. Anxiety releases adrenaline and the mouth gets dry, and there may be a distortion of the body or the world around them, which makes a person accident prone. Acute anxiety can feel like a heart attack but actually may be a panic attack.

The cumulative effect of anxiety can lead to anger. If the anger becomes overwhelming it may lead to a sense of numbness. Anger covers up how we feel, which is both vulnerable and threatened. Anger always feels justified to the person who is experiencing it, even if it is irrational. Venting anger is like fanning a fire—it can border on losing self-control and can be self-destructive. Intense and overwhelming anger banishes love. Both anger and numbness are last-ditch efforts to manage underlying emotional suffering. Chronic numbness can make one feel hopeless, inhuman, cold, and spiritually and emotionally dead.

## Impact of shame and guilt on constellation members

Shame and guilt have long been created by the secrecy attached to adoption and permanency. Secrecy has been used as an element of control over constellation members in the name of privacy. Society has promoted secrecy in adoption/permanency as evidenced by the following: Hester Prynne in *The Scarlet Letter*, by Nathaniel Hawthorne; the Freudian view of the "Unwed Mother" by Leontine Young; Carol Schaefer's book *The Other Mother*; movies such as *Philomena, Second Best, Mother and Child, Antwone Fisher, Secrets & Lies, Secondhand Lions, Martian Child, Problem Child, White Oleander, The Ten Commandments, Instant Family*; and the documentary by Sara Lamm, *Thank You for Coming*, the story of sperm donation and secrecy. Secrecy has driven policy and practice and is still supported through the stereotyping of constellation members and evidenced in the language used by books, movies, news and social media.

The very words that are used to describe constellation members are most often negative, stigmatizing and/or stereotypical. The authors, when presenting workshops, have requested that the audience share words that immediately come to mind when describing constellation members. Some of the responses are included below, and we invite you to think about the terms that come into your mind as you review these stigmatizing stereotypes.

- Children in foster care: "damaged," "older," "dark skinned," "angry," "abused," "drug affected." These very same children are seen differently once the adoption is finalized and, almost by magic, become different children: "lucky," "grateful," "good," "smart."

- Foster parents: "money hungry," "heroic," "babysitters," "too many children," "underpaid and overworked," "poor," "crazy for working with the child welfare system and courts and having their family invaded by outsiders." These very same foster parents are viewed positively if they adopt the children in their care.

- Birth/first parents who voluntarily relinquish their child: "young," "in school," "got caught," "smart," "white," "middle class or above," "female."

- Birth/first fathers: "uncaring," "sperm donor," "philanderer," "addict," "gang member," "threat."

- Birth/first parents whose rights were terminated: "addicts," "poor," "abusers," "mentally ill," "uncaring," "poorly educated," "homeless," "promiscuous," "undependable."

- Adoptive parents who adopt through voluntary relinquishment: "rich," "religious," "educated," "professionals," "infertile," "perfect parents."

- Adoptive parents who adopt through the foster care system: "low/ middle socio-economic status," "minority background," "good hearted," "heroic," "includes more diversity such as single parents, LGBTQ parents, older parents, parents with previous parenting experience."

- Parents who adopt internationally: "wealthy," "well educated," "wanting to escape dealing with the birth/first family," "resourceful," "heroic."

All of these words and phrases are occasionally true but most often limit the truth and disallow for the uniqueness of each individual constellation member. Labels and stereotypes that are repeated over and over again can be internalized and impossible to live up to (a saint) or live down (abusive). Stereotypes only reveal a fragment of a person's story and often distort the story. They create barriers to communication and limit empathy, individuality and the complexity of the individual roles that constellation members play. They create shame or guilt, which increases secrecy. Present laws, policies and practices continue to support the secrecy that leads to the shame and guilt that constellation members may experience.

In the United States, adoptees are fighting to gain access to their original birth certificates. It is common, when a child is adopted, that their original birth certificate is removed from public record and replaced with an amended version with the adoptive parents' names listed as if they gave birth to the child. The amended birth certificate becomes a legal lie that supports secrecy and is frustrating to adoptees. This policy and practice keeps adoptees in a child-like position where they cannot access what every other citizen has a right to access. This archaic practice denies adoptees the right to know their origins and leads to the secrecy that creates shame and guilt.

Years ago, a bill to allow access to original birth certificates for adoptees was being heard in Sacramento, California, by the Judicial Committee where it needed to be passed in order to be released onto the floor of the California Assembly. The Governor had agreed to sign the bill once it had passed both houses in California. The nine judicial committee members were men, six of whom had been touched by adoption in their families. After testimony by several members of the constellation, the panel voted six against and three for passing the bill to the Assembly. The panel members against the bill referred to the issue of confidentiality that they believed birth/first families had been promised. They voted against the bill in spite of the fact that several organizations representing birth/first parents stated that they were never promised confidentiality and supported the bill.

A search and reunion expert working in California shared that she had helped reunite some of the children of those committee members with their families of origin. She stated that the children knew that their parents had some shame about their infertility and rarely spoke about adoption. The adult adoptees had not shared their reunions with their parents because they had felt guilty about what they had done even though it had benefited them.

Secrets held in family systems can impede attachments, rob individuals of important facts that allow them to form a cohesive identity, and may negatively impact a person's self-worth. Secrets held by a community, or the larger society, deny people access to the truth.

Birth/first parents may experience shame and guilt when:

- they place a child for adoption or lose a child to the foster care system

- they are not able to provide for their child

- they are not able to save their child from experiencing pain, sadness and distress

- they are in a "lose lose" situation. If they raise their child under less than adequate circumstances, people will say that they are selfish and that adoptive parents would have so much more to offer the child. If the child is placed, people will say they are selfish and ask: "How could anyone give up their own flesh and blood?" They are shamed either way

- they are not able to keep their child safe from witnessing violence, being abused, or exposed to drugs/alcohol

- they are not able to provide food or shelter for their child

- they realize that their poor choices affected so many people and that they did not accept help or programs that were offered

- they realize the sadness, anger or pain that was experienced by the other parent or extended family members

- they are not able to complete the court's requirements in the time allotted

- they are unable to select and sustain healthy relationships, exposing their child to rotating partners or partners who are violent or addicted

- they do not know the identity of their child's father

- bad things happen to their children when they are not with them, such as abuse, molestation, bullying, multiple moves, group home care or being treated poorly

- their children later ask: "How did this happen?" "Why didn't you raise me?" "Where were you?" "Why didn't you work harder to get me back?"

- they have to explain to their future children why their sibling is not in their family

- they have to explain their past decisions and lifestyles to a future partner, spouse or relative

- the degradation of the court process publicly declares them as "unfit parents"

- what used to be hidden or secret is now public

- they lose more than one child to the foster care system or relinquishment

- they lie or withhold the truth to other parties involved

- they think and worry about what the resource/foster/adoptive or kin family is saying about them. Shame and guilt come from the judgments they feel others are making

> Maggie, a 60-year-old woman who placed a child for adoption when she was 15 years old, presented with all of the physical attributes of shame, guilt and anxiety. When we met her, she avoided eye contact, spoke very softly, wore clothes that were drab and too large for her body, held herself in a way that made her appear very small, and kept a distance between us that did not allow for touch. She appeared anxious as she shared her story. She explained that becoming pregnant with a high school boyfriend, sharing the news with her boyfriend, his family and her family and experiencing the demoralizing anger that was directed towards her by all those people was a devastating experience. She felt that everyone was ashamed of her, and she accepted, at the age of 15, that she was responsible for everything that was happening to the people she cared about and to the child. She had never married or had another pregnancy. She lived a very isolated life in a small community and limited any activities that would have given her pleasure. She was driven to help others and to be seen as a "good woman" in her community. "No one really knows how bad I am. I am ashamed of what I have done. I don't share that I'm a birth mother with anyone."

- they feel that they did everything possible and still lost their child

- if they gave birth to a child out of wedlock, there was a rape, or incest, or if they were promiscuous. They may see themselves as "dirty" and unworthy of a healthy relationship and may feel uncomfortable and ashamed of their bodies

- they have healthy sexual desires and needs. If healthy sexual desires created a pregnancy and loss of the child, sex and loss may be subsequently connected

- they ingest food that gives them pleasure and nourishment and feel undeserving of that pleasure, leading to regurgitation of food and the possibility of bulimia. Some birth/first mothers have described this experience of filling their belly until it is overly full and extended and then emptying their belly as a repetition of what happened to them during pregnancy and then placement

- they realize they denied their pregnancy, so neither they nor the baby received proper nourishment and medical care and they may have starved themselves in an effort to hide the pregnancy or continued to smoke, drink or use drugs

- they have been or continue to be party to a secret: never telling the father that a child was born; never telling their family a child was born and placed for adoption; keeping the child a secret from a future spouse and subsequent children; and telling others that they never had a child

- they feel relief and are able to move on with their life

- the children they are raising are impacted by this crisis and loss

- a family member offers to adopt or raise their child and they ignore or deny the offer

- they look back over time and realize that the decisions that were made did not unfold in the best interest of the child that they lost. The child did not have a happy childhood and/or grew up in foster care or had a negative adoption experience

- the birth/first father denies the pregnancy and the child and disappears

- the birth/first father does not support the birth/first mother through the pregnancy and placement of the child

- the birth/first father physically or emotionally hurts the birth/first mother or the child

- the birth/first father is told later in life that he does have an offspring and contemplates all of the things he should have been doing for his child

- the birth/first father does not tell his family about the pregnancy or the child

- the birth/first father is unable to support the birth/first mother/child because of age, lack of resources, distance, addictions or mental health issues or incarceration.

Adoptees and individuals raised in kinship/foster families may experience shame and guilt when:

- neither family of origin (paternal or maternal) kept them, wanted them, raised them or tried to get them back

- their siblings were kept and they were not

- they stand out and look different from their family. Other people stare at them and ask intrusive questions, and sometimes that feels embarrassing and/or shaming

- their family tells everybody that they were adopted. Being adopted is private and personal

- they are growing up in a family that has access to so much more than their family of origin

- siblings who are growing up with their family of origin don't have access to the same resources and lifestyle that they have been given

- they can't live up to the fantasies and expectations that their adoptive/ foster or kin family has of them

- they think they might have been "a mistake," and maybe shouldn't be alive

- nobody will tell them the truth about their beginnings because they believe the truth is that there is something wrong with them and all of this is their fault

- having experienced early abuse, neglect or trauma and they feel as if it was their fault

- they told the truth about the abuse and neglect in their family that caused the separation from their family. Their siblings are mad or upset with them because they told outsiders what was happening in the family

- they believe it is their fault that their siblings are in foster care or adopted. They should have done something to change the circumstances

- they do not feel gratitude or very lucky for being adopted or in foster care

- they experience divided loyalties—guilt and shame for loving their birth/ first family and their new family at the same time. They know that either family will be upset with them for loving or caring about the other family

- they ask their parents questions that make them feel uncomfortable, sad or angry. They want to put their own interests and curiosity first, which could make them uncomfortable. They are curious about so much, but their shame and guilt inhibit them asking questions

- they hear the words "illegitimacy," "bastard" or "mistake" in connection to their story

- their family is so different from other families. Their family is non-traditional: LGBTQ, bi-racial, multi-ethnic, single, kinship, foster and so on. They are embarrassed when friends ask them why their family looks so different or why parents are so old or why they have two dads

- their actions, behaviors and needs that come from their early life experiences cause problems in their family, neighborhood and school

- they no longer have the culture or language from the country of their origin. They can't communicate with the people they look like

> Juan was adopted by a Caucasian family at an early age and grew up not speaking Spanish, although a part of his heritage was Mexican and that is how he presented to the world. An incident occurred in a parking lot when he was 14 years old. He experienced both shame and guilt, accompanied with high anxiety, when a Spanish-speaking woman, who was in great distress, locked eyes with him and he realized that she was coming to him for help. He was ashamed of his inability to communicate. He realized in that moment that the reason the woman was reaching out to him was that he looked more like her than he did his adoptive mother, who was standing by his side. The woman could have been a relative but he could not communicate with her.

- they hurt their body because they experience self-loathing from their early physical/emotional/sexual abuse and neglect. Their body is bad and they hate their body. They don't want anyone touching their body and they do things to hurt and punish their body

- their extended family, birth/first or adoptive, does not see them as their "real" relative

- their first/birth family chooses to disconnect from an open adoption

- there are members of their family of origin, as well as their present family, that they do not like or trust

- they were never claimed permanently by any family and face emancipation without any home or family to connect to for birthdays, holidays or during a crisis. What is it about them that makes them so unlovable?

Joshua was 7 years old when he and his older sister went into foster care due to neglect and abuse. Their grandmother offered to parent Joshua's sister but said two children would be too much for her, so Joshua went into his first foster home. During his first few years, he went through four different homes and then into a group home for older boys. Feeling rejected and disconnected from his family, Joshua was sad and angry most of the time and would often lash out and become aggressive. When he turned 18, he couldn't wait to leave the group home and be on his own, without the "system" telling him what to do. Without any family to love and support him, his shame and isolation led him to join a local gang. Within three years after he emancipated from foster care he was in federal prison doing a five-year sentence.

Adoptive/permanency parents may experience shame and guilt when:

- asked "why" they adopted. They are reminded of their core losses and that they are parenting "differently"

- asked "where" did they get their children and how much did it cost

- asked why they didn't have their "own" children, as if the children they adopted are not their "own" children

- asked who the "real parents" are, as if their children are not their "real" children

- they lose their temper and do not understand their child or become embarrassed by their child's behaviors in public

- they don't like their child or the child triggers feelings in them that they dislike about themselves

- they withhold or distort information during the family assessment or in their conversations with the birth/first family

- they acknowledge that they do not like the birth/first family

- they break a promise to the birth/first family

- they close an open adoption because they made a commitment to the birth/first parents at the beginning of the adoption

- they realize the effect that adoption, trauma and/or birth/first family relationships are having on their entire family system

- they experience joy in response to the birth/first parents' grief and loss. In adoption and permanency, the "parenting parents" gain a lot of joy, fun and love from their child. The knowledge that they are benefiting from the sorrow and pain from what the birth/first parents are losing often triggers feelings of shame, guilt and/or anxiety

> The Brinker family decided to celebrate the finalization of adopting two children, aged 1 and 3, by inviting friends and family to an adoption celebration event at their home. During the event, they asked friends and family members to share their hopes and blessings as they welcomed the children into their family and community. The Brinker parents had written a poem that the adoptive mother read aloud, and at one point she tearfully stated, "I'm sorry that our greatest joy, becoming parents to two beautiful children, is someone else's greatest pain."

- having been assessed, trained and approved by professionals, they are still not able to meet the needs of their child

- they place their child in a residential treatment center, boarding school or hospital. "I feel as if I'm deserting my child and at the same time I feel relief." The knowledge that their child has needs that are so significant that they are not able to meet them within their own family can trigger feelings of shame, anxiety and guilt

> Laura and Pat, a couple with three biological children, adopted Jessica when she was 12 years old. Laura was a school teacher and Jessica was a student in her fifth-grade class. Jessica had suffered early, intense and chronic trauma that included extreme neglect and both physical and sexual abuse. Jessica entered foster care when she was 4 years old and lived in six foster homes and two group homes prior to moving in with Laura and Pat. The couple believed that because they had a lot of prior parenting experience, Jessica's "emotional and behavioral" problems would go away as soon as she settled into their family and felt loved. By the end of their second year of parenting Jessica, she had been admitted to two psychiatric hospitals due to suicidal ideations and self-harming behaviors and an intensive residential treatment facility. Both parents shared what a humbling and guilt-ridden experience it had been for them to admit that they needed a lot of outside support and guidance to help heal their daughter.

- they decide to return a child to the foster care system, dissolve an adoption or send the child away to a place from which the child can emancipate themselves

- asked why they didn't help the birth/first family keep the child

- a foster/adoptive parent realizes they did not do everything possible to help the child return to their family of origin

- they realize they did little to nothing to include the birth/first father

- they believe their infertility is a punishment from God: "Maybe God didn't want me to have a child," "Maybe God knew I would be a bad mom/dad"

- they cannot undo all of the trauma and problems their child has, no matter how hard they try. When parents have tried various schools, tutors, therapists, therapies, doctors and parenting practices and they believe there has been little to no progress, the feelings of shame and guilt can be overwhelming

- parents don't share the child's adoption status with them. The adoptee finds out at a later date that the parents have withheld or lied to the child about their true story. They feel shame and guilt because not only were they not able/willing to tell their child the factual story of their beginning, they also realize that withholding this information has created other issues for their child, such as mistrust, a sense of betrayal, profound grief and identity confusion

- asked if they would adopt or take in the siblings of their child and they decline

- they chose not to adopt a child in their care. Often parents come to this decision based on their own limitations and/or that the child's needs may be overwhelming the marriage/parents and family

- they receive money for parenting children who are placed from foster care/adoption

- they gain new information and knowledge, and may feel badly about some of the mistakes they made in their parenting.

The extended adoptive/permanency family may feel shame and guilt when:

- they have not fully accepted a child that joined their family through foster care or adoption

- they do not treat the child the same way as the children born into the family

- they realize the things they did or did not do to advise, help and/ or support their children through infertility, adoption, parenting and so on

- they were able to achieve a pregnancy and give birth when another family member was unable to because of infertility

- they did not have the financial ability to help their children with fertility treatments or adoption

- they are not able to be a consistent, dependable emotional resource through the process of foster care, adoption and/or permanency. Issues of geographical distance, health, age, finances or other life commitments may have been the cause but guilt and shame could still be experienced

- they do not step in to support the children or parents, even if circumstances gave them no choice in the decision.

All constellation members have experienced an assault on their self-esteem due to the losses, rejection and shame and guilt that are connected to their experiences of adoption and permanency. Constellation members can counteract these negative experiences by understanding the four pillars of self-esteem.

## Techniques to address self-esteem and self-worth

Like four pillars of a house that uphold its foundation, the authors believe that self-esteem is based on four pillars of *connectedness, uniqueness, power* and *role models*. If any of these pillars are not strong, the very foundation of self-esteem and self-worth is threatened.

*To establish connectedness:* a person must feel a sense of rootedness and belonging to a family, a clan or a community. This is based on reciprocal attachment to others: first, the parents must welcome the child into the family (offer themselves as "attachment figures"); second, over time, the child allows for their dependency and attachment needs to be met (accepts the offer to be vulnerable and attach). As the attachment with the primary caregivers deepens, the child can take the learned attachment skills and extend them to the extended family, clan and community. Identifying with and feeling a connection to one's past or heritage requires that one has knowledge, ongoing updates and honesty versus secrecy about one's past, story and lineage. People must feel that they are connected to something larger than themselves; they must be able to pursue their passions, identify their purpose and enjoy their interests and vocation. In addition, they need to feel pride in relationships with others and a connection to the community at large; know that the people or things they are connected to are considered positive and valuable by others; and feel that they are important to others and others want to be connected to them.

For children to feel connected, adults must claim them from day one and not wait for legalities to be completed. They must assume the role of parent without the certainty of the child growing up with them. They cannot allow their own prior losses or fear of loss to get in the way of meeting the child's emotional and attachment needs. Children are always communicating what they need through their behaviors. No two children are the same. Parents must listen, observe and learn *this* particular child's needs in order to establish and strengthen connections.

Another way to preserve connections for the child is to acknowledge and value all of the child's previous relationships, such as birth/first family, relative caregivers, previous foster families, and siblings. Families should maintain and preserve all photographs, letters, cards, clothing and toys that have arrived with the child as evidence of their prior lives with other families.

*To acknowledge uniqueness:* a person must feel that there is something special that makes them different from all others. The goal is to discover, with the support of others, their unique gifts and talents that they bring into the world. Everyone needs permission to explore and ask for support in order to cultivate their uniqueness; being acknowledged by others for one's uniqueness in a positive way is critical in this process. In addition, people need to feel free to express their unique self to others without apology; therefore, respecting themselves as an individual with unique gifts, interests and points of view. Individuals must be able to enjoy the feeling of being different without having to make others uncomfortable or diminishing others' uniqueness.

Without genetic mirroring and/or full access to both paternal and maternal family trees, how does an individual discover their unique talents, gifts and interests? Introducing children broadly to life's offerings through music, art, theatre, sports (both individual and team), travel, educational pursuits in math, science, writing, poetry and language becomes crucial when information is missing. There may or may not be a reflection of gifts or talents between the child and the family that is raising them; thus supporting a child to investigate and experience a variety of activities, interests and talents can generate a positive sense of being unique while still being a part of a family whose interests and skills may be different from theirs. This requires parents to set aside their fantasies about who they expect their child to be and accept the uniqueness of the child they are raising.

*To establish a sense of power:* a person must have a connection to a family and clan that has created a foundation of values, beliefs and spirituality that become touchstones as they choose how to use their power. Power helps us feel that we are in charge of our own destiny or life, which includes taking responsibility for those things that go well and don't go well; allowing us to make mistakes and use those mistakes as lessons learned. Therefore, the individual is able to use the skills they learned or have been taught in situations that require those skills to be activated, acknowledging that each and every situation offers individuals choice. As a result, people feel confident that they can distinguish right from wrong, good from bad, and understand that they have the ability to solve most problems by themselves or by reaching out to their support system.

Many individuals with traumatic loss struggle for power and control in their day-to-day lives. They may demonstrate their need for power through self-defeating actions that negatively impact on them. Examples of self-defeating actions include being passive-aggressive, bullying, being hostile, not taking direction from others, talking back, initiating power struggles and setting themselves up to fail.

Adults need to "share" power with children by giving them limited choices throughout the day—telling children that they are powerful and have rights and acknowledging when the child has exercised their power. Adults with a history of loss as children may need others to remind them that they are no longer "helpless children" but now have the power and maturity to make positive decisions on a daily basis.

*To create and sustain role models:* a person must have a relationship with people whom they feel are worth emulating. People need role models that reflect where they came from and who they hope to become in the future. Positive role models empower individuals by allowing them to see a reflection of themselves in others, which enables them to develop a positive self-image. Examples include seeing individuals of the same gender, sexual orientation, culture, ethnicity and race as people who reflect our life experience in adoption, foster care and kinship caregiving. These role models should be respected and valued members of the community. Role models enable us to make sense of our lives, find our purpose and understand our role in the larger community. For birth/first parents, foster/adoptive parents and kinship parents, this means having role models who can help normalize and light the path towards positive self-esteem.

Who do you look to for positive role models if the only thing you know about your heritage is that your country was too poor for you to be claimed by anyone; that your birth/first parent could not parent you due to addiction, poverty or war; that the people who conceived you were unable to parent you due to age, stage of life and/or life circumstances; or that your birth/first father never acknowledged or saw you? You may have positive role models from the family or clan that has raised you, but they may or may not reflect how you look or think or your sense of humor, temperament, interests or skills.

In order to imagine who an individual could become in the future, they must have role models that reflect their experience as an adoptee, former youth in care or a person raised by a relative. From the very beginning of the child entering the family, it becomes imperative for the family to provide access to peers, neighbors and relatives who have a similar lived experience. These individuals can offer a normalization of the child's feelings; diminish isolation; provide access to information and knowledge; and model coping strategies that allow the child to answer intrusive questions and respond to bullying, racism and/or cultural bias. The role models may also be a connection to the child's language, race and culture of origin, thus allowing for the development of positive racial and/or cultural identity as well as a strengthening of self-esteem.

## Self-esteem beliefs

A child/adult with a history of neglect may believe:

- I don't matter
- No one cares
- I'm not important or valuable or worthy
- I don't know who I am
- I don't know what is right
- I am a victim
- I don't know how to get close

A child/adult with a history of abuse/trauma may believe:

- I am bad, damaged, broken
- Everything is my fault
- I'm not important or valuable or worthy
- I deserve bad things to happen to me
- I am weak, not powerful
- I don't trust others; I stay isolated to avoid emotional closeness
- If people get close to me, they will see how bad or worthless I am

Self-esteem—positive beliefs:

- I am good, valuable, important and worthy
- I *was* a victim of trauma/neglect *and* I am strong and resilient
- It's okay to ask for what I need
- I deserve to have good people and things in my life
- I am lovable and loved
- I can trust and depend on others; others can trust and depend on me
- I have strengths and talents that I can nurture and share with others

## Additional techniques to address self-esteem and self-worth

- To challenge faulty beliefs, focus on assets and strengths, instead of weakness or limitation; give credence to a job well done and a challenge that was positively addressed, a new skill learned; acknowledge a mistake as an opportunity to learn and not as a failure, and a new friendship made.

- Positive focus on the little things done well makes a big difference. Positive reinforcement reinforces positive behaviors. For parents, this can be catching the child doing well, stating: "Good job sitting at the table," "I love how you have folded your clothes," "Congratulations on finishing your homework and completing your chores."

- Communicate unconditional acceptance for yourself and your child. Do not make your love and acceptance dependent on their behavior. Recognize improvement and effort, not just accomplishments.

- Let your child know their worth by respecting them as you would any other person, adult or child. This will lay the foundation for their self-respect. Be mindful of the language and tone of voice when speaking to others.

- Mean what you say and say what you mean. Keep your commitments and promises as a form of self-respect.

- Encourage cooperation as opposed to competition within the family. Every member of the family is valuable and has a unique and important role to play. Being given responsibilities within the family helps each individual feel like an important contributor to the family's well-being and success.

- Create achievable expectations for both yourself and others. Children who are expected to pull their weight in the family feel that they have an important job to do. Children feel a sense of accomplishment when they work hard to achieve a set goal.

- Avoid using demeaning or discouraging looks, comments and actions. Yelling, nagging, eye-rolling, turning your back, laughing or bullying others are all self-esteem killers. Comments like the following—"How many times do I have to tell you?" "What makes you think you can do that?" "You failed at that before." "You'll never learn." "You're going to turn out just like them." "You always…" "You never…"—can become self-fulfilling prophecies. These negative words, comments and feelings can easily become a part of a person's inner voice. For those who grew up with this negative input, learning to talk back to those voices, defending your inner child, are both important to the healing process. Saying it out loud and writing it down is much more impactful than ruminating about it.

- Choose friends who are playful and allow you to help your inner child feel joy, pleasure and laughter. Everyone needs time to play and be playful as a part of building self-esteem.

- Develop your child's and/or your own sense of humor and teach that happiness comes from within.

- Children and adults should practice being assertive and should understand that it's okay to take risks, make mistakes and even fail. That's how we learn.

- Permit your child to make decisions that are age appropriate and to solve problems that they create. Parents can help teach decision making by helping their child to identify the problem and offering solutions and options to be practiced.

- Foster creativity in yourself and/or your child.

- Discipline with respect, empathy and love. Each day is a new beginning—do not carry yesterday's mistakes and problems into today. Do not keep score!

- Teach your child to forgive themselves and others by modeling forgiveness of yourself, them and others.

- Take time to explore your own needs and desires, practice expressing them and risk being vulnerable and occasionally failing while learning to assert your authentic self.

## Techniques to address shame and guilt

Bessel van der Kolk (2014, p.104) states, "Shame is a by-product of chronic trauma. Self-blame is almost universal in chronic trauma because so many people are traumatized from their infant and childhood experiences. People need to be helped to make a very clear distinction between who they are now and that kid back then. They should not be defining themselves as that abused kid."

- Describe an embarrassing moment related to adoption or permanency.

- List five things you feel guilty or ashamed about. Do they relate in any way to adoption or permanency?

- For adoptive/permanency parents, describe how you think your child felt when you first told them the story of how they came to you.

- In what ways do you feel inadequate? Where do you think those feelings and beliefs originated? Are you still beating yourself up for mistakes and/or decisions made in the past? Accept "good enough" decisions and your worry, anxiety, shame and guilt will diminish.

- How do you address the feelings of shame and guilt when you experience them, and has that been effective?

- What more could you do to address shame and guilt? Do you have role models in life that help you gain perspective and hope?

- Have you talked to other constellation members who may have experienced shame or guilt?

- Do you know other people who hold a similar role in the constellation? Connecting to others who share a similar role can help diminish feelings of isolation.

- Cultivate friendships with individuals who have similar life experiences.

- Use therapy, write a journal and read blogs and books to help connect to your internal experience.

Sue Johnson shared the following from a video course on shame and guilt (National Institute for Clinical Application of Behavioral Medicine 2017): "Shame needs to be named, validated and talked about. Someone needs to turn on the flood light. To address shame, you need to create a corrective emotional experience as the antidote. Pick a person that you trust and love and talk about what you are ashamed of out loud to that person a minimum of five times. Ask the person to give you validation of your shame, love and support. Do this several times if necessary."

- Since shame embeds itself into the physiological system, physical activities may release toxic stress and shame from our bodies. Activities could include massage, yoga, running, meditation, praying, swimming, jogging, walking, cycling and so on.

- List ten things to nurture yourself. Being able to take in pleasure and practice good self-care is a critical component of healing. Treat yourself like your best friend.

- Happiness is living in the present and celebrating your blessings each day. Gratitude boosts dopamine and serotonin in the brain and creates a positive feedback loop in relationships.

## Notes to professionals

The first and most important mantra for every professional to keep in mind when working with members of the constellation is that professionals must be non-judgmental, accepting and validating of each individual's experience. The safe, accepting environment that the professional creates allows for the shame, guilt and anxiety to be identified and expressed. Remember, you are the primary intervention when working with any client, but especially those who have internalized shame, guilt and anxiety. These emotions can be deeply engrained, strongly defended and highly resilient to change.

As professionals attempt to address shame, guilt and anxiety, they can inadvertently push clients deeper into those feelings. It is not advisable to be working with these clients if you yourself have unresolved issues with these emotions, as they can be easily projected. The professional must be regulated and fully present in order to effectively attune to the needs of their client. In order to establish trust with a client who has deeply engrained shame, guilt and anxiety, the professional should position themselves at a 45-degree angle to their client, model a calm, mindful state through managing heart rate and breathing, establish gentle touch when accepted, use a calm, non-threatening tone of voice and a non-rushed cadence, and use intermittent, safe eye contact, as direct, consistent eye contact may be experienced as threatening or overwhelming. Remember that when addressing shame, guilt and anxiety, clients benefit most when the professional is authentic, dependable and honest in all forms of communication.

A reminder that much of the shame, guilt and anxiety has been generated in your client through the secrecy and stigmatization of constellation members touched by adoption and permanency. Negative language and mythology are still present in our culture and practice, reinforcing the very shame, guilt and anxiety that the professional is attempting to address. The client's shame-based core and self-loathing may lead them to be protective and hide their inner feelings and emotions. It is important to identify the shameful wound that came to them from the outside through parents, systems and society and was internalized into their belief system and identity. Accessing and deconstructing the shameful wound calls for the therapist to utilize tools that reach the pre-verbal and very young child within their client.

# Chapter 5

# Grief

Grief, I've learned, is really just love. It's all the love you want to give but cannot. All of that unspent love gathers up in the corners of your eyes, the lump in your throat and in that hollow part of the chest. Grief is love with no place to go. (Jamie W. Anderson, blogger)

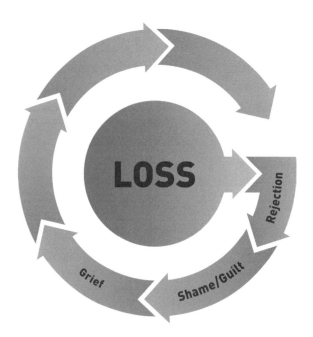

Grief is the third spoke in the wheel of the Seven Core Issues in Adoption and Permanency. Grief is the gateway to healing.

Most human suffering is connected to love and loss. Pain will be experienced as part of the reality of living and loving. Acknowledging loss and making room for the "work of grief" is essential to any healing process. The term "work" is used because grief is just that, it's messy, hard, labor intensive and feels never-ending. Grieving includes remembering, recollecting, feeling, questioning and reorganizing. People may wonder: "Will I get through this?" "How do I find the words to express what I'm feeling?" "Will my bones always hurt like this?" "Will I ever be the same?" "Why did this happen to me?" "Am I being punished?" "What did I do wrong?"

In today's culture, there are few models for healthy grieving. People live in a "quick-fix" society where individuals are expected to get over things rapidly and simply move on. Children are not taught how to cope with loss. Children are often teased, bullied or scolded for crying. People work hard to avoid the pain of grief. Unacknowledged grief and pain can accumulate, simmer and turn into bitterness, depression and anger.

Grieving is important because it allows people to speak their truth and express their feelings. Suffering and pain are part of living a full life. When people are free to express their feelings, it allows them to move through their pain so that they can eventually feel better. Grief is the healing process of the heart and mind. Acknowledging an overwhelming loss, and the accompanying pain and suffering, allows people to release the hurt and attend to the wound.

Grief is universal. Grief is a personal and highly individual experience. A person's grief process depends on many factors, including personality, gender, culture, temperament, religious and spiritual beliefs, coping styles, life experiences, the age the loss occurred and the nature of the loss. Everyone grieves according to their own timeline and in their own way. There is no recipe or prescription to shorten the process or make the suffering go away. Grief is not something you just "get over"; it is different for everyone; it is not linear; it is insidious and makes demands. It illuminates a truth in your life. Grief is about acceptance, adaptation and endurance; it changes you.

The work of grief may leave people feeling crazy, unhinged and alone; it is a rollercoaster ride with many ups and downs. The grief cycle is unpredictably predictable. Triggers for grieving are everywhere and can surprise people in unexpected ways.

> Both Ginger and Brittany have lost a baby. Ginger had suffered several miscarriages, as well as the death of a baby in her arms soon after she gave birth. Brittany held her baby in the hospital and released her to adoptive parents. Both women experienced profound loss and grief at that particular moment in their lives. Later, both women had the opportunity to parent newborns. When they first held their babies, the pain of the loss and the accompanying grief from their prior experience resurfaced in that moment. Loss remembers loss.

People who are grieving may find themselves wandering aimlessly, forgetting things, not finishing what they start and reading the same things repeatedly as they cannot concentrate and retain information. They may be prone to accidents as their brain feels "offline," distracted, overwhelmed and otherwise occupied. People may have physical symptoms such as a lowered immune system, tightness in their throat (a plum pit) and heaviness in their chest which may feel like they are having a heart attack, and may have headaches and intestinal symptoms. When grieving, people may do things in extremes, such as not sleeping or sleeping all the time, or having no appetite or unable to stop eating.

According to George A. Bonanno (2009), in 1917 Sigmund Freud compared grief and depression. Freud saw depression and bereavement as a longing for something that had been lost. He thought bereavement was not a pathological condition but that suffering was a normal part of the grief process. Freud added that a large amount of psychological energy is diverted towards the missing loved one and, therefore, grief becomes the work of reclaiming the energy that is connected to that missing person. Freud labeled this reclaiming of energy as "the routine of mourning" or the "work of mourning."

Although there were other intervening articles that were published by various psychoanalysts, it was another 50 years before the stages of grief were developed by psychiatrists John Bowlby, MD, and Elisabeth Kübler-Ross, MD. Bowlby's stages of grief were based on his observations of children who were separated from their mothers, which he then projected onto bereaved adults (Bowlby 1988). Kübler-Ross developed her stages of grief and loss while working with her dying patients (Kübler-Ross and Kessler 2005).

In spite of the lack of empirical evidence to support Kübler-Ross's stages of grief, they are the most commonly referenced. The authors believe that these stages resonate deeply with people who are suffering a life loss and that they have stood the test of time. However, this one model that is familiar to so many can be misinterpreted as being linear and completed when one reaches the stage of acceptance. We have included here some explanations of each stage:

1. *Denial, shock or numbness* serve as a form of "emotional novocaine." The purpose of the numbness is to buffer the physical and emotional pain of the loss. Shock may render people detached, not fully present in their bodies, dazed and in a stupor. When people are in great distress, denial can offer some relief. Denial serves an important purpose as it protects the psyche, allowing time for adaptation to occur. Some people may refuse to accept the reality of the loss; they may lie, avoid, minimize or rationalize the loss.

2. *Anger/anxiety* surfaces as the mourner moves out of denial and begins adapting to their new reality. This is the "go away closer" phase—comfort

me but don't touch me or get too close physically or emotionally. The intense emotions of anger and anxiety can be directed inward or outward in the form of blame. Anger and anxiety offer power and energy, although for some people it can be experienced as panic. Anger and anxiety are motivators and offer individuals an opportunity to "do something" with their pain. People may appear frenetic, hypervigilant, judgmental, irritable, easily angered, clingy or rejecting.

3. *Bargaining* is another aspect of the mourner's grief experience. It encompasses all of the "maybe ifs," such as "maybe if I had been there this wouldn't have happened," "maybe if I had been a better person," "maybe if I had had the right help," "maybe if I hadn't done that bad thing," "maybe if I had prayed more" and "maybe if I had been a better kid." Bargaining is an indication of desperation, a desperate attempt to make the nightmare, the pain, the suffering go away. It is often attached to faulty thinking, blame and self-blame.

4. *Depression/sadness* surfaces as the mourner realizes that nothing is going to make this loss go away. There is a deep yearning, a sense of emptiness, and a deep sadness for all the things that will never be realized or experienced again. This is the stage where the wound and its pain are deeply felt. Depression is a very lonely and scary place. It is a retreat into a deep, dark cave from which people may feel unable to escape. It can become frightening, and a person may turn to anger or anxiety in order to be re-energized. These two stages of grief frequently cycle as the mourner vacillates between despair and anger/rage.

5. *Acceptance* occurs as the mourner adapts to living with the loss and begins to accept that the wound is a permanent part of their life. The loss is never fully "resolved" and can be re-awakened during times of subsequent loss or during anniversary dates of when the wound was initially experienced. Acceptance is recognition that the mourner has done all that they can and must find a way to live with the reality of the loss. This requires the redefining of relationships and an acceptance of the loss of a role and/or an acceptance of a new label/role; for example, I was married and am now a widow, I was a parent and now I'm not, I was pregnant and lost a child or I was in the Brinker family and am now in the Hernandez family. Acceptance is being able to find peace, joy and hope again: I can now plan a future and can see myself living it.

Grief can come in waves of emotion that can encompass both sadness and longing as well as smiles and laughter. People may feel confused by these oscillating emotions. However, this is an adaptive behavior that allows a person to engage in contrasting activities that are both productive and healing. One set of behaviors is loss oriented, and the other set of behaviors is restoration oriented. Restoration behaviors allow for focus on the tasks and demands of everyday life, such as returning to the normality of a work routine and then returning home and collapsing in sadness.

"Anniversary reactions" are common when one has moved into the acceptance stage of grief. Anniversary reactions may be experienced over many years following a loss. They occur when a person experiences an increase in sadness and loneliness on the anniversary of an important date related to their losses.

> April, aged 9, Michael, aged 6, and Kendall, aged 4, were living with their parents who were neglectful and at times abusive. The children were taken into protective custody by the police on Christmas Eve and placed into emergency foster care. A month later, they were placed with a resource family. Their traumatic behaviors resulting from their early adverse experiences were diminishing over time as they adapted to the structure and safety of their new home and began attaching and trusting their foster parents. As the Christmas holidays approached, however, the children became increasingly agitated, fearful, insecure and angry. The trauma triggers for the children were Christmas music, the smell of Christmas fragrances, Christmas lights and decorations, presents under the tree and the excitement of the impending holiday. All of the joyous associations that the foster parents had connected to the holiday triggered the children's traumatic memories and associations.

One component of grief is to idealize the lost loved one. The gifts of that relationship loom larger when the individual is gone and subsequently becomes glorified. Fantasies flourish connected to lost loved ones as a way of keeping them alive in memory. People do not grieve the actual details of a relationship. They grieve only what they remember and their perception or fantasy of the individual. For instance, a widower, who like most people did not have a perfect marriage, now remembers his wife in an idealized way; she was never angry, was a great cook, always beautiful and a perfect hostess. Likewise, a child removed from their birth/first family for safety reasons only remembers his mother's loving smile and the fun things they did together, diminishing the present caregiver's positive qualities. Adoptive parents may fantasize that the children they would have created and given birth to only carried their best genetic qualities and characteristics. Birth/first parents may think of only the positive experiences that they shared with their children before the children were removed from their care.

People who get lost in their grief get lost in themselves and may withdraw from the world. It is complicated grief when the feelings of loss become incapacitating. The signs and symptoms include bitterness, inability to enjoy life, ongoing depression, trouble completing normal routines, feeling as if life has no meaning or purpose, irritability, agitation, and lack of trust in themselves and others.

Prolonged sadness can become despair when people see no way out of the pain; the feeling of resignation and hopelessness can become overwhelming. This feeling can deepen when individuals disconnect or lose faith in their higher power, which may be their faith in themselves as strong individuals or in God or however their spiritual connection is defined or named by them. A feeling of impending doom may keep them waiting for the other shoe to drop when another loss will surely occur. Because of this, people may decide to avoid getting close to others for fear of losing them. In this dark space, nothing really matters any longer and they may experience having no control over what happens to them or the people they love.

People who are grieving have little physical or emotional energy for others, which is appropriate as their emotional resources are focused on their own survival and healing. Barriers to their healing could include: being around angry people; having a demanding role as a caregiver or parent; restricting social and cultural expectations; their own personality or temperament; intense job or daily responsibilities; and lack of support. In addition, the grief process can be delayed, dulled or stymied through medications and addictions.

## Myths and facts about grief

- People "get over" their grief. It is not true that if you "do it right" you will have closure. *The truth is that emotional memory cannot be erased.*

- Pain will go away faster if it is ignored; keep yourself busy. In reality, the pain becomes a boulder in the road, a boiling pot that will overflow on the back burner. *The truth is that it takes a lot of psychic energy to not think about something. Addressing the grief is short-term pain for long-term gain.*

- It is important to be strong in the face of loss. Being stoic, minimizing your deep feelings connected to the loss or repressing the pain can superficially send a message that you have not been affected by something tragic. *The truth is that humans are built to connect through emotion; sorrow shared is halved.*

- Grief should last about a year and be finished. *The truth is that the second year after a loss may feel even worse as numbness has diminished and people's support may dwindle.*

- Tears are a sign of weakness. *The truth is that tears release intense feelings and remove toxins from the body that build up when you are stressed and sad.*

- People shouldn't talk about loss. The belief is that discussing painful feelings makes people feel uncomfortable. *The truth is that it is important to talk about all of our feelings, including the ones that are the most difficult to share or hear.*

- Children should be sheltered from grief. *The truth is that children need honesty, a loving presence, a comforting tone, and reassurance that everyone has losses. A family rule that may help a child in their grief is "our family grieves together—bring your pain, sadness or anger to Mommy or Daddy." Families that grieve together, heal together.*

- If you "finish" grieving and get on with your life, you will forget the lost person. *The truth is that love lasts beyond grief. Your lost loved ones live in you, in your memories and in your heart.*

- There is nothing to grieve—just be positive and have gratitude for the time you had together. *The truth is that if you try to avoid the grief, you will diminish the joy and positives you received from that relationship. When you numb the pain, you also numb the joy.*

- People can't grieve for people they didn't know. *The truth is that people can feel sadness never having known a person; they lost the potential of that relationship.*

- You will "get over it" and return to being the same person you were before the loss. *The truth is that profound loss changes people forever. It changes world views and how people live their lives.*

## Symptoms of grief

- As we are biological beings, grief hits a person's body first. Strong emotions impact the body before the brain makes sense of what is happening.

Humans are "feeling beings" before they are "thinking beings." Grief is painful physically and emotionally. Evidence of the pain can be seen when people wail, scream, hit or hurt themselves, pound their chest, ululate, collapse, freeze, dissociate or experience shock and numbness.

- Grief and mourning create stress within the body which leads to a build up of toxins. Grief leads to increased levels of the stress hormone cortisol in the body that must be eliminated. The body's wisdom uses tear ducts to release toxins through our tears as well as making our hair follicles oily, our skin break out and our breath unpleasant. This is the body's way of discharging the toxins as the person mourns.

- Grief has been found to aggravate physical pain, increase blood pressure, suppress the immune system and increase the risk of having a heart attack. "Broken heart syndrome" is a real thing. It happens when extreme emotional stress causes one of the heart's chambers to balloon, triggering symptoms similar to those of a heart attack. The condition is reversible and rarely fatal (Romm 2014).

- Grief disrupts and dulls the senses. Nothing tastes good and nothing feels pleasurable.

- Grief may lead to a person being overly strict with routines and rituals or being unable to accomplish anything. Examples include: neglecting self-care as in personal hygiene; an inability to complete daily tasks.

- Grief can increase anxiety, which leads to increased heart and respiratory rate. People may be extraordinarily busy, frenetic, unable to relax, unable to filter their thoughts or words, frustrated or engaged, and they may experience panic attacks.

- Grief can lead to depression. The body feels heavy or immobilized. Feelings of helplessness, hopelessness, worry and exhaustion can overtake the body and mind.

- Grief is painful, and in an effort to numb the pain, one may try and disconnect from what the body is feeling and needing. Addictive behaviors may be used as a way to create numbness and avoid the painful memories and emotions. Numb one feeling and you will numb them all.

- Grief takes up space in the mind. Mourning depletes intellectual focus. It becomes difficult to concentrate, retain new information, access old information, achieve positive outcomes at school or at work, remember the rules and make decisions.

Grief in both children and adults can easily manifest as "difficult behaviors." Many of the symptoms attached to grief may appear similar to other mental health diagnoses. Children who are grieving may be diagnosed with attention deficit hyperactivity disorder (ADHD), oppositional defiant disorder (ODD), reactive attachment disorder (RAD) or obsessive compulsive disorder (OCD). Children and adults can also be labeled with the following diagnoses: generalized anxiety disorder, bipolar disorder or major depressive disorder. These diagnoses may cause professionals and parents to miss the actual grief and loss issues. Misdiagnosing children may lead to medicating symptoms of grief and loss. As a result, the medications may interfere with normative and adaptive grief responses.

## Impact of grief on constellation members

Grief addresses the hundreds of losses that constellation members have endured. Dr. Gina McKernon-Cindrich's study on the Seven Core Issues in Adoption indicated that grief was a common affective experience for all constellation members.

Losses in adoption and permanency must be grieved in order to address the final three core issues of identity, intimacy and mastery/control. The grief experience may be intensified at times of subsequent loss or developmental transitions.

Adoption and permanency losses are too often left unnamed, un-acknowledged and "un-grieved." The losses may be difficult to acknowledge and mourn in a society where these forms of family building are seen as problem-solving events that benefit everyone. The culture perceives these families being formed as a solution to individual problems: a child needs a family, a parent can no longer parent, and new parents are created. This may be perceived as a "gain" for everyone, rather than an event to which loss is integral. Because of this point of view, it may be difficult to accept, discuss and express sadness.

Grief for constellation members is complex as they have experienced a profound loss that changed the trajectory of their life. In the rearranging of family trees through adoption and permanency, parents are grieving unborn children, children are grieving as their understanding of what happened to them unfolds, and birth/first parents are grieving for their child/baby who they hope is alive and well, but whom they are separated from.

**NEW LEGS**

I choose grief, that river that takes you somewhere.

Like when Charlie said it must be hard not to know the person you were born to.

And off I swept both hating him and loving him for saying it.

Floating upstream in anger to come swirling down in sadness and bumped
    against the bank to climb out on new legs.

Where would I *still be* but for that river and these new legs?

(Penny Callan Partridge 1999)

## Adoptees and individuals raised in kinship/foster families

Infants and children are the most impacted members of the adoption and permanency constellation. The adoption and permanency decisions that occurred in reaction to a crisis shifted their life at a time when they had no input. They may not have had the language, understanding or the rights to ask questions, to protest, or express their needs and desires, in order to influence the outcome of the crisis.

Children are adaptable, malleable and resilient. A child can learn any language, adapt to any culture and learn the cultural norms in order to survive. Babies are naturally resilient, which means they can bounce back from adversity or stress. For most babies, being in a home with unfamiliar caregivers is distressing, but because of their resiliency, they can adapt. If the caregivers can properly attune to the baby's needs while the baby is distressed, the baby can adapt more quickly.

Children are deeply aware and impacted by everything that is happening to them. When children are transplanted from one environment to an unfamiliar "other" environment or family, they are thrust into survival mode. Children must adapt to a whole new life that includes new smells, new sounds, new faces, new foods and new routines. Their very existence depends on them adapting to their new world.

However, children who repeatedly change caregivers lose their access to resiliency and adaptation as they are living in a state of chronic distress. Without the attunement that a consistent primary attachment caregiver provides because they know the unique needs of the child they are parenting, the child may remain distressed and dysregulated.

Amanda, a resource/foster mother and an experienced parent, asked for assistance because she could not comfort and soothe an 8-month-old baby girl who was newly placed in her care. This was the baby's third move and she had a strong attachment to her previous caregiver. Amanda stated that the baby cried and cried and would not allow anyone to hold, touch or soothe her. She reported that the baby would push away from her, not look directly at her, would not "mold and fold" into her body and was distressed by her very presence.

Babies and children grieve the loss of caregivers with whom they have developed a trusting and meaningful relationship. Caregivers are not interchangeable cogs in a wheel. Children's grief reactions and their ability to process and express their grief is contingent on their developmental stage, not their chronological age. For example, a 5-year-old who has experienced multiple attachment disruptions may be functioning developmentally at the age at which their first attachment disruption occurred.

Children's responses to loss and grief are typically very different from those of an adult. Children communicate their distress through their physiology and behaviors. Due to their social, emotional, cognitive and brain development, most children have not yet attained the skills necessary to verbalize their feelings. Subsequently, parents may see more "acting out" behaviors as children emote and discharge toxic stress, grief and pain. Parents are therefore tasked with decoding their child's behaviors and attuning with their internal emotional states.

Painful and distressing feelings in children are typically repressed and/or displaced. This most often leads to reactive and impulsive behaviors. Children who have suffered significant, life-altering losses often express distress and anger in response to the loss, crisis or disruption. Parents can easily misread the child's grief and adjustment response and respond to the child by being punitive, angry, withholding and reactive. It is helpful for parents to understand that it is typical for children to feel overwhelmed, angry and sad in response to their traumatic losses as they struggle to cope and adapt. The child needs reassurance that their grown-ups understand their distress and can respond in ways that comfort, soothe and relieve the distress, pain and/or confusion. The child needs assistance from their caregiver in learning helpful ways to both understand and express their upset, and their sad and angry feelings.

## Symptoms of childhood grief

- An apparent lack of feeling about what happened or relief.
- Physiological changes:
  - Complaints about their body hurting and accidents that require attention
  - Not eating or overeating
  - Changes in sleeping patterns; nightmares, night-terrors, insomnia; and fear of being alone at night
  - Bedwetting.
- Regressed behaviors; the child may appear to have lost skills and competencies that had been attained before the loss:
  - Overly clingy and needy out of fear and anxiety
  - Regressed language development; may revert to baby talk
  - Desire to be held and rocked, suck their thumb and be "babied."
- Disorganization, panic and fear:
  - Keeps forgetting things such as clothing, school work, toys
  - Trouble retaining new information
  - Separation anxiety; easily triggered during transitions
  - Forgetting normal patterns, rules and routines.
- Explosive emotions and acting-out behaviors:
  - Displacing strong emotions onto parents, peers, siblings and other adults; increased sibling rivalry
  - Appearing hyperactive, impulsive, reactive, irritable, destructive or aggressive
  - Appearing anxious and restless
  - Appearing oppositional and defiant as they search for control.

- Guilt and self-blame based on ego-centric and magical thinking.

- Increase in isolation, withdrawal and avoidance; may appear listless and/or lethargic.

- A change in functioning; good students become poor students; happy children become hostile; active children become withdrawn.

## Ways children cope with grief

- No reaction at all; no feelings are exhibited, could be numbness and shock.

- Anger and agitation at others as they adjust to the loss and change.

- Denial;  an excessive reassurance to themselves that nothing has changed.

- Justifying the loss and using an intellectual approach to exhibit acceptance and understanding.

- Compliance with their caregivers with an assumption that if they do what adults expect them to do they will not experience more loss, denying their true fears in order to minimize any demands that they might place on their new parents for fear of losing them as well.

A child who lacks a secure attachment relationship is alone with their overwhelming grief. If the child experiences additional losses, these coping strategies will continue and intensify.

Children's ability to understand their story, what happened to them and hence grieve is always connected to their stage of development. Therefore, children grieve again and again from infancy through adolescence and into adulthood as their understanding of their losses unfolds. It is important that parents and professionals do not label children's adaptive responses as unhealthy. These are normal emotional and behavioral responses to an abnormal crisis and/or series of events. Parents watch children grow and develop, and understand more and more as the child evolves and matures. For instance, children crawl, stand, walk and then run; they learn sounds, say a word, string words together and then talk fluently; and they learn their ABCs, read and then write. These developmental steps are unfolding alongside the child's understanding of their own story and the losses and gains attached to that story. Each developmental growth spurt deepens the understanding of any losses the child may have had, and grief attached to that newly understood loss needs acknowledgment and expression.

> An adoptive mother shared that when her child was 10 years old, he asked, "Why didn't my birth mother keep me? Do you know her name? Why did you want me? Did you know my birth/first mother?" At 16, he asked, "Do I have any siblings? Who is my birth/first father? How tall will I get? Will I get to meet them again? Am I going to be like them or how am I like them?" She added that as answers were given her son experienced a rollercoaster of emotions.

Children need to be developing language about how their family was formed, which then sets the stage for them to later ask questions about their story. Parents are setting the tone for open communication by providing a secure attachment relationship where the child can express their needs, thoughts and feelings in a non-judgmental and safe environment. By the parents modeling the use of certain words, clarifying what they mean and adding information during discussions of the child's story, the tone of communication, which should be relaxed, honest and non-judgmental, is set for all future intimate dialogue between the parent and the child. As parents, we will always need to have conversations with our children around subjects that are "emotionally loaded," such as death, sex, values, religion and adoption/permanency. For adoptive/permanency parents, talking to their children about the facts of the child's story can trigger the parents' own issues of loss. Parents often fear that they will say something incorrectly and hurt the attachment relationship they have built with their child. Many parents withhold complete information or are waiting for the "perfect moment" to share certain parts of their child's story. While it may be necessary to simplify the facts at certain ages, it is important for children to have all of the important fact-based information about their story and their birth/first family *prior* to adolescence, which thrusts the child into the complex journey of identity formation and individuation.

Late-discovery adoptees are unable to progress through these normative grief stages and adapt and integrate *all* the parts of their story into their identity and self-concept because vital information was withheld from them.

> Melanie was 18 years old when she finally found out the truth about her birth and adoption story. She had always suspected she was adopted because she looked so different from her parents. When she was 9 years old she asked her mom if she was adopted. Her mom said, "Of course not, stop talking like

that!" Melanie stated that she knew how much her parents loved her but didn't understand why they couldn't tell her the truth. When Melanie was 18 years old, her dad died suddenly of a massive heart attack. She was very close with her dad and the loss of their relationship was devastating to her. At his funeral, one of her aunts said to her, "You know, my brother loved you as if you were his real daughter."

## Grief through ages and stages
### Birth to 3 months of age

A newborn baby has already spent nine months in-utero orienting to a sensory environment. Babies attach through their senses. In the last three months before birth, the pre-nate has become accustomed to certain sounds, particular voices, circadian rhythms of day and night, and connection to their mother who responds when they kick, hiccup or move; and are being impacted hormonally and chemically by the mother's moods and emotions. Even if the newborn is placed immediately into another caregiver's arms at birth, a major loss has occurred; grief and adaptation will follow. Babies react dramatically to any change in an environment and caregiver. They typically become irritable, fussy and colicky, and may develop sleep problems, as well as other various physical manifestations such as diarrhea, upset stomachs and skin rashes. Strangers to the baby will find it difficult to comfort, soothe and regulate them into calmness. The necessity of having a minimal number of consistent and long-term caregivers is crucial. Providing a secure attachment relationship between the caregiver and baby will allow the baby to begin to trust their environment and learn that their needs will be consistently met, and eventually predict that the voice that they hear, the face they see, the smell they inhale, the familiar body holding them and what they are tasting are connected to a trusted and known caregiver.

Sally brought her 6-month-old child, whom she recently adopted, to an open adoption support group. The 6-month-old was awake in Sally's arms and was making steady eye contact with her mother while several other group members surrounded the happy pair, commenting how cute the baby was and how happy they were for Sally. The baby avoided looking at any of the new faces as she held her mother's gaze. Gloria, the birth/first mother, entered the group to see her baby for the first time in six months. She was at the opposite end of the room when she said "hello" and spoke to the group. The baby immediately began to squirm and shift her gaze towards the voice she recognized.

## Six months of age

Babies at six months show classic grief reactions when moved; they often react with tremendous physiological distress; they respond with rage and protest to the loss of their attachment anchor. They may regress and withdraw, become lethargic, and have trouble eating and sleeping. These changes create tremendous disorientation and toxic stress with no relief from the pain and suffering. This does not allow their biological system to experience pleasure, comfort or soothing.

When babies learn that their needs will not consistently be met and they experience an increased amount of pain and suffering from hunger and lack of touch, as in an orphanage, they may stop "crying out." They may appear placid, easy going, non-demanding and detached. The danger is that the baby is not cueing the parent that they are in distress and have a need. Any major change for a child ought to bring protest, fear and sense of disorientation.

## During the toddler years

At ages 1 and 2, introducing basic words about how the family was formed becomes important. At this stage, introducing the words "adoption," "foster care" or "kinship care" does not mean that the child understands the larger concept attached to those words. Reading books to children about adoption and permanency will help them to make a positive association with the words in the book. Showing signs of affection such as hugging them and stating "I'm so happy that I adopted or fostered you" will strengthen those positive associations. The word "adoption" is used in our society in relation to other living things, objects and concepts, such as "pet adoption," "adopt a highway," "adopt a cause" and "adopt a habit or trait." This can be very confusing for children. Toddlers may use the word incorrectly or indiscriminately and do not yet grasp its deeper meaning and how it relates to their personal story. If parents have introduced the words "adoption," "foster care" or "kinship care," have read children's stories with those words included and demonstrated warmth and caring when using them, the child will make positive associations with those words.

## The preschool years

In this phase, the child still carries the belief that their family is the same as all other families. Children at this stage of development have magical thinking. Therefore, all families are built through adoption, foster care or kinship care. If their physical image is significantly different from their parents in terms of skin color, eye color, eye shape, hair texture, hair color and build, they may hold the belief that they will become like their parents as they grow.

At this age, how parents frame the child's story is very important. Children need to know that they were born just like everybody else, that adoption is permanent and that their family is real. The introduction of basic information typically causes the child to ask some questions. Parents should answer the child's questions truthfully. No matter how difficult, it is important for parents to begin building the foundation of the child's birth and adoption/permanency story. It is important to share the truth of how a child became separated from their birth/first family in an age-appropriate way. A parent might say, "A man and a woman can create a baby even though they may not be ready to be a mommy or daddy."

As preschoolers, children's vocabulary should already include the basic words for how their family was formed, such as "adoption," "foster care" and "kinship care." It is now appropriate to use additional vocabulary, including "birth/first parents or family," "court," "country of origin" and "adoption day." Children are very concrete in their thinking, so parents need to choose their words very carefully. Again, storybooks and children's movies are helpful and can assist the child in having positive associations connected to how their family came together. Let the child know that it is normal to be curious and ask questions. Having friendships that include other families built in a similar way will help to normalize the adoption and permanency experience. From the very beginning, parents should set the tone for honest, open communications relating to both their child's story and the family's story. Introducing the words does not mean that the child understands the larger concepts attached to the words.

> Danny, age 3, used the words "I'm adopted" frequently and proudly. His parents thought he understood what the term meant. His favorite costume was a doctor's smock and a stethoscope. One day they realized that what he was hearing when they used the word "adopted" was, in his mind, "I'm a doctor."

Part of the darker history of adoption practice occurred when social workers told parents to not tell the child they were adopted if the child was placed directly at birth and was a close physical match to the adoptive parents. This practice occurred before there were significant advances in the fields of child development, brain development, attachment theory, identity formation and adoption and permanency research. What is known today is that *not telling* a child that they are adopted leads to the inserting of false information and the telling of lies in order to create the beginning of the child's story and history. Children cannot form a positive self-concept and identity from missing information or the incorrect information. Unfortunately, this practice still occurs and is often more linked to the parent's core issues or their desire to avoid the grief and pain that adoption and permanency inherently creates. For a child, long-term secrets mean that there is something wrong or bad happening. Secrets are connected to fear and shame. Parents can inadvertently connect their child's story of adoption and permanency to shame and fear, leaving the child unable to understand why they may be feeling confused, anxious, angry and disconnected. They become aware early on that there are certain topics in their family that are avoided. Many individuals know the information and truth of the child's beginning, which later, when revealed, feels like a betrayal. For the adoptee, it can feel like all of the people who knew the truth of their story were a part of a conspiracy. So, while it may be difficult for parents to talk about their child's beginning, which began with another set of parents, it is imperative that the child be given their entire story, over time, by those they trust and love.

## Entering school

At this stage, children begin to confront other people's beliefs about adoption, foster care and kinship care. Peers might say things such as "You're adopted because your mother didn't want you," "Foster kids are poor or stupid" or "Why is your mother so old?" Each of these questions may trigger grief for a child as they must now respond to the larger world's understanding, or lack thereof, of adoption, foster care and kinship care. Children at this stage of development will need assistance in knowing how to respond to these hurtful remarks. They have been observing their parents' responses to outsiders and have learned from those exchanges. For some children, bringing a baby picture to kindergarten, which is a pretty typical exercise, can be embarrassing or shaming if they do not have a picture available or if the picture triggers painful memories. Having parents of a different race or ethnicity, or being raised by a single parent or a grandparent, may also increase feelings of discomfort or distress.

Parents with children at this stage often ask what to tell the school about how their family was built. Information about the child's birth/first family and early life should be kept private. The downside about sharing how your family was formed with a teacher or school personnel is that some may carry negative bias and stereotypes about adoption, foster care and kinship care. This could negatively impact their expectations of the child and family. However, by sharing with the kindergarten teacher that adoption, foster care and kinship care are a part of your family, you may have the opportunity to educate them, provide appropriate books about the subject and share the vocabulary that you use with your child.

## Ages 7-10

At these ages, children are naturally curious about most things in their life and world. They are studying science, how things work, what's fair and not fair, who's part of the in-crowd and who are the outsiders. Their world view is expanding at the same time that they are comparing themselves and their family to others. Children at this stage want the facts. It is typical for children to have questions and be curious about their personal story, their birth/first family, what happened and why it happened. For instance: "Where did you find me?" "How did you get me?" "What did I cost?" "Why did you want *me*?"

If the parents have not been talking openly with their child and providing vocabulary around adoption and permanency, the child is waiting for their parents to open the topic and lead the conversation about these sensitive issues. Children at this stage are thinking about their story, even developing fantasies. They may be in a "holding pattern" as they wait for their parents to initiate these conversations and give permission to discuss them. It is tempting for parents to avoid bringing up difficult or awkward parts of their child's story, but these fact-telling, truth-telling conversations actually allow the child to know, understand and integrate all the parts of their story while still at home. "The telling" serves the dual purpose of facilitating the developmental understanding of the child's story and the grief process. In addition, it helps to eliminate unrealistic fantasies about what happened and why they were adopted. Fantasies flourish where facts flounder.

> Manny, an 8-year-old boy who was adopted as an infant, didn't ask many questions about his adoption, so his parents assumed he didn't think very much about it. One day, Manny and his mother were shopping and they walked past a woman who was quite pregnant. Manny said to his mother, "Why wasn't

I born like everyone else?" His mother asked what he meant, and he replied, "I know I didn't grow in your tummy. I came from a tube, right?" His mother knew that some of his confusion came from the fact that they didn't talk about his birth story, his birth/first parents and how he came into the world. That evening, she told Manny that his birth mother's name was Sara, and his birth father's name was Juan, and that he grew in his birth mother's tummy. Manny's mom said she could immediately see the relief on his face.

As children begin to understand the concept of adoption and permanency and that their life began with another set of parents who created them, they may more deeply feel the loss, rejection and potentially a sense of shame from that original separation experience. They may or may not be able to articulate these feelings. It is not unusual for parents to notice an increase in anxiety and agitation. Children are not abstract thinkers, they do not have internal insight into what they are feeling and why they are feeling it, especially if they perceive it being connected to something that feels "bad" or "wrong" or could hurt their parents' feelings if they ask questions.

Children may not be encouraged to identify and mourn their losses. Parents may inadvertently block their children's expressions of grief because the parents may experience their children's loss and grief as a personal rejection of them. Youngsters removed from abusive homes are often expected to feel relief and gratitude, not loss and grief. Adults may block or divert children's expression of pain by pointing out all of the positive things occurring in the child's life. Adults can make it more difficult for children to move into the grief process by telling incomplete truths to the child; spoiling, overprotecting or over-indulging the child who has a loss; forcing the child to be so busy that they have no time to feel their feelings; and distracting the child from their deep feelings or telling them not to be sad. It is important that children understand these feelings of grief and learn to name and express them without judgment. Children may think they will always be sad or mad and may begin to lose hope for a happier future. Children do not grieve like adults, and therefore adults must understand their particular child's style and mode of emotional expression or they will miss important cues in assisting their child's grieving style. Children may not say anything, but may demonstrate what they feel with physical distress such as stomach problems, headaches, a fear of leaving home and trying new things, sleep disturbances, frequent illnesses, hyperactivity, explosive behaviors or isolation. Newly placed children living in "survival mode" do not have the time or energy to work through their losses. Until the trauma is addressed and a primary attachment relationship is created, grief work is delayed. Children are essentially treading water to survive, as opposed to learning to swim. During this period of time, the child's physical and emotional resources are drained and they may not be successful learners or even physically grow.

## The pre-teen years

During these years, there is typically a dramatic shift in the child's ability to think abstractly. Children are emerging from their "magical thinking" and can more fully understand the concept of adoption and permanency and have insights into how crises cause children to be separated from their families of origin. Children now have a basic understanding of poverty, homelessness, mental illness, addiction, abuse and family dynamics, and they are now more able to grasp certain aspects of their own story. For example, a pre-teen may observe all of the many tasks their parents have to complete every day to keep the family going and could imagine that it would have been hard for their birth/first mother or father to do all of those things when they were 17, still in high school, mentally ill, homeless or drug or alcohol dependent.

At this stage of development, the pre-teen is more aware of their body image and more interested and influenced by friends and peers. For young people who have no reflections of their own face or body, race or ethnicity, this can be a confusing time. They may have difficulty feeling positive about their body when they don't know what their body will look like as they transition into adulthood. In addition, it is not uncommon for young people at this stage to talk less about adoption and permanency than they did previously. Parents should not assume that this means the teen is not thinking about their story—many of them are feeling and thinking about it quite a bit.

It is not unusual for pre-teens to be idealistic, judgmental and concerned about issues of fairness. They may feel upset or angry with their birth/first parents: "You don't give away something you love" or "You don't choose drugs over your child." They may also express agitation and anger at their adoptive/permanency parents: "You bought or stole me from them" or "You really wanted your own kids, not me." Loss issues surface as children understand that they have two sets of "real" parents. As the young person continues to age and mature, parents should look for opportunities to share the additional facts about their history while, at the same time, validating the young person's deepening understanding and strong feelings about adoption and permanency.

## Adolescence

Adolescents face two significant developmental tasks: separation/individuation and identity formation. For young people who were adopted, even as infants, these are the years where the grief feels the most intense. For the teen, there is a realization that they not only lost a birth/first mother and birth/first father, but they lost two entire familial trees; each with a unique history, culture, lineage, language and people who may look or act like them. As the adolescent becomes developmentally aware of their core issues, and gains the ability for abstract thinking, the intensity of their grief increases. Anger is a stage of the grief process and is the other side of depression. This does not mean that the adolescent is talking openly about what they are thinking, feeling and experiencing. In fact, many may feel quite overwhelmed by the intensity of what they are thinking and feeling, and may strive to avoid and minimize their pain and distress by isolating themselves and/or using substances to numb their feelings.

> "I just remember being angry all the time, even filled with rage," said Troy, age 19. "My anger really surfaced when I was about 14 and I admit that I was like a ticking time bomb. I didn't really know what was going on inside me, I just felt like I'd been 'wronged.' I was pissed and I would lash out at anyone. I know my anger came out in all the wrong ways and I said some really mean things to my parents. You know, it's the thing that adoptees are not really supposed to talk about, how much this all hurts. And I just didn't feel like I had anyone who could really understand what I was going through."

This intense grief work complicates the adolescent tasks of separation and individuation as well as identity formation. Some teens choose to "not think about it" and focus on their day-to-day life; some begin to search in earnest for their missing puzzle pieces; some begin to set up emotional barriers between themselves and their parents as a way of preparing themselves for the losses involved in leaving home; some isolate and express a great deal of anger about their life circumstance; some identify strongly with whom they consider other "outsiders"; and some test the boundaries of their family ties by making poor choices that could cause their parents to reject them and send them away. Some may consistently scan their environment for people who look like them. None of these coping strategies are consciously chosen.

Chapter 12, "A Child's Developmental Journey through Adoption and Permanency," includes a breakdown of developmental tasks, core losses, emotional and behavioral symptoms, and tools/resources.

## Note to parents and professionals

The ongoing sharing of the child's story, through each developmental stage, allows the child to address grief slowly, over time. The avoidance of talking truthfully and sharing openly the facts about the adoption and permanency story does not allow the child to grieve incrementally. When parents and professionals withhold the facts in order to protect the child from feeling pain or confusion, they may inadvertently be saving all of the child's unaddressed grief for their adolescent and young adult years. In addition, it may send the message that all of this is too "horrible" to discuss. The more information that parents honestly share with their child as they grow, the less intense the "grief work" may become during adolescence. Young people should not go off to college, join the military, get married or start a family without having been given all of the information that belongs to them.

There is no better place for an individual to address their grief than within the safety and love of their family. Parents should help their child to express grief, listen and observe, and offer comfort and hope.

## Birth/first family

The loss of a child whether through relinquishment or through the courts is lifelong and may lead to deep-seated feelings of the core issues of rejection, shame, guilt and anxiety. Birth/first family members may identify themselves as a failure or a loser. In society, there are fewer categories of individuals who feel more disenfranchised than birth/first parents. Most birth/first parents will never voluntarily share that they placed a child or lost a child to the court system. The stigma and shame that they may experience from their extended family and the community keeps them in hiding. Loss through adoption and permanency can feel like a thousand painful cuts to the heart.

Loss is the event, and grief is the processing of that experience. Culture, gender, age and temperament lead people to grieve differently. For instance, some cultures have biases against parents who lose their children to foster care/adoption or relinquish their children. Pre-teens or teens who become pregnant may deny their grief until a later stage of life. Some individuals may remain stuck in the developmental stage in which the crisis and loss occurred.

John Bowlby, the father of attachment theory, studied parental reactions to loss when children are diagnosed with a terminal illness. He found that parents began a process of mourning when they first learned of their child's diagnoses. It was common for parents to respond initially with numbness, punctuated with bouts of anger. It was typical for parents to disbelieve the diagnosis as they searched intensely for information that would prove the doctors were wrong.

It was common for them to direct their anger at the people who made the diagnosis.

These stages appear quite similar to what parents experience when they first learn they may lose their parental rights. Parents often do not believe the social worker, attorney or judge and may frantically search for information and allies who will support them and be on their side. Their anger is usually directed at the social workers and professionals who are talking with them about their rights, case plan and adoption/permanency. Parents often engage in a prolonged fight against losing their children and being labeled negatively as "abusive," "uncaring," "a failure," "a bad parent" and/or "neglectful." Some choose to bypass the final court hearing because it feels much like a "degradation ceremony." The pain, fear and anger are normal reactions to the potential loss of a piece of themselves, their offspring. Adoption or permanency without any contact with their children may feel like a "living death."

---

**Letter from a birth/first mother in prison**

It was nice of you to come and see me on Friday, even though all I did was cry—but crying can say it all.

How I feel:

⊙ Suicidal

⊙ Cannot cope

⊙ More depressed

⊙ Not being able to carry on

⊙ Knowing that my children are with other people. They are loving and caring and have responsibilities for my children. Doing the things that their mother should be doing for them

⊙ Not knowing whether my son is all right and if he needs any more medical treatment

⊙ Feeling really low

⊙ Crawling back into my shell

⊙ Not being able to concentrate

⊙ Feels like all of my insides have left me to be with my children

⊙ Wondering if I will ever see my children again, especially when they both get old enough to come looking, if they do

- Feels as if I am growing weaker instead of growing stronger

- Thoughts about next month. Do not want the anniversary to come at all

- Wondering what will happen when I get out of here—whether it is safe or not

- My past is haunting me and I cannot get it out of my head

- Still not been able to come to terms with anything that has happened to me

- Suffering badly

- Feel badly damaged on the inside

- Nightmares are coming back to me because I am having sleepless nights again

- Wishing that I could have done things differently

- Guilty

(Charlton *et al.* 1988, pp.13-14)

Birth/first parents who voluntarily place their child for adoption also experience deep and abiding life-altering losses. Many feel as if they had no other option but to surrender their child because of their youth, upbringing, religious beliefs, poverty and lack of support from family, friends or the other birth/first parent. Others did have the wherewithal to raise the child but made a decision that they were not ready to commit to parenting. Birth/first parents who voluntarily relinquish may not be prepared for how their decision and its accompanying losses will continue to impact their life. People who voluntarily relinquish their children are basing their decision on what they know about their life at a certain point in time. Even if something miraculous occurs at a later stage that would have allowed them to raise their child, they must live with the permanent consequences of their decision. If they make the decision in response to pressure from their family, the other birth/first parent, a religious community or professionals who are guiding them towards relinquishment, they may have strong feelings of anger and regret years later. Some birth/first parents also suffer secondary infertility at a time when they are actively trying to conceive and may find that the child they relinquished will be their only genetic offspring. Some marry the other birth/first parent at a later date and have children who are full siblings to the child they relinquished. Some parents who relinquished a child select a family willing to do an open adoption and later discover that they are excluded from that family and have no legal recourse.

Birth/first parents may undergo an initial intense period of grief at the time of the loss. They may be encouraged, by well-meaning friends and family, to move on with their lives and to accept that their child is in a better place. If the child loss is a secret, the birth/first parents may deny the loss for many years and bury their feelings, memories and thoughts. Many feel as if they need to suffer in silence because "they chose" to place their children or are ashamed of how they lost their children through the courts. The paradox for the birth/first parents is that their pain and grief are connected to their desire for their children to be happy, healthy and loved.

> "I gave birth to you, but you didn't come with instructions. I know that I made mistakes along the way, and for those I am sorry. I pray that you understand that they came from me not knowing and not from a lack of love. From the moment you were born my heart was yours. I looked in your eyes and saw all my hopes and dreams come alive in you. I love you more than you will ever know." (Anonymous birth/first mother)

Common symptoms of birth/first parent grief include any of the previously listed symptoms, as well as: dreams, nightmares, hallucinations such as hearing the child calling out to them or crying, unrealistic thoughts and fantasies about the child, strong emotions such as self-loathing, guilt, anger, depression, despair and sadness, self-medicating and difficulty forming healthy relationships. An ongoing experience of feeling helpless, hopeless and powerless may lead to strong dependency on others or isolation and thoughts of suicide. Grief can become pathological when adjustment to the loss is not achieved. Grief and isolation may unintentionally keep a birth/first parent connected to their missing child. Secrecy, judgments and lack of emotional support lock birth/first parents in grief.

Grief triggers abound for birth/first parents. For parents with no knowledge of where their children are, tragedies such as school shootings, plane, train or car crashes, fires, floods and/or earthquakes trigger feelings of loss and grief. Grief can also be retriggered daily for the birth/first parents: watching someone hold a child's hand as they cross the street; hearing a baby cry; watching a father and son play ball; and going to a movie and/or watching a television show that has themes of loss. Birth/first parents describe a feeling of a "missing piece" or a hole in their heart. Many birth/first parents do not believe they deserve joy and fulfillment in their lives.

Anniversaries, milestones and holidays may intensify the grief experience. Examples include: the child's birthday, a court appearance, Mother's or Father's Day, typical family gatherings around the holidays that celebrate family togetherness, and the birth of a subsequent child.

Some birth/first parents only allow themselves a short time period and then put their grief on hold for many years. In order to heal, birth/first parents need to share their story over and over again. The story needs to be witnessed and acknowledged by others with whom they feel safe. Complicating the grief work is a lack of rituals for mourning someone who is gone from your life but whom you hope is alive, well and happy. A lack of birth/first parent role models and guides who have successfully grieved and are living a fulfilling life may keep the birth/first parents isolated and without a roadmap for healing. At a later date, grief is often a motivator for search and reunion. Openness with the child and the adoptive/permanency family or a later reunion may help birth/first parents ameliorate their grief.

Some birth/first parents never accept the loss of their child. However, this does not mean that they cannot embrace the more uplifting aspects of their day-to-day lives. It is a bit like walking down the street with one foot on the curb and the other on the road. It feels awkward and challenging but is a skill worth mastering. Living with the double-dipped feelings of joy and sorrow in the same cup is complex.

The birth/first extended family may also experience grief connected to many of the same issues that the birth/first parents must confront. They too have lost a family member to whom they may or may not stay connected. They may also carry deep feelings about decisions made that affected them but over which they may have felt powerless. They may label themselves negatively and feel responsible for what occurred. For those who learn at a later date about a child that they did not know existed, both profound grief as well as joy may be experienced.

> With a big pot she would have plenty of room for all the memories, all the misgivings, and all the feelings and all the tears she needed to stew in the pot over time. (Schweibert and Deklyen 1999, p.40)

## Adoptive/permanency family

Adoptive/permanency parents may also have much to grieve despite having achieved the goal of parenting. Their losses are often not acknowledged by themselves or others.

Parents who adopt because of infertility remain infertile even when they achieve their parenting goal; being pregnant and becoming parents are two different goals. Adoption and permanency does not erase the losses that infertility created.

Infertility must be grieved; each child lost by failed fertility treatments, miscarriages, stillbirths or adoptions that never reached completion must be acknowledged. Acceptance that parenting through adoption and permanency is different from parenting through biological connections is crucial—neither better nor worse, just different. Infertility and parenting are parallel processes; they both exist at the same time. This parallel emotional process must be acknowledged. Grief connected to infertility continues over the years even while parenting a child that arrived through adoption/permanency. The grief of infertility may resurface every time someone asks why their child looks so different from the family; when they discuss their child's story with them over the years; when their child asks questions about how they entered the family; while having to discuss sexuality and their changing bodies; when preparing them to leave home; during discussions about searching and reunion; during re-engagement with the first/birth family; and as the children give birth to biological offspring, who still are not genetically connected to the adoptive/permanency family. Additional losses include the loss of their fantasy child that they may have carried in their mind and hearts when they were children or whom they dreamed about when they chose a partner—their "love child." Adoptive/permanency parents' grief may be triggered when their children are expressing their grief through anger, rejection or oppositional/defiant behaviors.

> My infertility resides in my heart as an old friend. I do not hear from it for weeks at a time, and then, a moment, a thought, a baby announcement or some such thing, and I will feel the tug—maybe even be sad or shed a few tears. And I think, "There's my old friend." It will always be a part of me... (Eck Menning 1988, p.122)

People who are not infertile but who choose to parent through foster care and adoption also have losses. The child described by the social worker at a pre-placement meeting is neither the child they imagined nor, ultimately, the child the social worker described. All members of the receiving family have fantasies, concerns and losses that need to be acknowledged. For example, grandparents will miss out on having the experience of their children creating and birthing a genetic family member.

Adoptive/permanency parents' losses are rarely seen as significant as those of other constellation members. Adoptive/permanency parents are viewed as gaining the most and losing the least. Society views them as having reached their goal of parenting; therefore the larger community does not identify them as having any losses. Adoptive/permanency parents' grief may be blocked by family and friends who are emotionally invested in a positive outcome.

Foster families also have much to grieve. The losses of each individual child whom they fostered must be acknowledged and grieved or it can leave the foster family with a limited ability to be emotionally available to the next child. Each child who arrives in the family has unique needs and a different personality that puts demands on the emotional resources of the family. Foster parents need time to emotionally recalibrate, coalesce their family unit and reflect and respond to their own needs before committing to another child. The losses of the children who remain in the family unit are frequently not addressed; they also grieve each change in their life.

If adoptive/permanent parents have not acknowledged their losses, including those that occurred before they added a child to their family, denial and avoidance of their pain may lead them to dread and defend against any further losses. Parents who deny and avoid their own grief and pain may be unable to assist others, especially their children. This avoidance may include their inability to acknowledge that their family was built differently. They may appear angry, fearful, anxious and not fully authentic. They may avoid participation in the larger adoption/permanency community; have difficulty asking for the information that will be necessary for sharing their child's story accurately and have ongoing fear of the birth/first family. They may also not be able to truthfully share the details of their child's story at each developmental stage, and have difficulty attaching to the child who has joined their family or accepting who that child really is as a person.

Denial creates tension in a family. For parents, the denial may often be connected to their natural desire to avoid causing pain for their child; to hope to avoid having their child view them differently from how any other child views their parents; making a mistake in how much and when to share the child's story; their concern that their child will choose to return to the birth/first family some day; and the difficult task of how to discuss the lifestyle and challenges of the birth/first family. As a result, the child's basic sense of self may develop around a faulty belief system. That flawed belief system is connected to the denial of the difference between being born into this family and arriving from a birth/first family. The denial can leave a child not understanding the words or concepts of adoption and permanency, perhaps believing that they were born from their adoption/permanency parents or that they were not born but somehow "arrived" magically into the family; that there is something frightening or shameful about being adopted or permanently placed with a family; that there is something intrinsically wrong with them or about them that created the adoption or need for placement; and that the truth is so "unspeakable" that no one talks about it. All members of the family can become dependent on the denial, creating a dysfunctional pattern of living and problem solving that is grounded in avoidance of the truth. The child's history and story becomes an obstacle to avoid, a weighty problem. This avoidant pattern inhibits the grief as it does not allow family members to honestly communicate, build healthy attachments based on the truth and address their fear, sorrow, anger and grief as a supportive family unit.

Adoptive/permanency parenting is the same as all other kinds of parenting except that it carries additional losses and adds important tasks that other families do not have to address. All parents deal with the tasks of changing diapers, helping with homework, disciplining, riding a bike and teaching values. In addition to these typical family tasks, adoptive/permanency parents must rely on outsiders in order to reach their goal of parenthood. They receive an infant or child that they may not know; attach and care for a child who may or may not remain with their family; learn to parent a child who may or may not look like the rest of the family; parent a child who arrives from another country who speaks a different language or carries another culture; and parent a child who joins the family, has experienced trauma and is grieving.

When adoptive and permanency parents acknowledge their losses and take the time to do their own "grief work," they may receive the gift of true joy that adoption and permanency brought into their family.

## Grief and resiliency

Life is amazing. And then it's awful. And then it's amazing again. And in between the amazing and awful, it's ordinary and mundane and routine. Breathe in the amazing, hold on through the awful, and relax and exhale during the ordinary. That's just living, heartbreaking, soul-healing, amazing, awful, ordinary life. And it is breathtakingly beautiful. (Knost 2016)

Human beings carry the gift of resiliency. Resiliency is the capacity to recover from an obstacle—being tough and possessing an ability to bounce back after a fall. Every obstacle individuals overcome can become a strength. Attachment can also build resiliency; childhood attachments and meaningful interpersonal relationships that are built over time strengthen and enhance resiliency.

Even with adverse childhood experiences and adoption/permanency trauma, children endure. Many youngsters meet normative developmental milestones and experience great success. Resiliency occurs within the gift of *one* committed, caring, long-term and meaningful relationship. That relationship can create healing as the child feels deeply connected, valued and loved.

Resilient people are less likely to use avoidance, denial, numbing and distraction. They are less inclined to avoid thinking about their losses and more able to accept and experience all their feelings, including grief. There are specific psychological characteristics that resilient people carry as well, including the ability to be emotionally and behaviorally flexible, to remain optimistic during difficult situations, to have faith and confidence, and to feel as if they have some control over the outcome. These people gather their strength, regroup and work towards restoration and balance. They can access their emotions, seek assistance from trusted others, think through a variety of options and clearly communicate their thoughts and feelings to a trusted network of friends and relatives. Everyone possesses some degree of resilience or they would not survive. People may demonstrate resiliency in some circumstances and not in others. Individuals can choose to build and strengthen their resiliency skills.

## Tools for all constellation members to address grief

Here are some questions to explore grief. You can choose to discuss them with a trusted friend or therapist, write answers, or share them with a support group.

- People confronted with pain and loss need comfort: someone to talk to, lean on and share their deep feelings. Who do you trust with your most intimate feelings?

- List five feelings you have when you experience grief. Describe the feelings according to your five senses.

- Describe ways you might avoid the work of grieving.

- People grieve differently according to gender, culture, age and spiritual beliefs. What were you taught about grief? How do you grieve? Pick one significant, specific loss and use that as a focus.

- Have you supported others during times of their grief? How did it make you feel?

- Who supports you during times of grief?

- How comfortable are you in using rituals as you grieve? See Chapter 10, "Rituals and Ceremonies for Healing," in Part 2 of this book.

*A Healing Ritual: FAIR, Families Adopting in Response, a northern California adoptive family support group, published a newsletter addressing the core issue of loss in the summer of 2005.*

## A Grief Shared... by Bonnie Malouf

Recently I attended a workshop led by Randolph Severson and Sharon Kaplan Roszia, therapists who work with adoptive families and members of the adoption community. The focus of the session was the use of ceremonies and rituals to help heal losses. At the end of the workshop, they invited us to participate in a ritual to help heal our losses. I would like to share my experience with you.

I initially went forward to join the circle of participants as an interesting way of experiencing the leader's methods and strategies. I soon found myself personally involved in the process and did in fact experience emotional healing.

Each of us who had chosen to participate first told what loss we were wanting to focus on. I chose the losses of infertility. Even though I have two children by adoption, the unsettled anxieties and longings of infertility still show themselves at times. I shared in the group that I grieve for my unborn children—the children I was never able to conceive—and for my inability to experience the connections with all womanhood that come through childbirth. As I spoke I felt again those old pains of loss and uncertainty.

Each one of us shared our loss—the death of a parent, the loss of a child in foster care, the loss of years not shared with children adopted at an older age, and some others who still carried with them the residue of the monthly cycle of infertility grief.

Directed to a table filled with objects, we were asked to choose one that somehow spoke to our own grief—a shell, a rock, a picture, a child's toy—there were so many to choose from. In silence, we chose. Mine was a rock—black and shiny—like the Earth, seemingly eternal and yet hard and real.

In turn, we shared our reasons for choosing as we did. As my hand closed around this object, my chosen symbol of love and grief, I felt something shift a little. There was something reassuring about holding that rock, something that made my loss tangible in a way that had not happened before.

A poem was read, we held hands, then lit candles to remember and honor our losses and our grief.

The ceremony was simple, nothing strange or too unusual. I had not left my grief there, it was still mine. In a way, it was more fully mine than before, a part of me, a little more integrated into the rest of me. And I had this rock. Funny that it should feel right!

I held onto that rock that day and the next. Then I put it on the living room mantle next to a flower pot. When I see it I am touched. This grief, this part of me, seems to be a little more at peace. Perhaps, that's what healing really is.

- Create a ceremony that honors the person, the role, the possibilities that you've lost. It should encapsulate your personal, spiritual and cultural belief systems.

- Create a loss history timeline that includes all of your significant losses and the age at which you experienced them.

- Going back as far as you can remember, make a detailed list of everything that you've lost in your life and in your journey to adoption and permanency; be specific, such as a teddy bear, a favorite pet, my brother, my foster mom who made great cookies, a miscarriage of a baby boy, attending your child's first birthday party. It is easier to grieve when you name the losses.

- Don't be afraid to reminisce; remembering can give you both pain and joy and, occasionally, a laugh.

- Create a space to honor what you've lost. It might be a scrapbook of pictures and treasured mementos. It could include a place that you visit regularly, a prayer that you repeat daily, a tree that you plant and visit and a poem or a story you write about the person that you miss.

- Repeat the story of what you lost to as many people who will listen. Their empathy and validation of your story can be healing.

- Find role models with similar losses who are further along in their grief work.

- On a daily basis make time to heal.

- Make new friends and keep the old. Be open to joining grief support groups and becoming a part of organizations that support people with similar losses.

- Write a letter forgiving yourself or another. Be compassionate.

- Be in service to others and let others be in service to you—both create healing.

- Think about what led to the loss and where you are now and all that you have accomplished because of your resilience.

- Celebrate being alive—a new day is a gift and a new opportunity to be in the present.

- Nurture yourself—eat well, drink plenty of fluids, shower, wash your hair, brush your teeth, and sleep as needed as grief is exhausting. Meditate, which allows you to slow your thoughts, relax and breathe. Get out in the sun every day for no less than 30 minutes or use a UV light daily. Breathe deeply, as people often forget to breathe when they're grieving. Go for walks in your favorite environment. Learn yoga or stretching. Use essential oils to soothe your senses and change your frame of mind.

- Experience your feelings—it is important to allow everyone the opportunity to express their painful feelings; we all need to be able to cry and discharge painful emotions.

- Use your support system. Be clear and specific about what brings you comfort and what makes things harder. People cannot read your mind. Alert your friends and family that this could change daily. You may be okay one minute but the next minute you may hit rock bottom.

- If two of you are grieving, do not judge each other. You are each dealing with your pain alone and may need others to support you as individuals.

- Don't compare yourself to others, judge yourself or let anyone else judge you. Try not to behave as others think you should, but only as you need to. Don't let others rush your grief because they're uncomfortable with your pain.

- Plan ahead for grief triggers such as birthdays and holidays.

- Find a good therapist or support group with an adoption/permanency focus, if you are feeling stuck or frightened.

- Reflect on the lessons learned about yourself while grieving: your coping mechanisms; your resiliency; your belief systems; and your friends and family. There are always gifts that surface after loss and grief. They can be hidden if we are not observant.

---

Stop punishing yourself.
Slow down.
Take a deep breath.
Relax and take a moment to wonder at your life:
    At the pain that shaped you,
    At the sorrow that taught you,
    At the misery that toughened you.
Despite it all,
You grew.
Own the story that made you who you are.
Use the lessons of the past to reclaim and rewrite what is yours.

(Maxon and Roszia)

## Physical activities to discharge pain and grief

- Get physical: twist a towel or pull on one with a friend; run; exercise; dance; play tennis or handball; do martial arts, boxing and kickboxing; do any sporting activities; tear up magazines; and/or hit a punching bag.

- Pound a drum or join a drumming circle.

- Buy old dishes, pots and pans and go somewhere remote with a friend or a few people and bang pans, make noise and break things.

- Make bread and knead the hell out of the dough—pound it until you are exhausted.

- Scream into a pillow or go to a remote place and yell, howl, growl, wail and sing at the top of your lungs.

- Listen to sad songs, see sad movies, and have a good cry.

- Belly laugh until you cry, collapse or are exhausted.

- Release the toxins that have accumulated in your body through deep massage.

- Paint, sculpt and draw your feelings. Working with clay can be a wonderful physical release. It isn't the outcome or the artwork that is important—it is the process and the release of the emotional pain.

## How to help a grieving child

- Allow the child to be the teacher of their grief experience. Children are always communicating through their body and behavior. Stop, listen and comfort your child through their distress.

- Create a safe environment where children can openly express their grief. Grieving children may look hyperactive, angry, frustrated and oppositional. It is rare that children walk around saying that they are sad. Children may not know that their deep sadness, anger and pain is temporary. Through their parents being emotional tutors, their children learn about hope, resiliency and how to cope with their intense feelings.

- Children, like adults, need to discharge their grief through some physical activity. Join your children in these activities.

- Children who are grieving may appear angry. It is important that they learn to identify and express those angry feelings. Get a big bucket filled with water and ten big sponges and have the child throw wet sponges at the garage door; with each throw of the sponge they have to yell, "I'm angry at…" With each throw, they can express those memories, losses and feelings that have been stored up.

- Use art to help children express their feelings. Have them draw a picture of sad, angry, hurt and scared feelings.

- Look for opportunities to allow the child to project their pain and sadness into movies and books. Find movies and books about loss, separation, abandonment, family conflict, adoption, foster care and kinship care. Movies about parental loss, such as *The Lion King*, *Instant Family*, *Bambi*, *Dumbo*, *Tarzan* and *Rudolph the Red Nosed Reindeer*, give opportunities for the family to share their sadness and tears together. It is much easier for children to talk about the characters in the movie and why they are sad than to talk about their own feelings. Books about adoption and foster care, fairytales and classics such as *Black Beauty* and *Little Women* all have powerful themes of loss and can be used to help a child understand that they are not alone in their grief.

- Pay attention and acknowledge every little ache and pain, fear and distress, illness and accident, and see it as a reflection of your child's pain and grief. For children who have had many losses that previously went unacknowledged, this is the opportunity to finally have their pain acknowledged, comforted and soothed. When the child falls down and scrapes their knee, the parent has an opportunity to use that small scratch to recognize the huge amount of pain that their child is carrying, sending the message that the child should bring their painful feelings to their parents. Stock up on fun bandages and ice packs, and get a rocking chair that allows you to rock, hold and comfort your child.

- Parents should role-model the healthy expression of feelings. It is important for children to witness that people can cry, be angry and very sad, and still be okay. If the parent says, "I am feeling really sad about what happened to your birth/first mother, it makes my heart hurt," they are effectively modeling appropriate grief reactions. If they say to a child, "This is the time of year that Fluffy our dog died. I'm so sad today and I'm missing him," they are modeling that losses that occurred in the past can still be impacting them in the present.

- In preparing children to hear difficult or scary news that triggers grief, parents need to begin by telling the child, "We have something difficult/ sad/upsetting to share with you." This will help the child to emotionally prepare to hear what the parents have to share. Parents should add, "Remember what we've always said, our family does their sad feelings together." This message to the child underscores that when they're feeling sad in the days that follow they should seek their parents out. Physical touch and closeness help a child to feel connected and safe during times of deep sadness. Be honest, factual and concise, and don't be afraid to show your own sadness. Children have difficulty absorbing painful information. They may misconstrue, mishear, misunderstand or immediately forget what has been told to them. Parents need to check back and ask the child what they heard the parent say. Parents may have to re-share the information several times.

- Children feel safe when their world is predictable. Be consistent in your expectations and continue with your usual routines as much as possible.

- Help children label and express their feelings: use a deck of "feelings" cards and play Go Fish or Concentration. When a player wins a pair labeled "sad," they must talk about a time they felt sad. When a player wins a pair labeled "happy," they must talk about a time they felt happy, and so on. Children are learning as they watch their parents label and talk about feelings, and are learning to label their own feelings. Expressing feelings is a learned skill that is best acquired through relaxed and playful interactions. It may also help to hang a "feelings" poster that links facial expressions to the names of feelings. When the child is upset, agitated or sad, it may help them to look at the poster to find the right words to identify and label what they're feeling. Children find it much more difficult reading the emotions of the men in their lives who have facial hair because it hides many of the facial muscles used to express emotions.

Parents have the most important role in helping their child understand and process grief.

## Notes to professionals

Professionals who understand the core issues that adoption and permanency creates for constellation members, and have a willingness to acknowledge, validate and honor the feelings and experiences of those intimately touched by adoption and permanency, are a specialized sub-group within the therapeutic community. Many families report working unsuccessfully with multiple therapists before finding a clinician who is trauma-informed and adoption/permanency competent. The professional who is working with any member of the constellation should always view them as being embedded within their unique familial system, which includes the family of origin, the family that raised the child and the child/adult. Without adoption and permanency competent professionals, many individuals move into crisis with no access to the specialized therapeutic support they need. The serious shortage of adoption and permanency competent professionals who fully understand and appreciate these complex issues frequently leads constellation members to feeling isolated, frustrated and hopeless. Everyone deserves the specialized mental health services that will assist them with their grief. In addition, adoptive and permanency parents need specialized mental health services that will assist them in effectively parenting a child with complex adoption trauma, relational and/or attachment trauma and/or developmental trauma. Too often, parents seeking mental health support for their child find that clinical providers do not understand the unique complexities associated with their life experiences and often intervene in ways that are unhelpful and that sometimes even compound their problems.

Professionals must do a better job in acknowledging the traumatic losses that adoption and permanency creates for the child, youth and family. For children who have suffered abandonment, abuse, traumatic loss and neglect, trusting and depending on new caregivers does not come easily. Utilizing a trauma-informed, attachment-based, family systems clinical orientation engages the entire family in the healing process; the family system is the healing mechanism for the child. Healing occurs *within* and *through* the context of a healing relationship.

So much of the work in adoption and permanency, for both therapists and social workers, is connected to loss and grief. It may lead to professional burnout. Practicing good self-care is imperative. In order to stay vital and effective with clients who are experiencing overwhelming grief, clinicians must have the emotional capacity to create a safe, loving, non-judgmental space for them. This work can be extremely difficult and draining. Suggestions include: consistently addressing the professional's personal grief; taking a break from the work if experiencing a personal loss; nurturing colleagues and support system and asking for support in return; and re-energizing by attending conferences, learning new tools and techniques and staying abreast of the latest research on adoption and permanency, trauma, attachment and child development.

Professionals bring their own cultural, professional training and religious lens when assessing clients for grief. Be aware that each culture, religion, ethnicity and race teaches a favored way to grieve. Each individual and family system brings their own personality, temperament, life experience and belief systems to their grieving process. Professionals need to stay open to learning from the client's unique perspectives and traditions.

Since these grief issues impact the family and children over time, it serves the family's best interests to have access to a trauma-informed, adoption and permanency competent professional, who can commit to the family over the long term. Families experience normative crises and issues throughout their family's lifecycle, and having a trusted relationship with a known professional who already knows the family's story may lessen the distress.

# Chapter 6

# Identity

The hero journey is inside of you; tear off the veils and open
the mystery of your Self. (Joseph Campbell, 1990)

Identity is the fourth spoke in the wheel of the Seven Core Issues in Adoption and Permanency. The pursuit for self-identity is at the heart of the human journey. Individuals are all on this quest to understand who they are, where they fit and how to be the hero in their own life. Humans have always told stories in order to understand themselves and their world. Stories that are broken due to historical or personal events can make it difficult for people to understand their story.

Identity, according to the Merriam Webster Dictionary, includes: the distinguishing characteristics or personality of an individual; our psychological identification; or the condition of being the same or like something else.

Synonyms include identicalness and sameness. Antonyms include difference, discrepancy, unlikeness and disparity.

Identity includes: our values, beliefs, spiritual identification, national and political associations, talents, intellectual capabilities, sexual self-image, gender, role, collective and social identity, personality traits, racial, ethnic and cultural heritage, age, personal expectations and our physical characteristics and career paths. All of these are facets of our identity. The words associated with identity, either self-described or attributed by others, can be positive or destructive. A person's mental model of themselves, a psychological identity, relates to self-image (one's mental model of oneself), self-esteem, and how a person sees themselves as unique. Identity is based on not only what we are, but what we are not. Identity springs from our experiences, perceptions and interpretations of the past; is reflected by others in the present by how we are perceived and labeled and how we understand ourselves in relation to others; and allows us to project who and what we want to be into the future.

Self-identity emerges from relationships. Before there is an "I," there is a "we." We are social-emotional beings, built to live in meaningful connection within our family and clan. In Dan Siegel's *The Developing Mind*, he states that "Human connections shape the neural connections from which the mind emerges" (Siegel 1999, p.2). People are built to get their needs met through the primary attachment relationship which lays the foundation for identity formation.

John Mayer's song "In the Blood" from his 2017 album *The Search for Everything* is a powerful representation of identity challenges as he explores what one gets from nature versus what one gets from nurture.

According to John Bowlby (1988), the creator of attachment theory, attachment allows the child to carry an "internal working model" or an internal representation of the attachment figure while moving towards individuation and separation. Children carry attachment figures in their mind as a "mental representation" that helps them to feel deeply connected, valued and secure, even in times of distress. Attachment precedes identity development and individuation. Thus, children with broken or disrupted primary attachment relationships may struggle with identity formation and separation from their attachment figures.

Developmental psychologist and psychoanalyst Erik Erikson (1902–1994) became one of the earliest psychologists to take an explicit interest in identity. Erikson's work aimed to investigate the process of identity formation across a lifespan. Identity can be charted in terms of a series of stages in which identity is formed in response to increasingly sophisticated challenges and deeper understandings. The process of forming one's identity is the major psychosocial task of adolescence.

Later, James Marcia, a developmental and clinical psychologist, refined and extended Erik Erikson's work. He focused on the twin concepts of *exploration* and *commitment* in identity formation. A person may either avoid the exploration and commitment to forming a cohesive identity or choose to use their curiosity and resilience to explore and commit to the task of identity formation. Marcia proposed that the adolescent's task is to explore and commit to an identity in a variety of life domains from vocation, religion, relational choices, gender roles and so on. Marcia's theory of identity achievement argues that two distinct parts form an adolescent's identity: crisis, such as a time when one's values and choices are being re-evaluated, and then a commitment to the new choices. He defined a crisis as a time of upheaval where old values or choices are re-examined. The outcome of a crisis leads to a commitment made to a certain role or value. As an outcome, there are four possible results: identity diffusion, identity foreclosure, identity moratorium and identity achievement. Note that the possible results should not be viewed as a sequential process.

Identity diffusion is the status in which the adolescent does not have a sense of having choices; they have not yet made nor are attempting/willing to make a commitment to an identity.

Identity foreclosure is when the adolescent seems willing to commit to some relevant values, goals or roles in the future. Adolescents at this stage have not experienced an identity crisis, meaning they have not questioned what has been given to them. They tend to conform to the expectations of others regarding their future, usually allowing a parent to determine the course of their life. As such, these individuals have not explored a range of options around their identity.

Identity moratorium is when an adolescent is currently in an identity crisis, exploring various commitments and ready to make choices, but has not made a commitment to these choices yet.

Identity achievement occurs when the adolescent has gone through an identity crisis and has chosen to make a commitment to an identity.

A more recent and unique concept is proposed by Andrew Solomon:

> Because of the transmission of identity from one generation to the next, most children share at least some traits with their parents. These are *vertical* identities. Attributes and values are passed down from parent to child across the generations not only through strands of DNA, but also through shared cultural norms. Ethnicity, for example, is a vertical identity. Children of color are in general born to parents of color; the

genetic fact of skin pigmentation is transmitted across generations along with a self-image as a person of color, even though that self-image may be subject to generational flux. Language is usually vertical, since most people who speak Greek raise their children to speak Greek, too, even if they inflect it differently or speak another language much of the time. Religion is moderately vertical: Catholic parents will tend to bring up Catholic children, though the children may turn irreligious or convert to another faith. Nationality is vertical, except for immigrants.

Often, however, someone has an inherent or acquired trait that is foreign to their parents and must therefore acquire identity from a peer group. This is a *horizontal* identity. Such horizontal identities may reflect recessive genes, random mutations, prenatal influences, or values and preferences that a child does not share with their progenitors. Being gay is a horizontal identity; most gay kids are born to straight parents, and while their sexuality is not determined by their peers, they learn gay identity by observing and participating in a subculture outside the family. Physical disability tends to be horizontal, as does genius. Psychopathy, too, is often horizontal; most criminals are not raised by mobsters and must invent their own treachery. So are conditions such as autism and intellectual disability. (Solomon 2012, p.2)

The self-identity quest is lifelong but expands in earnest in adolescence:

Constructing an identity is like writing a story. Both take time. Both are embedded in a particular culture and time. Both involve intersections between an individual and other important people. Having a clear sense of identity helps us feel that the different aspects of ourselves fit together in an understandable way. It helps us make meaning of the past, situate our self in the present, and anticipate the future. Identity does not develop in isolation. A liberating conclusion of current research and theory is that identity is not something done to us; it is something we shape, interacting with others, over a course of a lifetime. (Grotevant 2009, p.5)

## Impact of early trauma on identity

Neuroscience has informed our understanding as to the impact that early and chronic trauma has on identity formation. Early abuse, neglect, trauma and multiple attachment disruptions have a significant negative impact on all aspects of a child's development: physiological, emotional, social, cognitive and conscience development. The diminishment of any of these aspects of development will negatively impact identity.

The identity of adults with early trauma is shaped by the distress and dysregulation they experience early in life. Our earliest trauma and attachment experiences form a template for lifelong psychological, physiological, and relational patterns. Difficulties in the initial connection state of development undermine healthy psychological progression through all later stages of development, impacting self-image, self-esteem and the capacity to form healthy relationships. (Heller and LaPierre 2012, p.128)

Early trauma compromises their sense of safety, their right to exist and be in the world, and their capacity for connection. Therefore, they may not learn what it feels like to have a sense of self, to be connected to their body and they are left frightened of intimate connection. (Heller and LaPierre 2012, p.127)

If a mother is chronically depressed, angry, anxious, dissociated, or exposed to continuous stressors during pregnancy, the experience has an effect on the baby. Additionally, physiological stressors, such as drugs, alcohol, and even dietary deficiencies, create distress in the mother's system. The fetus reacts to the mother's states of distress with its own distress. The only way the fetus can cope when mother experiences chronic distress states is by going into contraction, withdrawal, and freeze. Biological distress lies at the foundation of psychological distress. (Heller and LaPierre 2012, p.133)

## Impact of the core issues on identity formation

Identity is the fourth spoke in the wheel of the Seven Core Issues in Adoption and Permanency. If constellation members have acknowledged and identified their losses, examined their feelings of rejection or fear of rejection, become aware of any issues connected to shame and guilt, and addressed their grief process, they have the opportunity to build a cohesive identity that includes their adoption and permanency status. The initial core issues that arise out of the multitude of traumatic losses that created the need for adoption and permanency can be a large and bitter pill to swallow. Those losses change the trajectory of one's life and impact the identities of all constellation members.

The sweet side of the core issues begins with identity. Healthy identity formation allows constellation members to experience the gains in adoption and permanency. If, however, constellation members have not fully addressed the initial four core issues, identity challenges may occur. The last three core issues are focused on creating empowerment and healing. It is a shift from losses to gains.

## Constellation members and identity

Adoption and permanency alters constellation members' identities. Adoption and permanency, for some, may preclude a complete or integrated sense of self-identity. Constellation members may experience themselves as incomplete or unfinished when important parts of their story, or actual people, are missing. Some share that they lack a sense of well-being and safety or a feeling of rootedness associated with a fully developed identity.

The norms, values and beliefs of a culture have a great impact on how constellation members are viewed. Constellation members are absorbing the spoken and unspoken messages of the society that they are embedded in and may take on the labels that are projected onto them in relation to adoption and permanency. The external messages can become internalized as birth/first parents, foster/adoptive/kin parents and the adoptee are bombarded with stereotypes that are projected onto them by family members, neighbors, teachers, the media, movies, books and news stories. If the culture views a parent who relinquishes their child as having made a loving sacrifice for the benefit of their child and to help another, more positive words and labels may be used. If the culture views parents who lose their children through the court system as having negative attributes and deserving of little respect and support, there is a diminishment of positive identity and self-esteem. If society views adoption and permanency as less valuable, second best and temporary, it can lead to the de-valuing of the roles that people fulfill and a diminishment of their identity. Constellation members may feel they are in roles as individuals or families that are viewed as "less real" by society.

Identity is defined by both what a person is and what a person is not. Birth/first parents are both parents and then not parents; adoptive/permanent parents are not parents to a specific child and then are parents to that child and children born into one family, then become part of another family and take on the new family's identity. Constellation members who carry more than one identity in the constellation, for example a birth/first mother who becomes an adoptive mother, have a more complex challenge related to identity.

Birth/first and adoptive and permanent parents frequently experience role confusion. Neither parent can lay exclusive claim to the child as the original family carries the genetic links, Solomon's "vertical identity," and the adoptive/permanent parents are the everyday parents, who influence the child's "horizontal identity." Both sets of parents have a lifelong impact on the infant, child, adolescent and adult who has moved from one family to another. Further complicating role confusion is society's use of the word "real" when referring to all members of the constellation. All constellation members have "real" roles to fulfill, but society tends to elevate some roles while diminishing others. Any negative stereotypes and descriptive words may stigmatize constellation members and impact their identity.

All people are tasked with creating an authentic identity. It is not about perfection or trying to be who or what you think others expect you to be. You must claim who you are, who you have been, and who you wish to be in the future. Define your authentic self for yourself.

## Birth/first family

The birth/first family are the only family of origin. They are parents and yet not parents to a particular child, even if they are parenting other children. They may label themselves in a negative fashion as baby-makers, baby-suppliers for infertile couples, unfit parents, losers, uncaring father, deserter, abuser, addict or bad. Factually, they may also have been young, immature, scared, unsupported, raped or a victim of incest, struggling with mental illness or addiction, grown up in foster care, having had no healthy parental role models, or living in poverty. In addition, they may also be a student, responsible, caring, maturing, talented, loving, hard working, resilient and a survivor. Birth/first parents may lose sight of the more positive dimensions of their identity. They may have a limited view of themselves because of their core issues. They may identify themselves as victims who have lost power or choice through the court system. Many have also been victimized as children. *All of these life challenges are things that happen to us, they are not who we are.*

It is not productive to define oneself by the things that happened or by the significant crises in life. If birth/first parents have addressed the previous core issues, they have the opportunity to heal by choosing those aspects of identity that serve them positively. Identity is not fixed and rigid. A person may choose to explore and be curious about those aspects of themselves that helped them to survive a crisis. People can re-empower themselves by making active decisions to choose labels and characteristics that highlight their strengths and attributes. A birth/first mother who thinks she is a "bad mother," and therefore a "bad person," can choose to say, "I have never stopped loving my children and I did the best I could with what I had." A birth/first father who labels himself as a "deadbeat dad" or an "irresponsible parent" can choose to say, "I was a young man who made mistakes, but I've been living a responsible life for the last five years and often think about my child."

For birth/first parents who participate in an open adoption, the issues of roles and boundaries may impact their identity. How they are identified by the adoptive family and the child will impact how they label themselves.

Are they called by their first names or labeled birth/first parents? Are they a family secret? Does the child know that they are the genetic parents? How do the birth/first mother and the birth/first father refer to each other? How do they refer to their child to the outside world? Can they publicly acknowledge that they are the birth/first parent of the child? How do they speak about the child who was placed to the other children they are raising? How do they label themselves when interacting with the child?

By exploring and redefining their identity in a positive way, birth/first parents can become role models for other birth/first parents who may be struggling with their roles and identities. Being in service to others boosts one's own sense of self in a positive way. Being a birth/first parent is such a unique and often isolating experience that having a peer who has experienced the core issues offers a guide to navigate complex terrain.

Reunions often supply additional puzzle pieces for identity formation. As new information arrives, the identity that was formed will shift. The words used previously to describe the self may no longer apply. If a birth/first parent has identified themselves as "bad" for having either lost or relinquished a child, the person found may display gratitude for the decision made, challenging the negative and shaming aspects of the identity. When identity shifts, questions may surface. What is my identity in relation to the people I find or who find me? How do we refer to each other? What roles do we serve in each other's life? Any fantasies, whether positive or negative, can be dismantled and replaced with facts, which allows for further strengthening of one's identity.

> "Oh, to meet you once again. To pick up the thread that I left dangling so long ago, to weave it into my life, to finally emerge whole. Oh, the peace and wonder of it." (Campbell 1977; Lee Campbell is the Founder of Concerned United Birth Mothers)

The birth/first extended family may choose to identify with their original role as grandparents, siblings, aunts, uncles and cousins. However, their role in that child's life has disappeared because they are no longer "grandparenting" or fulfilling the role of an extended family member, unless it is an open adoption where roles have been actively preserved. Siblings who remain with the original family are siblings and yet not siblings to the child placed outside the family of origin. Even in an open adoption, their role as siblings can be confusing because they are not being raised as siblings within the same family system. Depending on the age of the children who remain in the family of origin, and the memories they hold around the losing of their sibling to another family, they may question: Are we really siblings if we have different parents? Are we siblings if we do not live together or even know each other? Do half siblings count as siblings? How do I refer to those siblings to my peers and others, if someone asks me if I have any brothers or sisters?

## Adoptees and individuals raised in kinship/foster families

The foundation of self-identity begins in the womb, through sensations and feelings; the pre-nate and newborn experiences safety, nurturance and attention from the mother. It is initially a sensory experience of warmth, love and responsiveness to needs. The pre-nate and infant can internalize a feeling of worthiness and goodness when their basic needs are consistently met. This becomes both the basis for attachment as well as the foundation of identity formation. Because there is always a "we" before there is an "I," self-identity springs from within the intimate attachment relationships within the family system. While self-identity formation is a lifelong process, there are two crucial periods. Foundations of self-identity are laid in the first few years of life and expand during adolescence.

> For adopted persons, identity development involves exploration of alternative futures as well as coming to terms with the facts of one's adoption. Personal identity concerns the interconnected issues of uniqueness and similarity. How are we unique and also like others? Identity develops in the dynamic tension or balance between core (psychological sense of self) and context (sociocultural) in the midst of developmental change. The identity process becomes increasingly complex as layers of "differentness" are added such as adoption, trans-racial adoption, trans-cultural adoption, many homes. (Grotevant 1997, pp.3–27)

Adoptees face one of the largest tasks of any constellation member as they form their identity. Starting in childhood, they have the unwieldly task of integrating eight family trees—unless their adoptive or permanent family is a single parent, then they have six. There are two paternal and two maternal trees from the birth/first family, as well as two maternal and two paternal trees from the adoptive or permanent family. In terms of identity formation, the adoptee has the complex task of figuring out who they are in relation to all of these eight familial trees that each include a multiplicity of relatives who carry culture, ethnicity, racial identity, history, family stories, religion, medical history, unique talents, physical attributes, genetic information such as temperament and learning styles, genetic mirrors and world views.

From a society perspective, being in foster care or being adopted carries a stigma and added stressors. Various cultures, races and ethnicities ascribe these individuals a different, and at times negative, status based on their experience of being "fostered" and "adopted." These labels may infer that there is something wrong, different, bad, not "real," damaged, deserving of pity, lucky, needing to be grateful and loyal. These labels projected from society may become part of the individual's identity. For the individual to whom society has assigned these labels, additional questions are created. How do others view me because I am "adopted" or "fostered"? Would they view me differently if I was born into this family? Will I hurt my parents if I ask questions about my birth/first family because I'm curious about who I look and act like? Should I share that I'm adopted or in foster care? How will people view me when I do share my "adoption status" or "foster care status"? Who else knows about my adoption or foster care status, and would they treat me differently if they didn't know? As a teen or adult, do I have the right to search for missing pieces of my identity? When do I tell someone I'm dating about my adoption or foster care status, and will it matter? If I see someone who I look like, can I ask them if we could be related? What parts of my story are still missing, and how would the missing pieces affect my identity?

The more the adopted person differs in appearance from their permanent family and their surrounding community, the larger the challenge of forming a positive racial and ethnic identity. Body dysmorphia can occur when a child appears quite different from their family system, clan and community. A child who looks really different from their family or kin may begin to feel flawed in some physical way and go to exceptional measures to either hide or try and fix those aspects of their appearance that feel so different. They often experience existing outside the norm and may not be able to identify a specific group which they can join. This can be both an inner perception as well as an external experience as they receive messages from their surrounding community that they are different. This phenomenon could lead them to seek out other marginalized individuals who seem more like them in that "I don't fit anywhere either."

Joe, age 15, whose genetic lineage includes African American, Mexican, Native American and Russian Jewish, often experienced confusion and isolation in high school. He shared with his permanent family that he celebrated Jewish holidays, looked Mexican most of the year and looked African American in the summer after spending days at the beach. He did not speak Spanish and was not accepted into that peer group. He would often share how he felt as if he didn't really fit in anywhere, which also made dating difficult. Joe also reported getting bullied and being called derogatory names by various peer groups. His high school experience was frustrating and lonely.

When the adopted child learns, or fully understands, that they are *both* the child of their adoptive parents and the child of another set of parents, they must learn to hold both as true. Without connection to the birth/first parents, the child may retreat into an inner world of fantasy to try and understand who those birth/first parents are, why they did what they did, and to try and create some form of mental image with which they can identify.

Many infants are carefully matched at placement. According to Betty Jean Lifton (2009) in her book *Lost and Found: The Adoption Experience*:

> To a certain degree we were camouflaged, which made us relatively invisible…but they weren't protected at all but were psychologically affected by having to play what I call the "as if" game, "as if" they were born into the family. The *Adoption Game*, as I call it, requires adoptees to lead a split existence. (pp.12–18)

Anne Heffron (2016) also comments on this:

> I was four people jammed into one: I was the me that my Mom wanted; I was the me I would have been if my birth mom had kept me; I was the me I would have been if another family had adopted me; and I was the me that was just me. I couldn't commit to one, so I was a little bit of all four, and this made me unpredictable and unknowable both to those around me and to myself. (p.80)

The child cast as the mythical hero, who was "chosen" and is a "gift," must go forth into the world to search out their origins—this becomes a literal quest for the child/adult. The child/adult may feel as if they have thousands of identities and yet none.

Society's use of stereotypical language impacts the child's identity. If the child is "chosen," they have been acted on in a passive exchange. To be "chosen" or "special" both elevates and dehumanizes simultaneously. It puts the child in the role of being here in this family in service to others' needs. To be "chosen" or "placed as a gift" creates a burden, and to be labeled "special" becomes isolating. Because of this burden, children can be labeled either "good" or "bad" in their family roles.

> The good child is placid, obedient, didn't ask too many questions and was sensitive to his parents' needs to make believe he wasn't adopted. The bad

child was rebellious and continually acting out at home and at school...
For in all adoptees, there resides, simultaneously, the responsible child
along with the one who, being magical, is accountable, legitimate, and a
law-abiding citizen living alongside the outlaw. (Lifton 2009, p.54)

Identity formation is further complicated by the laws, policies and practices
surrounding original birth certificates and the issuing of amended birth
certificates. Original birth certificates are sealed and locked away from public
view. The amended birth certificate is issued after the adoption is finalized and
states that the new parents gave birth to the child. This practice further supports
the "as if" myth, pretending "as if" the adoptee was born from the adoptive
parents, which makes identity formation more complicated. The amended birth
certificate creates a legal document based on a lie on which an individual can
enter school, get a driver's license and secure a passport. Depending on which
state and country the adoptee was born in, they may or may not have access
to their original birth certificate as adults. This is a source of great anger and
frustration as adoptees are treated as second class citizens having fewer civil
rights as they are unable to access their original birth certificates as adults,
which every other citizen can do. Most adoptees want to hold their original
birth certificate, which is the document that attests to their birth and affirms the
truth of their beginning. The original birth certificate represents the beginning
of their story and validates that they were born like every other human being.
Holding their original birth certificate with names on it is a confirmation that
"real" people gave birth to them.

> The adopted are a break in the thread. We are a hole in the fabric, surrounded
> by love and care, but we just don't fit into that shape, that outline. Everyone's
> life ties back into family flesh, resemblance and history. (Blau 1993, p.9)

Children and adults who were raised in adoption and foster care are often left
with broken narratives which impact identity formation. When children are
moved and lose important caregivers who hold parts of their story, their ability
to build a cohesive narrative grounded in the truth of their story is limited.
Children need ongoing access to important caregivers who can assist them in
knowing their story and understanding it as they mature and develop.

Children lacking medical, genetic, religious and historical information are
plagued by questions such as: Who am I really? Where do I belong? Am I
lovable? What is lovable about me? Am I valuable? Do people really know me?

Do my opinions and feelings matter? Am I a good decision maker? Am I more like my birth/first family or the family that raised me? What makes me unique?

---

Further complicating identity formation for the male adoptee is the lack of information connected to the birth/first father and his family. The lack of identity may lead a child, particularly in the adolescent years, to seek out ways to belong in a more extreme fashion than their non-adopted peers. Not to live in knowledge of our full and rightful story can cause anxiety and disorientation, with no resolution. Adoptees are often teased as having been "given away," "not wanted," "a mistake" or being a "foster child." Teen adoptees are over-represented among those who join sub-cultures or fringe groups or become outliers. They also may run away, become pregnant to connect to a real-life blood relative, or to see if they could be a good parent, or they may even temporarily reject their adoptive family. They may try on the persona of the family of origin as they imagine it. They may know very little about their birth/first family and may cling to a small piece of information that they then try on and embellish as a way to feel connected and integrate that information into their identity. For instance, they may focus on the music, food, traditions, holidays and festivals, language and dress of a certain culture or country. My childhood wasn't perfect but there had been love, a brother and a sister, good schools, travel, books and the pantomime of Christmas. Wanting to find my birth parents had less to do with my childhood and more to do with yearning to learn the shapes of their faces, the gestures of their hands and the geography of their hearts. This concern for appearances would be superficial for most people, but as an adoptee starved of reflections of people who looked like her, visual similarity was the beginning of a new life. Not a new life exactly but a new sense of oneself as being fully alive and rooted in the world. (Burton 2008, p.2)

---

For children whose histories include rape, incest, sexual abuse, violence, murder and other horrific events that impact their identity, gaining accurate information becomes crucial. Parents and professionals often struggle with accepting and talking about the truth connected to these events. An inability to discuss the facts surrounding a child's traumatic history may leave a child feeling that something bad happened and it was their fault. Sometimes difficult information is withheld from the child only to be discovered or shared when they are adults. Although based on a desire to protect the child, withholding information may create an additional crisis for the adult who learns the truth and has already formed an identity based on inaccurate information.

Professionals have found that children who were adopted and are confused about their origins may suffer from "genealogical bewilderment." The lack of information and genetic mirror images leaves a child confused as they're missing access to parts of themselves that allow for the building of their identity. In referencing the earlier quote by Andrew Solomon, children receive vertical identities passed down through the generations that include genetic traits, strands of DNA, values, customs and culture. Adopted parents can provide much of the vertical identity but cannot provide the vertical identity components that come through genetics and genetic mirroring.

> The facts weren't always accurate, some weren't even facts; they were lies; the evidence was tainted. I didn't feel real—it was as if I was not quite here, often completely detached from the world around me. (Bohl 2018, p.xxi)

This bewilderment is often the generating force leading to search and reunion. It is not roots we are talking about, but being rooted in one's full identity. The search is an opportunity to generate a cohesive identity based on facts, not fantasy. The search is to find the missing parts of the self and may or may not include a relationship with the people found.

As adopted people collect their missing information and pieces of their story, they may appear different to themselves and others as they adjust and integrate these new facts. Loved ones connected to the adoptee, such as the spouse, children, parents and friends, are adjusting to the evolving and changing identity of their loved one. They may notice a person standing taller in their shoes, exhibiting higher self-esteem and becoming more assertive, or the person may appear hyper-focused on newly found relatives, be angry or depressed, or retreat into themselves or isolate themselves as they do the work of examining who they are and who they are becoming. It may raise questions, such as: How important are these newly found relatives in my life? Do I want to continue to search for others not yet found? How would I be different if they had never left me? Is blood thicker than water?

Reunions supply additional puzzle pieces for the adoptee's identity. As new information arrives, the adoptee's identity will change. The words used previously to describe the self may no longer apply. The same questions that the birth/first parents would ask if there is a reunion are also asked by the adoptee: What is my identity in relation to the people I find or who find me? How do we refer to each other? What roles do we serve in each other's life? Any fantasies, whether positive or negative, can be dismantled and replaced with facts, which allows for the further strengthening of one's identity.

Every individual experiences adoption differently and constructs different meanings surrounding their adoption and foster care story. These differences arrive through the complex interplay of what the person brings to the situation (curiosity, problem-solving ability, interpersonal skills, temperament and intellectual abilities) and the opportunities presented by key people in their social worlds, both their family and outside their family. Identity development is an active process. For people who were in foster care, kinship care or were adopted, and who lacked access to the complete truth of their story, healing and becoming whole are dependent on the task of finding and integrating what was lost into their identity.

## Adoptive/permanency family

For individuals or couples who choose to foster or adopt, their commitment to the children in their care, whether legal or informal, sets them outside the norm in most families and communities. They have dedicated themselves to all of the typical tasks of everyday parenting as well as the additional responsibilities that fostering and/or adopting brings to them and to their extended family. When parenting an infant/child/teen who was not born into the family, there are additional components and complexities that must be addressed—some of those tasks surface day to day and some unfold over time.

Societal views of foster and adoptive parents range from wonderful, positive, saintly and perfect parents, to "they must be crazy," desperate, in it for the money, "not real," needy or selfish. The very process of being assessed, trained, approved and certified before they are allowed to parent children who come from another family impacts how they view themselves as parents. They continue to be assessed, judged and supported by professionals for a period of time after the child is placed in their home. Community members hold these families to a high standard, which places stress on their identity and their parenting style. They frequently feel judged by teachers, social workers, therapists and even the extended family, and may have their parenting abilities and decisions challenged. These cultural views may undermine the very foundation of these individuals' identity. Are we a "second best" family? Do I have a right to claim this child as my own? Is it okay that I wish I had given birth to this child? Am I a "real parent"? Are we babysitters in that when our child turns 18 they will return to their "real" family? Are we a temporary or permanent family? Can I claim my grandchildren as my own?

These are all valid questions as adoptive/permanency parents claim their roles as parents. Stereotypes that are projected onto adoptive and foster parents can be damaging to their identity and may lead them to want to avoid, minimize or bury the truth of their family's formation and the claiming of their roles. Becoming an adoptive or foster parent is an alternate parenting path. In order to fully claim the adoptive/permanency parenting identity, roles and tasks, people should explore the following issues: Why would I choose the complex role of being a foster or adoptive parent? How will I be viewed as a foster or adoptive parent by my extended family and community? What stereotypes and labels do I personally believe about adoption, foster care and/or birth/first parents? How will those stereotypes and labels impact my view of myself as a parent? Do I deserve to parent someone else's child? If my stereotypes about adoption are negative, and I'm embarrassed about being an adoptive/foster parent, how will it impact my parenting? What are the labels that define my identity presently, and do any of them need to change as I become a foster or adoptive parent? Can I view myself the same as, or equal to, all other parents? Can I claim the role of parent with a child who is very different from me? Does my identity include the ways that I am different from others, and how do I feel about my differences? Can I nurture the differences in a child who is not like me?

There are many different reasons that individuals choose to become foster or adoptive parents. There are individuals who have raised their children to adulthood and are so proud of their parenting identity that they choose to start a second family through fostering or adopting. Kinship parents arrive at their role as a kinship parent through a crisis in the family that causes them to carry a dual identity, such as being both a grandparent and a parent to a child, or an aunt and parent to a child, or sibling and parent to a younger sibling. There are individuals who have been parenting boys but who also wanted to fulfill the identity of being a mother or father to a daughter. There are individuals who have a moral imperative connected to their identity that leads them to foster or adopt a child who needs a home. There are single, gay and lesbian individuals who want to choose parenting as a part of their identity and therefore choose to foster or adopt, or choose third-party reproduction. There are individuals who want to parent who have confronted the sadness of infertility, miscarriage and high medical or genetic risk, and who choose to meet the goal of parenting through third-party reproduction, fostering or adopting.

Challenges for foster, adoptive and kinship parents' identity are the additional tasks required of them by the role they assume. For example, the additional parenting task of talking to your child about their history and adoption becomes more complex when your identity as a parent is shared with others who carry the same role. This is true whether or not you are in an ongoing relationship with the birth/first family. Claiming your role as parent or any other family member, but accepting that it isn't an exclusive role, is crucial in helping your child piece together their more complex identity. You are the adoptive/foster mother or father, but you will never be the genetic parent—you are grandparents, aunts, uncles and siblings by adoption and foster care but you will never be the genetic extended family; children in foster care and adoption have the "extras" of everyone, whether or not they know them or see them. Children may also identify previous foster family members with labels such as foster mother, foster father, foster grandparent and foster siblings, with whom they also were meaningfully attached. Sometimes parents need to ask a child which mother, father or grandparent the child is referring to as they are actively trying to weave together their history and identity.

An additional task for foster, adoptive and kinship parents is differentiating when their parenting role is connected to feelings that can be attributed to their unique roles in adoption, kinship or foster care, and when it is an issue common to all parents. For instance, when I am upset about my child's progress in school, is it because I need them to do well to make me feel better as an adoptive, foster or kinship parent or would this be an issue for every parent on my block?

Children who are attached to their everyday parents need their parents to be secure in their parenting role. You are every bit as "real" as any other relative to your child and have a powerful impact on their identity formation. Becoming a mother or father and attaching to a child is a deeply intimate experience and a role not typically shared. This is one of the most difficult aspects of adoptive and foster parenting. Part of foster/adoptive parent identity is to claim the child through the day-to-day parenting role. Having to share the role with another mother or father, whether or not they are known and active players in the child's life, is a challenge. It is helpful to remember that primary attachment relationships are not interchangeable; you live inside your child's heart, mind and identity and cannot be removed or set aside by another person. All parents eventually share their children with love interests, spouses, in-laws and their own children.

Another complex task for foster and adoptive parents in relation to identity is adding a school-age child into the family with the intention of fostering and/ or adopting. An older child, who may be a total stranger, enters the family in need of parenting. The youth may not refer to a new parent as "mom" or "dad," may call them by their first name or may call them nothing at all. The child is a new face in the neighborhood and school. New parents have not yet done the work of building trust and forming a meaningful attachment relationship. The conundrum is that the new parent must function as a solid, committed, caring parent who can set boundaries, lovingly teach and guide, be true to their word, and embody the role of parent at home, at school and in the community. The role of parent has nothing to do with a legal connection and everything to do with a parent identifying themselves as this particular child's parent, whether the child is with the family for years, months or days. Children must be parented every day, and no parent has any guarantee as to whether any child will be with them forever, even if the parent gave birth to the child. For a child placed at an older age, the parent's ability to see themselves in the role of parent to this new child is based on their ability to commit before trust and attachment occur. The emotional commitment to the child often precedes any loving feelings the parent has towards this new child.

If the courts and other professionals have input into how you parent, be clear on what you can and cannot do and embody to the fullest those parenting tasks that fall to you. Nobody else is doing the job of being the "everyday parent"! The task for parents whose children are different from them ethnically, racially and culturally, or who look very different from the rest of the family, is to embody their roles as parents with no equivocation. Your family will stand out wherever you go, and onlookers will stare and ask intrusive questions of you and the child. Teachers and others at school will assume that you are not related. People of your children's race or ethnicity may question, "How did you get that child?" You may confront parental tasks that are unfamiliar such as caring for your child's body, hair, skin and specific medical needs. Examining your own racial and ethnic identity, and any privileges associated with your identity and life experiences, becomes crucial as you blend your child's race, ethnicity and culture with your own.

Everyone's individual identities shift as the family absorbs and blends each unique addition. Parents may need to reflect on the religious community where they pray, the neighborhood where they choose to live, the schools their children will attend, and the racial and ethnic make-up of the teachers in the school, the neighbors and the friends with whom they socialize. It should not be the child's task to adjust to an environment that does not reflect them—the parent's task is to provide the environment where the child feels comfortable and can assimilate a positive ethnic, racial and cultural identity. An adoptive or foster family who identifies as white and then adds a child of color must shift their identity from a white family to a non-white family, and will be seen as such by the larger society.

Infertility greatly impacts both female and male identity. For most people, our image of ourselves as a mother or father genetically connected to our children has been developing since childhood. The thought that we might not be able to create a pregnancy and bring our own offspring into the world feels unimaginable. We have fantasies about who we will marry so our children will look a certain way; how we will announce our pregnancy to our spouse and extended family; what the pregnancy and delivery would be like; what our baby will look like and what we will name it; how we will act as a mother or father; and all of the positive characteristics that our child will inherit from our genetic pool. Unless we grew up in a family where adoption was the norm, that world is unknown and foreign. Infertility disrupts a couple's life plan. They dreamt and planned to live in Australia and ended up living in Iceland. They didn't bring the right clothing, they weren't prepared for the language, the people were very different from what they expected and their bodies and minds had to adjust to the climate. Like this example, infertility requires a significant shift in identity. They will never be the genetic parent to a child. They will never see their genetics reflected in a child. This impacts the entire extended family and the couple may wonder why this happened to them. Their identity could become that of a couple who never parents; a couple who spend a great deal of time, money and emotion on pursuing becoming parents to genetic offspring through fertility treatments, donor insemination or surrogacy, or who turn to the unfamiliar world of fostering and adoption, becoming parents to a child not genetically connected to them.

In the process of losing the experience of giving birth to their genetic offspring, individuals may carry feelings of failure, blame, anger and shame as they build their family in a way that, in their minds, feels second best and inferior. Even when the infertile couple become parents through fostering or adopting, issues of infertility remain and play out alongside the joy they receive through becoming parents. They are both an infertile couple and parents simultaneously, and the task is to incorporate both facets into their identity.

For families who experience the conception and birth of their genetic offspring and then have secondary infertility when they choose to expand their family, many of the same issues are relevant. However, if the couple have produced an offspring, they have had the opportunity to fulfill some of their fantasies. The pain of secondary infertility should not be minimized by others and carries many of the same difficult decisions.

No matter how people arrive at foster and adoptive parenting, they will need to address the evolving practice of openness between the birth/first family and their family. These ongoing relationships that can better serve the child's identity formation create more complex identity issues among the rest of the constellation members. The reality of both the birth/first mother and father and the foster or adoptive mother and father coming together and negotiating the boundaries of their roles, the names they wish to be called, who gets to attend what functions and how they are identified to extended family and community goes to the heart of each individual's self-identity. Commonly, people accept extra sets of grandparents, aunts and uncles, but struggle with the reality in adoption and foster care of extra parents.

The complexity of identity formation expands when constellation members carry more than one role. Each additional role carries another full set of experiences and tasks connected to the core issues.

> Diane, age 35, and her husband have just completed a family assessment and were placed with a newborn baby for adoption. Diane's husband called the therapist asking for assistance because Diane would not hold the baby and was unresponsive to her cries. He was doing all of the parenting, hoping that his wife would come around. He hadn't told the placing agency what was happening. The therapist made an appointment to see the couple the next day and they arrived with the baby. Diane sat separately from her husband and the baby with her back to them. She vacillated between sobs and anger throughout the session and her husband pleaded with her to keep the baby as she repeatedly said she did not want "this baby." The husband left the office with the baby, which allowed Diane to be alone with the therapist who gathered information about Diane's history. Diane disclosed that she was adopted as a newborn directly from the hospital into a family where adoption was rarely discussed because she looked like them. She claimed that she never thought about her family of origin and had no desire to search for them.
>
> When Diane was 15 years old, she became pregnant through a rape, was sent to another town to be with an aunt and uncle, never saw the baby after birth, and the baby was placed into a closed adoption without her knowing whether she had a son or daughter. The advice given to her by her family was to go back to school and act as if none of it had happened. She was told to tell her peers that her family had taken her to another country for an extensive vacation. She never spoke of it to anyone and received no therapeutic support.
>
> Fast forward, she meets her husband and she is unable to become pregnant. She did not want to pursue fertility treatments as she assumed that it was her husband who was the cause of the infertility since she had given birth at 15. The husband suggested that they use a sperm donor, and she shared that she reacted in horror because in her mind having somebody else's sperm injected into her was like being raped again. The couple agreed to pursue adoption. The minute the baby was placed in her arms at the hospital, she handed the baby to her husband and went to the bathroom and vomited. The adoption and permanency competent professional working with Diane recommended that the couple return the baby to the agency so Diane could enter therapy to address her trauma. She needed to address her constellation roles in the order in which they occurred—first her own adoption, then the rape, then the placement of her child—before she would be able to parent through adoption.

## Tools to enhance identity

*Note to parents:* For the child, youth, adolescent and adult, the task for adoptive and permanent families is to collect and share accurate information so that the child can gain a sense of who they are and where they come from. Children need to understand the role of genetics, the influence of the parents who raised them (nature/nurture), and how they become unique individuals. The less information accessible to share with the child, the more support may be needed to help the child explore all their hidden talents, gifts, strengths and everything possible in order to form their identity—including sports, the arts, types and ways of learning, interests and various life paths.

- Who are you? List all of the words you would use to describe yourself.

- Which part of that list would you openly share with others? Which parts of yourself would you keep private?

- Go back over the list and identify where those attributes come from and which of them are unique to you.

- Identify any missing or mystery pieces to your identity.

- What was/is the most difficult aspect of forming your identity in relation to your specific role in the constellation?

- Create a lifebook that includes the narrative of your story; start at the beginning and include photos, timelines, memories and momentos.

- Write your story, in your own words. Go back to it in one week or one month and note the words that you used connected to your identity. Feel free to change your narrative as you gain new insights. How you tell your story is just as important as the facts within your story.

- Create an image of yourself that reveals various aspects of your identity. For example, paint, sculpt, photograph, make a collage, film, write or create a vision board.

- Make up a story or write a song or a poem about yourself. What did you learn?

- If you could change something about your identity, such as your looks, your name, your personality, your skills or your life circumstances, what would it be and why?

- For all parents: list 10–15 adjectives to describe yourself as a parent. How many relate to your role as a member of the constellation? How would your parenting be different if you had not been touched by foster care or adoption?

- When do you feel as if you are masquerading in a role, and do you fear others will see the truth behind your mask? Where, when and with whom do you feel authentic?

- Ask several people to describe you in ten words. Write down the words and note which descriptions are frequently mentioned. Which do you agree with and which make you feel good about your identity?

- Join or start a support group for constellation members where discussions of identity are openly explored.

## Notes to professionals

Support the lifelong process of identity formation by allowing for and supporting the reclaiming of the missing parts of the story. Join constellation members *where they are* and work to assist and empower them in telling their story, their way. Any of the above-stated tools can be used in therapy to explore and strengthen identity formation with any members of the constellation. Be mindful to not project your thoughts and feelings into their story or journey. Adoption and permanency creates more complexity within identity formation and family system relationships. Utilizing a family system's clinical orientation will allow the professional to understand, support and facilitate healing the ruptures that occur within strained relationships, which can easily impact identity formation.

Constellation members receive validation and support from their peers who have traveled a similar path (horizontal identity). Start an adoptee support group or a birth/first parent support group so those constellation members who are under-served can come into a healing environment with one another. Adoption and permanency can be a very isolating experience, as the culture views it as a one-time, problem-solving event. When constellation members are in an emotionally supportive environment with peers who have experienced similar core issues, they report feeling a sense of validation and mirroring.

For children, youth and adults who spent time in foster care experiencing rotating caregivers and multiple attachment disruptions, their narrative (story) can be broken and fragmented. This will impact identity formation. Support their "search for self" by actively engaging them in completing a lifebook and claiming their narrative as their own; empower them to retell their story with their own words, feelings, thoughts and beliefs.

Professionals often have the role of assisting and guiding parents as to the importance and complexity of identity formation with children and youth who are fostered or adopted. Children with racial, ethnic and cultural differences from their adoptive, foster or relative kinship family have additional components to understand and integrate into who they are (identity). It is common for parents to be "blind" to these dissimilarities as the child integrated and assimilated into the family (horizontal identity). Adolescence often brings these issues to the forefront, and professionals can best serve the child/youth by engaging the family system in the therapeutic process. It is not uncommon for the adolescent to struggle with issues connected to identity as they have a deeper understanding of their story and may be interested or conflicted about searching for missing relatives. If parents have not acknowledged their own core issues, it is more likely that they are not actively exploring these issues with their child or teen. Sometimes adoption/permanency is the great big elephant sitting in the living room that no one is talking about. A family systems clinician who is adoption/permanency competent can focus on strengthening the patterns of communication while addressing the core issues for each constellation member, including the parents who may feel rejected by their child's behavior.

# Chapter 7

# Intimacy

Every interpersonal skill that we need to feel deeply
loved and connected must be learned. (Maxon)

The fifth spoke in the wheel of the Seven Core Issues in Adoption and
Permanency is intimacy. The most complex organ in the known universe is the
human mind; imagine two human minds attempting to be intimate. Intimacy
involves risk, vulnerability and the belief that the self is valuable, resilient and
worthy of love. Intimate relationships play a central role in the overall human
experience. Individuals' most primary motivation is the drive to belong and
learn how to get their emotional needs met through human connections.
Intimate attachments provide the network through which all social, emotional,
physical and psychological needs get met. Intimate attachment relationships
require trust, respect, acceptance, empathy and reciprocity. The skills required

in order to create and sustain these meaningful intimate relationships are being learned from the moment we enter the world.

> Family life is our first school for emotional learning. In this intimate cauldron we learn how to feel about ourselves and how others will react to our feelings and how to think about these feelings. (Goleman 1995), p.189

Researchers have validated that infants need to be held and touched so that they can grow and thrive. Every experience creates an emotional memory that is embedded within the mind and the body. Emotional memory exists outside time so that the past is very present in all relationships. All expectations in relationships are conditioned by previous experiences. Emotions are first experienced through the senses, and, over time, people learn to "think about" and then "talk about" feelings; humans are "feeling beings" before they are "thinking beings."

Children need to experience physical and emotional closeness with another human being in order to learn the necessary skills that enable them to attach and get their *developmental* needs met. Children acquire an "internal working model," a belief system, based on their early primary attachment relationships that influence all future intimate relationships. The need for connection never goes away; it is lifelong. In its absence, symptoms of chronic emotional deprivation may develop, including anger, depression, addiction and physical or mental illness.

> Emotional hunger is a strong need caused by deprivation in childhood. It is a primitive condition of pain and longing that is often mistaken for feelings of love. (Firestone and Catlett 1999, p.105)

Intimacy requires that an individual be both a separate self and able to join "the other" in an emotionally meaningful relationship. Bringing an authentic self into an intimate relationship requires individuals to risk being who they are rather than who they think others expect or wish them to be.

Mature love includes kindness, respect, sensitivity, vulnerability, honesty and affection. Giving these gifts is often easier than receiving them, especially for those who carry early emotional wounds.

Intimate relationships are built over time through both verbal and non-verbal communication. Knowing each other means becoming acquainted with the subtleties and nuances in both ourselves and the other person.

Intimacy develops through reciprocal self-disclosure and candor. A healthy, emotionally intimate relationship is one in which neither party is afraid to speak their truth; neither party is asked to sacrifice who they are in order to stay in the relationship; or needs to betray their authentic self. Each person is able to safely express strength and vulnerability, as well as weakness and competence.

To assess the emotional intimacy within a relationship, explore the following questions: Does this person completely accept me as I am? Can I openly share my deepest thoughts and feelings with this person? Does this person care deeply about me, and how do I know? Are my thoughts and feelings understood and affirmed by this person? Am I capable and willing to provide all of the above for the other person?

Emotional intimacy is much like a dance. In this "dance of relationship," each person needs to first understand themselves—their needs, thoughts, feelings, expectations and vulnerabilities. An inner exploration of the self is essential as it sheds light on one's blind spots. Connections to others can be weakened by expectations that are hidden. In this intimate dance, we can step on each other's toes and cause pain.

In this intimate dance, it is much more than words that communicate feelings. Beyond words, emotions are revealed in how people hold their bodies, their willingness to make eye contact, their tone of voice, facial expressions and reactions to touch, and their matching of words, actions and physical expressions. The lack of clear communication may negatively impact a partner's ability to meet your needs and for you to meet theirs. The meeting of needs arises from the learned skills of empathy and attunement. Intimacy requires the absolute certainty that what a person thinks and feels is being heard, understood and valued. Empathy is an active behavior that requires undivided attention and the ability to feel what your partner feels. The ability to set aside one's self-interest and self-protective mechanisms in order to stop anticipating what the other person will say allows for a deepening of intimacy. Being able to fully listen to a dance partner's heartfelt needs and expressions allows for intimacy.

Our primary dance steps are learned in childhood and become more sophisticated over time. Two important qualities contribute to the creation of a secure parent–child attachment relationship, which sets the stage for all future intimacy. First, the parents need to be able to see their child as a separate being, not as an object, possession or a needed reflection of themselves. The second quality is the parents' ability to be emotionally available to attune to the changing needs of each unique child. Missteps and mis-attunements occur within all families. Missteps are a normal part of learning the dance of relationship and later may require "repair" through forgiveness. More significant family crisis such as divorce, death, addiction, abuse, an absent parent, parental mental illness or an overwhelmed parent can all negatively impact the meeting of a child's needs. This may cause the child to dance to a darker tune, as they personalize what happened and work to avoid further disappointment and emotional pain. The defensive coping strategies that develop from this darker dance of intimacy fall into four adaptive styles of relating that may be sustained well into adulthood:

- *Peace at any price:* this style incorporates a belief that one's needs are not important and that the person is here to meet everyone else's needs. They may have difficulty expressing true emotions and avoid confrontation, eager to please. They say "yes" to most requests. In an attempt to repress one's own needs, a person may actually appear to others as quite "needy." The neediness may be exhibited in underlying anxiety.

- *Critical fault-finder:* this style incorporates the use of generalizations, attacking and blaming others' characters and personalities. The person believes that the best defense is a good offense. They have not learned to speak on their own behalf without indicting others in the process. They may be in a constant state of agitation or anger as they live in a world that never meets their needs.

- *Detached thinker:* this style employs over-thinking and under-feeling. There is a detachment from their own needs and emotions and a preference to live with facts and statistics and to rarely admit mistakes. They hold themselves and others to a high level of expectation. Since they bury their own needs and feelings, they minimize others' needs and feelings. Others may perceive them as being self-centered, cold and self-assured.

- *Evasive distractor:* this style utilizes distraction from the issue or problem at hand. The person avoids confrontation by resorting to irrelevant comments, leaving a discussion, not giving direct answers, and avoiding eye contact. Topics may be changed if they are experienced as a threat to the self. Their perception of themselves is as an "innocent victim" who is picked on. Distraction and avoidance are the primary defensive strategy.

These learned coping styles are a response to pain, shame, anger and fear that have been incorporated into the dance of intimacy. Parents also have particular styles that teach the dance of intimacy to their children. Since parenting styles and attitudes exist on a continuum from parental acceptance and warmth to ambivalence, detachment and rejection, what the child learns about intimacy may vary.

Intimacy is the heart of a strong relationship. Adult intimacy is about trusting and knowing someone so deeply that people can be completely free in each other's presence. Intimacy requires that you and your partner are able to be open and honest with each other about your needs. It is such a personal emotional state that it is typically reserved for just one other person. Ideally, sex inside a loving relationship should be the physical embodiment of that love between consenting adults.

For all people, past experiences, childhood trauma and emotional conflicts impede intimacy. Trauma lives in the body and can be retriggered when an individual feels vulnerable, open and exposed. Additional approaches to connect to another are needed. There are many ways to express intimacy. Spending quality time together, listening to one another and enjoying physical but non-sexual contact such as massages, shared interests and activities all build intimacy.

---

**WHAT IS A HEALTHY RELATIONSHIP?**

I can be me

You can be you

We can be us

I can grow

You can grow

We can grow together

(Woititz 1985, p.20)

---

## Intimacy and constellation members

If individuals have acknowledged their core losses, noted where, when and with whom rejection surfaces, addressed feelings of shame and guilt, taken time to grieve and have embraced their identity, they are able to offer an authentic self in an intimate relationship. Identity and intimacy are linked. As a person clarifies and re-clarifies who they are, their ability to relate to others, forgive others, embrace others, trust others is enhanced. If the earlier core issues have not been addressed, an individual may not know themselves well enough to know what they "really need" or what they have to offer the other person in an emotionally intimate relationship. It is difficult for any person to feel deeply connected if fear of loss, shame and guilt, sadness or anger attached to grief is being experienced in the present. It is extremely difficult to be emotionally available to a partner or a child when one's emotional energy is being absorbed by the core issues.

All constellation members have been impacted by a core loss that changed their identity and may have led to intimacy challenges. The initial losses may have impacted self-esteem and created negative feelings, which may keep individuals from getting close to others. One way to avoid possible re-enactment of previous losses is to avoid closeness and intimacy.

Adoption and permanency inherently impacts intimacy as people are shifted on and between familial trees. These changes can send a message that individuals are easily lost, replaced, interchangeable and substituted, which may give a person the feeling that building attachments to others is risky and creates pain. When information is withheld or unavailable, intimacy can become hampered by the lack of personal information. Society's projected expectations about how constellation members should be loyal, live in the present, ignore the past and be grateful also inhibit honest communication.

Intimacy for constellation members can also be negatively impacted by adverse childhood experiences and relational trauma. Individuals who have experienced childhood trauma within their family system may lack healthy role models for intimacy and may have learned that getting close to others is painful. These experiences may lead to a desire to numb the pain through avoidance, medication or addiction, which creates further obstacles to intimacy. The feeling that life is unsafe and that the person must be "on guard" takes its toll.

Those who experience trauma in adolescence or adulthood, including incest, rape, loss of a child, domestic violence or death, may have limited emotional resources to put towards building healthy relationships. For some, co-dependency and excessive emotional or psychological reliance on a partner develop as an adaptive response to the trauma. True intimacy means that one develops a love relationship with another person where they offer—and the other offers in return—validation, understanding and a sense of being valued intellectually, emotionally and physically. Healthy intimacy does not require a person to lose themselves while being in a relationship and devoting all their emotional energy into the other person. People who are co-dependent are emotionally focused on "the other" to the detriment of themselves. They may be fueled by anxiety, excessive neediness, a chronic need for approval and an inability to function as a separate self. In essence, one person loses their sense of self and can be highly reactive, while the other person takes on the primary role of rescuer, supporter and confidant.

Very few people become members of the adoption and permanency constellation with any preparation for how it will impact their lives on an emotionally intimate level. Parents whose children may end up in foster care or adoption through the courts have the most intimate aspects of their lives examined under a microscope, including their lifestyle, mental health issues, addictions and relationships. Total strangers determine the outcome of their lives without having built any trust or meaningful connections to them. Some birth/first parents were physically raped, which brought them to the crisis of losing their child. Men and women who find themselves in the middle of the crisis of an unplanned pregnancy will experience strangers such as social workers, lawyers, adoption facilitators and obstetricians shepherding them through one of the most important decision-making processes in their lives. Some placements of a child can be experienced as a "business transaction" where no intimacy is present. Parents may transfer their offspring to total strangers without having built an intimate connection with the very people who will be parenting their child.

Couples who have run the gauntlet of infertility, where vastly intrusive medical procedures are employed and where having sexual relations has had to be done at a certain time in a certain way, may experience the diminishment of both their emotional and sexual intimacy.

The intrusion of a stranger into the private lives of prospective foster/adoptive parents as a part of a family assessment can be experienced as an emotionally intrusive process. Questions asked during the family assessment go to the heart of the couple's relationship or the prospective single parent's dating and love life.

For the child who was placed and is now an adult, intimacy issues may be evident in relationships with partners. Questions are connected to their conception, biological and genetic inheritances, concerns about their own bodies and sexuality. For children adopted at older ages who have experienced multiple disruptions, broken attachments, abuse and/or neglect, prior experiences may interfere with their ability to get emotionally close to others.

Adoption and permanency may also lead to a wider circle of available intimate relationships as they create a marriage of clans. Ideally, a relationship that begins with a group of strangers coming together for the benefit of a child will create intimate connections between all eight familial trees. Intimacy between people is based on contact over time, so trust can be built. For each break in connection to any familial tree, the child loses important facts about their lineage, which may lead to a diminished sense of identity, which can impact the development of intimacy skills.

People should explore the unique intimacy challenges that permanency, trauma and broken attachments create for constellation members.

# Birth/first family

All birth/first parents have suffered a relational crisis that brought them to the difficult place of losing a child through adoption or losing a child through a court process. This crisis and the subsequent loss of their child can create intimacy barriers because they may feel unworthy. They may also have lost their intimate connection to the other birth/first parent. Birth/first fathers may question their attachment to the child they helped conceive and think less of themselves if they were unable to assist and support the birth/first mother. They lose the future intimate relationship with their offspring. The birth/first mother is adjusting to an unfamiliar body that impacts on her intimate view of herself.

Growing another human being in one's body is the most intimate connection a woman can experience, and yet, at the same time, may be connected to the loss of that child. Mother nature in her wisdom allows for the release of hormones immediately after birth that cause the new mother to focus intensely on the needs of her new baby. She becomes a "feeling being" rather than a "thinking being" in preparation for motherhood at a time when major life decisions are being made. When deep intimacy between mother and child should be occurring, separation becomes the plan. Both baby and mother are vulnerable and thrust into crisis.

The crisis for some pregnant women may be addressed through denial of the pregnancy. The trauma of what is happening is so overwhelming that denial of the pregnancy becomes a defense mechanism. Pregnancy denial occurs when a woman denies either the fact of the pregnancy or the implications of the pregnancy on her life. A woman may be intellectually aware of the pregnancy but makes little emotional or physical preparation for the birth of the child. For others, denial occurs when a woman discovers the pregnancy in the third trimester and doesn't tell anyone or make any plans. This may lead to the baby being safe-surrendered at a hospital or fire station. For pre-teens and teens who may not know they are pregnant and suddenly deliver a baby at home or school, the shock may take many years to address as they move through the developmental phases of their adolescence and young adulthood. Teens and young women who were sent away to maternity homes, or to relatives or friends in other communities, or were hidden in their own homes while they were pregnant, may have lost the opportunity to make their own decision about whether or not they wanted to raise their child and were directed not to talk about the pregnancy and birth when they returned to school, work or college. Secrets and shame diminish intimacy. A birth/first mother who continues to carry the secret of a pregnancy and relinquishment from those she is most intimately connected to may live in fear and stress for decades that her secret will be revealed.

Men may also use denial of a pregnancy to avoid the impact and implications it has on their lives. Adolescent males most often have very deep feelings connected to the pregnancy they helped to create. Their emotions may swing from fear, guilt, love, shame, pride, embarrassment and a sense of being overwhelmed. They may not know who to go to for support and may quickly be eliminated from the decision-making process. Often the pregnancy is not disclosed to them. Even men at older ages experience similar emotions, though most can rely on stronger coping styles. The pregnancy starts affecting the woman very early on with hormonal and body changes, whereas a man can avoid the reality of the pregnancy because their body is not changing and it is not recognized by outsiders that they are becoming a father. For men, it might not be until the baby is separate from the mother that the true impact of what has happened is felt.

It is not uncommon in adoption and permanency for sex and intimacy to have a vague and/or misunderstood connection. The conception of a child may have been connected to a long-term intimate relationship, a desire by one of the parties to have a child, a form of manipulation to keep a partner involved, a one-night stand, or a rape. Sex without emotional intimacy is a basic physical act. Making love infers that there is emotional intimacy and connection between the parties.

The story of the conception has significant implications for the child to whom the birth/first parents have given life. Birth/first parents will be in a position to relate the story of the child's conception to others. Acknowledging the truth of a child's beginning is critical. There may be two truths, depending on who's telling their story. Depending on with whom the birth/first parents shared their truths, the stories may have become "cleaned up," reinterpreted, misperceived or shortened. It may be difficult for birth/first parents to recall the details of the conception story if it was connected to any trauma and/or embedded in their active use of drugs and/or alcohol.

Birth/first parents may blend future sexual relationships, pregnancies, emotional connections, abandonments and loss into one emotional bucket. Their fear of more loss, abandonment or rejection inhibits future relationships because one way to avoid possible re-enactment of previous losses is to avoid closeness and intimacy. Birth/first parents may find themselves in abusive relationships as a form of penance because the loss of a child has left them feeling they deserve punishment. Birth/first mothers may be afraid to give birth again for fear of losing their partner. Birth/first parents may worry they would not be good parents to future children. For some birth/first mothers, the search for intimacy through a series of sexual encounters may lead to multiple pregnancies and more placements or the loss of their children through the courts again.

For some birth/first parents, the search for intimacy leads to a desire to repeatedly conceive children. This may be connected to a belief that creating children is the one positive contribution that they may offer society. For a woman, the intimacy that is created through carrying and nurturing a child within her body serves to meet the need of feeling connected and important to another being. Being pregnant may be the only time that others intimately connect to her through nurturing and caretaking.

There are overlaying complexities if the prospective adoptive parents connect to the pregnant couple before birth with the goal of ongoing openness. The prospective adoptive father, who has no intimate relationship with the mother who may be carrying his future child, can create a false intimacy where boundaries become fuzzy. When out in public, the man may have his wife on one arm and the pregnant mother on the other, which may cause others to assume falsely that the woman carrying the child is his wife. Men may attend doctor's appointments for the pregnant mother or be offered the opportunity to be in the delivery room and perhaps even cut the cord or film the birth. Those are very intimate moments. Outcomes could include: the genetic father feeling that he has lost his role in the pregnancy and birth; the pregnant mother feeling as though she no longer has the option to change her mind about placing her baby because she has shared this intimate experience with the prospective adoptive parents; or a profound deepening of the intimacy between the genetic mother and father and the prospective adoptive parents that lasts a lifetime and binds them all to the child.

Individuals may develop crushes or deep feelings as the intimacy grows between the prospective adoptive parents and the birth/first parents. The powerful emotional intensity that occurs between the four individuals connected to this baby can blur the lines between what are socially acceptable boundaries and behaviors, and deep affection that can be misconstrued or lead to sexualized feelings.

Intimacy and boundary issues may also impact foster and adoption-built families. It is rare for foster and adoptive parents to have met the birth/first parents during the pregnancy or at the delivery; however, they may also be building intimate relationships with each other as they come together around their deep love for the child. Spending time meeting the needs of the child during the stressful court process intensifies everyone's emotions, which may include anger, fear, jealousy, distrust and resentment, all of which inhibit the building of intimate relationships. If these intimate relationships are not built, the child loses important connections no matter what the court decides. Without building a trusting and caring relationship, all four parties are at risk for losing connection to the child. If the court orders reunification, the lack of trust inhibits the foster/adoptive family from being seen as an ongoing support to the re-unified family. If the court severs parental rights, the lack of trust would inhibit ongoing openness between the parents and the foster/adoptive parents. In both of these scenarios, the lack of building a trusted, respectful relationship creates significant loss for all parties, particularly the child.

> Andrea was 21 years old when her 2-year-old son was taken into protective custody due to abuse and neglect. During her weekly visitations, she met Janet, the foster mother, who was caring for her son as well as Janet's own children. Although Andrea worked hard to meet her case plan, she was not successful and the courts terminated her rights. Andrea was relieved to know that Janet and her family wanted to adopt her son even though she was feeling a great deal of anger and sadness. Due to the relationship that was built between Andrea and Janet over that year, Janet decided to treat Andrea as an extended family member. Because Janet couldn't imagine never seeing her own child, her compassion led her to include Andrea in family gatherings, birthdays and special events. The trust that was built between the two mothers established the foundation that allowed for ongoing intimate connections.

Whether the birth/first parents had a nine-month in-utero relationship or parented their child for weeks, months or years, the intimate connection is broken and/or diminished when they are no longer the "everyday parents." For many, the loss leaves the birth/first parent feeling empty, lost, worthless and alone. For birth/first parents who have lost several children through the courts, their intimacy challenges are multiplied. Birth/first parents who have parented their children through multiple developmental stages, where memories and experiences have intensified their relationship, may have a limited capacity to tolerate or risk emotional intimacy again.

## Adoptees and individuals raised in kinship/foster families

Individuals who have lost their most intimate relationships, either at birth or as children, may learn to fear intimacy. They may believe that the breaks in attachment were their fault; they may be suspicious of anyone attempting to build closeness with them. Our earliest attachment relationships teach the skills of intimacy. If an infant or child's attachment relationships are disrupted, and occasionally disrupted multiple times, the impact on their ability to form meaningful emotional connections is reduced. They may employ a "go away closer" coping mechanism demonstrating their need to connect but also the fear of doing so, which is confusing to their loved ones. Parents may perceive their child as being oppositional, defiant, angry, rejecting and isolative when the child most likely is employing coping strategies to avoid further pain and distress they believe intimacy brings. If the parents can read the child's behaviors as expressions of what they are needing, move towards the child's emotional distress and avoid judging, reacting, distancing and blaming, the parent–child relationship can deepen. The more disruptions in attachment the child has experienced, the longer it will take the parent to build the necessary trust that creates emotional intimacy.

> For every week, month or year that a child has not been planted in permanency, that is how many weeks, months or years, plus one, that it takes for the child to believe that they are truly rooted in their family. They have to be longer with their permanent family than they were any place else. If a child joins their permanent family at age 10, it will take them to age 21 to really *feel* and *accept* that this is their clan. (Roszia)

Intimacy for children is complicated when they do not see themselves reflected in others and have concerns about their skin or eye color, facial features and body type. A child and teen may wonder whether they are in the "right family" if their family looks so different from the image they see in the mirror. How does a person become intimate with others when they don't love the image of themselves? Children are concrete thinkers and it is easiest for them to connect through similarities.

For adolescents who have just entered their new family, the paradoxical tasks of attaching and building intimate relationships simultaneous to individuating and getting ready to launch are overwhelming. Building intimacy through attachment with total strangers, while at the same time connecting to peers whose goal is independence from their parents, is challenging and exhausting and leaves the teen developmentally out of sync. The danger for the adolescent is that they prematurely launch themselves before they become deeply rooted into the family system. Alternatively, some later-placed youth may choose to stay longer with their family to develop these roots and be given the opportunity to address the unmet developmental needs connected to early loss and trauma.

Penny joined her permanent family at the age of 14. She entered her first foster family at 6 due to neglect and abuse. For the next eight years, she moved into six different foster families, due to no fault of her own. Because she had little stability and no permanency, her developmental age vacillates between 6 and 8. As a 14-year-old adolescent, she is tall, well developed, athletic and attractive, so her peers are drawn to her. Penny is able to maintain her adolescent demeanor while at school and in public. When home, her parents have observed that she easily regresses to a much younger age. She needs more assurance, she's more emotional and easily cries, she requires more touch and holding and she frequently retreats to her bedroom, where they overhear her "little girl voice" as she plays with her dolls and stuffed animals. Her parents have lovingly allowed her to enjoy the experiences that she missed while she was "treading water" in the impermanence of foster care.

Children, teens and adults may choose to reject others before others could possibly reject them. The need for distancing is based on distrust and fear of recreating the initial intimacy break. Maintaining control is an avenue of emotional self-protection.

The multiple ongoing losses in permanency, coupled with feelings of rejection, shame and grief as well as possible missing parts of one's story, may impede emotional intimacy. One way to avoid possible re-enactment of previous losses is to avoid any and all emotional closeness. Another strategy to avoid intimacy is to move from relationship to relationship and never stick around long enough to build true intimacy. Becoming emotionally intimate with another person requires revealing ourselves every day, in a thousand ways, to the other person. This process can feel overwhelming and scary if we fear that the other person will leave us.

For children entering a new family at an older age, where the parents look youthful, boundaries may become confusing as the new family member attempts to build emotional intimacy. A teen may develop a crush on their new parent or new sibling. Many children are developmentally out of sync with their chronological age due to breaks in attachment, trauma and/or institutional care. When they begin to get their physical and emotional needs met, it feels good and they desire more. For a 14-year-old who is developmentally functioning closer to age 8, receiving affection from his new mom may cause an erection. For teens, questions about how and where to touch new family members are juxtaposed against wanting to sit on their laps, climb into bed with them in the morning, be rocked, and give and receive hugs and kisses. The newly arrived child has not yet learned the boundaries around privacy, nakedness and incest that the rest of the family has already incorporated into their day-to-day lives. The youngster may peep in at windows, walk into occupied bathrooms, inadvertently expose themselves, or ask invasive questions. The confusion of a child entering a new family where the rules and boundaries are not yet clarified, and where they are not genetically connected and have no living history, may raise the question as to why they cannot have crushes or date their new siblings. Due to missed experiences, these awkward attempts at closeness may appear inappropriate and embarrassing for both the child and family members.

The dance of relationship is already established between the family members that this new child is joining. The child/teen must adapt and learn this family's unique dance steps and be given the opportunity to make lots of missteps and occasionally even stamp on someone's foot.

Many of the children who are joining their families through foster care and adoption have experienced different forms of trauma and carry that trauma into their new families. It is necessary to address how that trauma impacted the child's ability to connect. If they have experienced pain, terror, fear and shame within the intimacy of a relational dance, they will work hard to avoid closeness and connection until trust and safety have been established with their new family.

Trauma that occurs between authority figures or trusted adults and a child is called *relational trauma*. The child learns the lesson of false intimacy and betrayal, shame and oppression, and may incorporate that into their relational dance. If the youngster has been sexually abused by someone who is older, such as an older sibling, parent, extended family member or trusted community member, they have typically been coerced through fear and threats, which will embed secrecy, self-loathing and shame into their emotional dance. The child was objectified as they were used and manipulated to gratify the needs of another. The impact of the sexual abuse is dependent on the age of the child, where and with whom the abuse occurs, the length of time over which it occurs, and the type and intensity of abuse. Without therapeutic family or professional intervention, the relational dance of intimacy may be impacted for life.

The relational trauma that includes sexual abuse occurs on a continuum from voyeurism and exposure to pornography, sexualized verbiage, touch and fondling, to penetration and sodomy. If the perpetrator is a member of the family, the sexual abuse is called incest. The family system that includes alcohol addiction and/or drug addiction is fertile ground for all types of neglect and abuse, including incest. These issues typically play out intergenerationally as trauma is transferred from one generation to the next. Children whose perpetrator lives within their family system lose the ability to trust adults. They have no "safe harbor" to retreat to and typically experience "terror without solution." These early traumatic experiences may surface as flashbacks later in life while attempting to get close to another in an intimate relationship.

Permanency families, like all other families, have life challenges that include divorce, addiction, mental illness and death. Some adoptees report that their abuse occurred within their adoptive family. Sadly, some of their stories include being molested, physically abused and/or neglected. Others experienced breaks in their intimate connections because they were sent away to treatment centers and military or boarding schools and were never given the opportunity to return home. Adoption disruptions and dissolutions left other adoptees feeling disconnected and unwanted.

Despite the challenges to intimacy, research and experience show that adoption and permanency for the child and youth offers the most intense intervention that exists to heal intimacy wounds.

Children and youth who enter their adoption and permanency family with relational trauma have the opportunity to learn how to trust, love and be loved.

## Adoptees and birth/first families in reunion

Another unique challenge for the building of intimate relationships encompasses both the adopted person and the birth/first family through genetic attraction. During the experience of reunion, where long-lost relatives find each other as adults, the desire for a deep attachment is intense. Finnish anthropologist Edvard Westermarck (1891) originated the concept of the Westermarck effect. He defined it as reverse sexual imprinting through which people who live within close domestic proximity during the first few years of their lives become desensitized to sexual attraction; it is one explanation of the incest taboo. The reunion with genetic relatives who were not raised together gives individuals an opportunity to see themselves reflected in others who look like them and may trigger a sense of "falling in love"; first with their own face and body type, and second with the people who look most like them. Individuals begin to compare body parts to examine how they are alike and how they are different. Obsession may develop as the intensity of the new relationship can feel overwhelming. If the birth/first parent has been longing to see, touch, smell, hear and feel the child from whom they were separated, boundaries may be blurred when they reconnect as adults. If there were unresolved issues between the birth/first parents, reunions with the opposite-sex child may retrigger the unaddressed sexual feelings and loss. If the birth/first father and the found daughter who looks like the birth/first mother come together in a reunion, the birth/first father's unresolved issues may play out in the reunion relationship. The same risk may occur between the birth/first mother and the found son.

Jack became a birth/first father when he was 17 years old. His girlfriend of three months became pregnant, she was sent away to have the baby elsewhere, and the two of them were not allowed to have contact. Years later, at the age of 60, a 43-year-old woman calls him and says that she's his daughter. In their first face-to-face meeting, Jack is immediately struck by how much his newly found daughter looks like his first love. He feels like a teenager again and is embarrassed by his feelings of attraction towards her.

For the adult adoptee who has been starved throughout childhood of mirror images, the reunion floods them with sensory experiences, reflections of themselves and intense emotions. Connecting to members of the birth/first family validates that they are a "real person," born like everybody else, not "an alien," as they have a clan that reflects them. The tricky part is bringing two genetically connected strangers together as adults who wish to build an intimate emotional relationship, and fall in love with newly found relatives, without sexualizing the newly forming intimacy. There is a genetic magnetism that can feel intense during a reunion. This reunion experience has the potential to assist in creating deeper emotional intimacy with everyone.

Carol, a 42-year-old woman, had never met her birth/first father. He and her mother were separated before Carol was born. She was raised with her two younger half-brothers, her mother and a nurturing father who adopted her. Her passion had always revolved around horses and cowboys, unlike the rest of her family. At the age of 40, she searched for and found her birth/first father who was living on a horse ranch in Texas, her fantasy life. She arrived at the airport, met her birth/first father and shared that he was "the man of her dreams": he was a tall, dark and handsome cowboy. When she met her three younger half-brothers at the ranch, she was equally smitten. That first night at the ranch, she dreamt that she was in bed with her new-found siblings and birth/first father. She called a friend the following morning to share how shocked, afraid, disgusted, embarrassed and terribly uncomfortable she was with her own feelings. She also shared that she never wanted to leave.

## Adoptive and permanency family

No matter how individuals arrive at parenting, it is always a deeply intimate and personal experience. Before parenting, individuals need to reflect on the dance of intimacy that they were taught as youngsters in order to be intentional as they are creating their intimate dance with a child. In the parenting dance, we are apt to be teaching the same dance to our children that we learned from our parents. Parents should consider: Were your emotional and physical needs for closeness met as a child? Is there anything that you would want to change? Did you experience any trauma that could impact intimacy? Did you experience parental abandonment or rejection? Have your intimacy skills served you well? Have there been situations where building intimacy with an adult or child has been challenging, and if so, why? If parenting with a partner, are the two of you in sync with the dance steps you want to teach?

Whether you are approaching parenting for the first time or choosing to parent an additional child, these questions are worth exploring. If you are parenting a child with a history of loss and trauma, your own blind spots may inadvertently make the family dance more difficult. A deeper exploration of your intimacy style with this particular child may help deepen the relationship.

Parenting requires self-awareness, patience, commitment, time, a shifting of priorities, adaptation, outside support, a sense of humor, a willingness to learn, and forgiveness of self and others. Since each child has their own unique needs and strengths, each child offers a new parenting experience and an opportunity for parents to learn new dance steps, stretch and grow.

Adoptive and permanency parents must develop all of the typical parenting skills at the same time that they are creating the dance of intimacy with a child or children who arrive abruptly or as strangers. Children who come from a different culture, race or ethnicity, or those who have spent time in other families and may carry trauma, add complexity to the creation of the dance of intimacy.

Parents who are parenting by both birth and adoption/foster care form their intimacy to each child in different ways. These different paths do not mean one is better than the other. The process of creating, growing and giving birth to a child where nine months of connection have already established the emotional intimacy offers an easier path to attachment. Fathers become observers of the pregnancy as they see their wife's body changing, feel the baby kick and welcome their child into the world. These fathers have already established an intimate link to their baby. In addition, the fantasies that both parents carry connected to their future life with a child help to establish an emotional connection. Seeing a child who reflects them and their extended family is another intimate link.

Parents who adopt or foster take an alternative road as they build intimacy with a newly arrived child. As the decision is being made to expand their family, the very act of exploring avenues for family building, making deliberate decisions about moving forward and choosing professional helpers who will assist them becomes the start of an "emotional pregnancy."

The first trimester in an "emotional pregnancy" is devoted to paperwork, a family assessment, a study of their home to make sure it is safe for a child, a sharing of their most intimate history and relationship facts with total strangers, and taking classes in preparation for adoption and foster care.

The second trimester in an "emotional pregnancy" includes being "approved" to foster or adopt. Now there is hope for a child or children to join the prospective parents. This is where prospective parents begin to fantasize about who the child will be and what the child will look like, as well as what they will be like as parents. At this time, the "emotional pregnancy" is shared with others. Parents may join support groups and buy books about adoption and foster care as they further prepare themselves.

In the third trimester of an "emotional pregnancy," parents experience excitement as they get close to the "birth" of a child into the family. They look for signs of life everywhere through their social workers and attorneys. The house is being readied for the arrival of a child or children, and extended family members share both the anxiety and joy about the coming child. There is an ongoing fear that something will go wrong and a "miscarriage" will occur and that the child's "birth into the family" will not occur.

Labor and delivery in the "emotional pregnancy" begins when prospective parents receive a presentation of the specific child/ren that are a potential match and actually see pictures of the child/ren. The "labor" intensifies as placement visits occur. For any new parent, there may be doubts that surface about what they are undertaking once they meet actual children. These child/ren may not represent the child/ren of their fantasy. The overwhelming lifelong commitment, the fear that they are not up to the task, the possibility of disagreeing with their partner over these children, their fears of falling in love with a child they might lose and recognizing that these children are coming already attached to other relatives and former foster families may negatively impact their initial intimacy attempts. Celebration of the "emotional birth" is connected to the child actually moving into the family. A "later birth," solidifying the child's permanency, occurs at the time of adoption finalization.

Intimacy is much more anxiety producing for these families because there is a period of time when these parents must commit, love, treasure and attach to children who may or may not be adopted by them. If there are other children in the home who were birthed into the family or adopted at a previous time, these periods of anxiety and uncertainty will also affect them as they work to build intimacy with new siblings. During this time period, teaching the dance of intimacy to a newly arrived child needs to be a priority in spite of any legal concerns being addressed by the courts.

*All* parents need to show up and parent their child every day, no matter what concerns they hold, which could be based on legalities, medical issues, the age of the child at arrival, other losses or crisis, which might include divorce, illness, death or the loss of job. All parents need to show up each and every day despite any fears or crisis they may have. The development of intimacy begins the day the child arrives. The family that births a child begins with an act of love and the intimacy of sex, and is further assisted by the medical community during the pregnancy, labor and delivery. The family that fosters or adopts begins their "emotional pregnancy" in their minds and thoughts and intimate conversations with others, and continues it with the support of social work professionals, lawyers and courts. These are different avenues to achieving the intimacy of a parent–child relationship.

When families give birth to a child and return home with their newborn, there is a desire to build a cocoon and nest with their new baby. When becoming parents through foster care and adoption, that option may not be available. The invasive process that began with the family assessment continues after a child joins the family. The visitation of social workers in the home, many of whom change regularly, the keeping of records for attorneys and courts, having to abide by the state laws that impact parenting decisions, the constant threat that somebody could decide to remove the child if there was something they did not approve of and the possible visitation with the birth/first family all put added demands on the developing intimacy between the parents and child.

Telling your child their story also builds intimacy; every intimate relationship is built on trust and truthfulness. This trust building deepens between parents and children when the parents honestly share the information that belongs to the child, withholding nothing. It's commendable when parents want to protect their children from experiencing pain. However, parents who withhold the truth of the child's story and protect the child from grief lose an important opportunity to deepen intimacy. It is your deep emotional connection that sends the message to your child that they are not alone in their pain and can trust that their parents will not withhold information, even if the facts are painful.

Adoptees often report that they always knew their parents were withholding information about their lives or even lying to protect them, but they grew to resent the lack of honesty that inhibited true closeness. The more limited the truthful, open communication there is between parent and child about adoption, foster care, trauma and loss, the less likely it is that the child will share their own true and honest feelings with their parents. Adoptive and foster parents must set the tone for intimate dialogue. By modeling and initiating conversations about any emotionally loaded topic, parents have the opportunity to strengthen intimacy with their child.

> Rene, aged 43, was adopted at birth because her parents were infertile. Two years later, they adopted her brother. Rene reported that her parents sat her down and told her she was adopted when she was 6 years old. Her parents were clear that she was not to speak to others about being adopted, and in fact she was punished when she shared the "secret" with a neighbor. Rene stated that she kept all of her feelings, questions and thoughts about adoption locked away. Even today, when she says the phrase "I was adopted," it brings up all of the unexpressed and repressed emotions that she wasn't able to share with her parents.
>
> Her parents' denial that they were different from any other family or that their daughter was different from any other child produced secrecy and shame for all family members, including her brother. This dynamic led to intimacy barriers with her own children as she continued to keep the secret about her adoption in order to protect her parents. She reported that her brother struggles significantly with intimacy as he keeps many secrets from his wife and children, including the very fact that he is adopted, even though he is currently searching for his genetic and family connections.
>
> Over the years, Rene knew she struggled in being able to get close to other people and she sought out different therapists. She never talked about adoption, and the therapists never asked about adoption. She eventually married and had two children. As her children aged and commented on the lack of resemblance between her and her adoptive parents, Rene grew tired of keeping the secret and recognized how lying was impacting her closeness to her children. More recently, Rene told her 12- and 8-year-old children that she was adopted, finally exposing the family secret at the age of 43. She shared that it was a liberating experience to speak her truth and it set her on a path to search for the rest of her story.

One of the difficult topics that parents will need to discuss with their child is why they chose to adopt or foster. For many, this involves sharing their infertility journey, their pain, their disappointment, and their struggle to shift from wanting to become pregnant to wanting to become parents. The parents can use their own experiences of loss and grief to better understand and connect to their child's losses, sadness and pain, and therefore strengthen intimacy.

There are often marital difficulties that surface connected to infertility. If those ruptures in the relationship have not been addressed and healed, the parents' ability to deeply attach to a child may be limited. The adoptive parent relationship may never have recovered from the infertility assault, including hormonal shots, sex on schedule, invasive examinations, a constant sense of failure, anger at their body and loss of faith in themselves, each other and God. When parents share their journey of infertility with their child, the child may wonder about themselves being "second best" or a "second choice." A parental response that could strengthen their intimate connection to their child could be: "That was true and we were sad, but then we got to parent you and we can't imagine life without you." The truth is, no child would wish to lose their family of origin if things could have been different, which also makes adoption a second choice for them. However, now that the child is attached to their parents, the child also cannot imagine life without this family. That is the gift of attachment.

Moving from couplehood to parenthood shifts the dyad into a triad. The emotional resources that the couple gave to each other are now being channeled towards the child. Each parent brings their own style of intimacy and attachment to building this new relationship, and the child will respond differently to each parent. Over time, children may be more responsive to one style than another, which is often misinterpreted as the child loving one parent more than the other. When parenting more than one child simultaneously, a triad is developed with each individual child in the family, and they respond differently to the intimacy-building styles of the parents. A single parent may form a triad which includes a grandparent, an aunt or uncle or a caregiver.

The emotional pitfalls as the dyad becomes a triad could include: having little time to nurture the partner or themselves; becoming disillusioned by seeing how the partner functions as a parent; the primary caretaker being exhausted when the other partner comes home and wants to connect; one parent finding it easier to connect to the child than the other partner; the child treating the two parents very differently in public; one partner being unhappy with the decision to bring the child into the family; different parenting styles contradicting one another; or the partner who has done most of the adaptation to parenthood feeling trapped in the new role. The antidotes for these pitfalls include: practicing good self-care, determining what is needed and asking for it directly (the partner cannot read minds), using outside support systems regularly and making time to consistently connect to a partner. Think about how each individual child has their own unique triad established with each parent. The establishment of healthy emotional intimacy within the family is led by the parents.

Parents may be available for emotional intimacy but find themselves parenting a child who fears intimacy and is intimacy avoidant. A newborn who has been traumatized either before or after birth may not "mold and fold" into the warmth and comfort of a body. At a few months of age, the child may ride on the parent's hip, lean away from the parent's body, hold their arms in a rigid position against the chest of the parent and avoid eye contact. Babies and children exposed to overwhelming toxic stress carry that stress within their bodies and often do not know how to relax their muscles. Their bodies look and feel stiff and rigid. Parents may personalize their child's distressed behaviors as a rejection of them, leaving them to feel as if they are doing something wrong. In actuality, what the child most needs is the intimate emotional attunement that only a parent can provide. It takes time for the child to learn how to relax into the safety and nurturance of their parents' unconditional loving support.

Parents who choose to parent children at an older age may not learn for many years what actually happened that impacted their child so deeply. Parents may regret not being available to their children at an earlier stage of life and missing the opportunity to make intimate connections through bathing their child as a youngster, changing a diaper, blowing raspberries on their belly, brushing their hair and knowing their child's ticklish spots. Information about the body that includes scars and wounds, burns or bruises, or knowing whether a boy is circumcised or not, can create unanswerable questions. A trip to the dentist, seeing a doctor for a physical or the child's first exposure to a hospital may bring forth trauma that the parents were not anticipating. All of these naturally occurring events that build intimacy between parents and children have been missed. The opportunity to re-parent in order to fill in the gaps and be present during sad and scary experiences, as well as those that are new and joyful, deepens closeness. For some parents, the experience is akin to walking along a sidewalk and suddenly falling into an open manhole—they didn't see where the hole was until they had already fallen into it.

Foster and adoptive families are often in a position of parenting children who join the family at older ages, unpacking their suitcases of trauma into the family. Emotions that fall out of that suitcase are quickly absorbed into the emotional life of the family. Foster and adoptive parents should have the emotional capacity to receive and manage intense feelings such as fear, anger, rejection, rage, shame, sadness and despair. Intimacy can be deepened if the parents move towards the child's distress and strong emotions. When parents can decode the child's trauma-reactive behaviors, body language and words, they are less likely to personalize them. For a child who has been consistently alone with these intense and overwhelming feelings, having parents who do not retreat from their emotional pain and distress, and who show that they care, allows trust to grow. As these intense emotions are being expressed and responded to by the parents, siblings may become upset or frightened and require help in feeling reassured and safe, not only about themselves, but also about the parents who are experiencing the brunt of emotions.

Adoptive and foster parents carry a huge daily emotional challenge as they address the needs of their children. The intimacy task is to simultaneously build trust and attachment with the new child while maintaining their intimate connections with other children, their partners and extended family members. An additional hardship for single parents is that they have no one with whom to tag team when they are emotionally drained and no one to tell them what a good job they are doing.

Ruptures or breaks in intimate relationships can occur as the core issues surface. These are normal and expected reactions to the changes and adjustments a parent must make. Stretching and growing pains bring all of the core issues to bare on intimate familial relationships. When the core issues are acknowledged and addressed, it allows for authentic intimacy between all family members.

## Tools for constellation members to strengthen intimacy

- Explore how adoption and permanency has affected your intimate relationships. What do you expect from relationships? What do you expect from yourself in relation to others? What fears do you have about getting close to others? What obstacles do you use to avoid intimacy? To whom do you feel closest and why? What do you believe you have to offer others in an intimate relationship?

- Reflect back on your healthiest relationships. Identify what qualities the other person demonstrated that allowed you to feel safe enough to be vulnerable and open in that relationship. What did you bring to the relationship that allowed the other person to be open and vulnerable with you?

- Create daily connection rituals. Confiding with a trusted other, about both the big and little things in our lives, is the lifeblood of intimacy. Communicating daily builds the skill of non-defensive listening while strengthening the bonds of attachment.

- Touch and be touched daily. Loving touch is the foundation of our human connections.

- Take time every day to nurture yourself. Plan ahead and put yourself on the calendar. Taking care of yourself allows you to have healthy intimate relationships.

- Build trust:

  – Mean what you say!

  – Say what you mean!

  – Do what you say!

- Be still, breathe, relax, go inward. Connect to your inner thoughts, feelings and needs. This allows for clear communication with another person.

- Make a list of all the things that make it hard to connect to other constellation members. Identify the feelings that inhibit your reaching out and getting to know someone who identifies with a different role in the constellation. For example, if you are a birth/first parent, have you ever reached out and developed a relationship with an adoptive parent? If you are an adoptive parent, have you ever attended a conference or retreat geared towards the needs of either adoptees or birth/first parents? As an adoptee, have you ever joined a group with other adopted people or attended an adoptive parent support group? The Seven Core Issues in Adoption and Permanency bind all constellation members intimately.

- Honor the other person with your high regard, make them feel worthy by being attentive to both their verbal and non-verbal communications, and really listen to their thoughts and feelings. Be an "active listener" by reflecting back to another what you heard them say. This works well with both children and adults.

- Create reconnection when a relationship is ruptured. All relationships go through cycles of *rupture* and *reparation*. Being able to reconnect after a "rupture" strengthens intimacy. The ruptures are connected to "old tapes and messages" that are playing out in a present relationship.

- Imagine that the other person with whom you have built an intimate relationship disappears. Write down all the things you would miss about them. Have you ever communicated those things to them?

- Use what you have discovered from the previous question to construct a more rewarding relationship. Sit with the other person, share what you appreciate about them, communicate what you need from them, allow them to communicate what they need from you, and jointly negotiate the steps that will deepen intimacy.

- Identify or seek out relationship role models who demonstrate healthy intimate relationships.

- Create unconditional acceptance by releasing idealized expectations of the other and embracing your own and the other person's differences, flaws and limitations.

- Share your hopes and dreams with another. Hopes can range from everyday little wishes to major goals and fantasies. Create an actionable plan to accomplish your shared hopes.

- With your partner or a trusted friend, write down all the feelings you can think of and put them in an empty jar. It makes no difference if you repeat feelings, and you can add feelings at any time. Each day, each person picks a feeling out of the jar and talks about a time that they experienced that feeling as a child or adult. This is an opportunity to share past emotional experiences with another to deepen your connection.

- Use various expressive modalities to share your intimate feelings and build important memories with your partner. These would include taking an art class together, singing together, joining a drumming circle, going dancing and creating a meal together. All of these activities stimulate the senses and allow people to connect. It shifts emotional expression from thinking (left hemisphere) to feeling (right hemisphere).

- Pick an emotion and describe it by its color, its sound, its smell and its taste, and how it would feel if you could touch it. This form of description often heightens the understanding of your feelings by your partner and is an effective technique to use with children in helping them express their emotions.

- Consider the hopes and dreams you have that are unfulfilled regarding other members of the constellation. Imagine what you might do or say that would allow for those hopes and dreams to be realized.

## Notes to professionals

Social workers and therapists bring their intimacy skills and styles to their clients. The practice of social work and therapy is based on building trust and developing emotional intimacy with a client.

It is the deep connection between professional and client that allows for personal growth and change for both parties. This is not just about sharing what you know and giving advice to your clients, it is about becoming actively involved in the building of an intimate relationship. Clients and families deserve your compassion, empathy and full presence. As a professional, continue to work on and examine your own dance of intimacy. People continue to mature as they gain experience and move both personally and professionally through their own developmental phases over time. Where did you learn your dance of intimacy, and how has that dance evolved over time?

Individuals and families touched by adoption and permanency will return to a professional over the years because of the trust and intimacy that was developed between client and professional. Being available to families is crucial. Individuals and families return to therapeutic support during times of rupture, distress or crisis. A return to the trusted professional who previously established emotional intimacy through addressing and normalizing the core issues allows the family to address the rupture and do the repair.

No social worker or professional is able to intimately connect and work effectively with every client. The professional must assess each individual referral as to whether or not it is a good fit. "Good fit" is based on the following: their skillset, clinical competence, experience, interests, bias and comfort zones, based on their own personal history.

To effectively become an adoption and permanency competent professional, the person must be able to manage the depth of strong and possibly overwhelming emotions connected to the seven core issues and trauma that constellation members experience. Trust-building with clients in intense pain may be a challenge as the client projects their expectation of rejection, judgment, fear, neediness and anger onto the professional. This requires professionals to use their skills of emotional intelligence and attunement, self-care, patience and acceptance because the projection of the core issues may feel extremely intimate and personal to them.

# Chapter 8

# Mastery and Control

One can have no smaller or greater mastery than
the mastery of oneself. (Leonardo da Vinci)

The sixth and last spoke in the wheel of the Seven Core Issues in Adoption
and Permanency is mastery and control. Mastery is a proficiency, command
or grasp of a subject, skill or knowledge base. It includes mastery over one's life
circumstances, which is connected to self-awareness. Control is the power to
influence or direct people's behaviors or the course of events. The loss of control
over a person's early life journey diminishes their power to direct their future
life course. Words connected to the loss of control include frozen, constricted,
fearful, vulnerable, unsafe, helpless, powerless and impotent. Words connected
to mastery include active, proficient, learned, empowered and growing. Loss of
control is limiting, while mastery is expansive.

Traumatic losses and multiple attachment disruptions are a repeated assault on our need to feel empowered, secure, valued and connected. In order to cope with the trauma, individuals may have a need to over-control all aspects of their life or may withdraw from trying to get their needs met through human connection. The result could lead to an inability to create close, meaningful attachment relationships as the individual works to protect themselves from further psychic pain or loss. Alternatively, mastery requires an individual to be open to the risks of building deep, intimate emotional connections. This means addressing the impact of the traumatic losses and attachment disruptions on an individual's life and a willingness to let trusted others know what they need and allow them to see vulnerabilities. Mastery does not mean we're done grieving or processing the losses and complexities that come with adoption and permanency. It allows for the recognition that the experience is only a part of the story.

The ultimate goal for all members of the constellation is mastery. All constellation members lost power and control as they experienced adoption/permanency, so getting to mastery is no easy task. Every human being needs to feel powerful. Power is a strong component of resilience. Resilience offers us courage to recover from tragedy, fight for the things we believe in, resist peer pressure, push back against abuse of authority and overcome life's obstacles. We take on the strength of the obstacles we have overcome. Feeling powerful gives us the ability to have an effect on others, feel that we have authority and rights, be hopeful and create change. The loss of control and power may lead to feelings of hopelessness, fear, blame, distress, vulnerability and helplessness. Human beings feel secure and empowered when they have an element of control over their own destiny.

## Control

We live in a world that seems increasingly beyond our control. From the moment infants enter the world they want control. The desire for power and control over one's life unfolds through each stage of development and throughout adulthood. Think about all of the things you can control: your beliefs, your attitude, your reactions, your thoughts, asking for help, your smile, being honest, the friends you choose, the media you watch and read, your goals, touch and being touched, judging, the risks you take, gratitude, worrying, your activities, your decisions, how you respond to challenges, being accountable, respecting others, being kind, whom you forgive, what you eat, how you dress and when you sleep. What individuals cannot control includes: someone else's decisions, who likes them, how others treat them, past mistakes, others being honest and others forgiving them. In addition, people know that they cannot control the weather, the traffic, time, inflation and the price of gas.

One response when people experience a loss of control may be to retreat into passivity, because the less a person attempts, the less likely they are to fail in regaining control. Chronic loss of control may lead to a victim mentality where people feel they have no control of their life. People may feel sorry for themselves and attacked by the world, and may live with sadness and self-pity. When individuals stay stuck in these beliefs, they may feel like failures and don't believe they get validation for anything they do. The secondary gains from a victim mentality come from getting attention and help from others and avoiding taking responsibility for their thoughts, feelings and actions. Themes of complaining in either speech or thought are remnants of past experiences of feeling wronged. Holding on to those memories and reliving those complaints reinforces the victim mentality. Chronic complaining reflects the inability to move on from the past and an unwillingness to make a choice to stop one's own suffering.

A person's thoughts, feelings and body function as a united entity. Chronic negative thoughts that create painful feelings have an impact on the body. Lack of empowerment is demonstrated in body language by being afraid to take up space, keeping oneself small, trying not to make a noise, being hunched forward, holding a stiff position and crossing one's arms, mumbling, nervous laughter and avoiding eye contact.

A second response to the loss of control is to believe that the best defense is a good offense. In a dangerous, unpredictable or unsafe world, it may be beneficial to control, react and aggress against a perceived threat to maintain control. People learn to manage the underlying painful loss of control and power in many different ways: blaming, getting angry, using alcohol or drugs, being demanding, lying, complaining, yelling, being short tempered, arguing, becoming violent, being sarcastic, acting passive aggressively, being anxious and using threats that include abandonment, suicide and withdrawal of financial, emotional or sexual involvement.

Although some amount of control and power play is normal in order to fend off threats to people's self-interest, in some relationships the need for control is so pervasive and undermining of the other person that it becomes unhealthy and destructive. People with an extreme need to control are often fighting deep feelings of vulnerability, self-loathing and powerlessness, which may lead to a strong desire to be perfect. Such individuals may manipulate and pressure others to change so as to avoid having to change themselves and use power over others to escape an inner emptiness. An individual's controlling behaviors can result in creating whatever it is they were trying to prevent.

People use control in order to get their needs met and avoid further pain, yet by controlling rather than being kind and loving to themselves and others, they create the very pain they were trying to avoid. We have all learned ways to have control over getting love and avoiding pain. It is vitally important that an individual be compassionate and non-judgmental towards the controlling part of themselves. The "wounded self" is the part of an individual that operates under the false belief that people can control how others feel about them. People use both overt and covert ways of trying to gain control over others. An individual's "wounded self" may not be aware of what is driving the controlling behaviors, and bringing that into awareness is a step towards mastery.

## Mastery

> She is a beautiful piece of broken pottery put back together by her own hands. A critical world judges her cracks while missing the beauty of how she made herself whole again. (Storm, Facebook)

Mastery is a hard-earned proficiency. The achievement of mastery in various aspects of one's life is a process, a journey. People are born with an innate ability to adapt and learn. Mastery is available to anyone willing to commit to the hard, emotional work of the journey. People who seek mastery are open to learning, are curious, don't mind making mistakes and are committed to practicing. Constellation members often seek mastery in the following areas: learning to trust others, forgiveness of themselves, building meaningful attachment relationships, honestly and directly communicating their needs, identifying and managing their feelings, claiming, reclaiming and telling their stories from their own perspective, and any number of other skills that can bring healing and fulfillment to their lives. The problem is that our society continually bombards individuals with promises of immediate gratification, instant success, and fast, temporary relief, which may lead people in exactly the wrong direction, away from mastery. Learning any new skill involves relatively brief spurts of progress, each of which is followed by a slight decline on the path towards mastery.

To take the journey to mastery, one must practice diligently to attain new levels of competence. One must be willing to spend a lot of time on a plateau while practicing. Neuroscience teaches that people have a habitual behavioral system that operates at a level deeper than conscious thought. This habitual system is deeply ingrained, difficult to change and requires awareness and practice in order to create a new pattern of behavior. Learning generally occurs in stages; a stage ends when the "habitual system" has been reprogrammed to the new skill. This is why "practice makes perfect." It takes many repetitions for the sensory system to habituate a new skill. This journey to mastery is not about achieving a goal or getting to a finish line. It is about enjoying the process of learning and practicing every day. Mastery's true face is relaxed and serene, sometimes faintly smiling. We all have moments of mastery where we find ourselves peaceful and content.

## Steps to mastery

1. *Self-awareness.* Examining who we are at our core in order to discover our purpose, needs, desires and those aspects of the self that inhibit us from reaching our full potential.

2. *Gaining knowledge.* Using what was learned from our journey into self-awareness in step one to identify what knowledge, skills and teachers can assist us on our path to mastery.

3. *Practice.* Actively utilizing the knowledge gained from learning in step two and practicing integrating those skills into our everyday life.

4. *Mastery.* Being able to use, with ease and self-awareness, the newly acquired knowledge and skills from the first three steps.

*The first step* towards mastery is self-awareness. It is focused on the inner self; it is an inward journey; it is finding one's core self, going into the past and searching for the underlying patterns that have driven an individual to how they presently live their life. Finding yourself is actually returning to who you were before the world got its hands on you. It is related to un-learning cultural conditioning and other people's opinions, projections and inaccurate conclusions. It requires deep digging and recalling of your essence. Your true self has always been there. When we reconnect to our authentic self, we have the choice of continuing on our current path or choosing a different path. This journey has many twists and turns and is rarely a straight road. Being able to maneuver, make new choices and learn from mistakes are all important components of this step.

Through self-awareness, people can experience happiness, joy, satisfaction, fulfillment and gratitude, all of which originate from the inside. Developing self-awareness helps people observe and evaluate their emotional reactions and experiences without attaching value judgments. Self-awareness should lead to self-acceptance, which is when a person can graciously accept their faults, weaknesses, missing pieces and mistakes, as well as recognizing their own potential, strengths, talents and achievements. It also allows for the enlarging of one's self concept. Self-awareness will allow for authenticity—an ability to be comfortable in one's own skin and to allow others to see the "real" self.

For example, an adult adoptee who is seeking mastery in regards to knowing their complete story in order to feel deeply rooted and authentically grounded in their own truth might pursue self-awareness. This would include an inward journey that might begin with an exploration of the words and phrases that they use to tell their story and describe the various players; reflection on the truth of their story and the gaps or missing pieces of the story; consideration of their fantasies about who they are and what they might find; and an exploration of those aspects of themselves that they hide from others or do not acknowledge even to themselves.

> You can't go back and change the beginning, but you can start where you are and change the ending. (C.S. Lewis)

*The second step* to mastery is gaining knowledge. Once an individual has gained insight into their purpose, needs, desires and any inhibitors to reaching their full potential, they are able to address the second step, which is the gaining of knowledge. This requires identifying what skills and knowledge they need to learn in order to reach mastery. The brain is adaptable, malleable and ready to learn at every stage of life. It functions much like a dual-processing system. As information comes into the brain, it is always scanning for similarities, differences and connections between what it is currently processing and what it has already learned. Individuals have access to all the knowledge and skills that they have learned since birth. However, skills can be adapted, enhanced and changed. It is the transference of these previously acquired skills, along with the gaining of new knowledge, that leads to a new skillset. For example, looking back at one's life, one would notice that mistakes were made based on missing knowledge or skills not yet acquired. Being curious about oneself, one's beliefs and what one doesn't know about oneself is essential. On this step, a person must be open to being humbled; humility is one component of learning new knowledge and skills. On this step, individuals learn to embrace the darker parts of their story in order to experience the light. Learn to love your story, what it has taught you and the tools it has brought you.

For example, the adoptee from step one who is seeking mastery of their story might need to acquire knowledge and skills in the following areas: understanding their own core issues in relation to their own experiences and perceptions; gathering and assessing for accuracy the information they do possess; and identifying and searching for people, forms and systems that allow for the claiming and reclaiming of the full story. Part of this second step may include learning to be tenacious through frustration, disappointment and rejection, as well as being able to accept unpleasant or sad facts about the story.

*The third step* to mastery is practice. Practice includes actively utilizing the knowledge gained from learning in step two and practicing integrating those skills into one's life. Practice is a verb, it requires activity. It includes taking risks, making mistakes, falling on one's face, feeling the pain and using one's strengths and resilience to get up and try again. On this step towards mastery, individuals may begin to feel that the skill is beyond their capability and want to quit. Frustration is a sign of progress, and mistakes are an integral part of learning. In order to learn any new skill, practice and repetition are critical. When learning any new skill, a new neuronal pathway in the brain must be forged. The more complex the task, the more practice and repetition are required.

Find a tutor who can be both a support and a role model. Imagine this step as an apprenticeship to someone who has already mastered a skill. Making mistakes and feeling embarrassed and inadequate are all necessary aspects of learning. Experimenting with new beliefs and actions will allow an individual to overcome fears and habituated patterns that lead to automatic responses. Practice is related to focused intentionality. The result of practicing a new skill can result in openness to a new way of thinking, behaving and acting.

For example, the adoptee from steps one and two now must practice what has been learned. This might include actively searching for pieces of the story or long-lost family members, integrating newly found pieces of their story into their identity, discarding those aspects of their story that are no longer relevant and accurate, and sharing this information with others in a way that feels authentic and honest. They may practice communicating and integrating newly found individuals with present family members, using a role model as a guide as they practice integrating the new aspects of the story into day-to-day living, and practicing forgiveness of themselves and others, as emotional landmines are everywhere and will be triggered.

*The fourth step* is mastery—the use of a person's self-awareness and newly acquired knowledge and skills that have been practiced consistently and are now habituated and can be used with ease. Mastery is connected to intuition, which occurs when the mind is suddenly illuminated by some particle of truth previously hidden from oneself and others. When one reaches mastery, self-awareness and intuition become a power at one's command. Intuitive powers at the mastery level are both conscious and unconscious. Mastery is a form of personal transformation as previous ideas and perspectives are eliminated and replaced with new skills and knowledge. Mastery allows for a more realistic and honest view of oneself, the other and the world. Attaining mastery feels much like the shedding of an old skin to get to a new phase of growth. When one attains mastery in a specific area, the experience can be compared to a child-like sense of wonder and excitement, which is the ultimate form of empowerment. The Greek poet Pindar wrote, "Become who you are by learning who you are."

Mastery is about a specific aspect of oneself—as one masters a specific aspect, there may be other areas of the self that call out for attention and practice. Mastery is a lifelong journey.

Obstacles to mastery include: a lack of self-awareness, unaddressed core issues, trauma, a victim mentality, allowing others to define who you are, co-dependency and/or minimal emotional supports.

## Mastery and control and constellation members

All those involved in adoption and permanency have been forced to give up control. Because human beings need to feel in control to feel secure, the loss of control can have a long-term impact. Birth/first parents may emerge from the adoption and permanency process feeling victimized and powerless. Adoptive and permanency parents have lost control of over when, how and whom to parent. Adoptees had no choice about being adopted and must cope with the haphazard nature of how they joined their particular family. They may wonder, with all the families in the country that are looking to adopt, "How did I end up in this family?"

Mastery includes bringing into conscious awareness one's belief system about the self, others and the world. With increased self-awareness one gains power and control over decisions, feelings, beliefs, goals and actions. If constellation members have actively utilized the information and tools for each of the core issues, they are well on the way to mastery. The loss of control in adoption and permanency for all constellation members may have left them feeling that they are not the drivers of their own bus/life. Getting to mastery means the constellation member is in the driver's seat and is making the choices about where they want to go and how they want to get there. They are empowered to choose their goals and create their own outcomes. Self-awareness is always the key.

Another aspect of mastery is the knowledge that each constellation member "matters" to other constellation members. Michael Grand, author of *The Adoption Constellation: New Ways of Thinking About and Practicing Adoption* (2010), believes that "mattering" is a fundamental theme in the narratives of constellation members. The authors of *Seven Core Issues in Adoption and Permanency* recognize the importance of the concept of "mattering" and have included it as a form of mastery. "Mattering" is being of importance and having significance to another.

Part of the loss of power and control can be related to a question that is relevant to all members of the constellation: "Do I really matter?" People view other people's actual emotional investment in them as a reflection of "mattering." Mastery is acknowledging and acting on the fact that you "matter" to yourself and to others and that others "matter" to you. A sense of "mattering" occurs when we perceive ourselves as having an effect on others. "As an adoptee, do I occupy a valued place in relation to my birth/first family and/or adoptive family?" Adoptees may be in a position of not knowing whether or not they "matter" to those who brought them into the world. How does an adoptee know that their birth/first parents thought of them every day and loved them if there was not contact with them? Also, a child may be very different from their adoption/permanency family, but still need to know that their attributes, appearance, talents and achievements "matter" to the people they love.

Adoptees learn whether or not their family of origin "matters" to their adoptive/foster family through the language used in relation to the birth/first family. If the family of origin does not "matter" to the adoptive/permanency parents, the child may feel that where they came from is not valued and they may question whether or not they are valued.

When contact is occurring between the birth/first and adoptive/foster family, everyone's respect for everyone else's roles indicates that everyone "matters" to the child.

Adoptive/foster parents' goal is to "matter" to the child they are parenting. Parents may wait for the child to acknowledge that their role as parents "matters." For parents who adopted their child at birth, the "mattering" comes quickly as they meet their child's needs and attachment grows. This is not the case when adopting or fostering an older child. If a child has experienced multiple parents who did not keep them, they may perceive that they did not "matter" to those previous parents. If the current parents do not commit to the child, the child feels that they do not "matter" to these new parents, so trust and attachment may not grow. It takes time to build trust, create meaningful attachments and have experiences that show the child that they "matter" to their new parents. Examples that the parents "matter" to the child include the child first referring to the parents as "mommy" or "daddy," asking for help, and later, as adults, thanking them for being their parents.

Birth/first parents wonder if they "matter" to the child they brought into the world and to the family who is parenting that child. Do they "matter" to the other birth/first parent? Do they still "matter" to their family and friends?

All constellation members' stories "matter." People are storytellers by nature and seek to create purpose and meaning in the stories they construct about their life. All constellation members need to clarify, construct and claim their stories. Mattering to other constellation members requires accepting each other's stories and particular points of view, whether or not one agrees. Mastery is understanding that an individual's stories are personal, may change over time as information is updated and new insights are gained, and should not be judged or diminished by another. Everyone's stories "matter" and keep evolving.

> When we write our own story, we can access inner wisdom that may have been blocked through traumatic separations and losses. Taking back our story is an act of bravery.
> Take a pen into your hand and a blank piece of paper and write your story. It "matters" and it's yours to write! (Maxon and Roszia)

## Birth/first family

The crisis of relinquishing a child or losing a child to adoption/permanency is a major loss of power and control for the birth/first parents and their extended family members. Birth/first parents' experience of ongoing loss of power and control, during the crisis and afterwards, may leave them feeling victimized and powerless. The loss of control over their bodies, the intrusive control by outsiders connected to the court system and the loss of control over the direction of their lives, as well as other people's reactions to them during the crisis and afterwards, may disempower them and lead to a feeling of helplessness. The loss of control of birth/first parents will impact their lives as they may make demands for control in their relationships and friendships and with people in authority. It may also lead to problems with hanging on to unhealthy relationships too long or letting go of relationships too quickly and learning from mistakes.

Parents whose children were removed from their custody due to neglect or abuse enter a system that will not only take control of their children but also then prescribe what needs to happen for the children to be returned to the parents' care. Domestic violence, rape and incest are additional factors that lead to the removal or placement of children and are connected to intense feelings of victimization, powerlessness and loss of control.

At the beginning of the crisis, so much of the control is in the hands of other people—extended family members, lawyers, social workers, the courts and foster/adoptive parents. The birth/first parents may feel that everyone has taken some of their power and control away from them. To change their path from loss of control to mastery, they must commit to taking small steps each day by making decisions that are healthy. This practice feeds a habit that will build self-esteem and increase control in their life: for example, being empowered to say "no" to something that makes them feel uncomfortable or making personal choices that will give them pleasure instead of deferring to other people's decisions.

One of the challenges for birth/first parents on their path towards mastery is how much of the original loss of control remains connected to other members of the constellation. These constellation members may have been unknown or unavailable to the birth/first parents for years. It is possible that birth/first parents never met the foster/adoptive parents or there has been a lack of communication over time with the adoptive family or the child. The ongoing love and concern for the child automatically link the birth/first family to these other constellation members. Mastery may include contacting or re-contacting those constellation members and re-establishing communication. Also, mastery may be achieved through ongoing open connections or search and reunion.

Mastery includes the reclaiming of self-esteem and status within the community and family. Do others recognize them as being a mother or father, even if they are not raising the child? Mastery is the creation of a self-concept that is larger than the often limiting or stigmatizing definition of a birth/first parent. Mastery is achieved when the birth/first parent chooses to label and define for themselves who they are, setting aside shame, secrets and other people's definition of them, which may be frozen in the past.

Mastery can also occur when they take responsibility for the part they played in the creation and resolution of the crisis. For example, if their addiction was the cause of the loss of a child, being able to accept responsibility that their addiction created the circumstances of the placement is important. If the crisis was the reason for the separation from the other birth/first parent, part of mastery is to acknowledge how their decisions impacted the other birth/first parent. For example, if the birth/first father knew about the baby but did not assist in supporting the birth/first mother or participate in the decision-making process, mastery often requires an apology. If the birth/first mother did not include the birth/first father in the crisis and its resolution, mastery could require sharing the truth and apologizing, if safety is not a factor.

Mastery includes being able to tell one's story of the crisis and the outcome, honestly and authentically, including acknowledging one's part in the crisis that led to the separation. When telling the story to the child/adoptee, feelings of shame, pain, blame and anger should not be projected onto the child. The child/ adoptee who has been separated from the birth/first parents needs to hear the story of what happened without feeling responsible for the birth/first parents' pain, sadness, anger or shame.

Birth/first parents who were made aware of all their options and made a conscious choice to place their child for adoption do better over time as they retained a significant amount of control over the outcome of the crisis.

For extended birth/first family members, loss of control may be connected to the fact that they knew nothing about a lost family member, may not have had any input into decisions made about a lost family member and may never have been considered as a resource for a lost family member. Mastery is connected to forgiveness for either the secrets kept that later surfaced or the decisions that were made by others. Mastery may also be achieved by ongoing communication with other constellation members such as the foster/adoptive family and the child/adoptee.

## Adoptees and individuals raised in kinship/foster families

The constellation member who has lost the most control is the child. They lost control early in their lives as opposed to other constellation members who experienced loss of control at a later stage when they could use coping strategies. A major life-altering decision was made for the child without their consent. The decisions surrounding relinquishment and/or the termination of parental rights, loss of birth/first family, number of moves, choice of adoptive family and information to be shared or withheld from them were all made by others. Each time a child moves, they lose control of parts of their story, and they may lose control of their truth. They lose control not only of their story but also of the ability to access parts of their story. In addition, they lose control of their original birth certificate. Additional loss of control is related to the lack of ongoing information, privacy, access to important people and a lack of connection to their racial/ethnic/cultural heritage. All of these losses of control may leave adoptees feeling powerless. This feeling of powerlessness may cause adoptees to fear change, which could bring more loss of control. For children who were abused or neglected, there are additional issues of loss of control and power related to their victimization. Once permanency is gained and as the child grows, develops and gains a deeper understanding of their story, more losses of control accrue as they understand what they lost over time.

**Dear Adoption, This is What You've Done**
You are part of me
but you don't define me.
You chose me
but I didn't choose you.
You have given me a past of struggles, heartbreak and pain
but you don't determine my future to repeat my past.
You have shown ignorance from those around me
but you don't stop me from educating my peers.
You have impacted my world view
but I continue to see hope.
You have tried to make me victim
but I continue to proclaim victory.
You are strong
but I am stronger.
So, Dear Adoption,
continue to fight against me
because I will continue to fight back.

(O'Neill 2018)

The loss of control as children's lives are shifted may lead to additional hurdles in development and emotional growth. The change in their life trajectory may impinge on the development of their feelings of accomplishment, achievement, fulfillment, competence or completion, which are all related to mastery. A loss of control may lead to a strong need for independence, a need to control self and others, perfectionism, a focus on details, being stubborn and having a fascination with truth as connected to the use of words. Since others controlled the adoptees' destiny, they may have trouble understanding cause and effect thinking and have an unwillingness to take responsibility for their actions. Children may tenaciously work to control family and friends, conversations, activities, people in authority and parental attention. Their loss of control may set them up to want to fight for control, demand control and compete for control. Passive-aggressive behaviors are linked to feeling powerless and seeking control.

Since adoptees are sensitive to the loss of control, any secondary losses over the years, both large and small, may trigger a need to be back in control. For example, a best friend who moves away, a death in the family, a loss of a job or an accident may all intensify the need for control.

Mastery for adoptees is all about regaining control over what was lost and belongs to them. Mastery is a journey to the past, a reflection on the present and building a vision for the future. The ultimate goal on this journey towards mastery is searching for, identifying and claiming the authentic self. Aspects of the journey include life choices about the past, present and future. Reclaiming the past could be making a choice to emotionally adopt their adoptive family, maybe for the first time, by recognizing what they have gained from being a member of that clan; reconnecting with members of the family of origin to collect the parts of the story that were missing and perhaps building relationships with those family members; deciding who they are in relation to all their family members and what makes them unique; and deciding what their future will include and who they wish to become.

Mastery for children who have suffered early trauma and loss of control is possible within the context of permanent, loving relationships. Children do remarkably well in adoptive families relative to the trauma, neglect and abuse they suffered. "The opportunity to grow up in an adoptive family provides a nurturing and reparative family experience that can help to redress the impact of earlier adversity. Adoption offers children the most intense form of intervention that exists" (Steele *et al.*, as included in Oppenheimer and Goldsmith 2007, p.65). Mastery and the subsequent gains for children are accrued when parents:

- acknowledge the loss of control that children experience connected to the core issues

- become collectors, preservers and investigators of their child's story and authenticate everything

- stay connected to people who had a significant role in their child's life and preserve important parts of the child's history

- stay current and updated on the child's evolving information

- are open and honest about all the parts of the child's story and help them to understand their story as they grow

- encourage the child to ask questions about their birth/first family, both birth/first mother and birth/first father, their conception and birth, how they came to be adopted, and why, any siblings they might have and any difficult memories that might need clarification.

Mastery requires open and honest communication within the family. The fact that a child does not ask questions about their adoption story does not indicate that they have mastery over the important information that belongs to them.

Mastery, which includes forming a cohesive identity, is dependent on the full sharing of honest and accurate information beginning at birth and unfolding into adulthood. Knowing the facts of their story does not necessarily indicate that a person has mastered an understanding of the story or the feelings connected to it. No adoptee should launch from their home without having been told all the parts of their story.

---

A young woman, Johana Rivers, who spent the majority of her childhood in foster care, shared how she turned her pain into power. She stated, "Follow your dreams and never give up. Adversity comes so often it's like a neighbor. How you deal with adversity becomes your testimony. Each time I felt like what I was going through would break me; little did I know it was making me stronger."

The text below is from an article originally published in the *Chronicle of Social Change* on January 20, 2018.

"Here are the things that helped me get through adversities and push on for success:

- After every break down, was a break-through of some kind. Although my prayers were not always answered how I expected them to be, they were answered.

- Working through adversity also requires pushing through. The pain will come, the hurt will come but you're going to have to push through it. Most of the time you will find yourself alone.

- I just had to accept the fact that I'm hurt but I've still got to get up and support myself because that's whose life I'm in control of. I can't lose myself.

- Be true to yourself. Don't be scared to share your story. And when you do, be authentic about it. Own your narrative and use it to make a positive impact on others. When I wasn't sure about who I was, I would pretend, but that put me in a depression. The moment I stopped caring about what other people thought and began to believe in myself, that changed."

# Adoptive/permanency family

Adoptive/permanency parents' loss of control centers around the fact that they are parenting a child to whom they did not give birth. This is true whether it was due to infertility or a desire to parent a child needing a family. In both instances, parents may feel they had little control over the journey towards parenthood as others had most of the power. For some, it was a humbling experience that made them feel helpless. Once they have achieved the goal of parenting through adoption/permanency, they lose the control of being the only mother or father, and possibly being seen by the rest of society, or even their own family, as being the "real" parents. The process of achieving parenthood through adoption/permanency is intrusive and there is a loss of control over personal information that is now entrusted to strangers. Parents lose the ability to control their family's privacy as outsiders ask intrusive questions about them.

Adoptive/permanency parents may feel powerless over their child's perception of adoption and powerless to take away the child's pain, longing and curiosity connected to the family of origin.

Adoptive/permanency parents lost the ability to protect their child from abuse and trauma. The loss of control in being able to intervene early enough to save their child from suffering trauma is not something most other parents experience. Parenting an older child causes loss of control over the child's name, belief system, values, attachments, education and religious preference. Other parents largely have control over the pregnancy, the birth and the caregiving of their child. Many adoptive/permanency parents have lost control of their bodies, as they have had miscarriages, medications that impacted their well-being, failed medical procedures and/or the death of a child.

Some adoptive/permanency parents have lost control of parenting decisions while sharing the role of parenting with the court system. Adoptive/permanency parents lose the opportunity to function like all other parents because they are constantly being observed and held to higher standards. Other parents get to use trial and error as they are learning how to be parents, which includes making lots of mistakes. Adoption/permanency parents may have their mistakes judged and criticized and are constantly given advice by "real" parents. If the court decides to reunify the child with the family of origin, the foster/adoptive family loses ultimate control of the child's destiny.

The journey towards mastery for the adoptive/permanency parents begins the day the child enters the family and the adults step into their parenting role with this particular child. The initial facets of mastery include learning about this particular child and their needs, committing to the parenting role regardless of the legal risk and staying firm in the parenting role despite the child's behaviors of opposition, anger, lack of attachment and fear. Parents must choose to "show up" consistently to meet the child's needs; the child is still a stranger, with whom they have not as yet developed loving feelings. Caretaking of a child, taking responsibility for their needs while receiving little in return, eventually leads to the development of love and attachment.

Living the role of the "everyday" parent is a form of embracing the entitlement as a "mom" or "dad." There are other mothers and fathers who may have meaning for this child, but you are the "everyday" parent fulfilling all of the necessary tasks and are entitled to be acknowledged as the holder of that role. You are "mothering" and/or "fathering." A piece of paper from the court does not make someone a parent. Being the parent, showing up every day and "acting" the parent, and embracing the entitlement of that role, is mastery.

Mastering parenting through adoption/permanency requires practicing, failing, laughing at one's mistakes, finding peers who are further down the foster/adoptive parenting path, and continuing to learn until parenting this particular child becomes second nature. The arrival of each new child will call on the same steps to mastery since each child is unique. Parents who receive a sibling set are replicating this process with each individual child, which requires a cheerleading team to support the exhausting process.

Keep in mind that all parenting is a form of mastery. Since adoption/permanency parents have additional tasks, mastery is more complex and takes longer. All families must address the needs of developing children. Adoptive/permanency parents are also addressing the core issues and the child's deepening understanding of how adoption/permanency impacts their life. Finding other adoption/permanency parents, who are the only ones who will fully understand the tasks and challenges of being in the trenches, is imperative. These parenting peers, who can be mentors, offer horizontal identity in that they have lost control in similar areas and are mastering the tasks that non-adoptive/permanency parents do not have to address. Part of mastery is knowing where, when, what, how and with whom one can comfortably discuss adoption/permanency.

A part of mastery is understanding when an issue is connected to adoption/foster care or when it is connected to parenting in general. Being able to accept that one is a parent first and an adoptive/permanency parent second is critical. Both are important roles but different. Mastery is being able to discern the difference and adapt as needed. An example is a child who is getting into fights at school on the playground. The parent may wonder if the child's need to control is connected to adoption or whether all boys at that age fight. Adoption is not always "the" issue but is always "an" issue to consider. Mastery for adoption/permanency is being able to openly explore and check out all possibilities with the child.

The adoptive/permanency extended family loses control over what the family will look like in future generations, especially if the child is from a different race or ethnicity. They lose control over the decisions that other family members are making that impact the family tree. They may lose control over information about themselves and the rest of the family because as adoptive/permanency parents are being certified for the placement of the child they are asked to share information about their childhood, extended family and abuse or trauma in their family system. Extended family may not have any information about the child joining the family and may never be told.

> Because one believes in oneself, one doesn't try to convince others. Because one is content with oneself, one doesn't need others' approval. Because one accepts oneself, the whole world accepts him or her. (Lao Tzu)

## Tools to gain mastery

- List the ways you lost power/control in your life because of adoption/permanency.

- Have you lost power/control in other areas of your life? Does it feel the same or different? Identify who has empowered you.

- Make a list of the things in your life you can control. How important is it for you to be in control of yourself or others?

- What feelings do you have when you are not in control of yourself or others? How do you express those feelings?

- List your top five beliefs about life. Where did those beliefs come from? Are they true? Have you ever challenged any of those beliefs? Have you ever changed any of your previous beliefs, and if so, why? How do these beliefs make you feel? Who would you be without your beliefs?

- Identify what is likable about you.

- Identify what brings meaning and purpose to your life. Direct your energy, thoughts and activities in that direction. Stop wasting energy on things you cannot control.

- Identify your strengths and accomplishments. Use your strengths every day. If you improve by 1 percent daily, within a year you will have improved your skillset by 365 percent.

- Make a list of the lessons that you've learned. Celebrate your accomplishments.

- Acknowledge other people's successes and accomplishments.

- Our wounds keep us cautious—practice being open and curious about new experiences. Embrace change and take chances, take calculated risks and be open to learning from your mistakes.

- Write a one-page autobiographical narrative about your life story and include your strengths and positive attributes.

- Practice mindful meditation. Going inward and reflecting on one's inner experience allows for a quieting of the mind, decreases anxiety and depression, improves resiliency and strengthens optimism.

- Practice using confident body language. Your body language almost always says exactly what you're feeling.

- Smile—this releases endorphins. You can chase a feeling and move yourself from feeling down to feeling happy and joyful. Smiles are contagious.

- Try standing in your power. Stand with your feet shoulder width apart and raise your hands above your head, look up and smile and note how you feel. Stop saying you're sorry for who you are—feel free to say "No" and speak your truth.

- List the family and friends you value who are significantly different from you. Embracing people different from yourself diminishes prejudice and offers connection.

- Practice projecting your voice, speak up, let yourself be heard—you "matter."

- Observe yourself through audio or video while doing an activity, sharing a story or having a conversation. What did you learn about yourself? Would you change anything?

- Identify those individuals who you feel have mastery of their core issues. Be open to learning from their experience and wisdom.

- List three mistakes you've made and examine what you learned. No matter how embarrassing or awkward these experiences may have been, they can become valuable lessons. Reflecting on your life experiences takes you from passive observation to understanding.

- Write down the ways you have disempowered yourself. How have these actions served you?

- List the times in your life when you felt the most powerful.

- Let go of your need to be loved and approved by everybody. You "matter" to many people, so focus your energy on those who care about you.

- Make a list of the people you need to forgive or who need to forgive you. Holding on to bitterness and resentment is toxic for the body and mind. Peace of mind is the result of forgiving oneself and others. As an adult, you are responsible for your experience of life. There are grudges and there are feelings of joy—pick one!

- What do you hope to accomplish in the future?

- Volunteer, mentor, tutor and find a way to give back. Help others feel that they "matter."

- Make a "good enough" decision and be at peace with it; worry and anxiety will go down.

> Be mindful of what you allow into your world. Be conscious of what you watch, what you listen to, what you read and the people you choose to include in your life. Select wisely the things you take into your body emotionally, physically and spiritually. (Roszia and Maxon)

## Tools to help children gain mastery

- Focus on your child's strengths, talents and attributes.

- Consistently send the message that the child "matters," despite how the child acts, what issues they may have or the possible outcome of the foster/adoptive placement.

- Remember that parents' non-verbal communications are powerful. Touch, smile, laughter, gentle reprimand, guidance, play, rituals, family pictures, placing the child's drawings on the fridge and staying at home with an ill child all say to the child, "You matter to me."

- Use words of empowerment such as "Good choice," "Well done," "Much better," "Good job expressing your feelings," "You made a powerful statement," "I'm proud of what you accomplished."

- Acknowledge and support your child's deep emotional feelings, which include sadness, fear, anxiety, anger and possibly shame. Help your child know that their feelings "matter" to you. Don't forget to also accept their feelings of pride, joy, affection, accomplishment and silliness.

- Empower children, each day, by giving them limited choices throughout their day: "Do you want your blue shoes or your red shoes?" "Do you want oatmeal or toast?" "Do you want me to carry you upstairs or would you like to walk?" "Do you want to go to the store with Mommy or do you want to stay at home with Daddy?"

- Empower children by sharing control, teaching them that there are benefits to working together.

- Replace parental anger with empathy. Be a consultant, not a drill sergeant. Have empathy for your child when they make a mistake. Help them come up with options to solve their problems.

- Power struggles are created when parents order, nag and command their children routinely. Tell them what you will do, as opposed to telling them what you want them to do. For example, "Did you want to brush your teeth or shall Mommy brush your teeth?" "Do you want to get dressed by yourself or do you want Mommy to dress you?" "Will you be ready for school on time today so Dad can drive you, or will you be walking to school today?" All of these are examples of how to share control and power with your child.

- Take turns allowing your child to make the choices: "Which game would you like to play tonight?" "What would you like to eat for dinner?" "What do you want to do today?"

- Create a family tree that represents both the birth/first mother and birth/first father in the roots of the tree and both sides of the adoptive/permanency family in the limbs of the trunk above the ground. Put real pictures on the tree with as many details as possible. This visual will help the child to see all the parts of their story.

- Create a lifebook or a lifebox with your child that represents all the parts of their story. Continue to add to the child's story as new information is discovered. Be sure to ask the child if they have any questions about various parts of their story and check in with how they are feeling.

- Create a family collage that includes all members of the adoption/permanency constellation.

## Notes to professionals

Professionals should be consistently aware of the loss of control that all constellation members have experienced. Sharing control and offering choices to clients is empowering and builds trust. Being aware of any changes or upcoming losses that would trigger an elevated need for control allows for proactive planning with clients. Offering practical skills to empower constellation members, as well as challenging inaccurate or limiting belief systems that disempower clients, is part of assisting and joining them on their journey to mastery. Explore constellation members' behaviors that may indicate various types of controlling responses: what purpose do they serve; are they useful or not; and/or do they create barriers for growth and healing? Talk through various options that would empower the client to get their needs met. Continue to assess issues of mastery and control through body language, tone of voice, language, emotional expression, eye contact and/or any self-defeating or self-destructive behaviors.

Supporting constellation members in their journey of mastery requires time, patience, encouragement, and honoring both small and large accomplishments. Developing new habitual systems in both belief and action is not easy and requires an infusion of new information as well as the client being supported in their inner journey towards increased self-awareness. Your role as guide, mentor, confidant and role model assists clients on their path. All of the tools in this chapter can be used in your practice both for individuals and groups. Assist clients in finding their constellation member peers to support mastery.

Professionals need to bring their authentic self to their relationship with their client. The self is our most impactful and useful asset. Bringing our full presence to the relationship allows us to emotionally attune to the client's affect, needs and goals. The most valuable gift you can offer your clients is continued self-exploration and a growth mindset, which allows you to gain mastery of new therapeutic skills. The authors appreciate your dedication and commitment to strengthening your adoption/permanency clinical competence by the inclusion of the seven core issues into your practice.

Healing, for all of us, occurs within and through relationships. For clients who have suffered relational trauma, attachment disruptions and traumatic losses, the therapeutic relationship should be built on warmth, acceptance and unconditional positive regard. It is the quality of the emotional connection that makes all the difference!

## Conclusion

The language of adoption and permanency remains fluid, complex, limiting, stigmatizing, divisive and unifying. The Seven Core Issues in Adoption and Permanency trigger such depth of emotions that we as authors recognize that there is no way to put into words the feelings that all constellation members experience over time and no words that truly reflect each individual constellation member's unique experience. Words matter! Our words will not please all the readers, but please note that they come from the collective experiences and teachings we've gleaned from all the various constellation members over time.

Language can help our children honor all aspects of themselves, all their families, all their identities, all their languages and all their cultures. Words can be emotional landmines and can be hurtful, mean, divisive and destructive, or they can build bridges, create connections and heal.

We hope this book, *Seven Core Issues in Adoption and Permanency*, and all the resources and tools included give the reader a deeper, broader and more comprehensive view of the losses and blessings of adoption, foster care, kinship care, surrogacy and donor insemination. We want to remind the reader that we never want the core issues to be used to pathologize constellation members— they are to be utilized to normalize the losses, issues and tasks connected to moving children from one family tree to another. The issues of trauma and attachment are woven throughout the lives of members of the constellation. While there is complexity and inherent challenges, the opportunities for growth, joy and healing are always present.

Write your own story!

# ⦿ Part 2 ⦿

# **Practical Applications and Diverse Lenses**

# Chapter 9

# The Authors' Foundational Values and Beliefs

The authors of this book are anchored in a set of core values that guide our practice, learning and teaching. These values are based on our combined experience of over 80 years in the field of child welfare, adoption and permanency.

*Families built through adoption, foster care and kinship care are of equal value to all other types of families.*

All of these are alternative forms of family building. All these parents are "real" parents with no less value than any other parents. All parenting requires an emotional commitment to a child and cannot be reduced to a legal process. Families who commit to a child, such as foster parents and kinship parents, are just as valuable to the child as those who legally commit. Parenting is forever. A successful parent is one who demonstrates a lifelong commitment to an infant/ child/teen and adult even when the child/teen no longer lives with them.

*Adoption and permanency is a lifelong, intergenerational journey.*

The loss of any child to a family impacts the entire family tree: grandparents, parents, aunts, uncles, cousins and siblings. The loss of that family member from that family tree continues to reverberate throughout subsequent generations.

*Adoption and permanency should be about addition, not subtraction.*

The separation of a child from their family of origin should always be the last choice after exploring all other options of keeping that child connected to their birth/first parents. If the child needs to be raised by another family, all attempts to keep the child connected to their birth/first family and culture of origin should be attempted. Adoption and permanency should be primarily based on a child's need for safety and permanency. Adoption should be focused on gaining permanency for a child, not on finding children for adults.

For children, their first/birth parents will always be the holders of the genetic and cultural heritage. The "everyday parents" or the "parenting parents," which include foster/resource parents, adoptive parents and kinship parents, fulfill a necessary and important role either temporarily or permanently. Some parents also assume the role of legal parents through the courts. Each adult who fulfills any of these parenting roles has meaning to the child, and those roles are not interchangeable. Children can love *all* the parents in these various roles simultaneously, just as parents can love more than one child.

*Adoption and permanency should be about adaptation for the adults.*

The work of adoption and permanency must rest on the shoulders of adults; adults are better able to adapt and change. The primary goal is to meet the needs of a child who has experienced loss, trauma and/or attachment disruptions. Adaptations may be needed around the following points:

- These forms of parenting are different and require new parenting tools to meet additional tasks, such as telling the child their adoption story over time, attaching to a child who arrives as a stranger and learning new skills to parent a child who has been traumatized.

- These forms of parenting are more like a marriage, in that the children come connected to other people who are important to them, whether they remember them or not.

- This child is not the same as a child who would have been born into the family.

- Parents address the same parenting tasks as every other family but will also have additional complex tasks related to family formation, such as dealing with the public and extended family around permanency issues and language.

- Attachment is more complex, such as attaching to a child who joins the family at an older age, uses behaviors that push the new parent away or loves a parent who is already in the mom or dad role.

- Third-party assistance may be needed to build the family and there will be an ongoing lack of privacy through intrusive questions and input from family, friends and strangers.

*Families and professionals should honor and respect diversity, including sexual orientation, race, culture, ethnicity, religion, gender and age.*

All individuals and families have a culture, ethnicity and race. As children move from one family to another, they always have a trans-cultural experience and may additionally be with a family of a different race. As we move individuals from one family tree to another, cultural, ethnic and racial identities can be lost, merged, forgotten, assimilated or honored. The practice of adoption and permanency that includes ongoing open relationships with the birth/first family to benefit children addresses this need to an extent. The increasing numbers of bi-racial children entering foster care and adoption who are placed trans-racially, as well as children adopted across cultures nationally and internationally, creates the need for additional adaptation, knowledge and tools for both professionals and families. To quote Virginia Satir (1988), a noted social worker, family therapist and author, "We get together on the basis of our similarities; we grow on the basis of our differences." To grow, people must be willing to be "learners," uncomfortable, off-balance, vulnerable, fearful and curious.

*Families and professionals should tell the truth; knowing and telling the truth based on facts and not conjecture.*

Children have a right to their truth, to their full stories as age appropriate and to the facts about their history. Even if the information is difficult to share and could be hard to accept, it is of paramount importance to the formation of a well-integrated identity. Therefore, the most important task for parents is to see themselves as truth seekers and preservers of the information their child will need to become an actualized adult. As the truth seeker for your child, staying current with the facts is important so you have the most recent truths to tell. Sharing information allows the child to ask questions and express any feelings they may have. Truth is the foundation on which healthy individuals and family relationships are built.

*Birth/first family members count.*

The first two families (paternal and maternal) are the creators of the child's life. They are the progenitors of the child who carry important information regarding the child's genetic heritage, medical information, temperament and personality traits. Science has taught us that nature and nurture are Siamese twins. When the adoptive, foster and kinship parents acknowledge the value of the birth/first parent's information and history and allow the birth/first parent's role in the child's life to be validated, the child can claim their origin story and better understand themselves.

*Men count.*

The birth/first father's value as half of the genetic contribution to the child is often minimized, dismissed or forgotten. Too often, men are left out of decisions and play a lesser role in the unfolding of the permanency plan over time. Many times, birth/first fathers are not even told about the pregnancy and then become hidden figures. If acknowledged, they are not invited into the decision-making process and are often conflicted about what their role is since they are not carrying the baby. Without guidance they may appear uninterested, not know what their rights are and may not know how to support the mother through her pregnancy. If young, they may be encouraged by peers to not admit that they are the father. Many are afraid of the economic and legal repercussions and may not have access to an attorney.

Fathers whose children are in the foster care system or in kinship care are rarely seen as a possible resource for their children, and they can be stereotyped and maligned by the mother, relatives and even the social services system. Because they are single, working full time or have a history of addiction, mental illness, violence, being in prison or gang membership, they may not be offered the same services that the mother receives as they are not perceived as an important connection or resource for the child. They are frequently made to feel as though they are shadow figures in their child's lives and unworthy of connection. Professionals need to work hard to engage these fathers, which is especially challenging when there are so few male social workers and therapists, and when transportation and agency hours create barriers. Many of these men did not receive good fathering themselves and subsequently struggle to fulfill that role for their child.

It is important to note that, for many men, it is after the birth of the child that their feelings grow as the child is separate from the mother and they can see and hold their child.

Fathers by adoption, foster care and kinship parenting frequently take a more passive role in the process of family building as they find themselves immersed in a female-centric child welfare system. Both birth/first fathers and fathers through foster care/kinship/adoption should be given time and attention that would reflect their value in a child's life.

*Siblings matter.*

Siblings include foster siblings, adoptive siblings, birth siblings (both siblings present when the move occurred and those who entered the family later), siblings in orphanages, siblings in group homes, half siblings, and siblings placed into other adoptive homes. If the child considers another child a sibling, even if that sibling has no legal connection, the sibling relationship must be acknowledged. All kinds of siblings have meaning to our children.

Siblings are reflections of our own faces and our genetic family; siblings hold our memories for us, they understand our trauma, they have shared similar life experiences and they can help us make meaning out of our life's journey. Some siblings acted as parents, teachers, protectors, reporters and comforters. Even those siblings who were abusive, violent or sexually inappropriate carry pieces of a child's life story.

*Families and professionals should work towards keeping connections to minimize losses for children.*

Keeping children connected to people, culture, language, race and important objects that are meaningful and symbolic to them is critical. It lessons trauma and strengthens attachment.

*Value everybody's unique contribution.*

No two adoption and permanency families are the same. Be open to the unique qualities of any individual or family system you encounter. Let them teach you how they are the same as and different from others. Value the birth/first families who may be quite different from the adoption or permanency built family. Value the diverse needs of each individual child whose life you touch. Value the unique skills, talents, quirks, temperaments, intellectual capacities and interests of each child. Value the diversity between the ways two parents may parent differently. Value the unique contributions, talents and points of view of diverse constellation members.

*Adoptive and permanency parents require and deserve both pre-placement and post-placement adoption and permanency training and support.*

This would include ongoing classes, support groups and mental health services as their family is formed and evolves. The specialized training should include parent–child attachment tools, self-care, emotional intelligence, child development and the developmental understanding of adoption, therapeutic parenting for children who have experienced trauma, creating and preserving relationships with other constellation members, parenting across cultures and races, and the Seven Core Issues in Adoption and Permanency.

Even families who have parented other children may find parenting a child with a difficult history more complex. All families require support over time. Since adoption and permanency built families have additional tasks, they will need updated information on the most current research, books, respected websites, social media sites, magazines and local and national conferences.

*Child welfare workers and mental health professionals require specialized training and competencies to work effectively with adoption and permanency built families.*

To gain the knowledge base and practice skills to call oneself an adoption and permanency competent professional takes several years of being immersed in the field and working directly with members of the constellation. One must have the full perspective of all constellation members in order to be effective with any specific client touched by adoption and permanency. To become competent, one must pursue ongoing supervision, reading and training related to trauma, attachment, child development and neurobiology, as well as the latest research on adoption and permanency, and attend conferences and seek mentors from those experienced in the field.

Families and professionals who stand on the foundation of these values will have a road map to guide decision making and support all members of the constellation. Each value is an ethical touchstone to light the way.

# Chapter 10

# Rituals and Ceremonies for Healing

## Sharon Kaplan Roszia and Allison Davis Maxon

Rituals and ceremonies are symbolic forms of communication that incorporate participants' histories and traditions. According to Campbell (2008), "The ritual becomes an initiation ceremony, granting the participants membership into a new definition of himself or herself."

Some rituals and ceremonies, like holidays, anniversaries, weddings and funerals, are shared across families and cultures; others are more individual and private. Some are celebrated yearly, some only once, and some daily.

Ceremonies have many working parts that combine to create an emotional impact and a shift to designate an ending and new beginning. Rituals are typically smaller moments in time that may be repeated often but are connected to a much larger meaning, touchstone or memory. For instance, a wedding that includes music, dress, vows, rings and an officiant is a ceremony. The rituals of a wedding could include a pre-wedding rehearsal, a wedding shower, a blue garter for the bride, a bouquet of flowers, the throwing of rice as the couple leaves and "something borrowed."

Using rituals and ceremonies helps to acknowledge important shifts or aspects of the family's development, facilitate healing transitions and create connections. Rituals and ceremonies function as benchmarks, guideposts and bridges for events in people's lives. For birth/first, foster, kin and adoptive families, rituals and ceremonies help clarify roles and maintain relationships. Ceremonies have helped children and their families make sense of difficult life transitions: assisting in expressing and releasing such emotions as grief, anger, confusion and joy towards a situation or person; creating containers for memories and feelings; changing the environment in which a family functions; and allowing for acceptance of new rules, roles and relationships. Rituals and ceremonies are particularly relevant to children who are in transition from one place to another and for creating and strengthening new family attachments. Children who have no language for what is happening in their lives may experience a ritual that can help them conceptualize and give meaning to the events impacting them.

A ritual or ceremony can be developed that assists the extended family and community in welcoming and acknowledging foster or adopted children as new members of the family and/or clan. Rituals draw attention and provide an avenue to facilitate the claiming process of the child into the family system/ clan. Ceremonies provide a container, and the details of rituals draw attention and an avenue to facilitate the goal. Symbols are an important aspect in a ritual. Symbols are concrete objects connected to or representing a situation, experience or person. For instance, a picture of a person who is absent; a song or music that brings back a memory or creates a new one; a gift that represents an important person; a poem, vow or written statement; a scented candle; the holding of hands to create a sacred space; and ceremonial garb are used to externalize and express an internal experience. Symbols are also powerful activators of sensory memory (touch, sounds, smells), as they embrace meaning that cannot be expressed in words. Usually there is a trusted family member or community leader who conducts the ceremony. Often, religious leaders are willing to officiate at an adoption-related ceremony.

Children who are adopted, fostered or in kinship families benefit from a structured and predictable home environment where rituals for routine tasks are utilized to reinforce their sense of security, felt safety and continuity. These might include bathtime, bedtime and playtime rituals that help a child transition comfortably throughout their day. These embedded family rituals will allow the child to predict what is happening next. A certain prayer, a story, a song or a type of food may all give solace to a child.

One type of ritual does not fit the needs of all individuals, families or situations. Decide what the ritual is expected to accomplish; the type of ritual will vary according to the preferred outcome. Keep it simple, sensory oriented and focused on the goal. Create a sense of mystery meant to capture people's attention. For instance, young children respond to bright colors and ceremonial leaders who speak in hushed tones. Food, music and lighting can all enhance the ritual. A strong and trusted leader and a specific opening and closure create a safe container for the ritual. Maximize the ongoing effect of the ritual through capturing it with photos, video or audio. Put some thought into the time of day, the setting and the season of the year, and who will witness and validate the experience over time.

Rituals can be as simple as a set of songs and words to move a child into a bath and out; into bed and up in the morning; or leaving for school and coming home. It can include notes in a lunch bag or a special pebble in a child's pocket. Its purpose is to create structure, routine and safety for the child whose world has already been upended at least once. Even newborns need the comfort of routine and ritual.

Some of the bigger changes in a child's life—such as moving from foster care to adoption, even within the same family where you have lived for a long period of time; signing relinquishments; having rights terminated by the court; finalizing an adoption; adding or losing siblings; reunifying with parents; changing a name; and changing a role—have to be more carefully planned and are meant to be remembered. The impact of the ceremony on the core participants and the observers should commemorate life-altering shifts in individuals' lives.

There are many books on the creation of rituals and ceremonies, and they are useful to have as guides and resources to help individuals and families create rituals to move from infertility to adoption; let go of a child; welcome a child; build attachments; honor losses; acknowledge accomplishments; and commemorate the closing of one chapter and the opening of a new chapter in life.

# Chapter 11

# The Power of Forgiveness to Address Loss and Grief

## Sharon Kaplan Roszia and Allison Davis Maxon

Adoption and permanency are connected to both ethical and spiritual issues. When the practice of adoption and permanency takes into account the following issues—that there are long-term implications for these forms of family building; that they must be based on the truth for everyone involved; that money should be removed from the equation of family building as much as possible—and when the "golden rule" (as in do unto others as you would have them do unto you) becomes the guiding value, joy may be the outcome. If these aspects are absent, adoption and permanency built families can create pain and anger that trickles down through the generations.

Every person in the world is confronted with stress and it can be difficult to maintain one's moral or spiritual equilibrium. Members of the constellation have additional stressors embedded in their complex relationships that may lead to anxiety, simmering anger, emotional outbursts and a lack of patience.

Forgiveness or lack of compassion is firmly attached to the experience of the core issues. Further supporting the need for self-compassion and forgiveness of others are the feelings of rejection, shame and guilt that may impact our self-esteem and sense of powerlessness that originated with the losses. People's identities are also complicated as they harbor their unacknowledged grievances that fester. Individuals often define themselves by what happened to them because of adoption and permanency rather than seeing themselves for the totality of who they are. In essence, they define themselves by one aspect of their story. As they protect this painful aspect of the self, the individual may limit authentic intimacy in order to protect a more fragile or vulnerable self. Choosing forgiveness leads to a letting go of the victim role that may be part of their self-concept. Forgiveness requires ownership of their choices, mistakes and failures. This shift can lead to a different role in the family and community as a person moves from anger, sadness and fear to the embracing of their untapped potential.

Historically, strong feelings about the other members of the constellation have been divisive.

A grievance is a real or imagined wrong. It is a cause for complaint or a protest for unfair treatment. It leads to a feeling of resentment over something believed to be wrong or unfair.

Here are some examples of constellation members' unresolved loss and grief that may lead to grievances:

- Birth/first family members who are angry with: their own family for not supporting them, the adoptive parents, themselves, the other birth/first parent, the child, or people in the system such as judges, lawyers or social workers.

- Adoptive parents who are angry or upset with: the birth/first family, the foster parents, the child, and the people in the system.

- Adoptive grandparents who are angry or upset about having to share their relatives with the birth/first family, the foster family and the child, and for the trauma they bring into the family, as well as the people in the system.

- Adopted people who are mad at: the birth/first family for placing them or not fighting for them or hurting them through physical, sexual or emotional abuse or neglect; the extended birth/first family for not raising them; their adoptive parents for any number of affronts, real or imagined; and the people in the system.

- Siblings of the birth/first, foster and adoptive families who have been hurt by the choices that adults have made.

- Kinship caregivers who are angry with: the child's parents for being unable to meet the needs of their child; the other relatives who didn't offer to parent the child in need; themselves for mistakes that may have led to this situation occurring; the spouse who is not supporting the placement; and the people in the system who are not providing the support needed.

- Foster parents who are angry with: the birth/first family who don't act responsibly; social workers who do not take foster parent input seriously; child/ren who brought pain and chaos into the family; the community that sees the foster parents as "less than" other families and/or selfish; the judge and system that makes decisions that can be harmful to the child/ren they love; therapists and teachers who fail to meet the special needs of the child/ren they care about; their extended family and children for not being supportive of their commitment to be foster parents; and the people in the system.

- Social workers, lawyers and therapists who get angry with their clients for somehow letting them down, making them look bad or challenging their confidence.

Think for a moment about whether you, the reader, are holding grievances. Do you have a need to be forgiven or to forgive others or yourself? Is the grievance about a general thorn in your side like a system or is it about a specific person or people? Who is it or what is it that needs forgiveness? How long have you been holding on to this grievance?

How do we get to a place where forgiveness is needed?

- We took something *personally.*

- We continue to *blame* that person or ourselves for how badly we feel.

- We then created a *grievance story*.

The word "wound" comes to mind when we think of an act that requires forgiveness, either physical or emotional. Wounds make people suffer. Wounds keep people unwell and slow their progression through life. As longheld wounds remain untreated, they infect our lives and cause more suffering. This costs people a great deal. It is as if you are giving free space to another or others in your mind, heart and body. The more we blame and focus on regrets, the further we get from healthy thoughts, body and emotions. You can't be fully happy or present with your fist in a knot. Forgiveness can be learned, developed and practiced, and can, literally, rewire your brain.

Forgiveness sets you free—it actually means to "cut loose." Without forgiveness, we limit ourselves and our relationships. Forgiveness is not about condoning, forgetting, excusing, minimizing or reconciling. It is important to feel the feelings and acknowledge the pain before one forgives. To move forward, you must allow strong feelings of anger, betrayal, sadness and helplessness to emerge and be expressed.

Pride, fear, resentment, hopelessness and other people's expectations can hamper the process of forgiving. Some people conspicuously parade their anger, believing that, in so doing, they are punishing another. They attempt to get even by consistently appearing wronged and miserable. This stance may also be used to protect oneself from admitting personal or perceived mistakes by others.

Many constellation members have become defined by the role of victim. They tell the same story over and over again and their thoughts become repetitive.

They think about their grievances often and they seek out other people with the same grievances. This is an attempt to validate their side of the story and gain support from others with similar grievances. The story never changes.

Alternatively, some people blame their pain on themselves and can't forgive themselves for a decision made at a specific point in time, an action when they didn't have all the information or support they needed and had no crystal ball to envisage how this decision would impact their lives. Hindsight is twenty twenty.

Forgiveness is for *you*, not the offender. It is about reclaiming power and control. "Everything can be taken from a man but one thing: The last of the human freedoms—to choose one's attitude in any given set of circumstances, to choose one's own way" (Frankel 1946, p.86). It is about being the hero of your own story. It is recognizing that no one is perfect, not even you.

Research in 2001, conducted by psychiatrist Thomas Farrow and colleagues at the University of Sheffield in England, studied the brain while a person was asked to forgive a wrongdoing by another. While forgiving, blood rushed to the prefrontal cortex associated with emotion, problem solving and complex thought. It also surged in an area of the brain that weighs reward, therefore increasing pleasure, while decreasing stress.

Forgiveness gives people the gifts of a positive mood, physical well-being, a healthier outlook on life, happier relationships, the release of toxic stress and shame, and better learning abilities. Forgiveness changes a person's whole perspective on life, how they view themselves and others, and shifts world views.

# Chapter 12

# A Child's Developmental Journey through Adoption and Permanency

### Allison Davis Maxon

A child's developmental understanding of adoption/permanency changes and unfolds overtime as their ability to understand what adoption/permanency is generally (why some children are not raised by their birth/first parents?) and what happened to them specifically (why they are not living with their birth/first parents?). Babies, children and teens experience the traumatic losses associated with losing their connections to their birth/first families through a series of unfolding insights and understandings that often trigger the deep feelings, challenges and tasks associated with the Seven Core Issues. This developmental grid will assist adults in recognizing, guiding and supporting the child through the various stages of development.

| | Pre-nate | Infant | Toddler |
|---|---|---|---|
| Developmental tasks | Fetal sensory development.<br><br>*Sense of touch:* by 12 weeks, can perceive and respond to touch.<br><br>*Auditory system:* by 23 weeks, can hear and respond to sounds, loud noises and music.<br><br>*Vision:* by 26 weeks, the eyes are almost fully formed and eyelids will open and sense light.<br><br>*Taste buds:* by 15 weeks, can perceive taste. Mother's diet affects the flavor of the amniotic fluid and, by 20 weeks, the fetus is gulping and inhaling amniotic fluid and shows taste preferences.<br><br>*Sense of smell:* by 28 weeks, smell receptors in the nasal cavity can detect and respond to various smells.<br><br>*Sense of movement:* vestibular system (inner ear) is maturing, fetus experiences motion and gravity.<br><br>By 20 weeks, feels mother's movements; swaying and rocking comforts and soothes the newly forming biological system. | The infant becomes separate and independent from the mother's body.<br><br>Physiological adjustment to being outside the womb as they must learn to breathe, take in food and eliminate waste—all in an environment very different from the womb.<br><br>Activation of the infant's "attachment behavioral system" occurs; maintaining proximity/contact with caregivers allows for reduction of fearful arousal and an experience of felt security.<br><br>Infants/babies grow at a rapid rate across three major developmental areas:<br><br>*Motor development:* grasping and holding objects, sitting, crawling, rolling, standing.<br><br>*Language development:* babbles (ba-ba-ba-ba), coos, gurgles, laughs, vocalizes to mimic sounds.<br><br>*Social/emotional development:* by six weeks, will prefer the human face.<br><br>Social smiling and cooing, will learn and prefer the face and voice of primary caregivers. Distinguishes emotions by tone of voice. | The once dependent baby is now becoming more independent, walking, running and climbing as they explore their world. They prefer their "primary attachment caregivers" and are often shy around strangers. They use gestures, different cries and simple words to express their wants and needs.<br><br>*Physiological*<br>• Learns to regulate their biological need states, sleep/wake cycle, hunger, touch<br>• Walks, runs, climbs<br>• Dress self, eats with spoon<br>• Pulls toys while walking.<br><br>*Social and emotional*<br>• Security and trust in caregivers<br>• Able to express full range of emotions<br>• Imitates adult/caregiver behavior<br>• Learns reciprocity in social relationships<br>• Learns to delay gratification of needs and impulses.<br><br>*Language and communication*<br>• Can string words together<br>• Says "no" a lot<br>• Points to show others objects.<br><br>*Cognitive (learning, thinking, reasoning)*<br>• Knows common objects—fork, toothbrush, car, keys, etc.<br>• Can follow simple commands<br>• Begins to learn cause-and-effect thinking. |

*cont.*

|  | Pre-nate | Infant | Toddler |
|---|---|---|---|
| Core losses | A mother who may not want or acknowledge the child.<br><br>Traumatized, distressed, depressed or anxious mother.<br><br>Being in the womb with a mother who is psychotic, borderline or mentally ill.<br><br>Being in the womb with a mother who is using alcohol, toxic substances or drugs. | Connection to both maternal and paternal familial tree.<br><br>Familiar voices, familiar heart beat and familiar tastes are developed in-utero.<br><br>Balances in biochemistry and nervous system as the neurobiological system is impacted by the stress of needing to adapt to new caregivers.<br><br>Being in a relaxed (homeostatic) state, which can negatively impact the ability to feed/sleep/eliminate.<br><br>Unconditional love.<br><br>Feeling received by the familiar.<br><br>The sensory experience of having one's needs met and valued.<br><br>With each broken attachment (move), the baby's "felt security" is diminished and this can leave them in a state of objectification that impacts their sense of security and right to exist.<br><br>If the baby is exposed to drugs, alcohol or mother's stress, the ability to remain in a regulated state that allows the biological system to efficiently adapt to its new environment is negatively impacted. | Connection to both maternal and paternal familial tree.<br><br>"Primary attachment relationships" with birth/first mother and birth/first father.<br><br>Mirroring by familiar (faces, sounds, rhythms, rituals, language, food, etc.).<br><br>Felt safety in body (muscle tone, hyperarousal, tension).<br><br>With each broken attachment (move), the toddler's "felt security" is diminished and can leave them in a state of hyperarousal and/or toxic stress that impacts their sense of security and right to exist. Survival and adaptation responses are then required.<br><br>Sibling connections.<br><br>Birth order disruptions. |
| Secondary losses | "Dual unity" between mother and fetus; merged state between mother and pre-nate/baby.<br><br>Energetic exchange of chronic depression, anxiety, trauma and dissociation leaves physiological traces in the baby's experience. | Smooth transition from symbiosis with the mother to an emerging separate self.<br><br>Loss of ongoing mirroring—racial, ethnic and familial reflections that validate and feel familiar. | May believe self is undeserving of love/connection.<br><br>Belief that the self is "bad" or "unlovable."<br><br>Not grounded in permanency; adjusting to new name, new routine, new faces, new smells, new sounds, new world. |

| | | | |
|---|---|---|---|
| **Emotional and behavioral symptoms of distress** | Autonomic processes are hyperaroused; over-exposed to toxic stress, unable to calm or self-soothe.<br><br>When mother is distressed, the fetus is distressed. In response to stress/threat, the fetus goes into contraction and withdrawal reflex and related fear/paralysis, which impacts the entire sensory system; brain chemistry, organ systems, nervous and endocrine systems, skin and connective tissue and immune system.<br><br>Early chronic fetus distress undermines subsequent physiological and psychological development. | Central nervous system distress creates muscle tension (hypertonicity), inability to be soothed, excessive crying and wailing, abnormal sucking, excessive gas, colic, gastric reflux and an inability to take in or absorb nutrients, which can lead to failure to thrive and/or death.<br><br>Feeding issues—not interested in food or feeds quickly/excessively. Vomiting or diarrhea.<br><br>Sleep/wake cycle distress; most infants can sleep through the night by 2–3 months.<br><br>Excessive startle response, jitteriness and irritability.<br><br>Decreased soothability; the body has difficulty finding a "calm state" and taking in pleasure (touch/feeding). | Sensory processing challenges; sensitive to loud noises, touch defensive, etc.<br><br>Increased hyperarousal; easily triggered into a distressed state.<br><br>Decreased self-regulation, leading to:<br>• poor attention span<br>• motor agitation<br>• poor eye contact; gaze aversion<br>• increased "externalizing" behaviors: impulsive, reactive, aggressive<br>• increased "internalizing" behaviors: dissociative, non-verbal, does not cue when distressed or in "need" state.<br><br>Gross motor delays.<br><br>Depressed or blunted affect (is not pleasure seeking).<br><br>Delayed language skills.<br><br>Sleep/wake cycle impairment; increased nighttime distress or impulsivity.<br><br>Poor attention and focus. |
| **Attachment vulnerabilities** | Sensing constant threat.<br>Chronic hyperarousal.<br>Freeze paralysis response.<br>Withdrawal response.<br>Numbing.<br>Failure to thrive.<br>Traumatic symbiosis—the merged state between mother and child creates energetic exchange; states of depression, anxiety and dissociation in the mother leave physiological traces in the baby's core experience. | Crying, screaming, sympathetic hyperarousal (discharge of toxic stress).<br>Gaze aversion (poor eye contact).<br>Hypertonic (muscles are tense/rigid).<br>Poor sleep/wake cycles.<br>Poor feeding—increased internal distress decreases the "pleasure" of food intake.<br>Touch systems easily distressed; may not tolerate being held or rocked.<br>Failure to thrive; may not cry when hungry or distressed.<br>In-utero exposure to toxins disrupts normative attachment if infant goes through physiological withdrawals; overwhelming sensory distress.<br>A traumatized infant who is going through withdrawal and/or is in chronic hyperarousal has more regulation and attachment challenges. | Does not have a primary attachment caregiver; lack of "secure base" and "safe haven."<br>Lack of basic trust that primary attachment caregiver will meet needs; includes connection, belonging and identity.<br>Ambivalent/weak attachments—will go to anyone.<br>Increased hyperarousal: impulsive, reactive, distressed.<br>Decreased pro-social development and skills.<br>Fear-based self: protects against primary attachment and dependency.<br>Shame-based self: protects against intimacy and further rejection/shame.<br>"Primary attachment" deflecting behaviors established to avoid overwhelming distress. |

*cont.*

|  | Pre-nate | Infant | Toddler |
|---|---|---|---|
| Parent/Caregiver | A womb experience that allows the fetus to feel safe and protected; and move through its "need states" with an internal locus of control.<br><br>A womb experience where the mother is talking to her baby, reading, singing, and touching her belly.<br><br>A mother who has supportive connections that can help decrease any stressors and ensure that basic needs are met. | Claiming the infant's "need states" by becoming the external psycho-biological regulator of their internal affective states; parental attunement and responsiveness to the infant's needs and distress. The baby needs 24-hour access to their primary attachment caregivers.<br><br>Maximal parental empathy and responsiveness to infant's cues and needs. Early bonding and attachment is critical in order to reduce toxic stress on immature neurobiological system.<br><br>Provide nurturing "re-wombing" sensory experiences by attending quickly to physiological distress. Touch and movement with "primary attachment caregiver" builds the foundation for regulation skills.<br><br>Limit the number of caregivers that are meeting the needs of the child; ideally no more than two or three consistent caregivers.<br><br>Limit the number of people holding, touching, feeding, changing, bathing, comforting and/or playing with the baby. With each new person, the baby's immature, sensitive sensory system must adapt and manage their responses. Each "new" person looks, sounds, feels and smells different. | Provide a consistent, predictable, loving environment. Respond quickly to signs of distress and use proximity, calm voice and body language to assist them in feeling safe, relaxed and connected.<br><br>Assistance in calming when distressed or dysregulated. Holding, rocking, singing, comforting and soothing them back into a calm, relaxed state.<br><br>Structure and routine to allow the toddler to "relax" into safe, loving parental attunement.<br><br>Touch and movement to strengthen "primary attachment relationship." Children attach through their senses.<br><br>Play is the work of children at this stage; provide daily structured and unstructured play activities.<br><br>Non-reactive (non-angry) parenting and discipline; time-ins and logical consequences, maintaining proximity when toddler is distressed or dysregulated. |

| Tools/Resources | Support for the pregnant woman in crisis. Support to access prenatal care. Crisis counseling to address immediate safety needs and risk factors. 51% of all pregnancies are unintended. Find and access local and government programs to address food and housing insecurity, medical needs and/or mental health support services. Pregnancy counseling. Intimate partner violence (IPV), sexual violence or coercive reproduction can lead to an unintended pregnancy. Refer to the National Domestic Violence Hotline, www.thehotline.org. | Babywearing (such as a baby sling) allows the infant to feel connected to the sights, sounds and rhythms of their parent. Swaddle, hold, soothe, carry, touch; respond quickly to reduce and minimize infant's distress. Baby must learn that food is both a social and pleasurable experience; feeding time is an opportunity to deepen attachments between parent and child. As the caregiver holds, rocks and feeds the baby, the baby experiences the removal of distress and a painful, empty stomach and the pleasure of a full belly through human contact. Propping bottles and/or a distracted caregiver will not maximize the attachment opportunity. Zero to Three, Child Development resources at www.zerotothree.org. | Trust-Based Relational Interventions at www.child.tcu.edu. Center on the Developing Child, Harvard University, at www.developingchild.harvard.edu. Developmental screening and assessment. Physical and/or occupational therapy. Positive Discipline at www.positivediscipline.com. **Books:** *The Connected Child* by Karyn Purvis *The Whole Brain Child* by Dan Siegel and Tina Payne Bryson *We Belong Together* by Todd Parr *The Feel Good Book* by Todd Parr *My New Family: A First Look at Adoption* by Pat Thomas *The Invisible String* by Patrice Karst *I Love You, Stinky Face* by Lisa McCourt **Websites:** www.attach.org www.adoptivefamilies.com www.childtrauma.org www.adoptionsupport.org www.nacac.org www.aecf.org |
|---|---|---|---|

*cont.*

| | Latency | Pre-Teen | Adolescence |
|---|---|---|---|
| Developmental tasks | Identity: beginning to know who they are and how they fit into the world.<br><br>Personal power: regulating impulses better and learning how to get needs met.<br><br>Industry: learning to solve problems and figure things out.<br><br>Executive functioning (awareness, self-control, focus, flexibility) is being strengthened via experience.<br><br>Using family as base; children venture into the world and "do."<br><br>Building emotional resiliency as they overcome small stressors and challenges. | Developing complex social, emotional and cognitive skills.<br><br>Peer group is very important; finding where they belong. Strong need to fit in with a group.<br><br>Experimenting with activities; finding what they are good at, building mastery.<br><br>Internal working model: what they believe about themselves is becoming more fixed.<br><br>Self-image and appearance: more interested and aware of how they are perceived by others.<br><br>Adjusting to bodily changes: preparing for an adult role with an adult body.<br><br>Physical hygiene is much more important; they are beginning to practice better self-care as they are more interested in their appearance.<br><br>Becoming increasingly attracted to others; adjusting to these new thoughts and feelings. | Transitioning from childhood to adulthood.<br><br>Identity formation vs. identity confusion; may try on various identities as they understand themselves and experiment.<br><br>Abstract thinking: thinking deeply about their history, trauma, adoption, etc.<br><br>Becoming more autonomous and independent; less emotionally dependent on their parents.<br><br>Developing a strong peer group; social intimacy. Friends become an important resource for emotional support.<br><br>Learning to take responsibility for self.<br><br>Developing a sexual identity, dating and mating.<br><br>Developing a trajectory: What do they want to do? What are their strengths? |

| Core losses | Moving from unconscious to conscious awareness of adoption/permanency losses. | Increased awareness of adoption and permanency losses. | Paternal family lineage; relationships, history, culture. |
|---|---|---|---|
| | Awareness of what adoption/permanency means and how it occurs. | Knowing what it means to lose two family trees; a birth mother, birth father, extended family, siblings, a race/culture, etc. | Maternal family lineage; relationships, history, culture. |
| | A "waking up" to the losses; feels like rejection and/or abandonment. | Increased awareness can feel overwhelming, and losses are felt more deeply. | Identify formation; no mirrors. Who do they look like? Will they be a good person, mother, father? |
| | Loss of familiar and cultural mirroring. | Increased need for facts, truth, genetic mirrors as self-awareness is growing. | Why were they adopted? Why were they left? |
| | Lack of facts; who knows their story? | Body image challenges, lack of genetic mirrors; focus on external appearance; self-conscious and insecure about physical appearance. | Full awareness and understanding of what adoption and permanency means. |
| | | | Strong, deep feelings about the adoption and permanency experience but may not have the emotional competencies to express and articulate those complex issues and emotions. |
| | | | Sexual identity development; what parts of them are like their birth/first parents? |
| | | | Positive racial identity; lack of mirroring and mentoring. |
| | | | Understanding their developing body and sexual identity; how tall, menstruation, sexual activity and orientation. |

*cont.*

| | Latency | Pre-Teen | Adolescence |
|---|---|---|---|
| Secondary losses | The child may have a range of questions they need answers for:<br><br>What happened? How did I get adopted?<br><br>Where did I come from, really?<br><br>Where did I get my looks—face, height, nose, body type?<br><br>Where are my birth parents? Do I look like them? Do they think of me?<br><br>Do I have siblings? Where are they? Are they looking for me?<br><br>Could my teacher be my birth/first mother?<br><br>Could my coach be my birth/first father?<br><br>Peers and people may ask them questions about adoption:<br><br>Are those your "real" parents?<br><br>Where is your "real" mother? Why do you look different from your parents?<br><br>Why are your parents old? Do you live with your grandmother?<br><br>Where are the people who look like you?<br><br>Do you really belong here? | Feeling different in their day-to-day experiences.<br><br>Their family is non-traditional, they look different.<br><br>Is it okay to be adopted/in foster care/kinship?<br><br>Do they need to hide parts of themselves or their experience to avoid the embarrassment and shame of feeling different or marginalized?<br><br>Feeling "less than" other kids/families who look more "normal" or "traditional," as seen in images mirrored or reflected in the culture.<br><br>Questioning if they are being told everything about their story.<br><br>Who knows what about their story? Are people lying to them?<br><br>Feeling as if they are missing pieces of themselves.<br><br>If adopted trans-racially, they might wonder what they would have been like if adopted within their own race or kept within their original family. How would they be different? | Not having enough information about their history, story, facts or lineage to form a positive self-identity or a cohesive life narrative.<br><br>Finding it hard to ask questions; when talking about adoption/permanency they have deep feelings and are sensitive to rejection, abandonment and loss.<br><br>Who do they look like? May be unable to see themselves in the future, as genetic mirroring from mom/dad, grandparents is missing.<br><br>Being comfortable in their own skin. "Who am I really?" May spend time fantasizing about birth/first family and what would have happened if they had been kept. Where are the birth/first family? Would the birth/first family want to see them? Would they care?<br><br>They may be looking for their birth/first family, consciously or unconsciously, yearning and longing for mirroring and a place that feels familiar, accepting and unconditional. |

| Emotional and behavioral symptoms of distress | Hyperactivity and impulsivity; hyperaroused and increased emotional reactivity.<br><br>Poor sleep/wake cycle; increased agitation at bedtime (increased fears at night leading to anxious behaviors).<br><br>Internalized behaviors; quiet, closed-off, withdrawn, constricted.<br><br>May have little insight into why they are upset, sad, angry, scared or unhappy.<br><br>Children with a significant amount of trauma and/or loss often have displaced, denied or minimized feelings.<br><br>Emotional and behavioral regression can occur when demands are placed on them at home or school; they can become easily agitated, oppositional and defiant. | Increased moodiness and irritability with the onset of puberty, as the body and mind begin to transition into adolescence.<br><br>Fear and insecurity about where they belong.<br><br>May fear they don't belong anywhere. May struggle making friends as they feel more insecure, anxious and fearful in relationships and new situations.<br><br>Feelings of anxiety may surface around the new demands of being a teenager and impending separation from parents.<br><br>Self-loathing; feeling flawed, bad, damaged or unworthy. May not be sharing these feelings.<br><br>Academic problems are not unusual when the child has spent years surviving neglect, trauma, multiple placements in foster care.<br><br>They may have missed critical learning opportunities and milestones, and may wrongly assume they are "dumb" or incapable. | Without a conception and birthing story and with multiple moves, does not feel grounded, rooted or a permanent sense of belonging, and may feel empty or disconnected without all of their information.<br><br>Excessively moody, irritable, angry, depressed, agitated and/or negative.<br><br>If they feel as if they don't matter to anyone, they may not value themselves and may engage in high-risk or self-destructive behaviors; may drive too fast or experiment with drugs/alcohol. Some adolescents feel disconnected from their birth and wonder if they were born like everyone else or are they "beings" who cannot die.<br><br>Impulsive, reactive, oppositional, rebellious behaviors may intensify as they struggle with attachment, individuation and fear of impending launch into adulthood.<br><br>Emotional numbing may occur as a way to try and avoid feelings of rejection, shame, depression, fear, abandonment and/or anger.<br><br>Trauma triggers may surface or resurface; teens may isolate when in pain or distress. Watch for self-injurious behaviors like cutting, bingeing, promiscuity and other behaviors that are indicators of trauma/shame.<br><br>May use drugs, alcohol, sex/porn, gaming and other maladaptive strategies to cope with (avoid or repress) difficult feelings.<br><br>May engage in sexual acting out or promiscuity. |
|---|---|---|---|

*cont.*

| | Latency | Pre-Teen | Adolescence |
|---|---|---|---|
| Attachment vulnerabilities | May internalize feelings of rejection, abandonment, fear and shame leading to "attachment deflecting" behaviors such as oppositional/defiance, mistrust, avoidance, isolation and/or emotionally reactive or manipulative behaviors.<br><br>May provoke parent and strive to avoid the emotional intimacy of attachment.<br><br>Early losses, unmet developmental needs and attachment disruptions can lead to what are referred to as "developmental incongruities." | May be excessively clingy with parents or caregivers, or excessively detached and disconnected.<br><br>May isolate more as they become more introspective and abstract in their thinking.<br><br>May struggle in allowing others emotionally close to them, especially if trauma/neglect resulted in them feeling flawed, bad or damaged.<br><br>Touch may be difficult if they were physically or sexually abused, or if they were touch deprived. Humans attach through senses; it is important to learn to give and receive healthy, safe, loving touch.<br><br>Early losses, unmet developmental needs and attachment disruptions can lead to what are referred to as "developmental incongruities." | May not be able to articulate feelings of sadness, pain or distress.<br><br>May isolate and use anger to push parents away.<br><br>If later placed, the teen may be attaching to a new family at the same time they are individuating and preparing for independence—a difficult and complex task that requires sensitivity and empathy from the parent/s.<br><br>Relational trauma and feelings of rejection or abandonment can lead the teen to hold on to relationships that are unhealthy, abusive or destructive.<br><br>Sexual acting out or promiscuity can be used as a way to get close or intimate.<br><br>Early losses, unmet developmental needs and attachment disruptions can lead to what are referred to as "developmental incongruities." |

| | | | |
|---|---|---|---|
| **Parent/Caregiver** | Parenting a child who socially and emotionally appears to be 2, 5 or 15 on any given day is challenging.<br><br>Understanding child development and your particular child's losses and needs allows you to respond effectively to their developmental and emotional needs at any given moment.<br><br>The child needs consistent, predictable, nurturing and empathic parenting, and emotional attunement to their distress, hurt, anger and pain.<br><br>Create a structured and organized home environment, with increased predictability.<br><br>Give permission to make mistakes.<br><br>Start conversations about adoption, sexuality, family diversity, race, etc.<br><br>Check in with child about what they understand about loss, adoption, their story, and all of the feelings they may have (use movies, puppets and books).<br><br>Continue to deepen and strengthen a sense of belonging and connectedness by talking about the future, such as when they get their first car, their next birthday, when they get married, when they have children. | Parenting a child who socially and emotionally appears to be 2, 5 or 15 on any given day is challenging.<br><br>Understanding child development and your particular child's losses and needs allows you to respond effectively to their developmental and emotional needs at any given moment.<br><br>Set clear boundaries and expectations. Tweens still want to please their parents and have a strong need to feel a sense of belonging.<br><br>They need to feel confident and secure in their family/home. Create family rituals and activities that bring the family together in fun and play.<br><br>Eat dinner as a family. Talk about what went well and what didn't go well that day.<br><br>Listen and mirror back their strengths.<br><br>Continue to strengthen the emotional bond and attachment with your child. Have conversations about values, love, friends, dating, sex, loss, pain, trauma and adoption. It is important that they learn how to have conversations about complex topics with people they love and trust. Ask about their beliefs, opinions and feelings. | Parenting a child who socially and emotionally appears to be 2, 5 or 15 on any given day is challenging.<br><br>Understanding child development and your particular child's losses and needs allows you to respond effectively to their developmental and emotional needs at any given moment.<br><br>Adolescence can be a challenging stage of development for children who have experienced trauma, neglect, adoption and/or foster care. Prioritize the parent/child attachment relationship over all other behavioral issues that may surface. All children need to feel unconditionally loved and accepted for who they are.<br><br>Continue to fill in information about what happened, why it happened, and any/all details that are known about your child's story. The teen should know all of their facts before they leave the safety and love of their family.<br><br>Support their need to know all the parts of their story. It is normal to be curious about where we come from. Ask if they have any questions about their story, their birth/first family or adoption/foster care.<br><br>Continue to deepen and strengthen a sense of belonging and connectedness by talking about the future, such as when they get their first car, their next birthday, when they get married, when they have children.<br><br>Continue to fill in information in their lifebook about their history and any updates of information. Check in with them about how they are feeling and whether they have any questions. |

*cont.*

| Latency | Pre-Teen | Adolescence |
|---|---|---|
| Create a lifebook with your child that tells the story of their life from their beginning. Begin the lifebook at this stage with the basic narrative of their story, using language that helps them understand what adoption/foster care is and why it happened to them. | Continue to deepen and strengthen a sense of belonging and connectedness by talking about the future, such as when they get their first car, their next birthday, when they get married, when they have children.<br><br>Continue to fill in information in their lifebook about their story, birth/first family, why they were adopted or in foster care, and any ongoing information that is learned. Check in with them about how they are feeling about the information and whether they have any questions. | Many teens are thinking a lot about searching for relatives, siblings, birth/first parents, etc. It helps them to know that their parents support their curiosity and need to know. Some may not search due to feeling that it might be perceived as them being disloyal. |

| Tools/Resources | | | |
|---|---|---|---|
| | Adoption/permanency-themed books and movies/Disney movies. Loss themes—talk about the characters in the movie. How were they feeling? What happened to them? What did they do with their sad/hurt or angry feelings?<br><br>Feelings books and card games (label and share feelings): www.childswork.com.<br><br>*Fostering Families Today* magazine<br><br>*Adoption Today* magazine<br><br>**Books:**<br><br>*Kinship Toolbox, Foster Parenting Toolbox, Adoptive Parent Toolbox*, published by EMK Press<br><br>*Raising an Emotionally Intelligent Child* by John Gottman<br><br>*Adoption at the Movies* by Addison Cooper<br><br>*ABC, Adoption and Me* by Gayle and Casey Swift<br><br>*Adopted and Wondering: Drawing Out Feelings* by Marge Heegaard<br><br>*The Mulberry Bird* by Anne Brodzinsky<br><br>*Our Grandfamily* by Sandra Werle and J.P. Roberts<br><br>*Happy in Our Skin* by Fran Manushkin<br><br>*The Colors of Us* by Karen Katz<br><br>*W.I.S.E. Up Powerbook* for children who were adopted; *W.I.S.E. Up Powerbook* for children in foster care, at www.adoptionsupport.org | Timeline: beginning at birth to present, marking significant life events, moves and/or changes in caregivers.<br><br>Genogram.<br><br>Lifebook.<br><br>Social and emotional skill-building groups.<br><br>Grief and loss support group.<br><br>**Books:**<br><br>*Telling the Truth to Your Adopted or Foster Child: Making Sense of the Past* by Betsy Keefer and Jayne E. Schooler<br><br>*My Adoption Workbook* by Theresa McCoy<br><br>*The One and Only Me Lifebook*, published by Adoption World Publishing<br><br>*Lifebooks: Creating a Treasure for the Adopted Child* by Beth O'Malley<br><br>*I'm Chocolate, You're Vanilla: Raising Healthy Black and Biracial Children in a Race-Conscious World* by Marguerite Wright<br><br>*I'm Not Bad, I'm Just Mad* by Lawrence Shapiro, Zack Pelta-Heller and Anna Greenwald<br><br>*An Elephant in the Living Room* (to help children understand drug and alcohol addiction) by Jill M. Hastings and Marion Typpo | Timeline: beginning at birth to present, marking significant life events, moves and/or changes in caregivers.<br><br>Genogram.<br><br>Ecomap.<br><br>Lifebook.<br><br>Support group for teens with grief, loss, adoption, trauma, foster care: www.fosterclub.com.<br><br>**Books:**<br><br>*Twenty Things Adopted Kids Wish Their Adoptive Parents Knew* by Sherrie Eldridge<br><br>*The Real Me Teen Lifebook*, published by Adoption World Publishing<br><br>*Adopted: The Ultimate Teen Guide* by Suzanne Slade<br><br>*Three Little Words: A Memoir* by Ashley Rhodes-Courter<br><br>*Three More Words* by Ashley Rhodes-Courter<br><br>*Teens, Loss and Grief* by Edward Myers<br><br>*Adopted: The Ultimate Teen Guide* by Suzanne Buckingham Slade<br><br>*Grief Journal: Fire in My Heart, Ice in My Veins* by Enid Traisman | |

# Chapter 13

# The Seven Core Issues and Foster Care

## Sharon Kaplan Roszia and Allison Davis Maxon

Losing one's child, either temporarily or forever, can result from a crisis. That crisis leads to the need for an alternative family placement for a child who will be confused, terrified, traumatized and/or distressed. Resource families all serve a crucial role in helping to preserve the child's well-being and supporting the plan to reunify the child with his or her family. We identify the individuals who care for the children while they are waiting for reunification or permanency as resource parents, foster parents, emergency parents, caregivers and institutions, guardians and kinship caregivers. What the resource family does during that time can have a long-term impact on the child, the parents and their own family. The parents' crisis and the child's crisis move into a resource family, impacting siblings, aunts, uncles, grandparents, cousins, friends, teachers, spiritual leaders, neighbors, other community members and even pets—all can have deep feelings regarding a child's entry into and exit out of a family. It can be hard to resolve these feelings because the child may never be seen again, or the family may worry over time about the child being safe and nurtured. Losses are built into every placement. All of these families hold pieces of the child's life story and narrative. In order for the child to retain all the pieces of themselves, they will need ongoing access to all the parts of their story.

## Loss

Losses are built into every placement. Everyone loses important connections in their lives and a sense of stability. Everyone loses power and control to someone else. Resource families, parents and children feel helpless as their opinion is often dismissed by the court and by professionals. Losses are often experienced through a change in culture, values, rituals and religious perspectives, routines and familiar daily events, racial mirrors and unfamiliar language, including all of the nuances that feel different even when people speak the same language.

Each placement has memories attached to it that are connected to sensory memories—smells, tastes, sounds, images and so on. Children may not remember the names of the foster parents, but they do store, through implicit memories, feelings, experiences and attachments to specific things and people.

Being a resource family is stressful for everyone in the household as all are adapting to the new demands placed on the family by the child, the child welfare system and the courts. Resource parents often get little support from their friends, family or community, who believe that, since they chose to become foster parents, they shouldn't complain or need help. Others often don't know how to help or what to say.

People may lose important information about the other participants in this process and may not have full access to each other. There are "emotional landmines" everywhere, and it is easy to step into someone else's triggers, distress, unresolved losses or trauma reactions.

## Strategies for helping with loss

- Resource parents should document a child's experiences while in their home. Children in crisis do not always retain information, memories and events accurately.

- Make a photo album that includes all of the important people and their names, along with photos of the home, the rooms, the pets, the yard, their school, their friends and so on.

- Write about any significant stories, events and happenings that occurred that will help the child retain their memories.

- Resource families should take time between placements to reconnect with family and friends as well as nurturing and replenishing their own emotional resources as well as their family's and children's needs. The emotional demands placed on the resource parents are high, and taking time to replenish and practice good self-care is critical.

- As resource parents, only accept those children whose ages, behaviors and needs you are able to address and meet without depleting all of your family's resources.

- For parents with a case plan, ask for help when needed. Stay connected to your children through whatever means the court allows. Don't make promises that you may not be able to keep. Don't lose hope.

# Rejection

Losses generate feelings or fear of rejection. Feelings of rejection are experienced in the body as physical pain; this registers in the part of the brain where the body's pain receptors are located. Parents are scared of rejection by the courts, the child and the resource family, as well as members of their own family and the larger community. The child feels or fears rejection from their parents and family of origin and the resource family, and are often displaying a feeling of rejection of themselves as they feel as if *they* caused everything that is happening. Resource families initially fear rejection by the child welfare system as they might not deserve certification, and feel rejection when their voices are not valued by the professionals interacting with their family. They frequently feel rejected by the child and the child's parents, and possibly their own family.

## Strategies for addressing rejection

- Try not to take everything personally. What is coming at you emotionally may have nothing to do with who you are or what you did.

- Be kind to yourself. These feelings or fear of rejection should not be used as an excuse to reject yourself. Do something daily that gives you pleasure and is productive. Do something kind for another person every day, as that will lift your spirits. Get enough rest, eat healthily, take a walk in the sunshine, draw a picture, write a journal and take care of yourself physically.

- The child in foster care who has experienced multiple losses in primary attachment relationships may experience those attachment disruptions as rejection and/or abandonment and subsequently provoke rejection in the new caregivers. Be mindful that children carry with them a learned attachment pattern that will be activated as they are learning to trust and attach in their new home. They will need a lot of reassurance, comfort, nurturance and acceptance from their new caregivers.

- Be conscious of your self-talk. All of us have an inner dialogue, positive or negative. Our inner dialogue impacts our emotions and how we feel about our self. Include more positive affirmations in your self-talk and focus on the things you did well. Feed your strengths!

- Check out whether you are actually being rejected; ask questions, clarify and take control of what you are able to control. Take responsibility for any missteps that others may have read accurately or misinterpreted, and apologize.

## Shame and guilt

Shame is an emotion that begins at a very young stage of life and goes to the heart of whether we feel worthy or unworthy as a human being. Shame makes us want to hide, disappear and avoid interactions. Shame makes us feel less than others, flawed and unworthy of love and belonging. Simply put, shame makes us feel that there is something wrong or damaged at our core. Guilt is associated with having developed a conscious; it is a learned response after doing something wrong.

Being a resource family, a child in foster care or a parent who is unable to parent at a certain point in time impacts one's sense of guilt or shame and can lower self-esteem as society in general overlays myths and stereotypes that are negative.

Everybody carries some shame or guilt about what is occurring and what they are able or not able to do about it.

## Strategies to address shame and guilt

- Be aware of when your feelings of shame are triggered; when shame is driving behaviors, you are more likely to self-sabotage. Shame is typically passed down from parent to child. See if you can become more aware of the roots of your shame. You were not born with shame. Increasing your awareness of your thoughts (inner dialogue) allows you to begin shifting your thoughts away from self-shaming or self-loathing into thoughts that are more affirming and positive.

- Identify what was within your control at a time when your action created guilt. Decide what you are responsible for and make amends. The avenue towards making amends would include a person-to-person discussion, a phone call, a letter or a prayer or ritual. Remember that no one is perfect, we all make mistakes, and none of us has prepared for the roles that we have assumed as resource parents, parents or children touched by the court system.

- If forgiveness is part of the journey, take the time to read the chapter in this book on forgiveness of both self and others.

- Children are still forming their identity when they are repeatedly labeled a "foster child." This pejorative and negative term can help them feel "less than," "damaged," "ashamed," "different," and an outsider. Remember, they are children first. Using child-first language helps us to always see the child first and not label them with a term that is so negatively loaded in our society. The resource family can work hard to not use this negative term and to help the child feel like a valued member of the family, school and community. Claiming the child by putting pictures of them on the wall showing the child in all family rituals, events and festivities, and adding the child's heritage and rituals, such as favorite foods, to family gatherings, are all ways to help the child feel a sense of belonging.

## Grief

Grief is a necessary response to a loss. Since everyone has substantial losses in this process, grief becomes a challenge to be met by all parties. Our society is not kind towards people who it feels have caused their own losses. Grief requires an acknowledgment of loss, the expression of sadness and anger, and time to feel the feelings and process the emotions, and gain support from others.

Taking into account people's culture, religious beliefs and values, gender, stage of life, trauma history and intellectual or developmental capacity, there must be an acceptance that no two people grieve alike or at the same pace. There is no timeframe associated with the grief process.

Even if the child is reunified with the parents, adopted by the resource family or moved to yet another family, everyone will have losses attached to these outcomes that must be grieved. Note that children and young people do not have the same self-awareness that an adult would have, and their ability to identify and express their grief, hurt and pain is a learned skill.

## Strategies to address grief

- Don't label children's behaviors as being "bad," as their impulsive, reactive, demanding, angry or isolative behaviors most likely are an indicator of their sadness and grief. Children get labeled as hyperactive and oppositional/defiant as they struggle to cope with overwhelming grief, sadness and loss. They may present as easily agitated, disruptive, rejecting or provocative as they struggle to adapt to their new world. Remember that children need time to attach to new caregivers, learn to trust and allow you to assist them with their intense feelings of sadness, hurt and isolation.

- Be clear on what you are feeling and how you want to express your feelings. Do not compare your grief process to someone else's.

- Nurture yourself as grief impacts us on an emotional, physical, psychological and spiritual level. We can be exhausted, ill, irritable, anxious and short-tempered, and have difficulty remembering and learning. We tend to do things in extremes, such as not being able to sleep or sleeping too much; not being hungry or constantly eating; or wanting to create isolation or never wanting to be left alone. Destructive forms of avoidance of grief include self-medicating through drugs and alcohol, cutting ourselves off from support, hurting ourselves and endangering ourselves.

- Attend grief support groups, either in person or online. Engage with a therapist. Seek comfort from those you trust. Read books on grieving. Start a grief journal.

- Turn to a spiritual leader, religious rituals and/or prayer that would give you comfort.

- Children need the closeness and emotional support of their caregivers and should not be left alone when they are experiencing overwhelming or intense feelings. Remember that the angry child is really a very hurt child. Underneath all that anger and distress is a great deal of pain. Children do not have insight into these feelings and will need your "emotional tutoring" to assist them in expressing these feelings of grief, loss and distress. Read children's books that are focused on teaching kids about their feelings.

## Identity

If you have not taken the time to address your losses and grieve, it is far more difficult to identify who you are. This experience will require significant adaptation to your identity. There are three kinds of parents: genetic parents, legal parents and "everyday" parents. In the court process, the parents remain the genetic parents and legal parents, but lose the role of the "everyday" parent. The resource parents are the "everyday" parents but not the legal or genetic parents. Even as "everyday" parents, they are still limited by the court, which is currently acting as the legal parent and will set parameters around what the resource parents can and cannot do.

Everybody has changed roles and lost a specific identity in the process.

Who are we to each other? What do we call each other? Some roles are in conflict if the resource family is actively supporting reunification and hoping to adopt the child. What is my role in relation to the decision-making individuals such as lawyers, social workers and court appointment special advocates? Am I a member of the team with a valued opinion? Who is my main boss? Do I really matter in this process and in these relationships? What are my rights and obligations in regard to the parents of this child and the child? How do I explain to the public who I am and what I am doing?

## Strategies to address identity issues

- Becoming an accurate historian and a gatherer of facts allows individuals to piece together a story or narrative about themselves that is fact based and cohesive. This is an ongoing task. We all need to help inform each other's identity through asking questions, listening to other people's perspectives and wishes, stating our needs and remembering the experiences and stories of our time together.

- Examine the language you use in describing yourself and other people who participate in this journey. Language can inform identity, especially in children who are in the process of developing and forming their identity. For instance, children should always be referred to as children first, not "foster children." The more children hear this disparaging phrase to describe them, the more it can become a part of how they see themselves. They are children stuck inside a foster care system. Children also struggle with all the people who are called "Mommy" and "Daddy," especially if they have moved often and have lost many "Mommies" and "Daddies." It would be more useful if a resource parent could combine their first name and their role, such as "Mommy Jenny" and "Daddy Mike," as opposed to their actual parents who are "Mommy" and "Daddy."

- Be intentional about how you define your role in public and how much information you disclose to outsiders. For example, do you share with the grocery store clerk that you're a foster family or do you just say that you're a family? The style in which you address outsiders models for children how best to answer intrusive questions from peers and adults.

Children's circumstances and their private information and foster care status should not be information that is shared publicly.

- Everything should be done to clarify the roles of the parents and resource parents so that all parties can develop a dialogue that builds bridges between them and doesn't create anger that breaks down communication and doesn't benefit the child. Each needs to be sensitive and supportive to the other's role.

## Intimacy

Intimacy is a challenge when bringing together a group of strangers who must interact around the special needs of a child. Resource parents must address the intimate emotional needs of the new child that they have accepted into their family. Part of creating a deep, meaningful attachment relationship with this new child is an awareness of who this child is already connected to and building on those attachments to diminish the number of losses for the child. Building on those connections will increase the child's trust, allowing them to accept you as a safe, caring and loving adult. To really embrace a child in a family, one must attempt to include all the people who are important to that child. Safety concerns, availability and proximity, and a person's desire to play an ongoing role in the child's life, all must be taken into consideration. There is always someone who can support the child's connection back to their community and/or family system. If the parents are currently unavailable, extended family members, mentors, spiritual leaders, school teachers, coaches and neighbors may be able to fill this role in the child's life. The more broken connections the child has experienced, the more difficult connecting to new caregivers becomes.

Depending on the age and stage of the child on arrival, rules and boundaries must be put into place. Children who bring into the family a history of sexual abuse require the resource family to be vigilant about the needs of the child as well as the needs of the other children in the home. Various cultures have different values concerning touch, eye contact, appropriate ways to display affection, words to describe body parts, and dialogue about sex and dating.

Resource parents in the beginning of placement with a child are building and creating a "primary attachment relationship" with the child. This will promote and strengthen intimacy and interpersonal skills for the child. A challenge would include the parents and the resource parents being in conflict around the loyalty and allegiance of the child. If either parent speaks negatively about the other, it can create distress and conflict for the child, diminishing the child's emotional intimacy with one or both parents.

## Strategies for strengthening intimacy

- Parents who have lost their role as the "everyday" parent to their child can work to keep communication with their child open and consistent, as much as the court will allow. This can include sending postcards and notes, keeping phone calls and visitation appointments, being open to communication with the resource family, not making promises that can be broken, keeping the child aware of what they are doing with the goal of bringing the child home, and asking other parents who have preceded them in this journey for advice and support. Do not overwhelm the child with things but bring small tokens that help them feel connected and that they are thought of, such as a small picture of yourself, a small book or a picture that you drew.

- Resource parents can establish daily routines that help a new child feel safe and connected and quickly allow them to experience their new world and family as predictable, safe and loving. List up to five rules in the house on the refrigerator, and what happens when the rules are broken. Give all kids chores to ensure that everyone in the family participates. Spend alone time with each family member, perhaps as a bedtime ritual or a special date that each child has once a week with the parent. Families can wear the same colors, such as matching shirts or wristbands, when going out as a family. Pictures can be taken of individuals that the new child will be interacting with on a regular basis, with their name and role written under the picture, and these can be put on a bulletin board inside the room. Discuss with the extended family what they want to be called and how they want to be introduced, and be sure to explain that this child's birthday and other special events should be celebrated and acknowledged just like any other child in the family. Ask the child what rituals are a part of their holidays and birthdays and include them during special times of the year.

- For parents and resource parents, attend to your adult intimate relationships which should be supportive and healing. Take time to nurture yourself and your relationships. Intimacy takes ongoing attention and planning.

## Mastery and control

The outcome from all these losses and core issues can be feelings of powerlessness that cause people to grapple for control in all areas, helpful or not. The more helpless, powerless and out of control someone feels, the more demanding, provocative, manipulating, avoiding and agitated they may become.

Mastery is the goal and is connected to the gains in this experience. Being able to integrate the lessons that the core issues have revealed or brought to awareness is the task and the gift. Claiming our own power starts with being able to take responsibility for our actions, feelings, thoughts and behaviors. The ability to know ourselves deeply and authentically allows us to communicate clearly and intentionally about our needs, beliefs and feelings. It also allows us to attune to the needs and feelings of others.

## Strategies for gaining mastery

- Practice mindfulness—staying present in the moment.

- Seek out others who have lived experience and who can support and mentor you through this journey.

- Because of the amount of work required, find a therapist who is trauma informed and permanency competent, who knows the seven core issues, and who can support you as needed over time. Additional losses surface in life and can retrigger these core issues.

- Assess your spiritual belief system and access what would be most useful for you.

- Make a gratitude list before bed every evening.

- Practice forgiveness of self and others.

- Attend to your physical well-being.

- Gather friends who are seasoned, healed from trauma, hopeful, supportive and a have a wicked sense of humor.

# Chapter 14

# The Seven Core Issues and Kinship Families

## Joseph Crumbley and Allison Davis Maxon

*Kin: relatives, relations, family, connections, kindred, of the same blood.* For centuries children have been raised informally by kin when their parents were unable to care for them. Currently federal policy upholds the bonds children have and develop with their relatives by giving priority to "kinship caregivers." Our most basic need is the need to belong; to feel we are among *kin*. It is no surprise then that 32 percent of children in the child welfare system are placed with grandparents, aunts, uncles and/or siblings.[1] The most obvious benefit of kinship care is family preservation. Keeping a child within their familial system preserves a continuity of care, relationships and environment that is essential to a child's overall well-being. Kin guardianship and adoption offer greater stability and permanency than temporary foster care. When a relative attains legal guardianship, legal custody transfers from the state or parent to the caregiver without severing parental rights. There are both benefits and challenges within kinship families. The intensity of the emotional response to kinship care will vary according to the circumstances that led to the placement, including severity of abuse or neglect, age, developmental stage, personality, temperament, history and life experience. For example, grandparents may have a less negative response if the child is placed with them at birth than if they received the child at age 4 after he or she has suffered neglect and/or abuse. And while there are many benefits to kinship care, it is important to acknowledge that *loss* is central to the kinship experience and each family member will have issues emanating from that initial core loss.

---

1    Child Trends 2016: www.childtrends.org

## Loss

Grief and loss permeate the experience of the kinship caregiver, the birth/first parents and the child. The core issue of loss is often easily triggered and reacted to in these intimate and sensitive familial relationships. Some kinship families are loaded with painful experiences: poverty, parental drug or alcohol addiction, incarceration, abandonment, mental illness, abuse and/or neglect. Loss can easily become a central theme within kinship families as there is the initial loss, which leads to many secondary or sub-losses.

Losses for kinship families include:

- Loss of typical family roles—roles have shifted and are now outside the "norm."

- For children, the loss of growing up without their parents. Being raised in a "non-traditional" family. "Our family looks different from most other families."

- Loss of typical lifecycle development—grandparents are now parents.

- For birth/first parents, loss of their child and their parenting role with their child.

- For caregivers, loss of freedom and disruption of daily life activities.

- Loss of dreams—how we "thought and hoped" things would work out.

- Loss of the "other" birth/first family as they may disagree about who should be parenting the child, or become disengaged.

- Loss of relationships—various friends and family members may become resentful and/or detach from individuals or the family.

- For caregivers, a loss of financial resources that may be diverted to caring for the child/ren. This could lead to delayed retirement and additional family stressors.

## Rejection

In an effort to minimize losses and the painful emotions they can create, individuals try to regain a sense of control by trying to figure out "what they did or didn't do" to create the loss. They may become very sensitive to perceived criticism or rejection, and may anticipate rejection where there is none or even provoke rejection based on this fear and need to control. Birth/first parents often feel a sense of rejection by society for having "failed" their children and they may feel they have to spend the rest of their lives being the "black sheep" or the "outcast" within their own family.

Children most often experience their removal from their birth/first parents as abandonment or rejection. Their egocentric thinking may leave them blaming themselves for the events that led to the removal and separation, which can intensify their feelings of rejection. They may say things like "This is all my fault" or "I deserved what happened" or "I'm bad, so no one should love me." Children may carry these thoughts and feelings, and if left unacknowledged, they can impact future life choices and relationships.

Kinship parents may fear rejection from the birth/first parents, their own children or relatives, extended family, social workers, the judge and society. They may have fears that if they attach to the child, their relative will be angry or reject them. There may be loyalty conflicts within kinship families that are not typically present in foster care placements. Kinship caregivers may experience a sense of rejection if they get "too close" to the child, attach and enjoy parenting. They may feel a conflicted loyalty towards the birth/first parent, as they are actively parenting their relative's child.

## Shame and guilt

The feeling that one deserves to be rejected, abandoned and treated poorly can generate feelings of shame, guilt and anxiety. Intergenerational trauma, neglect, mental health issues and/or addictive patterns can be co-occurring challenges for kinship families. Kinship family members may all share in these similar emotional experiences yet may never directly share those feelings with their family members. For example, a child who lives with his grandmother may not have the words to share that he believes it is his fault that his mom went away, which leads him to feel bad about himself, maybe even feeling that he is flawed or damaged in some way. Kinship caregivers may have feelings of shame and/or guilt about what they did or did not do to support the parent who is no longer parenting the child. The parent who has lost their "everyday" parenting role to a family member may have deep feelings of shame and guilt about not being able to parent the child they brought into the world. Even if they originally reached out and asked their relative to parent the child, actually witnessing the child becoming attached and thriving in a relative's home can trigger feelings of shame and guilt.

While feelings of guilt, shame and embarrassment may surface, it is important that kinship family members are able to ask for the support they need. Many grandparents who are raising their grandchildren share that they feel isolated. Being a non-nuclear family can be a challenge at back-to-school nights, soccer games and birthday parties, where they may feel different and not "in the club" as they observe younger parents connecting and sharing a similar developmental phase. Aging often brings with it physical challenges that make it more difficult to parent active children. Educational methods and even forms of discipline have changed significantly in the last decade, which might impact their ability to support and parent the child.

The broader culture has not always been accepting of kinship families. There are negative stereotypes and biases that kinship families experience which may lead to increased stressors and a desire to avoid reaching out for connection and support. To combat the shame and guilt that some kinship families experience, it helps to remember that kinship caregivers desire *respect* and *acceptance*, just like all other families.

## Grief

Assistance with grief and loss is key to healing and successful relationship building in kinship care. Children with traumatic loss often feel anger, hurt, fear, abandonment and confusion. Because young children experience the world *through* their relationships with parents and caregivers, those relationships are fundamental to the healthy development of the child's physical, emotional, social, behavioral and intellectual capabilities. Kinship caregivers may be parenting children who have been exposed to multiple and/or chronic neglect and/or traumatic experiences. The placement of children with their relatives does not erase the effects of trauma and the lifelong issues connected to the loss of their parent/s. Grief and loss will surface for the child through each developmental phase as their ability to understand what happened and why they were placed in guardianship or adoption with their kin deepens.

A kinship parent's grief is often complex as it is connected to the child, the parent of the child and their own losses in relation to being a kinship parent. Kinship parents may grieve for the pain and suffering that the child they are parenting experienced. This may be intensified if they feel somehow responsible for contributing to the circumstances that led to the maltreatment or placement of the child.

Losses for kinship families may be difficult to grieve as they are largely unrecognized or ignored. The view is that the child went from a negative, unsafe or abusive environment and is now in a safe and stable home, so the problem has been solved. Each loss for kinship families must be acknowledged and grieved. The process of grief is more complex when there are no rituals or ceremonies or public acknowledgment that a loss has occurred. Support groups for caregivers *and* children with professionals who understand the core issues can assist in normalizing some of the experiences unique to kin families as they support one another.

## Identity

Kinship care changes family members' roles and relationships to each other. Family members may wonder where they "fit" in the family and may struggle to adapt to the shift in their new role and identity. Grandparents may change their role and relationship with the child they are actively parenting. Are they still a grandparent? Are they a mom/dad? What should the child call them? What if the original parent of the child hears the child refer to their kinship parent as Mom/Dad? Does the extended family support the shift in the role/identity? How does the shift in roles impact the original parent of the child? How does being in two roles—parent and grandparent—impact identity? What kind of family are they? What is a kinship family?

For some kinship families, these identity challenges create emotional landmines that permeate their experiences and relationships with one another. Being able to openly explore these challenges and issues with other kinship families who have gained resiliency and coping strategies allows for both normalizing and mentoring.

## Intimacy

One of the greatest benefits of kinship care is family preservation. However, it is important to not minimize the various losses kinship families experience which may leave individuals feeling rejection, shame, grief, anxiety and anger and can negatively impact their desire and availability for emotional closeness. Family members may decide that it is easier to simply avoid getting too close than to risk being vulnerable and possibly hurt again.

It is typically easier for children to attach to caregivers with whom they have a familial connection or a prior relationship. However, breaks in attachments for children will impact their ability to trust and connect to their caregivers. Birth/first parents, grandparents and other relatives may also be suffering the residual effects of broken attachments, grief, loss, shame and rejection, and may invest very little in creating emotional intimacy with another person. All parties in kinship families may struggle with loyalty conflicts and dual relationships, which can impede intimacy. It is important to note that emotionally intimate relationships and meaningful attachment relationships do not automatically occur in kinship families. These relationships must be based on safety, trust, respect and emotional availability, and need to be built over time.

## Mastery and control

Many grandparents and relatives are raising two, three or even four children, and some are doing it on a modest or fixed income. Kinship care shifts relationships, roles and identifications. It puts individuals on a different life path where they must learn to adapt, navigate obstacles and accomplish various tasks. Many kinship parents receive a crisis call to pick up a relative child or children with little to no preparation or support. This type of "unplanned parenthood" shifts roles and responsibilities quickly, and often drastically. Kinship parents may have gone from having no children to three children in one day, with a home and a life that were ill-equipped for children. They may suddenly find themselves working with social workers, therapists and attorneys and may feel their lives have been turned upside down by something they had no control over. Feelings of helplessness, frustration, anger and resentment are common as they begin to make significant adjustments in their life and adapt to the demands of the court process and the needs of the children.

There are also significant opportunities for growth, change and healing. The steps to mastery include missteps, practice, more missteps, more practice and then increased insight and mastery. Learning to forgive ourselves and others as we fumble through this process allows for healing and growth.

In order to find joy in the present moment and overcome the many troubling memories and challenges that surface, one can use levity and humor. Emotions are contagious; it's easy to "catch" an emotion. One of the most effective tools caregivers can use daily to de-stress their home is to laugh often and frequently. Incorporating playful rituals into the home environment, such as a joke night at the dinner table, all-day pajama day, feelings charades and Tuesday game night, will all help to model and teach healthy coping strategies. Families that learn to de-stress together build in strengthened resources that help to sustain them through times of crisis.

Being around other kinship families decreases the sense of isolation that many kinship caregivers feel. The experience of being a kinship family is unique and includes additional tasks and challenges as well as opportunities. Peer support allows members to share their collective experiences and provide and receive support from others with similar life paths and challenges. Community networks that *welcome* and *celebrate* the unique contributions that kinship caregivers make become a powerful partner in helping to support and sustain kinship families.

# Chapter 15

# The Seven Core Issues and LGBTQ Families

## Abbie Goldberg and Cynthia Roe

The Seven Core Issues of Adoption and Permanency provides a framework to understand the issues that all members of the adoption constellation live with every day. Here, we explore these issues as they manifest in families headed by parents who identify as lesbian, gay, bisexual, transgender or queer (LGBTQ). Additionally, we acknowledge and aim to be inclusive of individuals who define their sexual orientation and/or gender identity in more fluid terms—really, all of us who don't fit neatly into any box that defines who we love and who we are. We are sure to see an increased visibility of gender non-conforming people who are or want to become parents in the future (James *et al.* 2016).

LGBTQ people have been parenting children presumably for as long as there have been parents and children (Goldberg 2010; Lev and Sennott 2013). However, historically, the sexual and gender identities of these individuals have been hidden or disguised as something else. Many families headed by sexually and gender non-conforming parents were formed through kinship care arrangements, some of which were made via formal and legal arrangements, and others via non-formal and non-legally binding agreements. Our hope and goal with this chapter is to bring into the light families that have been hiding in the shadows for far too long. Of course, many readers will say "Isn't it okay, now, to be gay or lesbian and be a parent? Isn't it a thing?" And the answer would be yes…and no. We live in a perilous time for families who don't fit into a heteronormative mold. At the same time that sexual and gender minorities are more visible in society, and are creating and sustaining families in many forms, they face constant challenges to their right to parent—and indeed their right to exist.

Over the past ten years alone, the United States has seen the growth in referenda, laws, policies and both public and underground practices and religious edicts that stigmatize families who dare to publicly come out. LGBTQ couples and families with children cannot go through a single day without at least one news story about some new restriction on adoption, marriage or legal rights that heterosexual cisgender Americans can expect without question (e.g. Politi 2018). Our children are bombarded with each election cycle with anti-gay lawn signs and political ads, as well as highly publicized restrictions on where people can go to the bathroom or go to church. Recently, an award-winning elementary school teacher in Texas was suspended and eventually resigned for sharing with her students that she was going to marry her girlfriend. The decision to suspend this teacher was based on the complaints of one parent. As long as events like this keep occurring, the decision to come out will continue to be okay, but fraught with risk—especially if one works with children.

The risks that LGBTQ people face are shaped by the intersection of their sexual orientation, gender and gender identity. Gay men and transgender women are at high risk for being assaulted just for being out in the world. Lesbian woman are at high risk for economic hardship just because of who they are. The risks that LGBTQ people and especially parents face are impacted significantly by where they live. Being an LGBTQ parent is especially "not okay" if you live in Georgia, Mississippi, Tennessee, Colorado, Kansas, Oklahoma, Michigan, North Dakota, South Dakota, Texas and Virginia. In fact, in 2019, only eight states and the District of Columbia have explicit non-discriminatory laws on the books. If the authors of this chapter—as members of families about which these discriminatory laws are written—want to move, they have to consider the laws of where they will live and their willingness and ability to risk discrimination in housing, education, employment and so on.

This book is focused on the Seven Core Issues of Adoption and Permanency. Whenever we—as professionals working in academia or in direct practice—consider the core issues, we are continually asking ourselves, "How is the world we live in impacting the core issues of the people we serve?" Cynthia Roe is a therapist who has worked with families and individuals of all stripes in a variety of settings. Abbie Goldberg has been doing research with LGBTQ adoptive families for a decade and a half. Thus, we see and interact with families every day who are living the core issues in their daily lives.

For example, when a 13-year-old biracial teen, Leah, adopted at birth by her two Caucasian mothers in suburban Southern California, sees a Proposition 8 advertisement[1] to pass a law that would delegitimize her family in her neighbor's front yard, consider which issues—or what wounds—are being touched, and how:

*Loss:* Loss of control, and loss of a sense of security and belonging.

---

1    Proposition 8 in California amended the state constitution to define marriage as the exclusive right of opposite-sex couples.

*Rejection:* Rejection by Leah's own community, perhaps by her schoolmates, teachers and neighborhood playmates.

*Shame and guilt:* Leah might be asking herself, "What is wrong with me? What can I do differently to make people accept me? I wish I didn't have two moms but wishing so makes me feel guilty because I love them, and I know they love me."

*Grief:* Grief over the loss of her first family and the "what if" fantasy of "What if my birth parents had loved me enough to be able to raise me in a 'normal' family?" "What if I had been adopted by a man and a woman?" "What if I didn't have to feel this pain?"

*Identity:* Leah is likely plagued by the "who am I?" question that every teen asks themselves—but the process of navigating this question is made exponentially more difficult because of the complications of having been adopted *and* adopted by two same-gender parents. Leah likely asks herself: "Am I going to be seen as gay because my parents are? What if I am gay, is it their 'fault'? Am I 'normal'?" Such questions are often pondered by youth with LGBTQ parents, especially in adolescence (Telingator 2013).

*Intimacy:* The rhetoric associated with the Proposition 8 agenda has turned the intimacy that exists between Leah's parents into something "dirty," "unnatural" and "against God's laws." How does this impact Leah's identity development— both in terms of her sexuality as well as her identity as a friend and community member?

*Mastery and control:* This real-world story of "Leah" is that of one of the author's close friends and seems to epitomize the feeling of being out of control in one's world. Leah became increasingly angry, suicidal and self-hating after months of the ads and signs and a growing schism between her family and certain neighbors. Leah's sense of mastery, already tenuous as an adopted person of color in a predominantly white neighborhood—and as an adolescent finding her way in the world, and as a victim of early interpersonal trauma—was blown up. In turn, Leah became increasingly out of control, emotionally and behaviorally, with the advent of Proposition 8 being the demarcation, the before and after for both her and her family members.

For both authors, the issue of living within a family structure that is seen as "non-traditional" is not merely an academic area of study or a focused area of practice. It is our lives. One of us was raised by a mother who for ten years had a same-gender partner. In turn, she had to learn how to negotiate a path through childhood on which she was required to explain or define the unconventional structure of her family every time there was a new situation: new school, new neighbors, camp, graduations or other formally marked transitions, new friends coming to her home to play, and so on. The other of us was raised by a single mom at a time in history when this was a rarity, and grew up to fall in love and eventually marry someone of the same gender. They went on to adopt two sons, both survivors of the foster care system. Looking at our lives through the lens of the Seven Core Issues of Adoption and Permanency, and having the opportunity to write about it, presents an opportunity for us to help other similarly constructed families to normalize their experiences and perhaps make sense of feelings, thoughts and experiences that occur alongside as well as inside a heterocentric society.

While the primary focus of this chapter and the discussion of the seven core issues is on the problems and challenges faced by LGBTQ adoptive families, the discussion would be incomplete if we didn't highlight some of the advantages to being raised in LGBTQ parent families. While working on this chapter, one of us had the privilege of attending a high school graduation for her nephew, the son of her wife's sister—who also happens to be a lesbian. Her son was surrounded by people who love him: his three moms (that is, his biological mother, his biological mother's former partner, and his biological mother's wife), his birth father (a good friend of his birth mother, a gay man who has been as involved in his life as a dad can be), siblings, grandparents, aunts and uncles, cousins, friends and other extended family. Also present was a contingency of friends, among which was one transgender young woman and young people of different ethnicities and backgrounds (and diverse sexualities). It was a gathering that revealed to this author the beautiful and abundant possibilities for acceptance, inclusion, love and growth when we are able to expand the definition of family and kinship. Consistent with this, research shows that children who are raised in LGBTQ parent families can be more accepting of differences and are more able to engage in healthy relationships with all types of people (Goldberg 2010). They may be at an advantage in terms of their ability to compromise and negotiate, and to experience empathy and exercise compassion. Heterosexual parent families can learn something from these families that they can then teach their children—for example, lessons about inclusion, diversity, acceptance and compassion. We believe strongly that these lessons learned have the potential to make the world a happier and safer place.

| | Child | Adult adoptee | First/birth parents |
|---|---|---|---|
| Loss | The child experiences the loss of imagined, fantasized, or idealized heteronuclear family structure that includes a "mom and dad." This is more likely to be an issue among children adopted from foster care who have pre-formed ideas about ideal and "normal" family structures.<br><br>The child may perceive the loss of a same-gender role model and may seek models in teachers, coaches, older peers, media figures and sports figures. Manifestations of loss show up differently at different stages of development, e.g. transitions like graduations, births, significant birthdays, onset of puberty. | For the adolescent and adult adoptee, the absence and loss of a same-gender parent (i.e. a woman for a girl with two dads; a man for a boy with two moms) may be uniquely felt. For example, during puberty and menstruation, and during one's reproductive years, females raised by two dads may acutely feel the loss of a female parental figure. Likewise, a girl raised by two mothers might find that her sense of loss is amplified and intensified when she gets married and there is no "dad" to walk her down the aisle. The birth of a child, especially the first child, may open up a profound sense of loss as well as wonder, as for many adoptees this is the first time they have looked on a face that looks like theirs (or if the child doesn't look like them, the wonder is also tinged with loss: "I thought having a baby would help diminish the sense of loss, but it has in fact made me feel it more deeply"). Additionally, having a biological child gives the adult adoptee an experience that it is likely neither of their parents has had. This can be felt as the loss of shared parental and adult experiences. | Birth parents who choose same-sex parents to parent their children are often drawn to the many positive qualities that these parents possess, including a strong desire to parent, and socio-emotional, financial and educational resources. They may also wish to place their child with a couple whom they view as encountering additional barriers to becoming parents. At the same time, they may experience a sense of loss for their child surrounding not being able to "give" them a father or mother. |

| | | | |
|---|---|---|---|
| **Rejection** | Feelings of rejection by the birth mother may be uniquely felt by children placed with two dads—especially if they have no contact with their birth mother. Likewise, feelings of rejection by birth dads may be uniquely felt by children placed with two moms. This sense of rejection is wrapped up with feelings of loss; that is, feelings of loss of a parent of a particular gender may intensify one's sense of rejection.<br><br>The child may fear or in fact experience rejection by peers, teachers, coaches and others in their life who may reject the "lifestyle" of the child's parents. Additionally, the child may anticipate rejection by peers because their family doesn't "look like" the families of peers. | The adolescent in an adoptive family headed by same-gender parents may actively reject their adoptive parents because they are LGBTQ. As the adolescent struggles to establish their own identity (including their sexual identity), they may decide that the only way to do that is to reject the identity of their parents.<br><br>The adolescent may also experience (or anticipate) the rejection of peers and adults in their life because of the fact that they have LGBTQ parents. The adolescent may behave in ways that keep others at a distance in order to avoid rejection or that pull others close into co-dependent/enmeshed relationships (also to avoid rejection).<br><br>The adolescent may fear rejection by their birth family because of the structure of their family. The youth may reject their adoptive family in favor of their birth family because "at least they are normal." | The birth family may feel rejected and concurrently judged by their child's adoptive family because of the consequences of their sexual behavior/choices. Conversely, the birth family may reject the child's adoptive family because of their LGBTQ status.<br><br>Birth parents may experience self-rejection for not being able to provide their children with a "normal" family, feeling as if their children were placed with an LGBTQ family because that was the only type of family that would accept them. For some, it might feel like a "third choice" (behind kin and heterosexual cisgender parents). |
| **Shame/Guilt** | Internalization of idealized versions of family life (i.e. in society and the media) may lead children to feel that their families are inadequate, which may exacerbate feelings of shame and guilt. Such feelings may then be magnified by guilt over not appreciating, or being grateful for, their adoptive parents "enough."<br><br>The adopted child may feel that they are the "second or third choice" because their parents couldn't conceive, therefore "settling" on adoption. "There is something wrong with me, so I was placed with a family there is something wrong with." | Feelings of shame/guilt over not appreciating their adoptive parents (and wishing for a mom or dad) may be accentuated in adolescence and adulthood as adoptees become more cognitively and emotionally mature. If the adopted person already has an internalized concept of themselves as flawed, this sense of "something is wrong with me" grows as the individual gets older and is reminded intermittently that they didn't really have a "normal" childhood and don't have a "normal" family. | Birth parents who place their children with same-sex parents may at some point experience regret, shame or guilt around their decision—or at least wonder if they did the right thing. Although such concerns may be rare overall, they may be activated during periods of significant societal debate and unrest surrounding the rights of sexual minorities, or when reading or learning about events that involve the persecution of sexual minorities. They may feel as if they have placed their child into a "double jeopardy" situation by placing on them the perceived stigmas of having been adopted and then being adopted by gender non-conforming parents. |

*cont.*

| | Child | Adult adoptee | First/birth parents |
|---|---|---|---|
| Grief | The ability to grieve for one's losses may be compromised by the added sense of growing up under a microscope, whereby adoptees feel pressure to "do good" as children of same-sex parents, so as not to reify negative stereotypes about LGBTQ parenting. The adopted child may feel that it is not okay to be sad about not having a family that looks like the families of their peers. This repressed grief may show up as perceived ingratitude, emotional and behavioral problems, substance use and other issues. These types of challenges may continue into adulthood, as expression of any feeling becomes difficult and, in some cases, threatening. | Along with the typical feelings of grief experienced by adult adoptees, the adult child of sexual and gender minority parents may feel a heightened sense of sadness, especially for individuals acutely aware of societal scrutiny surrounding their families (especially if they live in less progressive/more conservative areas). The birth of biological children may intensify this grief as the adult adoptee may feel the absence of a same-gender parent to guide them through the childbirth experience (this can be true for both men and women). | For birth parents, the sense of loss and grief never really ends. Throughout the life cycle, birth parents think of their biological children as both the children/babies they remember and the adults they are becoming over time. Each life transition brings new ways of grieving. In situations where the birth parents are aware that the child has been placed with a gender minority family, there may be a heightened sense of grief. The birth parents' desire for their children to have a "normal" life may be held up to the perceived (or feared) marginalization of their children because of the double stigma of having been adopted into a sexual or gender minority family. |
| Identity | Not "looking like" the typical family may create challenges related to identity and finding one's place in the world—particularly when an adoptee with two dads or two moms does not know any children with a similar family structure. Not having a same-gender parent as a role model may also create certain challenges in terms of identity, identification and forming a sense of oneself as a gendered and sexual being—particularly if they have few close relationships with same-gender adults (e.g. grandparents, aunts, uncles, birth parents). | The adult adoptee may experience different developmental stages of identity as they integrate their understanding of who they are as adoptee and who they are as someone who has been raised in an LGBTQ family. The young adult may struggle with the understanding that they may be "watched" by others to see if they "turned out" to be gay or gender non-conforming. They may feel pressure to "prove" that they are "normal" (regardless of their actual sexual orientation or gender identity) "in spite of" or even "because of" the fact that they were raised in an LGBTQ family. As the adult adoptee gets older and engages in intimate sexual relationships and begins to create their own family, the struggle may be with how to define the family from which they come to a potential partner's family, to their children's friends and their families and to the community at large. In essence, the adult adoptee may feel that they need to "come out" on a regular basis, that the job of revealing their family to others is never really done. | The birth parents' struggles related to the issue of identity are ongoing and may at times be related to the fact that their biological children were placed with and adopted into an LGBTQ family, and at times may be unrelated to that fact. In the case of a birth mother whose child was placed with and adopted by a male couple, she may feel that she retains her identity as the mother. In the case of a birth mother whose children have been placed with and adopted by a female couple, there may be an added struggle in terms of defining her role as one of three mothers and she may hold on tighter to her identity as the "real mother." Conversely, the birth father may struggle with these same issues, particularly in the context of defining his role amid a two-dad family. |

| | | | |
|---|---|---|---|
| **Intimacy** | Intimacy challenges may arise as children enter the teenage years and enter into intimate or romantic relationships. They may be acutely aware that heterosexual relationships and couplings are idealized and normalized in society. This, in the context of their own parents' same-sex relationship, may cause heightened sensitivity or anxiety surrounding their own same-sex crushes. Indeed, at the same time that such attractions may be normalized in their households, children and adolescents may worry about outsiders' assumptions about the "influence" of their parents on their own emerging sexuality, causing intensified feelings of shame and guilt (see above). | The adult adoptee with same-gender or gender non-conforming parents may struggle with honesty and transparency in intimate relationships. Out of a fear of rejection, there may be hesitance or fear on the part of the adult adoptee to reveal the truth about their family, thereby setting up a pattern of emotional dishonesty or inauthenticity in developing relationships. This dishonesty can carry over into sexually intimate relationships. The adult adoptee may pull away from parents and/or extended family, impacting the quality of parent–child intimacy. Unfortunately, the potential for the adult adoptee to set up rigid boundaries between their intimate partners and LGBTQ parents can carry over into the next generation where connections between grandparents and grandchildren are negatively impacted. | The loss of a child to adoption, whether it be "voluntary" or through court action, always impacts birth/first parents' ability to experience genuine intimacy. When sex, whether it be by choice or an act of coercion or violence, results in an unplanned pregnancy and loss of the child, heterosexual intimate relationships can become forever linked with pain and loss. The birth parent may believe that they are protecting their children from this kind of pain and loss by placing their children with same-gender parents. Birth mothers may choose lesbian parents for their children to protect them from the same kind of loss and pain they experienced in the context of relationships with men. |
| **Mastery/Control** | For the adopted child, there can be an overwhelming feeling of not having control over the circumstances of their lives. They didn't get to choose whether they were adopted, and they didn't have a say in the family into which they were placed. As children get older, this feeling of not having a choice about their family can manifest in anger over not being able to choose to live with a "normal" family. They may also fear that having gay parents will make them either be gay or be perceived/labeled as gay. This is also something over which they may feel a loss of control. | Some of the issues faced by the child adoptee carry over into adulthood. The adult adoptee may exercise control by protecting their family and themselves by limiting access from outside forces (people, institutions, ideas). A sense of fatalism may develop, with the adult adoptee telling themselves, "Why bother, because everything is out of my control anyway." This can show up as passivity and even recklessness. | The birth parent experiences a profound sense of loss of control, while at the same time being given messages that they are "choosing" adoption for their child. When a child is placed with a gender non-conforming family, this sense of having no choice may be exacerbated with the birth parent being left with the feeling "I couldn't even find a 'normal' family for my child." |

*cont.*

| | Extended birth family | Adoptive parents | Extended adoptive family |
|---|---|---|---|
| **Loss** | The extended birth family may experience loss surrounding the absence of a heteronuclear family structure; the loss of a grandchild, niece or nephew may be intensified if they feel the birth parents made the "wrong choice" by placing the child with two moms or two dads. | Lesbian or gay parents may experience loss associated with the fact that they cannot have a child with both parents' genetic material. This awareness may be accompanied by loss associated with unsuccessful insemination attempts (among female couples) or frustrated attempts or desires to pursue surrogacy (among female and more often male couples). | The adoptive family—and specifically the parents of the adoptive parents—may feel an additional sense of loss as they may have grieved the loss of a heterosexual child, and now they experience the loss or the imagined loss of a biological grandchild. |
| **Rejection** | The extended birth family may feel rejected and betrayed by God, especially if they are against LGBTQ parenting. They may reject the child because they are in an LGBTQ family. The extended family (especially grandparents) may also fear rejection, not only based on the fact that their children lost or relinquished their grandchildren but also due to the differences in economic and cultural circumstances that are often present when children are placed into LGBTQ families. | Lesbian or gay parents may experience a sense of intense rejection by adoption agencies (who are less likely to work with them as LGBTQ prospective parents) as well as birth parents (who are less likely to choose them as the parents of their children). This may be particularly intense among two-mother families, who are often told that they can expect the "longest waits" for a child. LGBTQ families may also feel rejection by other members of the adoption community, many of whom adopt as a religious calling and may be opposed to LGBTQ parenting. | The extended adoptive family may also experience or fear rejection because their children/siblings are LGBTQ and are now welcoming children into a life they fear will be difficult for their siblings, children and grandchildren. The extended adoptive family may have rejected their children because of their sexuality or gender identity, and experience conflicted feelings about their adopted grandchildren. For some adoptive grandparents, the arrival of children may make it easier for them to embrace and accept their LGBTQ adult children. |
| **Shame/Guilt** | The extended birth family may experience shame or guilt around the child being placed with two moms or two dads and may wonder if they should have "stepped up" to parent the child—especially if they are anti-LGBTQ parenting. | The adoptive parents may internalize societal notions of the "shortcomings" of LGBTQ parents, whereby they feel guilty about depriving their child of a mother or father, or possibly exposing them to additional stigma. They may wonder how their family structure will affect their adopted child's sense of self or identity, perhaps especially if they are different in other ways/facing multiple stigmas (e.g. due to race). This feeling of shame may push the family to present themselves as functioning better than they actually are, to appear to be the "ideal" family and to ignore or minimize normal family challenges. | The extended adoptive family may experience shame around the fact that their LGBTQ child/brother/sister is now a parent; this may bring greater visibility to their sexuality among extended family members, who may not be ready to be "outed" as the parent or sibling of an LGBTQ person. They may be struggling with long-term internalized shame over having given birth to an LGBTQ child: "This is our fault, and now our child wants to be a parent/is a parent, and if those children suffer it will be our fault as well." |

| | | | |
|---|---|---|---|
| **Grief** | If there has been rejection from either end of the adoption equation, there may be grief over not being able to be engaged as grandparents, aunts, uncles and so on. Because of a perceived or actual aversion to LGBTQ individuals, there is a sense of grief over the loss of relationship or the possibility of relationship. | May experience a "blockage" of any grief related to not having a biogenetically related child, insomuch as, as LGBTQ parents, they may internalize the notion that they should "just be happy" to be parents. That is, they do not have the "right" to grieve the loss of a biogenetically related child since they are not heterosexual. | The extended adoptive family, particularly grandparents, may experience grief over the loss of genetic progeny because their children are LGBTQ. They are reminded again of this loss with the arrival of adopted children. |
| **Identity** | As in any situation where biological children are lost to adoption, birth family members struggle with how to identify themselves and may hold fast to their identity as the "real" family of the children. This may be further rigidified by a child's adoption into an LGBTQ family if the birth family does not think of the gender-variant family as a valid representation of family. | LGBTQ parents may struggle with entitlement—the "right" to be parents. They may struggle with not feeling like "real" parents, and with not "belonging" or "looking like" a "normal" family. | Feeling like a "real" grandparent, for example, may be challenging for some parents of LGBTQ parents, especially if they currently or in the past rejected their LGBTQ child or distanced themselves from them or their sexuality. |
| **Intimacy** | As with other members of the adoption constellation and regardless of the adoptive parents' sexual or gender identities or relationship structure, the birth parents experience intimacy challenges. If the child's adoption has been kept a secret, then the ability to be honest and authentic in relationships in general is impacted. | LGBTQ parents may find adolescence a difficult time, if and when a different gender child is experiencing physical and sexual development in ways that they have difficulty relating to. They may also find it uncomfortable to have discussions with their children about sexuality because their children might ask questions about their sexual lives. | There may be members of the extended adoptive family who are more accepting of the fact of their kin's gender identity/sexuality and are therefore more accepting of their adoptive family. This may set up a conflict with other family members that shows up in relationship and family intimacy challenges. |
| **Mastery/Control** | As with other members of the adoption constellation and regardless of the adoptive parents' sexual or gender identities or relationship structure, the birth family experiences a loss of mastery and control. When the children are placed with an LGBTQ family, this feeling may be intensified. | Additional pressures to be "perfect" parents may create challenges in parenting for LGBTQ parenting. Parents may be "holding on" so tightly that challenges are ignored or minimized to the degree that they intensify and can become larger problems. | As with other members of the adoption constellation and regardless of the adoptive parents' sexual or gender identities or relationship structure, the extended adoptive family experiences a loss of mastery and control. When the LGBTQ children adopt, these feelings may be intensified. |

◉ Chapter 16 ◉

# The Seven Core Issues as Seen through the Eyes of the Latino Family

## Dee Dee Mascareñas

What is family? What is family if you are a Latino? First, you must ask yourself, what is a Latino? If you have worked with anyone from a Latin American- or Spanish-speaking country, you will have already run across this question. Depending on who you are speaking to, you will get a variety of answers. If you are speaking to a third- or fourth-generation Mexican-American, they may define themselves as Mexican, or Mexican-American or Chicano. If you are speaking to a first-generation Mexican, they may see themselves as Mexican, or as Hispanic or Latino. If you are speaking to an immigrant from Cuba or Venezuela or Costa Rica, they may say they are Costa Ricans or Latinos, or Hispanic. A Puerto Rican may say they are a Puerto Rican or they may simply say they are an American. Still others prefer to refer to the region they come from in their country of origin. In truth, all Latinos from North or South America are Americans. The United States has usurped that term as if they are the only Americans that exist in this hemisphere.

Some Latinos are bilingual or trilingual; some are monolingual, which also greatly impacts their sense of identity. Some terms are political, some terms are cultural, some terms are racial. Even within the Latino community, there is prejudice or bias, and while we may all speak Spanish, the dialect has been changed from country to country and region to region. I would simply say, ask the audience you are speaking to about how they prefer to be identified. For the purposes of this chapter, and as a personal preference, I will use the term Latino.

With regard to the Latino family in adoption, I am speaking not only of couples or individuals who are of Latino descent who decide to adopt a child, but also of the Latino family that decides to adopt the child of a family member, that is, a grandparent adopting a grandchild, or a sibling adopting a niece or nephew.

Latinos are the fastest-growing population of immigrants in the United States. The US Census Bureau estimates that roughly one in three Americans will be Latino in the year 2020. Latinos have a long-standing practice of having large families and of being family or group centric—a term known as "familialism." As in many agricultural societies, large families, including the extended family, created a large workforce necessary for survival. An agricultural family did not go hungry. Another significant influence was the Catholic Church, which subscribed to the philosophy of "bearing fruit." Depending on how assimilated Latinos have become to the majority culture, the Latino experience of the seven core issues is colored by this history.

For a Latino, family is not *only* the nuclear family as in the United States, but also includes extended family, such as grandparents, uncles and aunts, cousins, and often those who are not related to us by blood but whom we have in essence "adopted" into our fold. Adoption, therefore, is not a term foreign to the Latino family; however, adoption has predominantly been informal. It was not uncommon for a child to be brought up by a grandparent, when parents were forced to work outside the home for long hours or even to emigrate in order to better their family's life circumstance. Other family members would readily step in to nurture and care for a child. In the United States, however, there has been a push to make these informal adoptions formal so they can access a number of available resources. It has also become strikingly apparent that children benefited from the stability of knowing that they had a "forever family."

Kin adoptions are common in the Latino community. There is a sense of trepidation that if a child is adopted by someone other than their blood relations, these other parents will not be as loving, kind or caring as a family member. Often, the anxiety or concern is so great that even when grandparents seem unable to care for their grandchildren because of health or financial challenges, they still do so. It is also important to note that many of these grandparents still hold fast to traditional Latino values and the women see their worth or importance only as a parent—even more than a wife. The individual is almost non-existent as the group or family-oriented focus is paramount in Spanish-speaking countries.

Conceptually, we also must consider how the Latino family will be impacted by the core issues. The further away they are from their country of origin, whether they are the first generation to arrive, the second or the third, impacts their experience of the world, themselves, others, their ideas of family, ways of communicating, education, intimacy, self-worth, and the expression of emotions. Even a family who may be third- or fourth-generation immigrants may exhibit steadfastness to ideas promoted by their grandparents or great-grandparents in some areas of their lives as these ideas or concepts have been promulgated, endorsed or disseminated throughout the family in a myriad of different ways through foods, sayings and traditions. Their adherence to some of these traditions or ways of looking at the world is often unconscious, despite their level of assimilation to the larger culture in other aspects or areas of their lives.

*First generation:* Refers to the individual who was born and lived for a time or was raised to maturity in a Latin American country.

*Second generation:* Refers to the children of those individuals. They themselves have been born and raised in the United States and have been exposed to more of the normative values and culture but have also been raised by parents who hold fast to their own country of origin's language, values and mores. These children struggle more than their predecessors with the process as they try to negotiate two cultures. Learning to create an internal and external balance between two cultures—the one they live with at home and the one they live with in the larger world—can be challenging. Most, but not all, speak Spanish and many, but not all, have visited their country of origin.

*Third, fourth and later generations:* Refers to the children of the children of immigrants. They are further removed from the original country of origin. Many of them do not speak Spanish and know only some of the cultural ideals and traditions that have become a part of the tapestry of their lives.

## Seven core issues

### Loss

If the child is placed in a family that is not theirs by birth, then they have lost connection with their birth/first family and the history, customs and traditions of that first family. If they are placed in a Latino family, it helps to circumvent some of this loss, yet there is still a loss in not having day-to-day contact with their first family. If they are adopted by a relative, then they have that sense of connection; however, if they are not involved in an ongoing relationship with the members of the other parent's family, then they still experience the loss of half of their DNA information—their history, traditions, customs and connections. If the child speaks Spanish and is placed with a family that does not speak the language, the child has lost significant access, on a deep level, to their heritage. If the adoptive family does not speak Spanish, then it is imperative for them to be committed to living their lives surrounded by friends, colleagues and other individuals of Latino descent who can serve as positive role models, mentors, teachers and preservers of language for the child—the whole family benefits.

As is customary in the Latino culture, a woman tends to see her value and worth as someone's wife and mother and therefore no sacrifice is too great. Any losses a woman may experience often go unacknowledged and unaddressed. It is not surprising, therefore, that they are repeatedly caught unawares as to how to handle the losses their children have over the years and subsequently do not know how to acknowledge or address these issues or concerns for themselves or the child/ren.

Adoptive parents may also lose face in their own family because they did not give birth to their "own" biological child or, if they were able to conceive initially, were not able to conceive a second or third child, so they opted to adopt. Giving birth to children, especially for women in the Latino culture, is tantamount to an edict. Adoption therefore is seen as "second best." Adoptive parents may lose the support of family or friends who do not agree with or understand adoption as being a legitimate way to create a family.

For the Latino birth/first parents, the inability to acknowledge their own losses and the accompanying feelings leaves them in an ongoing state of distress. They are also often unacknowledged by the Latino community as well as the overall culture because they are seen as having caused the damage or loss to the child and are at times treated like outcasts.

## Rejection

All children experience rejection when they become separated from their birth/first family, no matter the reasons. Some exhibit those feelings through anger, not trusting others out of fear of anticipated rejection. Other children, in order to fend off the fear of rejection, will become compliant and work to look "perfect" or be "good," believing that they can control whether the parent loves or claims them because of their exemplary behavior. This kind of exemplary behavior is greatly applauded in the Latino culture. A child is expected to be compliant; a child should not create a scene or problems or bring unnecessary attention to the family. The result is that the child's hidden fears and worries go unaddressed or unacknowledged. The Latino culture's tendency towards cooperation and familialism, as opposed to acknowledgment of the individual, creates innumerable difficulties.

Further, the child can use any cultural differences as a way to distance themselves from or reject the adoptive parent. In some cases, they may actually reject their own culture because they think in absolute terms. So, the adoptive parents and their culture can be seen as "good," as opposed to their biological parents and their culture, who may be seen as "bad," and can become yet another impediment to self-acceptance. A young teen I was working with was adopted by a Caucasian family and brought to the United States from a Latin American country at a young age from an impoverished situation. The adoptive family was prosperous and exposed the child to many things that he had never or might never have experienced in his country of origin. This caused in him a profound struggle, where he began to reject his culture and deny his Latino identity in favor of the Caucasian identity. This was a difficult task at best, but more so because physically there was no denying his heritage. His parents, lacking a deep appreciation for this dilemma, left this need unaddressed and he remains in a constant state of distress.

For the Latino adoptive parent who is adopting a child because of infertility, especially for those who are first- or second-generation immigrants, they see their bodies as defective and themselves as being tainted or unworthy. This is especially true for the Latino woman who is essentially taught that their value and worth comes from being a mother. The focus is not even on the relationship with their partner, in that they are someone's wife, but more so that they are someone's mother.

The biological parent may also struggle with self-rejection, rejection by their own family and rejection from a culture that says, "You are a bad person if you abandon your child." As noted above, Latinos who have no children are somehow seen as incomplete.

## Shame and guilt

Some of the children I have worked with struggle to deal with thoughts and feelings that they are bad and that there is something wrong with them. To deal with their discomfort, they may accept the "wrongness" in them and even amplify it: "If I'm bad, then I will act badly. I can't help myself." They see themselves as weird, alien or different and embrace those differences by glorifying them or associating with others whom they perceive as different as well. They become a part of the "outsiders" club rather than being alone. The child is left feeling at fault and is not comforted or soothed, nor are their thoughts or feelings validated. Instead, they are once again abandoned, albeit on an emotional level. This is the classic "blame the victim." In the case of Latino families, because they do not often understand the dynamics of abuse, there is often a direct or indirect message that somehow the child created the situation. For instance, if the child were sexually abused, the parents might think that it was what the child was wearing, or that the child should not have gone over to that person's house, or that the child should not have accepted anything from that person. This puts the onus of the abuse on the child and not the perpetrator. This is a parenting style that utilizes guilt and shame to control the child.

Shame and fear in the Latino community is an acceptable means of controlling or parenting a child. For a time, I worked with a Latino family (first-generation immigrants) who struggled to address the extreme anxiety their daughter was experiencing. Their parenting style was guided more by their sense of embarrassment and frustration than their ability to understand their child's fear and effectively calm and soothe her. Instead, they begged, cajoled and shamed their child into appropriate behavior. This is a traditional parenting style for many Latinos and creates even more complications for the child in that they are left emotionally unattended by this form of parental intervention. It leaves the child feeling unsafe in the world, as their parents are perceived as weak and easily manipulated by their child's inappropriate behaviors. In short, all parties are left frustrated, often exhausted, resentful and at times fearful.

For the biological parent, they too struggle with guilt and shame about the choices they made. As Latinos, they are overwhelmed with cultural shame and guilt as well. In addition, many Latinos follow the doctrines of the Catholic Church that also often focus on shame. The sinner is shamed, the sinner must repent, and the sinner must be redeemed. Consequently, the biological parents carry enormous guilt and shame about their lives, their behaviors, thoughts and feelings, and their inability to be a positive influence in their child's life. They are often placed in a double-bind—they feel guilt because they chose or were forced to relinquish their child, and they feel guilt or shame if they do not relinquish their child when they know they are incapable of parenting them. Even if later the biological parents are able to change their lives, they are riddled with so much guilt and shame that they do not make overtures towards their children or are unable to maintain healthy connections with those children.

The biological parent in the Latino community is seen in a negative light. Interestingly enough, Latino males are often treated better than their female counterparts. That is to say, if they cannot care for their children, their parents often take responsibility for the child. If the father does not participate in the life of his child, he is somehow seen as exempt from that responsibility. Whereas for the Latino woman, more is asked of her, even if her parents intervene and help, and there is a higher level of expectation that she will participate in her child's life. Women in the Latino community are taught from an early age that they are here to serve. Their value and worth comes from their ability to be a "good" mother. Men are not held to the same standard. Because of these cultural beliefs, another layer of guilt and shame may be heaped on a biological mother.

## Grief

Latinos are not readily given permission to grieve. Often, the period of grieving is either cut short or unacknowledged. Some might consider a child's outward expression of grief, sadness or angst as "wallowing" instead of a natural response to a painful or difficult life circumstance. Often in the Latino family, they are not permitted to express emotions that are considered negative or they may not or do not allow themselves the time to experience these feelings because of life's obligations or challenges. For many, these daily responsibilities become a welcome escape from thinking or feeling and it is an acceptable way to rationalize their behavior.

In the Latino community, expression of certain emotions or self-analysis is discouraged or perceived as lacking in value or being a waste of time. Why focus on feelings and thoughts that will only take you into further pain or discomfort when you can be doing something productive? There is a sense of inevitability about life, as illustrated by a common saying, "Si Dios lo quiere," or, "If God wills it so, then it will be." The underlying idea is that we have no power over life, and complaining about it serves us no good. The idea of being proactive rather than reactive is foreign in many Latino homes. Whether the family is educated or uneducated, this can still be an influencing concept.

The biological parent may still struggle with issues of grief and loss, but as Latinos, they may have learned to sublimate or dismiss these feelings and consequently developed unhealthy or inappropriate behaviors to address these feelings. The culture does not legitimize their feelings and they have few resources to soothe their spirits and create productive and fulfilling lives.

The adopted child is grieving the loss of living and growing up with their biological parents on a daily basis, even if they are being parented by a relative. There is a smell in the air, a physical energy, a sound that accompanies life as a Latino that one cannot easily manufacture, especially if one has never been exposed to it. There is a comfort in sharing these connections with others, a sort of shorthand. Latinos are traditionally helpful, accommodating, attentive and obliging, and this permeates their everyday life experience with the world. For others, it can be perceived as passive or subservient. At times, it can be experienced as quite positive and comforting to see oneself as part of a community, a whole and not so much as an individual.

In the case of language, the child who was exposed to Spanish in their formative years not only speaks Spanish consciously, but also unconsciously. Their emotional life lives in their initial language of origin—even as they grow older and learn to become fluent in English, there is still a strong identification with Spanish on a subconscious level, and if adopted by non-Latinos or non-

Spanish speakers, another loss occurs for the child. During a period when a therapist I was consulting asked to do some hypnosis work with me, I was surprised that she proceeded with the session in Spanish. At the end of the session, I asked her why she had done so, and she said to me, "For the first five years of your life you only spoke Spanish."

One family I worked with who had adopted a child from a Spanish-speaking country believed that their child (adopted at age 9 and who was now 13) was fluent in English and did not need to have a bilingual therapist. A child who struggles with grieving can also readily hide that grief if they are not with a therapist fluent in Spanish or who understands the Latino culture.

## Identity

If a child is adopted by a family of a different culture or race, they must face the profound question of identity without assistance, especially if their adoptive parents are not culturally or racially aware or live their lives in a multi-cultural manner with regard to friendships, food, music and customs. One Latino child I worked with had been doing fairly well in her adoptive home until she turned 15. She became sullen, depressed and often combative. She had asked her Caucasian parents if she was going to have a quinceñiera[1] for her upcoming birthday like many of her classmates at school. Because this was not their tradition, the parents said that she would have a big sweet 16 party. This crushed her. The parents did not fully understand the importance of this event in the life of a girl of Latino heritage. It marks her introduction into adulthood. She is now considered a young woman, and, next to her wedding, it is one of the most important days in her life. This can be experienced as yet another loss for the adopted Latino female child.

Latino adoptive parents experience infertility as a major identity shift within their cultural context since their children by adoption may not be seen as their "real" children. If the family adopted Latino children, the fact of the adoption may be hidden so they never get asked questions, which allows them to avoid disclosing that they are an adoptive parent and hide a significant part of their identity. In the process of hiding their true identity, the children they adopted may be given a false identity as stories are conjured to avoid the truth.

The birth/first parents who were parents to a child are now not parents to that child. Whether they parent other children or not, they remain people who have lost a child they brought into the world. In a culture that shames that

---

1    A celebration of a girl's 15th birthday, marking her passage from girlhood to womanhood.

experience, the biological parents are forced to hide an important part of who they are.

## Intimacy

Intimacy can be greatly impacted by the tendency in the Latino culture towards co-dependency in their intimate relationships. Latinos focus on the highly prized value of "familialism," so the individual is de-emphasized and not as esteemed as the whole or the group. The child's judgment is clouded as a result of their early childhood experiences as well as this cultural edict as they seek not only a healthy self-image, but also to develop deeply profound connections to others. They will either hold themselves apart from the "love object," forcing them to "prove" their love time and time again, or they will acquiesce to every want and need of their "love object" with the hope that if they are able to please them, they will be loved and never abandoned. As there is a strong tendency toward co-dependence, often Latinos see the expression of their needs, wants, thoughts or feelings as hurtful, ungrateful, undeserving, judgmental or selfish. Instead of moving towards intimacy, this moves them away from it, because of emotional shutdown or self-loathing. Intimacy is often seen as merely being sexual, and the emotional component is all but ignored, and is sublimated into self-effacing behaviors, addictions or other emotionally or physically harmful behaviors and interactions with others.

Intimacy issues can arise in the parents' relationship to their child, their relationship with each other, or their ability to form new intimate relationships with others, because the Latino culture does not typically value the "relationship." This is also true with regard to friendships. In the Latino culture, outside friendships are not encouraged. Your family is your source of friendship. I often hear mothers telling their children, "I am your best friend." This should not be the case because a parent must take on the role of guiding, directing and correcting as well as comforting, consoling and assuming full responsibility for the child in all aspects of their development. This is different from the parameters that typically define a friendship.

The biological parent may not be able to develop loving and lasting relationships with others if they are not able to resolve the loss they have experienced. Often they continue to have unhealthy relationships and may become pregnant time and again with the hopes of being able to keep and parent one of their children. If they are not afforded assistance in addressing their intimacy issues, they will continue to look for connection and esteem from people or situations that continue to leave them plagued with feelings of unworthiness. As friendships are built within the family and community, the biological parents, who feel shamed or rejected from that family system and community for losing a child, may struggle to gain the necessary support to heal. If the child is placed in a non-Latino adoptive family who offer openness in the adoption and extend their hand in friendship, the Latino biological parents may not have the experience, skills or mindset to embrace this opportunity for connection.

## Mastery and control

The adoptive parent who struggled with infertility may feel inadequate because they could not master the act of procreation, which is highly valued as a Latino. When they enter the adoption process and are faced with the myriad of requirements and components involved, they can often feel angry, resentful, confused, unsure, out of control and inadequate. If they do not have effective ways to address these stressors, they can often adopt unhealthy ways that only serve to exacerbate the experience. Their child will need their assistance as these are similar feelings to those that they will be experiencing in their own lives.

The adoptive parent may also become engrossed in having control in the family, seeing their role as parent from a more authoritarian perspective and also seeking legitimacy. So when the child appears to be argumentative or antagonistic, they see it as a personal affront rather than a cry for help. In the Latino community, the parent is meant to be the ultimate authority. Children are to be seen and not heard. Children must be obedient, devoted and grateful to their parents. The kind of devotion the Latino parent requires is often rooted in shame and guilt and only serves to further erode the adopted child's positive sense of self, albeit unintentionally. The child's initial foray into feelings of safety and trust was acutely negatively impacted when their world began with a sense of rejection by their biological parent. The child believes that they can only trust themselves, as inept as they are as children, so they struggle with letting go of control. This is particularly difficult for the parentified child—the one who may have cared for their siblings when their biological parents were unable to or incapable of doing so. This child may believe that their job, title or position in the family, or even in life, is being usurped by the adoptive parent. They must relinquish this need to be in charge in order to receive what they so desperately need and want—to be safe and to be loved and cared for. If they are able to do so, the child will learn to let go of their deeply rooted need to manipulate, influence or otherwise dominate situations or people.

The kin adoptive parent in the Latino community deals with issues of mastery and control from a more submissive or passive-aggressive stance. They will try to cajole or bribe their child into acceptable behavior and entirely miss the dilemma the child is attempting to address. Latinos are not naturally taught to assert themselves; they are taught, usually by modeling, to obtain what they want by self-sacrifice, over-indulgence, manipulation or passive-aggressive behavior because the individual and their needs, wants and feelings are not respected in comparison with those of the group. Often these parents are unable to adequately address their child's needs because they themselves have not successfully dealt with this developmental task. Surprisingly, I have seen many adoptive grandparents in the Latino community learn to become more assertive and proactive because they are fighting for the rights or safety of their grandchildren, but there are still many who struggle to grasp and develop these abilities in themselves and therefore in their children.

The biological parent, often riddled with guilt and shame, will also wrestle with the issue of mastery and control. This is why many of them continue to have children and believe they will be able to parent them without any change in their lives, resources or in their own psyche. They may become combative with their families, with others, with the court system and even, at times, with their own child. This is because of their personal struggles with self-worth, identity, intimacy, loss and control. They will often struggle with family, friends and strangers because of their need to gain some semblance of control and will fail to self-actualize because they are in a state of survival versus thriving.

The Seven Core Issues in Adoption and Permanency, when acknowledged and addressed within the context of the Latino culture and community, offer a path to mastery through which the benefits and gains of adoption can be realized by all members of the constellation.

# Chapter 17

# The Seven Core Issues and the African American Family

## Lynne White Dixon

When writing about any specific racial/cultural group, one must remember that no group is a monolith and that within the group there is significant diversity. An African American individual's experience with the Seven Core Issues in Adoption and Permanency may often be influenced by the intersectionality of socio-economic status, education level, region of the country they may live in, personal family experiences and their individual experiences with racism and prejudice in America. Being raised and living in a country where your racial group has a long history of being targeted and marginalized by the majority population and the systems they developed impacts an individual's life experience. Entering the world of adoption is one of those life experiences.

|  | Child | Adult adoptee | First/birth parents |
|---|---|---|---|
| Loss | An older child who spent time with the biological family prior to adoption will experience loss of familiar cultural/class differences in terms of socio-economic status, educational values and so on. The child may see the new family as "acting white" and feel very uncomfortable with the new environment or lifestyle. If there is significant difference in skin tone and hair texture, the child experiences the loss of looking like their parents. | This may be the first time the adult realizes losses generated from adoption, especially if the adoptive family saw being adopted as "the same" as being born into the family. Depending on the messaging from the adoptive family about "who is family," this can deny feelings of loss and minimize the need to address these feelings. | The birth parents' feelings of loss may be minimized if it is a planned placement and they see new parents as a "step-up" (economically and educationally) from themselves and their family. If they feel that a biased and racist system "took" their child from them, this may minimize their feelings of loss and cause them to focus on anger. |

*cont.*

|  | Child | Adult adoptee | First/birth parents |
|---|---|---|---|
| Rejection | If their physical appearance differs greatly from the adoptive family (skin tone and hair texture), the child may experience feelings of being rejected, or "not the same." This overt difference is a consistent reminder to the child that they are not "blood" related, which can make them sensitive to feeling or fearing rejection. | Unhealed experiences with rejection in childhood due to looking different from the adoptive family or messages of not being blood relatives may result in the adopted adults distancing themselves (emotionally and physically) from the adoptive family. They may search for the first/birth family and over-compensate for feelings of rejection by having poor boundaries with the newly met birth family. | Fear of rejection by the extended family or community because the birth parent "let the system take their child" may motivate the birth parent to "fight the system," not focus on the child's needs and perhaps miss an opportunity to mitigate loss to the child and themselves. |
| Shame/Guilt | The child may feel shame if they look very different from their adoptive family in skin tone and hair texture (especially if female). Negative messages by the majority media/community regarding black females bombard all African American girls. If the adopted child doesn't look like the females in her family, these messages can be harder to combat and can exacerbate common shame issues for adopted children. | Given the "collective community" feelings and values present in African American individuals, the adopted adult may feel guilt that they had a "privileged" life compared to other African American children who were in foster care or came from the same socio-economic status as their birth families. If the adult is in reunion with their own first/birth family, these feelings of guilt can be exacerbated by this contact if birth family members have had challenges that the adopted adult did not due to their being adopted out of the family. | Many African American birth parents whose children are in the foster care system have a history of intergenerational trauma and poverty. These experiences create feelings of shame, which are then further exacerbated by the removal of the child and subsequent adoption placement. Feelings of shame and guilt, impacted by early history, can prevent the birth parent from engaging in a relinquishment. |

| | | | |
|---|---|---|---|
| Grief | If the child sees adoption as being better for them (out of traumatic experiences, more resources, etc.), then they may deny losses and need to grieve the circumstances of their adoption. They may become "stuck" in the anger phase of grief, and displays of anger in black children are often seen as behavior and conduct issues. Displays of anger in school and community settings often result in black children getting harsh and biased responses from these settings. These responses can result in the child's grief issues never being acknowledged or addressed. | If the African American adult gets "stuck" in the anger stage of the grief cycle, they can be misread and mistreated as an "angry black man/woman." Displays of anger by African Americans are often responded to in a more negative and punitive way by the dominant culture. Also, displays of sadness and depression in the African American community are often not recognized and addressed, so anger may be the emotion that is comfortable to display. | If adoption is from foster care and involuntary, the African American birth parent's anger at the foster care system can contribute to them becoming stuck in the anger stage of the grief process. Experience with perceived bias, racism or prejudice reinforces the anger, masks other feelings and can derail the parent from moving through the grieving process. |
| Identity | If there are significant physical differences with adoptive parents (skin tone, hair texture), the child may struggle with identifying as part of the family. They may experience being "outed" by peers with comments such as "You don't look like your family." | The adopted adult may overly identify with the birth family if they have not resolved feelings of guilt about being adopted or feelings of rejection due to physical appearance differences with their adoptive family. The adopted adult may reject identifying any similarities with the birth family if they fear that the birth family's issues can be genetically based and "in the blood." As adults, African American adopted people will have the same struggle as non-adopted African American adults in managing to maintain a positive identity when dealing with issues of racism and discrimination. These issues are more frequently faced in adulthood. | The importance of family and connection in the African American community may sustain the birth parents' identity as the child's "real" parents. The birth parents' sense of identity may interfere with acceptance of the adoption and limit willingness and ability to participate in openness in the adoption process. |

*cont.*

| | Child | Adult adoptee | First/birth parents |
|---|---|---|---|
| **Intimacy** | Issues with identity, shame, guilt and unhealed grief can interfere with being close with parents. Experience with racism and prejudice may impact developing trust with both peers and adults from the white community. Distrust in cross-cultural relationships can be due to experience with racism and prejudice in addition to adoption. | Unresolved issues with identity, shame and unhealed grief can interfere with the adopted adult's romantic relationships and friendships. In the African American community, challenges in male–female romantic relationships and with LGBT identities and relationships can add to the complexity of this core issue for African American adopted adults. | Experience with intergenerational trauma, maintaining of identity as the child's "real" parent and unresolved grief may keep the birth parents from trusting a relationship with the adoptive parent or professionals. Mistrust of helping professionals and systems can deter the birth parents from engaging in therapy to help process the core issues. |
| **Mastery/Control** | If self-esteem challenges exist because of physical features being different from adoptive parents, the child may seek out either positive or negative behaviors or attire to accentuate their difference as a way of taking control or mastering their difference. | Adopted adults may seek out becoming adoptive parents to gain mastery over their adoption issues or unconscious feelings of loss, guilt or identity. A sense of "collective community" may motivate adopted adults to give to their community by adopting from the foster care system and "saving" children from the child welfare system which they see as being harmful to African American children. | Overall experience of being an African American and dealing with racism and prejudice, which one cannot control, can enhance a need to control experiences with systems that have historically disenfranchised African Americans. Birth parents may exert control by using anger towards individuals, being uncooperative with professionals, and maximizing legal rights by prolonging the court process. |

|  | Extended birth family | Adoptive parents | Extended adoptive family |
|---|---|---|---|
| Loss | Traditional African American values of keeping family together and the importance of community can enhance the feeling of loss for the extended birth family. Because of this, the extended family may not support a relinquishment adoption outside the family. With foster care adoptions, the African American extended family may view the foster care system as racist and "illegally" taking the child from the family. They may deny feelings of loss and only focus on anger. | Adoptive parents may experience the loss of the dream of giving birth and having children like other members of their family. As family and children are key values in African American families and having children is generally seen as easy and natural, becoming a parent the "non-traditional" way can be experienced as a great loss. The African American community may be less familiar with the "formal" adoption process, and thus the adopted parent may feel additional loss in having to explain and educate their community more than white adopted parents would have to do. | The extended adopted family may minimize feelings of loss, as the family values the addition of children to the family (by any means) as a positive. Some may display feelings of loss as an objection to adoption because of discomfort with the possible genetic unknowns (strangers) or circumstances of the birth family. |
| Rejection | Because of traditional African American values of keeping family together, the extended family may be rejecting of the birth parent because they "let the system take their child." Feelings of rejection by the extended family can impact the extended family's interest in having any type of openness with the adoptive family. | Adoptive parents may fear rejection from the black community due to the community lacking knowledge of the unique needs of adopted children. They may be seen by the community as being "too lenient" or "wrong" for parenting children using a trauma-informed, therapeutic approach. They may experience rejection from the adoption community because of that community's lack of exposure or understanding the needs of African American children, especially in communities without a strong African American presence. | Discomfort and fear of possible genetic unknowns and/or birth family circumstances may predispose the family to be hypervigilant for "problems" with the child and not be accepting of a trauma-informed view of the child's behaviors. These fears may be communicated via negative behaviors and comments that can be interpreted as the child being "different" from the rest of the family. |

*cont.*

|  | Extended birth family | Adoptive parents | Extended adoptive family |
|---|---|---|---|
| Shame/Guilt | If the adoption is through foster care, the guilt can be more intense for African American families because of a sense of failure in having "lost" the child to the system that is seen as historically detrimental to African American families. Experience with intergenerational trauma and/or poverty may intensify feelings of shame. | If adopting from the child welfare system, adoptive parents may experience guilt because they are completing their family by working with a system that has disproportionately removed black children from parents. They may feel shame that they are working with a child welfare system which historically and systemically prevented black children from reuniting with parents. They may feel guilt that others may see them as "stealing" someone's child and that they have colluded with a system known to engage in racist practices to "get" their child. | Extended family may feel guilty about having adopted grandchildren, nieces or nephews from the child welfare system because they see the system as being biased/unfair towards African Americans. May feel they are benefiting from a system that has mistreated their people for decades. |
| Grief | The extended birth family may join with the birth parent in expressing their grief with anger. Their experiences with racism, intergenerational trauma and biased systems may reinforce denial of other feelings associated with grief. Historical mistrust of helping professionals may support not seeking therapy or support to grieve losses. | Grief may be felt that another black child is being removed from their first family, and this can add to grief over the challenges and impact of historical racism on the black community. The adoptive parents may feel grief that their child will have to process and understand their removal and integrate this into their identity. They may also feel grief that their child's behaviors, due to early trauma, will be seen as behavioral and conduct issues and thus be easily targeted by the school and community. A single parent may grieve not having the "traditional" two-parent family. | If the family tends to minimize their losses from adoption then they may ignore or deny the need to grieve the loss. Because of African American individuals' possible distrust of the helping systems, psychoeducation about grief and referrals for grief therapy or support may not be accepted. |

| | | | |
|---|---|---|---|
| **Identity** | Importance of family and connection in the African American community may sustain the extended birth family's identity as the child's "real" family. Adherence to this view may prevent the extended family from engaging with the adoptive parents. Also, this strong identity as the child's "real" family may support a protective response to ensure the grandchild is treated well, and so the extended family may decide to engage with adoptive parents. | With the increase of adoptions by single, professional African American women, there is a growing community to identify with and from whom to get support. However, single black females may fear they will be seen as choosing adoption because they "could not get a man" and are perpetuating the stereotype of the "black single mother" in the African American community. These associations may contribute to some insecurity in their role. Difference in skin color between child and parent could contribute to the parent struggling to identify as the child's parent. | Possible issues with rejection, guilt and shame (listed above) can prevent the extended family from claiming and identifying the adopted child as truly a part of the family. If African American extended family members have a traditional view about child behavior and discipline, they may use the child's behavioral issues and challenges as "evidence" that the child is not a "genuine" family member. |
| **Intimacy** | Experience with intergenerational trauma, maintaining of identity as the child's "real" family and unresolved grief may encourage distrust and prevent the extended birth family from developing a relationship with the adoptive parents. Alternatively, strong identity as the child's "real" family may motivate them to engage in openness with the adoptive family. If there is openness and the extended family feels as if they are the "real" family, they could engage in actions that undermine the relationship between the child and adoptive parents/family. | Black adoptive parents may be reluctant to accept the trauma-informed/adoption experience information and interpret the child's behaviors negatively, maintaining distance in connecting with the child. Also, feelings of guilt, shame and rejection may keep parents from developing relationships with other adoptive families who could be supportive, especially white adoptive families. | If the extended adoptive family doesn't claim or identify the child as part of their family, relationships can remain distant. Grandparents may not claim their role in the child's life, which may keep them from feeling as if they are part of the "grandparent" club. Being a grandparent is also a huge and respected role in the African American community. Because of this value, African American grandparents may easily be predisposed to eagerly and energetically take on this role with the adopted child. |

*cont.*

|  | Extended birth family | Adoptive parents | Extended adoptive family |
|---|---|---|---|
| Mastery/Control | Overall experience of being an African American and dealing with racism and prejudice, which is not controllable, can enhance the need to control experiences with systems that have historically disenfranchised African Americans. These experiences may cause extended family members to encourage birth parents' efforts to control or assert anger. | Due to the history of prejudice and discrimination within the child welfare system and private agencies, African American adoptive parents may lack trust in the assessment process and may doubt if they're being treated fairly. This can lead to feelings of loss of control and trigger behaviors in parents that may be seen as controlling, challenging and angry. This possible interpretation by professionals can lead to unconscious bias by professionals and increased defensiveness from African American adoptive parents. Because of a history of mistreatment by medical systems and lack of culturally competent resources, African American adoptive parents may not engage in therapy that could help them with managing the unique needs of their children and themselves. A lack of engagement in appropriate therapy can interfere with obtaining mastery. | In African American families, grandparents are often seen as the matriarch or patriarch of the family and can have significant control over the family. Their view about the adoption, the child and the process can have an influence over other family members' reactions and attitudes. |

# Chapter 18

# The Seven Core Issues and the Multi-Racial Family

Lynne White Dixon

Transracial adoptions historically have been identified as white families adopting black children. However, a more accurate definition would be when a parent adopts a child and the child's ethnicity or race is different from that of the parents. In America, the majority of transracial adoptions are white families adopting children of color (Latin, Asian or African heritage). In the world of transracial adoption, most studies, writings and controversial discussions have involved white adults adopting African American children. It appears that when a child of Latin or Asian heritage is adopted by a white parent, these children are seen as easier to "assimilate" into the white family's culture. In fact, some studies have shown that if a white family chooses to adopt across racial/ethnic lines, Asian and Latin heritage children are preferred over African American children. These preferences both within white families and within white culture can make the adoption experience of the adopted child of color different, depending on their heritage. In transracial adoptions, issues of race and racism impact the child, adoptive family and birth family experiences. The extent to which these issues impact the experience may be dependent on the community of color from which the child originates. Since most transracial adoptions in the United States are between white parents and African American or Latino American children, the grid that follows will focus on the experiences of members of these communities of color.

| | Child | Adult adoptee | First/birth parents |
|---|---|---|---|
| Loss | The child will experience the loss of looking like their parents and grandparents; of living with people who understand how to care for hair and skin; of the anonymity of being an adopted child; of having cultural history, rituals, norms communicated in a daily "matter of fact" way; of having someone who lives with and looks like them, and can explain and understand experiences with racism and how to cope with these experiences. | As they move into the world and away from their white family, young adults may realize new losses or the magnitude of the losses they had identified. Their increased experience with people from their racial/ethnic community may exacerbate the loss of not knowing much about their heritage and the subtle "community" education that they missed being raised in a white home. The feelings of loss may drive the adult to connect more with their culture of origin through: cultural education; adopting cultural music, dress and values; or living in a more diverse community than the one in which they were raised. These changes can create challenges in the adult's relationship with their white parents and family members. | Since most black birth mothers choose to relinquish their child to black families, most children in transracial adoptions have come from the foster care system. Therefore, the loss for these birth parents may be more devastating because their child has been placed with a white family. The birth parents fear not just the loss of their child but the fear that their child will lose all connection to their culture and perhaps be raised as a "white" child in brown or black skin. The loss of power that many birth parents experience is exacerbated by having their child placed in a white family and white culture, which the birth parents view as historically disempowering to people of color. These feelings of loss are further complicated if they feel that a biased and racist system "took" their child from them. They may focus on feelings of anger instead of sadness and loss. |

| Rejection | The child may experience possible rejection from members of the adoptive family's extended family because they are a child of color, especially a black child. Societal messages of rejection and racism may be directed at the child or at people who are members of the child's racial or ethnic group. There may be rejection from peers from their racial group because they do not "act" the way peers believe they should act if they are members of the specific racial or ethnic group ("You're not black enough"). | As they move into the world and away from their white family, young adults may experience rejection by their community of origin. These rejections may be subtle in the form of questions and comments about "being white" because the adult adoptee's presentation is more in sync with the white community than the community of color from which they came. If the adult adoptee enthusiastically embraces their cultural heritage, they may experience rejection by their white family who may feel the adult is "choosing" their culture over them. As adults, transracial adoptees may have their first experience with overt racism. They may be unprepared for how to recognize and how to respond to these situations, further deepening the feelings of rejection such an act inflicts on a person of color. | Fear of rejection by the extended family or the African American community because the birth parent "let the system take their child" may motivate the birth parent to "fight the system" and not focus on the child's needs, perhaps missing an opportunity to mitigate loss to the child and themselves. Depending on the birth parent's experience with the white community and past experiences of rejection by members of this community, their fear of or feeling of rejection by their child's adoptive parents could be intensified. Personal experiences with racism and discrimination may create an expectation by the birth parent to experience rejection by the white adoptive family. |
|---|---|---|---|

*cont.*

|  | Child | Adult adoptee | First/birth parents |
|---|---|---|---|
| Shame/Guilt | Negative messages from the majority media/community/government directed at African Americans can contribute to feelings of unworthiness and shame. Visuals and statements that reflect stereotypes of the child's ethnic group contribute to that group being seen as "other" and not acceptable. Black females, especially dark-skinned girls, are bombarded with messages that they do not meet the acceptable standard of beauty in America. All of these messages lead to increased feelings of shame for the adopted child. White parents may fail to see these messages or believe their impact and thus not prepare the child with counter-positive and affirming messages which could combat feelings of shame. The child's feelings of shame or guilt may keep them from sharing these experiences and feelings with their white parents for fear that the white parents won't understand or may feel uncomfortable with the discussion. The child may feel guilty when they see members of their racial community not having the resources they have or having a very different day-to-day experience. | Given the "collective community" feelings and values present in African American individuals, adopted adults may feel guilt that they had a "privileged" life compared with other African Americans. Further understanding or raised consciousness about the disparity of treatment/access to resources of people of color, especially those from lower socio-economic status, may deepen feelings of guilt in the adult adoptee. If the adult is in reunion with their first/birth family, these feelings of guilt can be exacerbated by this contact if birth family members have had challenges that the adopted adult did not due to their being adopted out of the family. Being adopted by a white family can create feelings of shame, because the adult adoptee may feel they have "betrayed" their race by being raised by the dominant culture that historically has oppressed their group. | Many African American or Latino birth parents whose children are in the foster care system have a history of intergenerational trauma and/or poverty. These experiences create feelings of shame, which are then further exacerbated by the removal of the child and subsequent adoption placement. Placement of their child in a white home creates increased guilt and shame as they may perceive their actions resulting in their child being raised by the "oppressor." This may be especially true for African American birth parents. Black birth parents may feel as if they have "betrayed" their race by having their child being raised by a white family. |

| | | | |
|---|---|---|---|
| **Grief** | The child may deny their losses in an effort to "fit in" and cope, and thus grieving these losses may be denied also. They may feel guilty for having feelings of sadness or loss and won't share these feelings with parents. Children may get "stuck" in the anger phase of grief. Displays of anger in children of color, especially black or Latino children, is often misread as behavior or conduct issues and responded to with fear and harshness. Focus on "stopping" the behavior instead of understanding the underlying feeling or message (grief) can result in the grief issues going unaddressed for years and maybe into adulthood. Black children are often mis-diagnosed or labeled as having conduct issues or being oppositionally defiant. White parents' fear of the anger may trigger unconscious negative thoughts about "angry black people" and impact their empathy and responsiveness to their child. | Experiences with loss, grief and rejection that may have been addressed while a child can recycle as an adult and create new feelings of grief. If an African American adopted adult gets "stuck" in the anger stage of the grief cycle, this can be misread and they may be mistreated as an "angry black man/woman." Displays of anger by African Americans are often responded to in a more negative and punitive way by the dominant culture. This can also occur with Latino adults, but not with the same frequency as with African American adults. Also, the adult of color who may be newly reunited with their culture of origin may feel that displays of sadness and depression are not acceptable in their community of color and thus may hide these feelings and decide that anger is the comfortable emotion to display. Adults may be in denial of their grief because they feel they "should" be happy because they have "resolved" their identity issues and reconnected with their community of color. | If adoption is from foster care and involuntary, the birth parents' anger at the foster care system can contribute to them becoming stuck in the anger stage of the grief process. Experience with perceived bias, racism or prejudice reinforces anger, masks other feelings and can derail the parent from moving through the grieving process. A transracial placement may be seen by the birth parent as justification for their anger and support their belief that the "system" has stolen their child to benefit "white" people. The African American and Latino community's reluctance to seek services due to past negative experiences will contribute to birth parents not seeking grief counseling or therapy. |
| **Identity** | This can be a huge struggle for the child, as one's identity is usually first confirmed by appearance. In transracial adoptions the child does not look like their parents and cannot "pass" as being their biological child. In addition, identity development is a complex issue in the African American community and a constant and at times controversial discussion. The struggle in the black community around identity can probably be traced back to slavery when the cultural and social identity of being African was stripped from the slaves, leaving no history or language from which slaves could build a positive identity. | All people of color (adopted or non-adopted) have the task of developing a positive racial identity as part of their personal identity. Since identity development starts in the family, being adopted by a white family can make developing a positive racial identity more of a challenge, because natural role models and experiences are not part of the adoptee's day-to-day life. The transracial adult adoptee may overly identify with the birth family if they have not resolved feelings of guilt, shame and rejection about being adopted by a white family. | The importance of family and connection in the African American and Latino communities may sustain the birth parent's identity as the child's "real" parent. In a transracial adoption, that belief of being the "real" parent is further supported by the child being raised by a white parent who will be perceived as inadequate for raising a black child. *cont.* |

*cont.*

| | Child | Adult adoptee | First/birth parents |
|---|---|---|---|
| Identity (cont.) | Instead, slaves had to form an identity surrounded by negative and degrading messages devoid of any positive history or experiences. What it means to be "black" is a question that can be challenging for most black people in America to think through. If you are a child being raised by white people, you don't have a parent to help you sort this out; thus the child may be left to depend on the messages in the media, books, comments from friends and family to figure this out. The child may choose obvious and explicit representations of their culture of origin with which to identify or may deny any cultural representations as being meaningful or relevant to them. Some children may struggle with accepting their physical appearance that links them to their cultural heritage. Statements about disliking their skin tone or hair may be made along with wishing they were not part of the racial/ ethnic group to which they belong. The first response may confuse, embarrass or anger white parents if they are not comfortable with or knowledgeable of their child's racial and cultural heritage. The second response may bring relief to white parents and allows them to remain "colorblind" and not put any effort into helping their child of color develop a positive integrated identity. Often in adolescence when the child is struggling to define their racial and cultural identity, that distance between the child and parent can grow and the relationship can be tested to the point of rupture. | They may also overly identify because they feel some relief and comfort in being around people who look like them. Adoptees may struggle with identifying with some characteristics in their birth family if they access unhealthy attitudes and behaviors. They may have a deeper sense of "betrayal" if they don't completely "claim" all of the attitudes and values they perceive as being "their culture." This struggle impacts the adult adoptee in developing a positive racial identity. Transracial adult adoptees may continue to struggle with accepting their physical appearance that links them to their cultural heritage. For some, an internalized racism can develop, which creates additional challenges to developing positive identity and self-esteem. The search for identity and community can become stronger in adulthood as the adoptee has more control in this search than when a child. Adult adoptees of color will have the same struggle as non-adopted adults of color in managing to maintain a positive identity when dealing with issues of racism and discrimination. These issues are more frequently faced in adulthood. | Birth parents of color may hold a sense of entitlement and superiority over white parents because of their shared cultural and racial history with the child, which the white parent can never attain. The birth parents' lack of a positive identity may interfere with acceptance of the adoption and limit their willingness/ability to participate in openness in the adoption. |

| | | | |
|---|---|---|---|
| **Intimacy** | The child's unaddressed or unhealed issues with loss, shame, grief and identity can impact their closeness with parents and other relationships. Lack of positive racial identity can impact the child's choice of friends, romantic relationships and overall comfort with closeness. Black or Latino children, who have only been around white peers growing up, may feel uncomfortable and awkward when around black or Latino peers who have been raised within their cultures. They may feel rejection or fear rejection and thus distance themselves from those connections. However, they can also feel distant from their white peers because they do not share their exact same experience either. In adolescence, the child may struggle with whom to date (within or outside their race/ethnicity) and, depending on where they live, messages of acceptance, of either choice, may or may not be present. | The adult adoptee may feel more comfortable with white people than with members of their community of color. Experiences with rejection and unresolved identity issues may alienate the adoptee from their community of color and thus close relationships may only be with people from the white community. Struggles with internalized racism may drive the adult to further distance themselves and feel a deeper discomfort when in the presence of members of their racial and ethnic group. Adult adoptees who have fully and positively embraced their cultural identity may feel comfortable having close relationships with members of both the white community and their own community of color. However, being raised in a white family, they may not be aware of some of the challenges their community may have in male–female relationships and with LGBT identities and relationships. Should the adult adoptee be a member of the LGBT community, they may not receive the support from their community of color that they have from their white family or peers. | Birth parents' experience with white people/white supremacy/racism will directly impact their beliefs and comfort level with their child's white parents. These experiences can support feelings of distrust and maintain a distance between birth parent and adoptive parent. Experience with intergenerational trauma, maintaining of identity as the child's "real" parent and unresolved grief may keep the birth parents from trusting a relationship with the adoptive parent or professionals. Mistrust of white helping professionals and systems can deter the birth parents from engaging in therapy to help process core issues. Feelings of shame associated with having their child adopted by a white family may keep the birth parent from developing subsequent close relationships with members of their community of color. |

*cont.*

| | Child | Adult adoptee | First/birth parents |
|---|---|---|---|
| Mastery/Control | In efforts to master or control feelings of insecurity about identity, or being a transracially adopted child, the child may choose to engage in actions and activities completely counter to their white parents' perceived values, experiences and behaviors. Children may call their parents "racists" when the parents say anything about the child's inappropriate behaviors that the child feels are "part of their culture." This name calling can be due to the child's discomfort with their racial identity and lack of education about racism and racists. White parents' reactions of powerlessness or anger to this name calling can give the child a misplaced sense of control and impact their sense of security. | In seeking mastery over their transracial adoption experience, adult adoptees may study their community of color's art, literature, heroes and so on to feel more connected and to develop a positive defense against negative experiences from the present or past. They may use their experience to educate adoptive parents and children who are involved in the transracial adoption experience. They may become adoptive parents, but choose children from their racial or ethnic group to adopt. They may become advocates for same-race adoptions to help children avoid what they may have experienced. They may confront their white parents' racism or denial of issues involved in their transracial adoption. They may demand that their white parents expand their consciousness and awareness and not practice "colorblindness." | Overall experience of being an African American or Latino and dealing with racism and prejudice, which one cannot control, can enhance a need to control experiences with systems that have historically disenfranchised African Americans and Latinos. Birth parents may exert control by using anger towards individuals, being uncooperative with professionals and maximizing legal rights by prolonging the court process. A transracial placement can motivate a birth parent to fight harder and longer for control. They may see the stakes of "losing" as even higher because the child will be raised by a completely different culture that is experienced as hostile to and dismissive of the birth parent's racial and ethnic group. |

| | Extended birth family | Adoptive parents | Extended adoptive family |
|---|---|---|---|
| Loss | Traditional African American and Latino values of keeping family together and the importance of community can enhance the feeling of loss for the extended birth family. The extended family's experiences with racism/discrimination may intensify their feelings of loss when the child is being raised by a white family. Not only may this be viewed as a loss of connection, and an opportunity to share family culture and experiences, but the family may feel that the opportunity to have any of the losses mitigated is lost because the child will be with a white family who is perceived as unaccepting of the child's culture and history. With foster care adoptions, the extended family may view the foster care system as racist and "illegally" taking the child from the family. They may deny feelings of loss and only focus on anger. | White parents lose their white privilege when they adopt a child of color, especially if they adopt a black child. If they are with their child, they lose the experience of never having to think they are being treated differently because they are the parent of a black child. They lose their privacy of being adoptive parents. They lose the experience of looking like their child. They lose the freedom of not having to worry that their child will be safe and not discriminated against when they are away from them. They lose being able to be "colorblind" and believe that skin color doesn't matter or that racism doesn't exist. They lose the security of feeling "entitled" to their child. | The extended family lose their white privilege when a family member adopts a child of color, especially if they adopt a black child. When they are with the child, they lose the experience of never having to think they are being treated differently because they have a familial relationship with a black child. They lose the privacy of not being questioned about the diversity in their family and judged because of it. Grandparents may experience the loss of having their "family lineage" carried on in the way they had envisioned. The extended family may lose the ability to be comfortable and ignore issues of racism or prejudice. |

*cont.*

| | Extended birth family | Adoptive parents | Extended adoptive family |
|---|---|---|---|
| Rejection | Experience with and view of white people can heighten the extended birth family's sense of fearing or feeling rejection. Their past experiences with white people may have left them anticipating rejection by the child's adoptive parents and they may defend against this by proactively rejecting the white parents first. Loss of the child to a white family may also intensify the extended birth family's rejection of the birth parent and may communicate to the birth parent as the ultimate betrayal to their race/ethnicity. The extended family may also fear or feel rejection from their own community because they "failed" to save their extended family member from being "lost" to the system and be raised by whites, who may be seen as "enemies" of the racial/ethnic community. | White parents can experience rejection from both the white community and their child's community of color. White parents may be faced with feelings of rejection when they are asked, in different ways, to confirm that their child is theirs. Parents may experience rejection when members of the black community make negative comments about their child's appearance (hair or skin) or ask several questions to determine if the white parent is competent to parent a black child. Parents may experience rejection when they are asked by their child, and both the black and white communities, why they chose to adopt a black or Latino child. Parents experience rejection when their child brings up the history of mistreatment of blacks by whites or calls them racists or refuses to engage in family activities that the child perceives as for "white people only." Rejection may be experienced when the extended family make negative comments about the adoption or overtly treat the child differently from other members of the family. | The extended adoptive family members may feel rejection by their friends when friends make comments that indicate negative views about the racial group their grandchild/nephew/niece is a member of. They may experience rejection by the child when the child makes comments about their "whiteness" in negative or judgmental ways. They may experience rejection from the adoptive parent when they question the parent's embracing of the child's culture and engaging in activities to help the child stay culturally connected to their heritage. |

| Shame/Guilt | Shame and guilt can be more intense for African American families because of a sense of failure from "losing" the child to the system that is seen as historically detrimental to African American families. Given the strong value placed on family and community in communities of color, the extended family's shame may be intensified by their inability to take in the child and keep them in the family. The shame is further deepened if the child is placed transracially and raised by a white family. The historical relationship between blacks and whites in America has included the shaming of blacks by whites. Thus, a transracial adoption could be seen as the embodiment of the shame dynamic that has been historically present. Experiencing this level of shame could motivate the extended family to never acknowledge or verbalize the impact of the loss that triggered the shame. | White parents may feel guilty that they kept a child of color from living with a family that shares the child's racial or ethnic background. They can feel guilty when they have thoughts of wishing they hadn't adopted transracially, especially as they experience more complicated and challenging situations connected to their child's race or ethnicity. They may feel shame when they realize they underestimated the prevalence and impact of racism and discriminatory experiences their child will endure. They may feel shame when they examine their own implicit bias or racist thoughts of which they were unaware. | Depending on their personal views about black and Latino people and experiences with these groups, the extended family may experience shame that a person of color is now a legal member of their family. If their views are based on a long history of racist beliefs, they may feel the adoption has shamed the family and scarred it forever. Transracial adoption may bring first-time awareness to a family member of their bias and racist views and they may experience shame and guilt for having such feelings. Family members may experience guilt when they witness mistreatment of members from the child's racial/ethnic group. This guilt can be triggered by direct witnessing or from media and news. |

*cont.*

|  | Extended birth family | Adoptive parents | Extended adoptive family |
|---|---|---|---|
| Grief | Loss of racial and cultural heritage present in a transracial adoption adds to the intensity of the typical losses in adoption and may not be grieved with sadness but with anger. African American extended family members may feel the loss of the child to the white culture, which mirrors the experience of black children being sold to white slave owners. Though rationally they know it is not the same, emotionally it may feel the same. In addition to anger, there may be expressions of emotional pain with tears and sadness, similar to emotions displayed at funerals. However, emotional responses, other than anger, may be viewed as "weakness" in dealing with a system they see as racist and biased. Historical mistrust of helping professionals may support not seeking therapy or support to grieve losses. | There may be grief for the loss of their fantasy child who looked like them. White parents may not acknowledge loss of privilege, "colorblindness," privacy or appearing similar to their child as true losses that need to be grieved. Parents may avoid these issues that surround transracial adoption and stay in the denial stage of grief. White parents may deny feelings of grief due to fear they would be judged by others as regretting their adoption or being ashamed they have a child of color. | Family members may not realize or acknowledge losses to grieve or that they have anything to grieve. If they are stuck in shame, they may not feel they have a "right" to grieve any losses they may perceive from the transracial adoption. Family members may deny feelings of sadness because they witness the happiness of the adoptive parents. Family members may experience grief if they witness mistreatment of the adopted child or adult due to racial prejudice or bigotry. |
| Identity | The extended family may see themselves as the "experts" in their racial/cultural heritage and not acknowledge or be dismissive of the white parents' attempts to keep their child connected to their cultural heritage. They may see themselves as and verbalize that they are the child's "real" and "only" family. This view may motivate them to be very protective of the child and critical of the white parents' parenting or care of the child. Their strong racial identity may interfere with their developing a relationship with the child's white parents. | Not looking like their child means the white parent may have more challenges with their identity as the child's parent. Continual questions about their entitlement to their child or comments indicating doubt that they can parent a black or Latino child can cause the white parent to doubt their identity as the child's "true" parent. White parents may question their right to "claim" their child as theirs. Parents may worry that the child does not claim them as their parents, further diminishing the parents' identity. | Transracial adoption changes the family from being homogeneous to diverse. This shift may be uncomfortable for family members to integrate into their family and individual identity. If they are uncomfortable with this identity shift, they may not acknowledge the adopted child/adult as a member of their family to others. Family members may make hurtful statements to others or the child that indicate they do not accept the familial role the adoption places on them. |

| Intimacy | Experience with racism and discrimination, maintaining of identity as the child's "real" family and unresolved grief may encourage distrust and prevent the extended family from developing a relationship with the white adoptive parents. Strong identity as the child's "real" family may trigger interest in openness with the adoptive family; however, feelings and beliefs about white people may create obstacles to pursuing openness. These conflicting beliefs will impact the level of engagement between the extended family and the white adoptive parents. If there is openness and the extended family feels they are the "real" family, they could engage in actions that undermine the relationship between the child and adoptive parents/family. | Unhealed feelings of shame, grief and identity may impact the parent's ability to form a secure attachment with the child. Fear of not being sanctioned as the child's parent may cause the parent to recoil in forming a connection and intimacy with the child. This self-doubt can also cause parents to isolate and not connect with other parents or reach out and connect with members of the child's racial/ethnic community. Being a transracial adoptive parent may put a strain on previous friendships and familial relationships if the parents determine that these friends and family members may be prejudiced and may mistreat their child. | Unaddressed or unresolved issues with shame, grief and identity will impact the family members' relationship with the adopted child/adult. Feelings of shame and guilt that go unhealed may motivate the extended family to limit associating with the child. Limited contact may be chosen as a way to cope with the feelings. Refusal to accept a certain role identity with the child (grandparent, aunt/uncle, etc.) creates a barrier to any secure and safe relationship being developed with the child. Refusal to accept their new role can also distance and rupture the relationship with the adoptive parents. |

*cont.*

| | Extended birth family | Adoptive parents | Extended adoptive family |
|---|---|---|---|
| Mastery/Control | Overall experience of being an African American or Latino and dealing with racism and prejudice, which is not controllable, can enhance the need to control experiences with systems that have historically disenfranchised African Americans and Latinos. A transracial placement may motivate extended family members to be more intense in efforts to prevent the placement from occurring or to support the birth parent's efforts to assert their control. Feelings of shame, exacerbated by the potential loss of the child to "white people," may provoke family members to engage in both overt and covert controlling behaviors directed at social workers and adoptive parents. Historically, the African American community's ability to reframe situations of adversity into something with which they can cope is a type of mastery. In transracial adoptions, extended family members may reframe this adverse experience and cope with it by deciding to pursue openness with the white adoptive family to oversee the child's development and ensure some ongoing connection to their family of origin and culture. | Fear of their child being exposed to or hurt by racism and prejudice may cause parents to overly control their child's experiences and the information they receive. Parents may become too protective and deny teaching their child protective strategies for dealing with racism and prejudice. Parents acquire mastery when they intentionally and openly embrace their child's cultural heritage and integrate it into their family in a balanced and positive way. Parents demonstrate mastery when they acknowledge their white privilege as a fact and begin to view the world through the eyes of a person of color. Parents demonstrate mastery when they seek out and find help from members of their child's racial/ethnic group to be role models for their child and to teach them and their child how to successfully navigate a racist and discriminatory society. | If family members object to the transracial adoption, they may use their influence and position in the family to control the adoption being finalized or, if finalized, may try to control how other family members accept or interact with the child or adoptive parent. Fear of rejection by friends and acquaintances may result in controlling where or when they are seen with the child. They may try to overly control the child's behaviors if they interpret them to be "unacceptable" because they are seen as a reflection of the child's racial/cultural heritage. Similar to adoptive parents, the extended family achieves mastery when they intentionally and openly embrace the child's cultural heritage and integrate it into their family in a balanced and positive way. Mastery is also demonstrated when the family members choose to defend the child if they witness mistreatment or when they choose to educate others about race/racism/prejudice. |

# Chapter 19

# The Seven Core Issues in International Adoption: From an Asian Adoptee

Huyen Friedlander

When I'm asked to speak about my experience as an international adoptee, there is a part of me that hesitates. Each adoptee's experience is unique, and my single voice cannot adequately represent the experience of thousands of people from varying countries and varying ethnicities. That being said, there are some common themes that have emerged in my conversations with other transracial adoptees and in the research I've come across: a crisis of identity, internalized self-hatred, internalized racism, feeling out of place, struggling to fit in, feeling less-than for not being white, and even sometimes developing body dysmorphic disorder. When I encounter other adoptees who share similar wounds to my own, there is a recognition of community and a resonance—a found family of people who understand this sometimes painful space we grew up in. In the spirit of hoping to alleviate suffering for future international adoptees, I want to share my story with you.

## Loss

I was born in 1971 in Ho Nai, a small refugee camp located just outside of Sai Gon, Vietnam. Growing up, I had little information about the first four years of my life, other than what was offered in the affidavit my birth mother provided before she relinquished me in April 1975, just days before the end of the Vietnam war. My paperwork indicated that my birth father was most likely an American GI, and my birth mother was concerned for my safety because I was mixed race. My birth mother was also worried that I would become domestic help for the family who would adopt me. I was part of what is now commonly referred to as the first-generation Vietnamese adoptees; I came to the United States by way of Operation Babylift. My placement was conducted by the Friends of the Children of Viet Nam; after being processed in Guam, I eventually landed in a makeshift adoption center in Denver, Colorado.

We aren't certain of the exact timeline, but my family thinks that there were about two weeks between the time I left Vietnam and the day that I met my adoptive family in Sacramento, California (on Mother's Day, May 10, 1975). In that two-week period, I lost everything about myself: my mother, my extended family, my home, my language, my food, my culture. I lost my self. In attachment theory, we talk about how the caregivers are the first to reflect a child's sense of self through interaction. All my caregivers were suddenly gone; I no longer had any context for who I was. It was absolutely traumatic, though I didn't have words for it at the time. My new parents created a photo album of my arrival to give to my grandparents, who couldn't be at the Sacramento Municipal Airport the day I arrived because they lived in Los Angeles. Growing up, I loved to look at that photo album every time I visited my grandparents; I thought the photos were precious and adorable. I look at the same pictures now and I see a completely traumatized child who is dissociating, looking off, not making eye contact with these complete strangers who are overwhelming her. As a child, I couldn't have thought that because it would have been acknowledging there was some sadness on that day that I became a member of the family. Children are resilient. We figure out all kinds of ways to survive.

During that two-week period when I was between families and had no clue what was happening, I started to build a mental wall that disconnected me from everything that came before May 1975 and everything that came after May 1975. There was a brief window of time when I would talk about having two mothers, both women with long black hair. I would talk about the pig who lived beside our outdoor kitchen. And I would talk about sitting in the dirt in front of my house. I couldn't remember faces, and soon I couldn't remember any of the language. That mental wall protected me from the deep pain of what I had lost, kept me from not wanting to be where I was, and kept me focused on just wanting to belong to my adoptive family. Due to the war ending and the ensuing cease in diplomatic relations between the US and Vietnam, I grew up thinking that I would never be able to return to Vietnam—and this was another wall that kept me separated from my past. This geographic distance and political climate made my country of origin feel more like something in another dimension, rather than an actual location that I could ever access.

## Rejection

Being resilient (or maybe driven to survive), I became the perfect child within my new family. By "perfect," I mean I was compliant, obedient, quiet, not demanding, easy. These qualities were only heightened in contrast to my adoptive sister (the biological child in the family), who was full of energy, tested boundaries, and needed a good deal of attention. My behavior was an unconscious process, which I now understand was propelled by my fear of being cast out or rejected, re-abandoned again. To my 4-year-old mind, there was no logic to the first abandonment, and therefore a second abandonment could happen again. Although seemingly irrational, you can imagine a child thinking, "If I am perfect, if I never give them a reason to want to be rid of me—then I will be okay." This unconscious dynamic was often validated by other adults commenting to my parents that they would adopt or become parents "if they could get a child just like Huyen." Looking back, I can see that I was a safety-seeking child. I preferred to hang out with grown-ups, rather than play with other children (who might get me into trouble). I was an avid reader and a daydreamer, both avenues for my dissociative tendencies. I now know that children who have experienced trauma often engage dissociative strategies as coping mechanisms. Despite being outwardly well adjusted, my over-compliance and chewed-up fingernails were telltale signs of my underlying hypervigilance and anxiety.

## Identity

What's in a name? Of course, I knew I was adopted and I knew I was from Vietnam, but no one I knew had a clue about what it was to be Vietnamese. When I was 9 years old, my father took me to a Vietnamese restaurant to celebrate my birthday. While dining, a Vietnamese couple struck up a conversation with my family. Much to their credit, my family had kept my first name because I had lived with that name for four years, and they didn't want to take away my birthright. Through the course of conversation with the couple in the restaurant, we learned we had been saying my name wrong. The couple explained that Vietnamese names were one syllable; my name should sound more like "Hwen," not "Hu-Wen." Following that, I asked everyone to call me "Hwen." My name continued to be challenging (and still is to this day). Like most kids, I just wanted to fit in. I longed to be like one of the five Jennifers in my third-grade class. I hated being "different," a euphemism for non-white.

Growing up, I loved fairytales. And not the Disneyfied tales but the original ones with hardship, suffering and redemption through some kind of growth or show of courage. I was partial to stories about exiled princesses who had to journey far and sacrifice much to reclaim their true identity. However, it was a more innocuous story that turned out to be the one that best represented my experience growing up in a transracial adoption: *The Ugly Duckling*. In case you don't know this story, it is a story of a little duck who is different from the rest of his family. He is essentially unable to truly fit in, but never quite understands why—until one day he grows up and realizes that he is a magnificent swan, different from the ducks who raised him. For me, this core issue of identity development in a transracial adoption and its impact on self-worth is one of the most crucial elements for adoptive parents to understand. The family being "colorblind" or not acknowledging a child's ethnic or racial identity is actually harmful to the child's ability to develop a healthy identity.

When I was growing up in Northern California in the 1970s and 1980s, the standard of beauty was Caucasian, tall, thin, "fine" features, light-colored hair, blue eyes. My adoptive family members very much embodied this standard of beauty. My father was 6 feet 3 inches, my mother was 6 feet, and my sister was always tall and thin and grew to be 5 feet 10 inches. They all had blue eyes. I was always the smallest in my class, and my most fervent wish was to grow beyond 5 feet. My eyes were brown, my hair was brown, my skin was a light brown. At a very young age, I internalized that "brown" was boring, unattractive, not very special. The culture at large emphasized the ideal (it was hard to avoid the message in advertising, television and movies—where people of color were rarely represented), but I also received this message within my own family. Height was equated with beauty and power; it mattered. Relatives often commented on my sister's willowy body with admiration, characterizing her as beautiful. My small stature was more often characterized as "cute." Once I realized that I was going to be short, I began hating that part of myself. If I had been able to surgically lengthen my legs at that time (as they do now in parts of the world), I probably would have begged my mother to let me go through that excruciating pain for a mere three additional inches.

I equally hated other parts of myself that were different from my family: the "bump" of my round stomach and my nose (which was sometimes described as flat or broad—both had negative connotations for me). I often had the experience of being surprised to see myself in the mirror or in photos; in my mind's eye, I perceived myself as more "white" than I actually was, so the image of the Asian person that was reflected back to me was jarring. This is what internalized self-hatred looks like. From an early age, I fantasized about surgically changing myself so that I could be "more attractive." This is where the story of the ugly duckling feels so relevant. There was nothing unattractive about my nose, or being short, or having a round stomach—these features just highlighted how I was different from the people raising me. And perhaps those differences felt like a neon sign pointing out to everyone, "This person does not belong here. She is not really one of us."

## Shame and guilt

Another reason why it is so important for adoptive parents to be proactive about nurturing their child's ethnic identity development and being able to talk to their child about race is because of the reality of the world beyond the family doorstep. Let me just pause to say that the reality is, you won't be able to really protect your child from insensitive comments even when you are standing right next to them at the grocery store, at church, at the mall or at school. At least, if you are paying attention, you (as a mature adult) will have the opportunity to speak up or provide a teachable moment to the other person in question. However, you won't always be there to protect your child. One example of this was when I was in the fourth grade: I was walking down the hallway at school, when two girls who I thought were my friends (one girl had even been over to my house for sleepovers several times) approached me. The girl I knew the best asked, "Huyen, why do you have a nose like a pig?" Honestly, I don't know what happened next. I may have smiled and laughed. However, I clearly remember how I felt: a deep sense of shame and embarrassment. I was completely shocked and unprepared. I didn't tell my parents what Jennifer (yes, one of the five Jennifers) had said to me at school because it was just too shameful. In a sense, Jennifer was calling out the fact that I was different, and she was calling out that my features were not "white." If I were to bring that to my parents, they might have to acknowledge my difference, too.

Of course, that was not an isolated incident. There were too many micro-aggressions and aggressions to count. The most upsetting encounter took place when I was 14, at my first high school dance. It was a casual dance on a Friday night, and I had arrived with my best friend. We were milling about, socializing. At one point, I found myself in a corner by myself, watching people dancing. A boy named Eric (actually someone my best friend had gone out with the year before) approached me with a group of friends not far behind him. I was slightly excited and nervous because I thought he might ask me to dance. Instead, he walked up very close to me. Right when he was about six inches from my face, what I thought had been a smile turned into a weirdly smug expression as he sputtered out, "Gook!" He spun around and walked away, to the laughter and approval of his friends. Again, I was flooded with a feeling of shame and embarrassment. I remember quickly looking around to see if anyone had witnessed my humiliation, and I felt relieved to see no one else seemed to have noticed. I spent the rest of the dance hiding in the girl's bathroom, not really understanding what a gook was, but totally comprehending that I had been the target of a mean joke. Again, I didn't tell my parents what had happened. We had never talked about how I might experience racist encounters. Looking back, what I needed from my parents wasn't just conversations that might have helped me to prepare myself. I needed them to understand that I didn't hold the same white privilege that was available to them, and because of that, I would be subjected to both subtle and overt forms of racism, especially when I was on my own.

It's interesting to note just how much guilt and shame plays into a family's ability to have a dialogue around this painful topic: I felt too ashamed to talk to my parents when incidents occurred, and now I wonder if my parents' unconscious sense of guilt and shame (for having white privilege) was a barrier to freely talking about systemic racism with me.

## Intimacy

From an early age, I expressed an interest in romantic love. In elementary school and middle school, this just amounted to having crushes and pining away for the object of my affections. By high school, I was in full pursuit of an idealized relationship that provided me with a sense of unconditional love. In this way, I was precocious for my age as I approached relationships with a degree of seriousness and commitment that was unusual. My most significant early romantic relationship began when I was 16, and it continued on-and-off until I was almost 24 years old. During those eight years, my partner and I established a painful pattern of getting together, idealizing one another, breaking up, feeling devastated, and getting back together again. For the most part, I was the one who was being rejected over and over—I just couldn't seem to get out of this pattern because I was so hopeful that this other person would see my worth and we would live happily ever after.

This pattern finally ended when I realized that I had been re-enacting an abandonment scenario that was really about the pain of feeling rejected by my birth mother. As it happened, the travel embargo to Vietnam had been lifted around the time of the "final" breakup, and I decided to go back to Vietnam and search for my birth mother, rather than try to make this unhealthy romantic relationship work again. I spent a year working, saving up money for my trip and planning how I would search for my birth family. It was an empowering phase of my life, as I finally gave myself permission to focus on healing my adoption experience by returning home and seeking answers. This is how rejection, intimacy, identity and mastery and control all played a part in my decision to go in search of my identity, roots and truth.

## Mastery and control

The same year that I was saving up to go back to Vietnam, I also began the process of becoming a licensed marriage and family therapist by applying to graduate school. When I started graduate school, I focused on the issue of adoption and what type of counseling support would be most useful to families. I developed a research proposal to address ethnic identity development in transracially adopted children. The proposal was a 12-week course for adoptive parents with the following goals: to help them understand their own ethnic identity development, to increase awareness of the impact of systemic racism, to develop a rich understanding of their child's ethnic and cultural background of origin, and to create a plan for how they could help foster their adoptive child's ethnic identity within the context of their new family. Ultimately, after creating this deep understanding, the adoptive family's identity would shift to now include their child's ethnic identity, as well. In addition to my graduate school work, I was also sharing my story and relaying this information to adoptive families through public speaking opportunities. I was reclaiming my narrative, going from "orphan" to educator. Eventually, I pulled back from doing this work because I felt overly identified with adoption, which had shaped so much of my life. I needed to see what work I would be drawn to do, without the adoption focus. I landed in the field of trauma, grief and loss.

## Grief

Adoption, like grief work, isn't something that happens to you and then goes away. With each milestone or life event, aspects of adoption can resurface for you to work through in a new way. When you graduate from college, get married or have your first baby, you may grieve for or reflect on some of these core issues of adoption. When I was in my late thirties, my husband was diagnosed with a rare, incurable cancer—which he ultimately fought for five years before dying. Interestingly, I never felt abandoned by my husband because I was absolutely clear that he would never have chosen to leave his family. As my husband was approaching death, I dreamt that I was visited by the grim reaper (in the form of a friendly old man). He matter-of-factly told me that my time was up, and my first thought was: "No! I can't die broken." I had the incredible fortune to have this dream while I was at Satir Family Camp, an intentional community that meets for one week a year for personal growth work. With the help of seasoned facilitators, I was able to immediately process this dream in a very meaningful way.

What I took away from the work was this: when my birth mother left me at the US Embassy in Saigon when I was almost 4 years old, the person I would have been died. I became the compliant, safety-seeking, serious child who was afraid of anger and afraid to displease people for fear of rejection. Through this work, I could grieve the loss of who I might have been—maybe someone who was more playful, silly, funny, bold, confrontational. I could also honor the wisdom of the 4-year-old who just wanted to survive, while recognizing that I no longer had to live that way. From this work, I made it a goal to connect more with my anger and to try to communicate my difficult/unlikable feelings. This work didn't "fix" me, but it did add to my understanding of myself and why I tend to respond in a certain way to conflict. I think this particular example reflects how adoption truly is a lifelong process, which continues to unfold in complex ways.

## In conclusion

Reading all this, you may wonder what my attitude is about adoption at this point in my life. As an adoptee, I don't think adoption is something you choose—sort of like I didn't choose for my children to lose their father to cancer. It's something that happened to me, beyond my control, and I have learned to accept it and live with it. That being said, when I imagine myself selling vegetables in Vietnam or growing up with both my birth parents in the United States, I don't long for those scenarios, either. Here is another example of the complexity of adoption. Despite all the pain related to the core issues of adoption, I believe that I was raised by the people I was meant to be raised by. Some people might call it God's plan, or karma, or the universe working in mysterious ways, or plain dumb luck. I think of it as soul work; that I would land in a group of people with whom I had no connection at all, that they would turn out to be the family I needed them to be, and that we would love and support each other through the rest of our lives. I'm grateful to have reached a place in my life where I feel a sense of peace about my adoption experience, with a deep love and appreciation for all the members of my adoption triad.

# The Seven Core Issues in Adoption and Permanency in Tribal Communities

## Kathryn England-Aytes

*If there is another group of people in America who have faced all the forces this society and its government could bring to bear in destroying their identity and fundamentally reshaping them in the image of the dominant society, I would like to meet them.* (Wildcat 2001)

There are currently 567 federally recognized tribes in 35 states in the United States.[1] According to the US Census Bureau, American Indians and Alaska Natives represent about 1.5 percent of the population—around 4.5 million individuals. In 2014, approximately 25 percent of the Native population lived on reservations or other tribal areas; 30 percent were below the age of 18; and the median age was 30 years old. Native Americans experience the highest rate of poverty of any racial group—almost twice the national average—as well as the highest rates of crime, addiction, abuse and suicide of any ethnic group in the United States (Lechner, Cavanaugh and Blyler 2016). According to Native American scholars, these issues are best addressed by recognizing the impact of separation and disconnection from tribal cultures and connections.

The nature of adoption for Native Americans must be considered in the context of the historical and intergenerational trauma experienced by adoptees, birth families and tribal communities. It is important to understand the roles that adoption, slavery and expansionism played in competing claims of land, liberty and citizenship in US post-revolutionary policies. These created a complex socio-political environment for Native peoples that shaped ideas about sovereignty, race, procreation and family systems. The new federal government

---

1    www.census.gov/history/pdf/c2010br-10.pdf.

pursued an aggressive expansion into Indian territories, following a previous century of uneasy co-existence and evolving economic relationships.

As an alternative to outright genocidal policies, federal policies began to stress assimilation through adoption of Native children into European homes, a practice that represented both a literal and metaphorical way to control Native American populations within expanding territorial borders. In 1813, during an invasion of Muscogee Creek territory, future US President Andrew Jackson discovered a Creek infant orphaned by his troops, and, "moved by an unusual sympathy," sent the child to be adopted into his plantation household in Tennessee. Author Dawn Peterson's *Indians in the Family* (2017) tells the stories of white adopters, adopted Native children and their Native parents, and the role that adoption played in efforts to subdue Native peoples in the name of nation building. Such efforts ultimately set the stage for new political struggles which began with the Indian Removal Act of 1830, and culminated in another century of forced removals, allotments, reservations and residential schools across Indian country (Peterson 2017).

Throughout the 20th century, assimilation policies encouraged the relinquishment and/or removal of Native children from tribal communities and their placement into residential schools or non-Native American adoptive homes. Citizenship was promised to those Natives who took advantage of an allotment and education policies designed to bring Natives into "civilized life." Education away from parental influence was considered essential, and the principal of the first boarding school for Native children at Carlisle, Pennsylvania, boasted that the goal for each student was to "kill the Indian in him and save the man." An estimated 300,000 Native children were placed in residential boarding schools. Infectious disease was widespread due to malnutrition, overcrowding and poor sanitary conditions. Students were punished for speaking their Native languages, and accounts of sexual, physical and emotional abuse were common.

Before the passage of the Indian Child Welfare Act (ICWA), approximately 25 percent of all Native children were removed from their homes, many of whom were adopted into non-Native families. The Bureau of Indian Affairs and the Child Welfare League of America partnered in 1958 to establish the Indian Adoption Project, which deliberately placed Native children from western states in non-Native adoptive homes in eastern states. Eventually, the Child Welfare League incorporated the program into the Adoption Resource Exchange of North America for "hard to place" children. It was not until the ICWA to prevent the unwarranted removal of children from their homes and communities passed through Congress in 1978 that federal policy provided increased tribal jurisdiction in matters of child placement and adoption. The latter part of the century saw a period of cultural revitalization and economic development for many tribes, with increasing emphasis on sovereignty, self-determination and cultural preservation. Relationship remains the cornerstone of tribal communities, and expression of community is that connection to the communal soul of their people (Cajete 2000).

Native Americans of the 21st century have been shaped for survival and resilience throughout generations of war, oppression, failed federal policies and outright malfeasance. Despite the hardships, they have survived. Clearly, this endurance is a sign of the strength represented in Native American peoples. Supporting a connection to that "communal soul" for Native American adoptees honors that resilience for future generations.

## Addressing the Seven Core Issues of Adoption for native adoptees

> *Having heard all of this you may choose to look the other way, but you can never again say that you did not know.* (William Wilberforce (1759–1833))

### Loss

Losses are experienced in every adoptive placement. For Native adoptees, losses are heightened by the loss of culture, racial identity, religion and language. Early federal policies, based on the idea that when Native people learned US customs and values they would merge peacefully with the dominant culture, resulted in the removal of nearly 25 percent of Native children from their homes to be reared in non-Native settings. This philosophy had a disastrous effect on Native communities.

### *Strategies for helping with loss*

- Seek *knowledge* about Native cultural values, historical legacies, contributions and achievements.

- *Learn* about a Native adoptee's birth community and seek ways to connect with that specific community as real people—with both a historical and contemporary context.

- Clearly *acknowledge* the unique loss of culture that adoption represents for Native adoptees.

## Rejection

Losses generate feelings or fear of rejection. Feelings or fears of rejection can negatively impact self-esteem, a sense of belonging and an awareness of one's unique role in a family, in a community and in the world. Native adult adoptees describe a desire to connect with their adoptive families, while simultaneously experiencing a desire to explore and understand their lost cultural identity and tribal connections. To meet this challenge, Native adoptees must feel that adoptive families can claim and parent them without dismissing or being in competition with their birth families.

### Strategies for addressing rejection

- Promote *cultural connections* and maintain relationships whenever possible with Native communities that go beyond a superficial understanding of pan-Indianism.

- Be *aware* of social norms that may differ in Native and non-Native cultures, such as interpretation of eye contact, body language, proximity during conversations, and speech patterns.

- Take *responsibility* for missteps and press on beyond misunderstanding or misinterpreting cultural cues.

## Shame and guilt

Native adoptees may experience shame as a toxic reaction to the belief that something must be intrinsically wrong with them. Guilt is a learned response. Everyone carries some shame or guilt about what is occurring and what they are able or not able to do about it. Maladaptive behaviors to guilt and shame may include a denial of Native identity and internalized racism, and may increase as adoptees become familiar with the history of indigenous peoples.

### Strategies to address shame and guilt

- Increase *awareness* of thoughts of self-shaming or self-loathing.
- *Reject* labels that denigrate a Native adoptee's identity, and address any indication that they are feeling damaged, different or an outsider in the family or community.

- *Learn* about a Native adoptee's birth community and seek ways to connect with the community as real people—with both a historical and contemporary context.

## Grief

Grief is a necessary response to a loss. Everyone has substantial losses, and grief becomes a challenge to be met by all. For Native adoptees, grief requires an acknowledgment of cultural loss, the expression of sadness and anger, time to feel the feelings and process the emotions, and support from others who have weathered similar losses.

### Strategies to address grief

- *Recognize* the full picture of Native birth families.

- *Encourage* spiritual rituals and/or prayers for comfort and emotional support.

- *Honor* the diversity, history, culture and contemporary realities of Native communities.

## Identity

Adoption changes the role of everyone in the adoption constellation. Tribal communities place great value on children as gifts from their Creator. Losing a birth child may result in a loss of identity for birth parents. Native adoptees may struggle with identity, particularly in adolescent years, and seek out ways to create a feeling of belonging, sometimes with extreme measures, such as totally rejecting the birth parents.

### Strategies to address identity issues

- Become an *accurate historian* and a gatherer of facts to allow Native adoptees to piece together a story or narrative about themselves that is fact based and cohesive.

- *Examine* the language used in describing all members of the adoption constellation. Language informs identity, especially for developing children.

- Be *sensitive* to how roles are defined in public and how much information is disclosed to outsiders. Protect children's circumstances and private information.

## Intimacy

For the Native adoptee who has been disconnected from racial, ethnic and cultural heritage, and who may feel dissimilar from family and the larger community, emotional intimacy can be a challenge. For adoptive families, creating intimacy with a Native child requires that cultural heritage be accepted and honored. There is always someone to support an adoptee's connection to their community and/or family system. The more broken connections the child has experienced, the more difficult connecting to a new family and community becomes.

## *Strategies for strengthening intimacy*

- Be *willing* to discuss the "dark side" of adoption, which involves the struggle with intimacy. Native children who struggle with attachment difficulties due to unresolved losses or feelings of rejection often create further rejection, and may present as ever cautious and watchful.

- *Establish* consistent routines to help Native adoptees feel safe and connected. Enquire about routines and rituals that are important to the child and incorporate them whenever possible.

- *Create* links with Native professionals, agencies and communities to support a Native adoptee's development of cultural identity.

- *Attend* to all intimate relationships within the family. Model relationships that are supportive and healing.

## Mastery and control

Mastery requires the ability to integrate life experiences, and become responsible for one's own feelings, thoughts and behaviors. The ability to "know thyself" deeply and authentically allows one to communicate clearly and intentionally, and to attune to the needs and feelings of others. Native adoptees lost control of their lives within the larger context of historical and contemporary trauma. Many embrace this legacy of loss as they work through adoption issues, developing an inner resilience that allows them to survive extraordinarily difficult experiences, and find healing and forgiveness.

## Strategies for gaining mastery

- *Practice* mindfulness, with past experiences acknowledged and honored, and model the ability to stay present in the moment.

- *Seek* out those who have lived the Native experience and can become sound supports and mentors. Life will present other losses to be worked through, and a supportive mentor will be essential in this journey.

- *Model* successful communication, problem solving and advocacy, as well as forgiveness of self and others.

It is a great mistake to think that the Indian is born an inevitable savage. He is born a blank, like all the rest of us. Left in the surroundings of savagery, he grows to possess a savage language, superstition, and life… Transfer the savage-born infant to the surroundings of civilization, and he will grow to possess a civilized language and habit…and gradually take on those of the side to which they have been transferred. (Capt. Richard Henry Pratt 1892)

They made us many promises, more than I can remember, but they never kept but one; they promised to take our land, and they did. (Red Cloud, Oglala Lakota)[2]

---

2     Red Cloud's speech was made in 1890 at Wounded Knee, following the massacre of 150 Lakota people, primarily old men, women and children.

|  | Adopted child | Adult adoptee | First/birth parents |
|---|---|---|---|
| Loss | The historical nature of adoption for Native Americans must be considered to understand the losses experienced by individual adoptees, their families and their tribal birth communities. Assimilation policies encouraged the relinquishment and/or removal of Native children from tribal communities and placement into orphanages, residential schools or adoptive non-Native homes beginning in the mid-19th century. Between the years of 1941 and 1978 when the Indian Child Welfare Act was passed, some 25 percent of all Native children were removed from their homes. This legacy must be included in any consideration of the contemporary experience of adoption for Native children. While all adopted children encounter the loss of birth family and community, Native children adopted into non-Native families experience many losses on a profound level, including birth culture, racial identity, legal status, religious heritage, and language. | For Native adoptees, losses are heightened by the loss of culture, racial identity, religion and language. Early federal policies, based on the idea that when Native people learned US customs and values they would merge peacefully with dominant American culture, resulted in the removal of nearly 25 percent of Native children from their homes to be reared in non-Native settings. This philosophy had a disastrous effect on Native communities. Adoptees describe a sense of not belonging in a primarily "white" society. A native adoptee shared the following: "My self-concept was so negative. I felt so ugly and unwanted and lonely. I did not have an Indian face to reflect my image. However, somewhere deep within myself I had a sense—as small as it was—that I was Indian and that it was a good thing… I did not know how I was going to get out, but I felt that I would." Adult adoptee losses can manifest in emotional, physical and spiritual areas of their lives. | Native birth parents experience loss in the context of both historical and future losses. Early child welfare policies were based on the idea that when Native people learned US customs and values, they would be able to merge peacefully and successfully with American culture. The removal of nearly 25 percent of Native children from their birth parents, often for "neglect" based on poverty, had a disastrous impact on tribal communities. The legacy of these adoptions and removals to orphanages, residential schools and non-Native adoptive homes is a part of every tribe's written and oral history. Contemporary Native birth parents experience the loss of adoption in the long shadow of this history in Indian country. These birth parents are among an extended constellation of grandparents, aunts, uncles and cousins who grieve the loss of a Native child. The grief is both historical and contemporary in nature, representing the family's loss of past and future generations. |

*cont.*

|  | Adopted child | Adult adoptee | First/birth parents |
|---|---|---|---|
| Rejection | Native children adopted into non-Native families describe feelings of never belonging within their families. One native adult adoptee shared her childhood experience as: "It was the feelings of being different, of not fitting in, because I didn't look like anyone around me. This led to unbearable feelings of isolation. I did not grow up looking into Indian faces, looking at Indian bodies." | Native adult adoptees describe a desire to explore tribal communities to understand their lost cultural identities, and a way to address the loss of both their history and future as a Native person. Feelings or fears of rejection can negatively impact self-esteem, a sense of belonging and an awareness of one's unique role in a family, in a community and in the world. To meet the challenges of adoption, adoptees must feel that adoptive families claim them and can parent them without dismissing or being in competition with their birth families. | Native birth parents describe feelings of rejection and confusion about the adoption experience and the placement of their children. Some birth parents may struggle with forming and maintaining relationships, perhaps due to lingering feelings of loss and guilt, or to a fear of repeating the loss of their children. Other birth parents may attempt to quickly fill the loss by establishing a new relationship, marrying, or giving birth again—without having dealt with the grief of the adoption placement. |
| Shame/Guilt | Shame and guilt may arise out of an adoptee's sense of rejection.<br><br>As Native children experience the dominant culture's rejection of their birth culture and history, they struggle to reconcile this with their own developing identity. Some adoptees describe early experiences with shame in educational settings. One native adoptee described his experience in a boarding school this way: "Can you imagine an Indian kid sitting in a classroom with all-white kids, and your history book is telling you what dirty, filthy, heathens Native Americans were?" Others describe feelings that they were unlovable within their own birth family and culture, and were therefore placed in non-Native families. | Adult adoptees who experience a continued sense of shame and guilt can find it debilitating. They may understand that birth parents have grown-up reasons to relinquish a child, but unresolved feelings that their adoption was a reflection of not being "good enough" for a mother to keep can bring deep shame. Toxic reactions to the belief that something must be intrinsically wrong with them may include a denial of Native identity and internalized racism. Maladaptive behavior may increase as they become more familiar with the history of Native Americans in the dominant culture. | Many Native birth parents live in silent shame over the events which led to their child's relinquishment, removal or placement in an adoption setting. In recent years, Native adoptees have repatriated to their tribal families and communities, and some birth parents have shared stories. "Many broken-hearted mothers did hand over their children. Many were coerced with shame by being told, 'You don't have anything to offer your child.'" This experience of Native birth parents must be understood with any consideration of tribal adoption. |

| | | | |
|---|---|---|---|
| **Grief** | There is no opportunity to grieve lost cultural identity or unknown tribal communities. Native adoptees may struggle to accurately label and grieve feelings such as numbness, sadness, anger, depression, emptiness or anxiety. Young children may exhibit anger, or demonstrate little expression or excitement about life in general. Some may be excessively nervous or shy, and worry more than is typical. Grieving occurs within the context of one's culture. The loss of their native culture robs them of access to understanding their grief within their culture or origin. | Adoptees may not fully appreciate the impact of their adoption losses until adulthood. Delayed grief can drain resources and manifest in a variety of ways, including acting out through substance abuse, depression or aggressive behaviors. Native adult adoptees describe a resurfacing of grief across time, especially at times of other loss or at anniversaries of other losses. Confronting and talking about inner issues like grief renders the benefit of taking the issue outward and reshaping one's perceptions about it. | Native birth parents grieve the loss of a child to whom they are genetically connected in communities that place great value on family lineage, tribal connection and community relationships. There is little opportunity for them to grieve, let alone to publicly acknowledge, their children. Birth parents have described grief as washing over them in stages or waves, particularly at times of other losses or developmental transitions, including the birth of other children and the loss of family members. The important role they have as parents in tribal communities, and their forfeiture of this role, will reshape the entire course of their lives. |
| **Identity** | For Native children, identity is intertwined with legal, cultural, religious and political constructs.<br><br>Born into one family, Native adoptees lose an identity as they acquire one from their adoptive family. If that family is non-Native, questions of identity are further complicated. A person forming their identity within their Native community creates a different outcome from a child who is Native and gaining their identity from non-Native parents and extended family. The non-Native family does not understand and cannot offer a Native cultural identity and is less apt to have role models to help the child gain access to that part of their identity. | Adoption can threaten one's sense of identity. Native adoptees' identities are further complicated by legal, cultural and political considerations. Identity formation for Native people can include resisting definitions and rejecting stereotypes while seeking to construct a positive identity with their own voice. Native adoptees who have been repatriated to their families and communities describe a frustration of learning who they are as Native people from the voices and writings of others. This often pushes them to reconnect with birth families, and to seek "official recognition" of who they are as Native people. | Native identity can be as complex for Native birth parents as it is for adoptees. Tribal communities place great value on children as gifts from the Creator, and birth parents may believe they have lost an important part of their identity when a birth child is lost. Adoptive parents and birth parents also experience a common role confusion. Neither set of parents may lay full claim to their child, nor may they gain distance from issues which arise with the adoptee. A struggle with identity may lead adoptees, particularly in adolescent years, to seek out ways to create a feeling of belonging, sometimes with extreme measures, such as totally rejecting birth parents. |

*cont.*

| | Extended birth/first family | Adoptive parents | Extended adoptive family |
|---|---|---|---|
| Intimacy | For the Native adoptee who has been disconnected from their racial, ethnic and cultural heritage, and who may feel dissimilar from both their family and larger community, emotional intimacy is more of a challenge. If adoptive parents are unable or unwilling to discuss this "dark side" of adoption, children will struggle alone, wary of close intimate relationships. Children who struggle with attachment difficulties, due to unresolved losses or feelings of rejection, often create further rejection. Native adoptees describe that they are aware of holding back part of themselves in relationships, being ever cautious and watchful. | Adult adoptees' issues with loss are particularly evident in intimate relationships. Some state that they have never truly felt close to anyone because that would require knowing themselves, their story, their history and their cultural lineage. Native adoptees describe their early experiences of cultural losses as impacting their intimate relationships as adults. One native female adoptee shared: "There was a time when I felt that my feelings of isolation and confusion were solely a result of the abuse. But that's not true. They are a result of not being connected to that spiritual center as an Indian woman." | Birth parents who did not voluntarily consent to their child's adoption may experience increased anxiety and shame about children whom they view as "stolen children," a term used to refer to Native children removed during the adoption era. The additional challenges that led to the separation of parent and child may also impact intimacy, i.e. addiction, poverty, mental health issues, trauma and historical trauma. Shame that comes from a person's sense of unworthiness and/or originates from the community surrounding the individual leads to a diminishment of trust in self and others, which inhibits true emotional intimacy. |
| Mastery/Control | Native adoptees are keenly aware that they were not party to the decisions that led to their adoption. This knowledge must be understood in the context of historical and contemporary trauma for Native people around the issues of child removal, and its impact on past and future generations. The unnatural change of course has a profound impact on Native adoptees' feelings of mastery, accomplishment, achievement, fulfillment and competence. | The knowledge that adoptees lost control of their lives at a very early age must also be understood in the context of historical and contemporary trauma for Native people around the issues of child removal. Even so, Native adoptees describe some gains as they have worked through adoption issues. Many describe the development of an inner resilience that allowed them to survive extraordinarily difficult experiences, finding healing and forgiveness in the process. | Contemporary Native birth parents experience the loss of adoption in the shadow of a history involving the forced removal of their children. Even those birth parents who have consented to their children's adoption may feel they did not have control over the outcome. Their grief is historical and contemporary in nature, representing the family's loss of both past and future generations. Some birth parents describe reunification experiences as painful reminders of past events. Those who have overcome a sense of powerlessness cite an emphasis on healing and forgiveness as part of their journey. |

| Loss | With 568 federally recognized tribes in the US, comprising under 2 percent of the population, there is no generic "Native American," and the experience of being Native in the US can be very different. Native people, however, may share common values and world views, with an essence of Native American knowledge as the understanding of how all things are interrelated and continuously interacting. Within traditional Native cultures, there are similarities in the way culture and societal values are learned by children. While tribal groups may vary in beliefs and practices, traditional child-rearing among Natives often includes the practice of children modeling and imitating the behaviors of important people in their lives.<br><br>The losses for Native children include intergenerational practices of child rearing, and are both contemporary and historical. | Before the 1978 Indian Child Welfare Act, most Native children were placed in non-Native homes. Without connections to Native communities, adoptive parents could not provide their children with an opportunity to learn and maintain Native culture and beliefs. Throughout the 18th and 19th centuries, this was largely seen as a benefit for Native children, who were removed from tribal communities as part of assimilation policies. Though unnamed, the loss of these opportunities to instill pride in themselves and their culture may be a struggle for adoptive parents as well. | Extended family networks in non-Native adoptive families differ significantly from Native kinship systems. Child care is generally part of specific gender and family roles, and extended families do not have direct responsibility for supervision or correction of children. Loss for extended family members has not received a great deal of attention, but for these family members, the adoption of Native children may highlight differences among birth grandchildren, nieces and nephews, and the roles they have in extended families. Acknowledging the loss of an adopted child's birth culture and its replacement with an adopted family's non-Native culture and traditions may affect relationships among all family members. Adopting Native children may be viewed as a family's effort to "rescue" a child. |

*cont.*

|  | Extended birth/first family | Adoptive parents | Extended adoptive family |
|---|---|---|---|
| Rejection | Children raised in traditional, tribal communities are viewed as a gift from the Creator. Some tribes view children as coming so recently from spiritual culture that they have a special connection with spiritual matters and they should be listened to by all family members. Native families include multiple generations of grandparents, aunts, uncles and cousins who share in child care and supervision. When a Native child is removed from a tribal family, the community feels the loss of these intergenerational connections, which include a loss of culture, historical identity and language. Regardless of the circumstances of the placement, birth/first families may view the loss of their child as a rejection of their Native culture and tradition. | Non-native adoptive parents may experience feelings or rejection simply because there is often a marked difference between their child's birth culture and their own. Connections with positive role models from both cultures can assist non-Native adoptive families in parenting a Native child. Establishing such connections can be difficult if the adoption was contested. This conflict must be addressed by adoptive parents if they are to open a door to Native culture for their children, who may feel they belong in both cultures. A true sense of belonging comes from the adoptive family claiming the child and feeling entitled to parent without dismissing or being in competition with the birth family. This can be challenging for non-Native birth parents who have adopted Native children. Seeing children develop their own sense of uniqueness, their abilities, looks and special talents, may feel like rejection of adoptive parents, particularly if they differ greatly from those of the adoptive parents. | Non-Native extended adoptive family members may experience some form of rejection with the adoption of a Native child as they seek roles in the child's life. Identifiable differences may highlight the roles they have with other children in the community. Extended family members may experience challenges in engaging tribal leaders and Native birth and extended families to support their child. They may have trouble figuring out how to build relationships with Native people and communities even though they are eager to do so. It is important to understand that tribal leaders have many good reasons for being reluctant about engaging with non-Native adoptive families resulting from conflicts with state child welfare systems, and significant historical distrust. Building relationships takes time, especially if tribes have experienced the forced removal of their children by state and federal governments, policies. |
| Shame/Guilt | The public policies behind the removal of Native children in the 18th and 19th centuries were described as an attempt to "rescue" Native children from poverty and challenging social conditions and give them access to the resources of the white middle class. In reality, it served as an effort to nearly eradicate the Native American population.<br><br>Many who survived struggled with a sense of shame and guilt over the dominant culture's rejection of them. Birth families may struggle with guilt that they were not able to keep a child within the community, and that the loss of that child reshaped the entire course of the community. | Non-Native adoptive parents may experience feelings of guilt and shame arising out of the historical and contemporary hardships experienced by Native communities which resulted in Native children being removed from their homes and communities. Native children placed in non-Native homes may experience great difficulty with their identity as they mature and find themselves members of two cultures. Adoptive parents may struggle to find accurate information about their child's birth culture and traditions, especially if there has been no contact with the community. | Extended adoptive family members can also experience feelings and guilt from an awareness of the historical policies regarding Native Americans in the US. They can also be a resource for one another and their adopted child by educating themselves about their child's birth community and seeking ways to connect with the community as real people— with both an historical and contemporary context. Creating a full picture of birth and adoptive families, communities and cultures can address guilt and shame, and be an invaluable resource. |

| Grief | Family kinship systems form the foundation of tribal communities. Many traditional societies considered aunts and uncles as mothers and fathers, while cousins were brothers and sisters. All members shared with parenting responsibility and no one person had sole responsibility for a child. Children could be corrected by anyone in the community and the supervision was everyone's job. Children are valued members of tribal societies, representing the renewal of life and the continuation of culture. The loss of a child to a family represents a loss of a child to the community. The impetus for the Indian Child Welfare Act included the Native perspective that children "belonged" to their tribal community. While every loss in adoption must be grieved, this community loss is particularly difficult. There is no way to resolve this within Native communities, as children are irreplaceable connections to the future. Birth families may experience an intense period of grief at the time of the loss of their child, but are unable to express it in the face of commonly held beliefs that a child is better off without them. The grief does not vanish. | For Native children, grief may be connected to unacknowledged and unspoken feelings regarding cultural loss, as cited by a repatriated Lakota child who was adopted into a non-Native family at the age of 4 in 1966 (Wood 2011): "We were on the front page of the newspaper, along with lots of good talk about…adoption. We were brought up without our culture, which took a terrible toll on our lives. I grew up angry and miserable." In the case of parents who have not grieved their own losses regarding an inability to have birth children, this "misery" of an adoptive child can add additional grief. Adoptive parents must address their own grief as well as that of their children, particularly at adoption anniversaries and times of subsequent loss and grief. Such grief may continue as a child grows up, since they can never fully meet the fantasies and expectations of their adoptive parents. | Extended adoptive families may find it difficult to acknowledge the experience of grief and in many instances may be unaware of it. Some may have encouraged family members to adopt children to replace the loss of birth children, or the inability to have birth children, as if they are interchangeable. As a result, family members may ignore or minimize grief as they do other loss issues, particularly if they are expressed at a time when other cognitive or developmental processes for adoptees arise. Extended family members may be unaware that the adoption of Native children highlights differences among birth grandchildren, nieces and nephews, and the roles they have in those families. They may also expect that children who have been removed from abusive homes will feel only relief and gratitude, which can complicate the expressions of loss or grief for all members of the adoption constellation. |

*cont.*

| | Extended birth/first family | Adoptive parents | Extended adoptive family |
|---|---|---|---|
| Identity | Many researchers have noted that Native people often experience identity as a part of "collective selves." Group membership is central to collective identity and is different from "individualistic selves," which is seen as autonomous from other groups who value individualism more highly. A collective world view values kinship as the foundation of social life, and it is within this kinship that Native American children learn cultural and societal values and identities. While tribal groups in the US vary in their traditional child-rearing beliefs and practices, there are some similarities among the groups with regard to encouraging children to model and imitate the behaviors of important people in their lives. In tribal societies, children are valued members and represent the renewal of life. Traditional education of children involves the use of stories, humor and theater. Experience is emphasized as a primary tool for learning, and children are taught to be responsible to the community.<br><br>When a child is lost to the birth/first family, irrespective of the events which led to it, there remains an empty space once occupied by that child, no matter how briefly. | Adoptive parents take on the task of assisting their Native adopted child to develop an identity that is likely to be very different from their birth families. If they attempt to preserve their child's Native identity, it is likely to be very different from their own identity. Child development professionals emphasize the importance of supporting a child's natural curiosity about their developing identity and how they fit into their cultural environment. As Native adopted children gain a developing sense of identity, their adopted parents can provide opportunities to discover and claim identities in both their birth and adoptive cultures. This may be difficult for adoptive parents who struggle with what it means to be Native, or who may struggle to obtain complete and accurate information about Native cultural identity generally, and their child's Native birth family specifically. | Extended family systems, whether Native or non-Native, birth or adoptive, may place great value on kinship systems in successfully parenting their children. Native communities teach their children that collective kinship systems are strengthened by individual members, and group members are responsible to and for the collective group. This is a crucial factor in what it means to truly recognize and respect tribal sovereignty. Adoptive extended families can help Native adoptees develop an identity that includes both their birth and adopted families, as well as their Native and non-Native families. This is vital for children who may have been removed from situations that cannot provide actual links with birth communities. The need for extended families to reflect who that child is and where they come from does not change simply because the past is painful. Repatriated Native children describe the need for this connection even when adoptive families and communities have been loving and accepting: "Even in loving families, Native adoptees live without a sense of who they are. Love doesn't provide identity." |

| Intimacy | Extended birth/first families may experience intimate connections differently with parents who have lost a birth child than they did before such loss. There may be a stigma for birth/first parents who have voluntarily relinquished a child, and some may question their ability to parent any child successfully. Extended family members may suggest a "replacement" child for both the parents and the community. Native children are often cared for by parents, grandparents, aunts and uncles, and attachment to another child may play an important healing role in addressing the loss of a child through adoption. Conversely, attachment and bonding with other children may be difficult after a loss. Native families who have experienced multiple losses may experience difficulties bonding with other children. Extended birth families may find themselves challenged to move beyond the loss of children who are important parts of the tribe's future, and who have taken that future with them. Coming to terms with that loss can take years as the community incorporates the stories of those losses. | Adoptive families may find that Native adopted children seem to be reserved in their connections to parents and siblings, holding back a part of themselves in family relationships. This issue can have a residual effect on family relationships, including the adopted child's perception that they are somehow to blame for any dysfunction or maladaptive behavior in the adoptive family. All imagined losses can take years to address, and can affect intimacy in multiple ways. Native distinctiveness joins the intersection of infertility and adoption as part of the unique story of adoptive parents and their family's creation. | Traditionally, the education of Native children involved the extended family, with direct care of children, the telling of stories and humor, sometimes for correction. The removal of Native children from this community represents a loss that cannot be substituted with a non-Native nuclear family where intergenerational relationships exist, but are not closely interrelated. Native children are taught a deep appreciation for the meaning of extended family, particularly elders, within their community.<br><br>Extended adoptive family members may not understand the history of displacement that some Native communities have experienced, and the legacy that such children share. For some of these children, their adoptive placement may have included disrupted early bonding and attachment, which will impact intimate relationships for their whole lives. An associated anxiety may impact relationships for the child within the extended adoptive family. They may remain ambivalent or avoidant towards a family which, in turn, holds them at some distance to avoid potential conflict. |

*cont.*

| | Extended birth/first family | Adoptive parents | Extended adoptive family |
|---|---|---|---|
| **Mastery/Control** | Birth/first families did not plan for any of their children to leave the community. All contemporary adoption stories come with the unfortunate legacy of Native families losing their children, not because they chose to place them, but because they were viewed as an impediment to their children's well-being, "civilization" and assimilation into mainstream American society. Native adoption must be understood in the context that birth communities surrendered not only their children, but also their volition, and the feelings of victimization and powerlessness that were generated in a community became themes with which many still struggle. There can be significant healing for birth/first families when tribal communities work through issues of loss with a focus on tribal sovereignty. Native people have faced enormous struggles to survive. Their resilience is both an individual and a collective resource in their communities. | Child-nurturing practices embedded in the traditional Native social structure can be trusted and effective. The recognition and acknowledgment of these practices by non-Native adoptive parents can help Native children find a place in both worlds. Adoptive parents should avoid power struggles while acknowledging their own feelings about lack of control. Rituals and ceremonies are ways to facilitate a painful letting go and regain a sense of control for everyone. Adoptive families can seek a broader perspective of Native issues, both historical and contemporary, to assist them in successfully parenting Native children who represent the future of a resilient and honorable people. | Extended adoptive families for Native children should understand that Native adoptions originated from the traumatic legacy of removing children from their Native communities. Serving as replacement extended families can be painful when viewed in this context, and family members may struggle to comprehend the historical trauma of the communities which produced the child they now claim and love as theirs. Extended family members can support the healing of those Native children with an informed acknowledgment of the history, as well as supporting contemporary connections with Native community members who can address the physical, emotional and spiritual losses suffered. Terry Cross, Seneca Nation of Indians tribal member and founder of the National Indian Child Welfare Association, is quoted as follows: "Mainstream society's services are so fractured. Medical doctors get the body, psychologists get the mind, judges get the social context, and clergy get the spirit. But, in fact, we are all whole people, and real solutions have to address that." |

## Further information

www.adoptivefamilies.com/talking-about-adoption/adoptees-seven-core-issues-of-adoption

England-Aytes, K. (2012) *Memories Hold Hands: Understanding Historical Trauma in Contemporary Populations in Indian Country*. Tribal Law and Policy Institute, Indian Nations Conference. Palm Springs, CA.

"Native American Cultures: Family Life, Kinship, and Gender." *Encyclopedia of the American West*. 4 vols. Macmillan Reference USA, 1996. Reproduced in History Resource Center. Farmington Hills, MI: Gale.

Pratt, Capt. R.H. (1892) *The Advantages of Mingling Indians with Whites*. Reprinted in Pratt, R.H. (1973) *Americanizing the American Indians: Writings by the "Friends of the Indian" 1880–1900*, pp.260–271. Cambridge, MA: Harvard University Press.

www.wearecominghome.com/ComingHome.php

# Chapter 21

# Siblings and the Seven Core Issues in Adoption and Permanency

## Heidi Staples

I was adopted as an infant in Massachusetts to a Protestant middle-class family in 1957. Catholic Charities was the adoption agency. A year and a half after my adoption, they contacted my parents to inform them that they had another Protestant baby and would they perhaps like to adopt again? This is how my sister and I came to join my adoptive family, which consisted of my father, a college professor of mechanical engineering, and a college-educated stay-at-home mother, who had a smart 7-year-old birth son at the time I joined the family. When I was 7, my parents gave birth to another boy, and that is how our family was formed, two girls and two boys, two by adoption and two born into the family. The town where I was raised was near idyllic and times were simple but happy. My sister and I were always aware that we were adopted and had been "chosen" to join the family in a special way. Of course, later we had to come to terms with what that meant in terms of who we were and who "unchose" us, which we handled in very different ways. Many of my parents' friends had also adopted, so we had a natural community in which adoption was not seen as all that strange or in a negative way. Who would have thought that there were any issues that would come up for any of us?

The adoption agency had given my parents some information about our birth mothers' situations. Both had come from homes for unwed mothers and had been pregnant out of wedlock in their late teens—a crisis, especially in those times. Nothing was in writing, so we had to rely on my mother's memory of those prior verbal disclosures by the agency years ago.

Yet, as I learned over time, adoption is not a one-time event that solves many problems (a child needs a home, parents want a child, a parent can't care for their child) but rather a lifelong process for all of those touched by it, including not only the triad members (adoptee, birth parents, adoptive parents) but all the other children and family members in those homes, as well as the children in any kin, relative or caregiver homes who may have cared for the children prior to their adoption or come to care for them after their adoption. It is like a stone hitting the water of the pond near our summer camp on Cape Cod, watching the ripples go out into a larger body of water.

When I became a social worker, then moved into child protective/welfare work and then became an adoptions administrator, I learned over time more about adoption, but it was when I read and heard about the Seven Core Issues of Adoption and Permanency that all of it fell into place for me. I then understood that *of course* we all go through these stages, no matter how we are adopted or at what age, that all of the members of the triad as well as those close to them are affected, and that understanding these issues is the key to working through them successfully towards a well-balanced and happy life. Adoption has shaped me and my family, both the one I came from as well as my adult children's families, as well as how I deal with life, the profession I chose, the lens through which I view the world, my values and my passions. It has made me stronger and more empathetic for others, and I certainly know how to walk in others' shoes (as my shoes were changed for me, so to speak). Yet it also presents unique challenges and issues, for which the best preparation is information and insight. That is the gift of the Seven Core Issues of Adoption and Permanency, crafted so brilliantly decades ago by Sharon Kaplan Roszia and Deborah Silverstein, and I am grateful that now Sharon and Allison Davis Maxon are bringing these issues forward in an expanded and updated version to share their revealing and insightful truths for adoptive families and the professionals who work with them in order to assist them in their adoptive journeys.

I was honored to be asked to write about sibling relationships as it is so complicated and so often overlooked. I have had incredibly close relationships with my adopted brothers, but a complicated relationship with my adoptive sister. She was born into a different birth family with closed relationships and has subsequently reunited with birth siblings as well as distant ones. This has affected me and all my siblings, as well as all of our families. I also have step-siblings and in-law siblings as well—so many types of "sisters" and "brothers" who have enriched my world.

Growing up, my older brother Russell, being seven years older, was almost like another parent; he was thoughtful, smart, fun, gifted athletically and intellectually, and a natural leader who was much admired but who always remained kind and gentle. He would tease me with kindness, watched over us three younger kids and was movie-star handsome. Often compared to Robert Redford in looks and demeanor, he always made us feel safe, loved and special. He was good at so many things, a great athlete who taught skiing at Colorado ski resorts, a gifted student who graduated from Tufts with a degree in engineering, and an accomplished sailor and tennis player. He befriended a young man with a terminal illness in high school who looked different and was often excluded by others; they shared a close friendship until that young man died in their senior year. My brother never tolerated bullying or discrimination, without being preachy or judgmental. I always felt that I won the sibling lottery with Russ. He married the love of his life, Suzanne, also an adopted person, in a lovely ceremony on Christmas Eve in a chapel, with roses wound through her beautiful brown hair; they were a stunning and happy couple for ten years. When Russell was killed by a drunk driver at the age of 36 on the way home from work, I had to find my father on a road trip in the middle of the night and tell him his first-born son had died. It was a family tragedy that none of us ever fully recovered from, but I felt that I was so very lucky to have had Russ as a big brother for as long as I did.

Being adopted was something that we all knew about, but it did not determine how close we felt as siblings. The intensity of the loss reverberated not only throughout our family but our friends as well; one of them recently told me, 30 years later, that she could remember exactly where she was when she heard about Russell's death; it was similar to the JFK assassination or 9/11 to all of us, in terms of remembering where we were in relation to this highly traumatic event.

My sister in my adoptive family struggled mightily as an adolescent and ever since, much of which may have been related to grappling with self-esteem and identity issues as part of being an adopted person, as well as the disintegrating state of our parents' marriage during our adolescent years. Yet who is to say that these struggles are related solely to being adopted? Or solely to being in a family that was undergoing troubles at a critical time in her life? It is not exclusively one or the other, nor is it so different from the challenges any family might face. Awareness of the issues that adoption brings and seeking help with professionals knowledgeable about adoption topics can certainly help address these areas, but does not mean that events will not happen, as they do in all families. It did help my sister to find her birth family and she did indeed feel an affinity for her siblings. Her children also have enjoyed the relationships with their birth grandmother and aunts and uncles as well. It is enriching to know more people with whom we share a biological bond as well as those with whom we have a shared history. Adoption certainly from an early age shaped my future, in everything from relationships to career path to fundamental beliefs and lifelong interests, including a love of history.

I used to play cards for hours on end as a young adolescent. We would play in the sand and swim in the lake and then plunk down for hours at a time and play Hearts and other card games, often barely stopping for meals. Much laughter and all manner of joking and trash-talking ensued! I recently ran into some of the friends with whom I spent those hours of card playing and we felt an instant connection even though 40 years had passed. It is how I sometimes feel with my birth sister Lorna, who I met first in my thirties. We often see the world in a similar way and will talk for hours. We are close—closer than we are to some of our siblings in our birth or my adoptive families. That is also not so different from the complexity of relationships many experience with childhood friends and families of origin when we may be closer to one sibling than another, or familial relationships which may ebb and flow over time. There is comfort in the familiarity of both a shared history and experiences as well as a shared ancestry and biology. It is Lorna who was able to explain why I had inherited issues with my feet that landed me firmly in several podiatrists' offices, being asked about hereditary foot anomalies—these are not details often covered in adoption disclosure meetings! And she can tell me things about the family history as well as our birth mother, who I never met, as she had passed away before I was reunited with my birth family. It was Lorna who told me that "our mother loved to play cards, it was like an obsession with her; she couldn't wait until we kids were old enough to play with her." I of course immediately identified with that, as a child and as a parent. It is in these and a myriad of other ways that I am grateful to have found such a wonderful birth sister.

My older and younger brothers in my adoptive family, although 14 years apart, were almost identical in appearance as well as mannerisms. My sister and I were definitely different from them, and from each other. Although I was more similar in appearance to my adoptive family than my sister was, I was different in terms of interests and abilities. My sister, with her red hair and freckles, was the most different looking, but she was more similar to the rest of the family in terms of her athletic abilities, as she was a much better skier, tennis player and swimmer than I was, and these were big interests in my adoptive family. I enjoyed reading, dancing and card playing, all lifelong interests for me. My sister wanted to be a singer, and many years later, when I met her birth mother, with her red hair and freckles, she talked about my sister's birth father having such a love of singing and performing, which is also shared by my sister's daughter a generation later.

All of this has led me to think about how much of our lives are shaped by adoption, but also how all families have in them those who have shared interests and abilities, as well as differences. In my adopted family they played bridge, and my mother loved to read and garden, which I also enjoyed. My mother, like her mother before her, was very artistic and talented, traits I did not share. I came to feel that so much of what shapes us is determined by the acceptance, understanding and appreciation of the similarities, as well as the unique characteristics and abilities, of each child. This allows children to succeed in families whether formed by adoption or birth, and to understand that love of siblings is not formed solely by birth or by adoption. In all families, special talents and interests can be nurtured and developed if they are appreciated and given opportunities to be explored, and each child brings their unique set of abilities and inherited traits that need to be nurtured in order to develop.

These are a few snippets of my story, which I share to exemplify that *everyone* has their own story, each of which is unique, special and deserving to be treasured. Relationships with siblings need to be recognized and honored, as they are foundational to one's place in the world, and some of the strongest and most long-lasting ties throughout a person's lifetime. It behoves everyone to be broadly inclusive and thoughtful in our concept of sibling relationships, including those in foster, kinship, step-, adoptive and blended families. Non-traditional families are more accepted today as there is a move to embrace the concept of family diversity. This must always include recognizing the value and importance of sibling bonds.

As a social worker, supervisor and manager of a large adoption program, I saw hundreds of scenarios, each unique but with common themes, involving siblings of children placed for adoption from foster care. These included those in which children were removed under emergent circumstances from their birth families and placed in relative or foster homes; some of the children were subsequently moved several times, sometimes with little notice, to different homes and ultimately to adoptive homes. Although social service agencies generally understand that best child welfare practices dictate that there should be planning and pre-visitation when moving children from home to home, there are times when that is not possible, such as when there are accusations of abuse or neglect in the caregiver's home, or if a foster parent or relative has a medical emergency or something similar, when an emergency change of placement is required. Some of the most significant relationships for a child involve their siblings, including those with whom they were raised prior to removal, the "emotional" if not legal siblings they share a bond with in foster, relative or kin settings, and their adoptive families. These relationships should be considered and brought into planning whenever possible. This will only happen if *all* types of sibling relationships and bonds are valued and considered by the professionals and families involved in the child's case.

When I supervised or talked with staff as an administrator, I was often taken aback by the lack of concern about separating siblings in adoption or foster care, or in not trying to place them in the same home when they entered the system years apart. The response was often "Oh but they never lived together." This lack of concern was predicated on a lack of awareness and understanding rather than a lack of diligence, and was often indicative of a lack of adoption-informed training. However, I found it chilling. In response to that and other knowledge/practice gaps, I brought in the experts to teach about adoption-informed practice and the Seven Core Issues of Adoption and Permanency, having discovered them in many ways and through multiple avenues over the years. I had also identified a lack of adoption-informed practice among local therapists who were treating foster and adopted youth, so we devised an eight-month program of one-day classes to address these gaps. On one Friday each month for eight months, the majority of the adoption staff attended all-day, off-site trainings with Sharon Kaplan Roszia, Deborah Silverstein and Allison Davis Maxon. That same dream team met on Saturdays with local therapists who received similar training, geared towards their role.

The impacts were significant and dramatic. There was a new use of shared adoption-appropriate language. The adoption social workers, who were either assigned to working with children or with the adoption applicant adults, passed on their new knowledge and skills to their clients. We revamped our training to include the new knowledge and skills, and developed advanced training sessions that were adoption informed. Morale improved as the staff felt that they were receiving highly valuable and relevant training that indicated the high level of value in which they were held by the agency, and it improved their level of professionalism and commitment. They had reading and homework, and actively participated in these training sessions, which increased their confidence as well as their sense of being a team. A year later I was in court and was excited to observe a fairly young staff member confidently and capably testifying about the Seven Core Issues of Adoption and Permanency and how these were impacting his client, and what services were needed to address those challenges.

When I spoke to groups or classes of social workers, or in one-on-one or group consultations, I would often ask, "How would you feel if you suddenly learned that you had a sibling out there in the world who you just learned existed? Even if you had never met or lived with that person?" Of course, the responses were not "Oh that doesn't matter" but rather an overwhelming and urgent response that, yes, they would want to meet them or assist them, to learn about them, to make and maintain contact. It is a normal and very human reaction to want to know who you are connected to! Biological relationships and family are important to all of us. Where we come from helps define who we are. Our biological families gave us life; our adoptive families cared for and raised us. They are not mutually exclusive. As Sharon famously says, "Adoption is about addition, not subtraction." No truer words could be spoken.

Siblings are a bonus—be they foster, adoptive, birth, kin or step, sibling relationships are critical to maintain and value. Once we think about it, of course it makes sense to us, for we only have to think back to our own experiences as a child. The vulnerability we feel when any of those crucial sibling relationships are threatened or lost can shake us to our core.

The grid below helps us organize the different types of sibling relationships which we can encounter as adoptees or as the professionals. Siblings may have lived together and then be separated. Some siblings may remain with birth families and no longer have contact after adoption. The core issues affect them all!

A child may be placed in an adoptive home while siblings are placed with a relative, birth, foster or adoptive home. The adoptive family's interest in maintaining contact may change over time and is generally at their discretion after the adoption is finalized. I have seen adoptive families who begin in fear and only have contact with birth parents due to being required to do so as foster parents, only to later learn what a positive gift that contact is for their adopted child. It allows adopted children to not have to wonder about where they came from, who they look like, where their talents or skills or medical conditions came from and so on, because they can ask someone who knows. It can also help them better understand what happened to them and the reasons and circumstances of their adoption.

Siblings are often overlooked but always important. In cases of both voluntary and involuntary adoptions as an infant, often there are subsequent siblings born to the same birth parents, who may be subsequently placed for adoption or may grow up within the birth families. Establishing those relationships, even years or decades later, is often a treasure trove of benefits and joy to all parties involved and their families. While it may be initially awkward or challenging, having adoption-informed professionals involved can assist in helping to navigate any issues and manage expectations, boundaries and roles.

For many adoptees who never located their birth or adopted siblings, a void can be present that no one else can fill. The ability to grieve these losses with understanding and adoption-informed family members, support people and professionals can help adoptees and birth, kin and adopted siblings better cope with these issues.

For foster and kin siblings who do not share a common biological or legal tie with someone with whom they lived for some time in a sibling-type relationship, it can be difficult to grieve a relationship that is not well recognized by others. The grid below helps us categorize and recognize the various types of issues which may arise and how these may affect the parties. Maintaining contact, providing and sharing pictures and honoring those relationships by recognizing their value and meaning can help all parties work through those losses or forge a new way to maintain contact or to reunify.

Throughout my personal life and decades as a professional social worker working with children and families, the Seven Core Issues in Adoption and Permanency has been a beacon, providing a critical framework through which professionals and family members alike could recognize and understand the impact on multiple family members in the constellation. I am very appreciative indeed that the various subtleties and nuances involving siblings will be part of that crucial lens moving forward.

| | Birth siblings—separated No contact | Birth siblings—separated Contact/visits | Adopted siblings |
|---|---|---|---|
| Loss | There can be a longing and magical thinking for siblings, especially if there is no contact with birth parents or they are deceased, wondering what life is like for them, what they are like, how are they, if they are cared for, if they are like the adoptee. Longing may be more intense after the death of adoptive parents, due to a desire for birth connections. Adoptees who do not have information about whether they have siblings can feel a sense of being robbed of that birthright to have that information/contact. There can be a pervasive ongoing sense of loss throughout life. | Longing for increased contact and difficulties dealing with contact limitations can cause resentments about different family settings among siblings. Increased contact and the ability to be flexible to accommodate changing needs over the lifespan can be helpful; adoptive parents being receptive and welcoming to this contact may be very helpful to adoptees. This may be complicated if some siblings remain in birth families or adoptive families don't work well together, or some siblings are adopted and some grow out of foster care without permanency. | The child may lose birth parent order, i.e. going from oldest in birth order to being a middle child, or from a family with many children to being an only child or vice versa. They may not share common abilities, interests or appearance with adoptive siblings and may differ on how they perceive their adoptions, or may have a differential response if some are adopted and some are birth children, so sensitivity by adoptive parents to these issues is key. |
| Rejection | Having no contact can contribute to sense of not being as good as, not deserving of having these relationships that are normal for other people. For siblings who previously lived together or who have knowledge of each other, there can be a sense of perceived rejection if lack of contact continues and if there is not an age-appropriate explanation about the lack of contact. Sensitivity to questions and issues as they arise will help adoptees navigate these issues from childhood through adolescence, early adulthood and on. | Visits/contact may not always be comfortable or stress free, particularly if all parties are not equally comfortable with contact, visits and roles, including adoptees, siblings and adoptive or birth parents. Adoptees may have changing needs or wants regarding contacts over their lifespan and in different life stages, so flexibility and assistance with navigating relationships can help. Some may have success with establishing traditions or structured frequency, visitation or time-of-year contact. As in most family/relationship situations, if the parents set an appropriate affective tone and handle issues appropriately as they arise, it will work better for the children involved. This can be complicated but rewarding if handled well. Levels of contact may vary over time but should be maintained at some level in most cases. Not doing so or not handling issues well as they arise can lead to feelings of rejection. Professional intervention can assist intermittently if needed. | The adoptee may not be fully accepted by all siblings in the adoptive family, whether they are also adopted or are the birth children of adoptive parents. They may feel closer to some siblings than others, but it can be pointed out that this happens in many families. Other issues, such as birth order or personality issues or interests and aptitudes, also come into play. Adoptive parents who have strong parenting skills and adapt to each child's needs may have more success in addressing issues. |

*cont.*

| | Birth siblings—separated No contact | Birth siblings—separated Contact/visits | Adopted siblings |
|---|---|---|---|
| Shame/Guilt | Secrecy or lack of contact can contribute to a sense of shame and guilt. Adoptees wonder what is wrong with them that they are not worthy to have these basic relationships with people in their life. Lack of information can make it worse. Even if there is no contact, it is better for the adoptee to have information about their birth siblings. | The adoptee may be in a more economically optimal situation/family than their birth siblings. The adoptee may be ashamed not to be brought up with the birth family or feel worry or guilt for their siblings in other situations. Birth siblings may be ashamed that their sibling was given away or that they were not told about the adoption until the reunion with the sibling later in life. | The adoptee may feel shame/guilt that they are not as good as their adopted siblings, despite the adoptive parents' best efforts to protect them. The feeling of guilt/shame has more to do with the circumstances of loss, of being "given up," than the home of their adopted family. However, adoptive parents should be informed and sensitive about how to recognize and address adoptive issues and ensure that siblings are sensitive. Siblings may resent perceived special treatment or celebrations of adoptive events or attention to the adoptive child's needs. However, good parenting is individualized to the child's needs in all families. |
| Grief | Intense and pervasive feelings of loss and emptiness can occur with lack of contact and create a void that cannot be addressed. Concern or wondering about birth family/siblings and lack of control regarding contact and information can create a sense of intense sadness, anger and/or acting-out behavior, which may be episodic. | If formerly living together but no longer are, siblings may feel intense sadness for the loss of the former sibling relationship. They will have to adjust to a new type of relationship, and belonging to different families with different rules and expectations can cause concerns and resentments as well as a lack of understanding how this could happen with a sibling relationship. Throughout life, they may grieve change in the nature of relationships or issues may arise with the level or type of contact. This may be more intense if some siblings remain with the birth family and others with the adoptive family/families. | Adopted siblings do not share the same history with each other, may look different and may have different abilities, talents and interests. (Of course, this can be the case in all families who share the same biology, so sorting out adoptive issues can be infinitely interesting and challenging.) There can be a sense of sadness that there is not a shared history or that the adoptee has a different/special history that their siblings cannot be a part of, and vice versa. This requires ongoing awareness and management, and feelings may ebb and flow over time. |

| | | | |
|---|---|---|---|
| Identity | Adoptees may have difficulty in sorting out identity and sense of belonging, at both conscious and unconscious levels, when there is little or no information about siblings. Early adolescence may be troubled and they may act out due to unaddressed issues. Wondering if commonalities with birth siblings, shared interests or thoughts, appearance, abilities and so on can occur. | When former relationships are altered, it can erode a sense of security about who one is and where one belongs in the world, as placement within a family may change from being the oldest child to being an only child, or the middle or youngest child, etc. | When siblings look different, have different ethnic/racial backgrounds and have different interests/abilities/talents, it can be confusing for the adoptee and their adopted siblings in terms of sorting out who they are and where they belong in the world. This may come up with family tree projects, celebration of adoption traditions, or over time as children go through developmental stages. Yet adopted siblings share a commonality of upbringing and circumstances that can forge very strong, lifelong sibling relationships. |
| Intimacy | The adoptee may find it difficult to trust/fully open up to others as they may "disappear" as siblings/birth parents/family have. There can be a fear of dating someone who could be a sibling—this may be at a conscious or unconscious level—and they may date outside their race/ethnicity to avoid potential violation of incest taboo. | The adoptee may experience difficulty managing relationships or relying on others, with a fear of being vulnerable or not being able to count on someone else to be there for them. Visitation/contact may be challenging as there is a shared biology and perhaps past history and shared ancestry, but not a shared upbringing/daily experience, and this can create awkward or forced relationships. It is good to be flexible and aware of fluidity/changes in relationships. | It is important adoptees do not feel that they are treated or loved less or differently in their families, though in all families, all children have different and unique needs and issues. This requires adoptive parents to maintain an adoptive-informed environment in which siblings also have an age-appropriate knowledge and understanding of adoptive issues and truth about their own circumstances. |
| Mastery/Control | There may be an inability to hold on to important people in life, a perception that they can't count on anyone else because the most important relationships can disappear. They may experience difficulty managing relationships or relying on others, have a fear of being vulnerable or not being able to count on someone else to be there for them. | There may be an inability to determine how much contact there should be and the nature of the contact with siblings, despite longing for more or a different type of relationship/contact. They may worry about siblings' circumstances and can feel unrequited longing. | Adjustment to differing stories of birth families and ways that they joined families can create feelings of uncertainty. There may be significant differences in appearance and temperament, and timing/order can affect relationships. |

| | | Later found birth siblings | Never found siblings | Lived/kin siblings (foster/group care) |
|---|---|---|---|---|
| | Loss | Sadness for lost siblings if there was a prior relationship or if they lived together formerly can be very intense, with shared background and memories. They may be worried about how their siblings are doing and long for the prior closeness or relationship. There can be a great and lifelong sense of loss if there is no further contact. If a reunion occurs late in life, there may be a sense of lost connections/time together. | Even for those with unknown siblings, there can be a longing and magical thinking for siblings, especially if there is no contact with birth parents or they are deceased. Longing may be more intense after the death of adoptive parents, which can create a desire for connections. A sense of great sadness and longing can be lifelong, of being robbed of their birthright or of siblings, what could have been, and the closeness they could have had. | There may be an inability to grieve, and recognition of the importance of the relationships that may have gone on for a long time and/or been intense, but not perceived by others to be important as they were not blood or legal siblings. Connections may be lost suddenly and without any way to maintain contact or reunite. |
| | Rejection | Birth siblings may not welcome contact with the adoptee if they were not told by the adoptive or birth parents about the adoption; it may be difficult for adoptees and their siblings to navigate these issues without professional assistance. Sometimes the adoptee may suddenly contact birth siblings and they are fearful or need time to process information before they are ready to move forward, but either side may perceive rejection or lose contact information and then the reunion or ongoing contact can be difficult. | Adoptees may feel a sense of rejection if they never meet birth siblings, wondering why no one came to look for them. These feelings may spill over to other relationships if the adoptee tries to protect themselves from rejection by building walls. | If the adoptee lived with a former foster family and then is moved from that placement to an adoptive home, they can experience more losses if there were foster siblings with whom the adoptee has shared part of their childhood but they are not viewed as important relationships as they are not legal siblings. There may have been a sibling/kin relationship emotionally, and if there is not contact afterwards or even a changed level of contact, this can feel like rejection or as if another important relationship has been taken away. It may be harder to forge future sibling relationships if the adoptee feels those also may not be permanent. |

| | | | |
|---|---|---|---|
| **Shame/Guilt** | Shame about the circumstances surrounding adoption may arise when contact is made later. This may be guilt that the adoptee was given more opportunities than the birth siblings or vice versa if family situations, economic circumstances or other hardships or good fortunes greatly differ. | There may be a sense of shame/guilt about not having such a basic relationship honored throughout their lifespan; self-esteem can be affected, and issues need to be worked through so that the adoptee does not feel "less than" and a sense of not being worthy or good enough to have these relationships. | The adoptee may feel shame at having been a foster child or in a kin relationship, and may have foster or kin siblings who are not biological or legal siblings, so it is hard to explain so that others understand what it is like. This can lead to feelings of shame/guilt that the adoptee is not worthy of having a "normal" situation. Fortunately, definitions of family have greatly expanded over recent years, so more unconventional family relationships are now more accepted. |
| **Grief** | Intense loss/sadness can be felt at time lost when there was no contact. The adoptee can feel more sadness if perceived hardships were endured by any of the siblings over their lifetime, and wish that they could have helped. There may be shared grief over issues of birth family/parents which led to the adoption or aftermath. Reunion/information about the birth family can be healing, even when it occurs late in life, and can be a source of great joy. | There may be feelings of great sadness at never having found and connected with biological siblings. This can represent never finding someone else who shares common biology, ancestry, appearance, interests, abilities and so on. These feelings may come up differently and with varying intensity at different times throughout their lifetime. | The adoptee can experience feelings of grief if moved out of a foster or kin family (sometimes more than one) if there is not satisfactory closure or ongoing contact with foster/kin siblings who lived in the former foster parent/kin caregiver's home. This can result in feelings of loss and sadness or uncertainty about trusting others in a new family if this issue is not addressed sensitively. |
| **Identity** | There can be a gap and missing information for the adoptee when there is no contact with siblings—from family history to medical issues to skills, aptitudes and interests. All adoptees want to know who they look like, and siblings are a key source of information here after parents. Siblings can fill in the gaps if the birth parents are missing or deceased. | Contact allows adoptees over time to learn at age-appropriate intervals about connections with a birth relative who shares one or both parents; adoptees may feel connected and find similarities in appearance, tastes, interests, aptitudes, expression, thought, abilities and so on, as well as shared family background and genealogy. | There may be a shared sense of growing up with adoptive siblings, which the adoptee often does not have with birth siblings. They may be very close to adopted siblings who may be the birth or adoptive children of the adoptive family. These can be lifelong relationships and helpful in allaying a sense of shame, if siblings are supportive and informed of adoptive issues for their adoptive siblings. |

*cont.*

|  | Later found birth siblings | Never found siblings | Lived/kin siblings (foster/group care) |
|---|---|---|---|
| Intimacy | It may be difficult to trust or open up to others when relationships with the birth family don't occur. However, when reunions do occur, there can be a commonality of appearance, ancestry, ethnicity/racial composition, sharing of stories and so on with siblings, even when those reunions occur after years. There is not a shared common upbringing and experiences, which can make it challenging to connect, and it may take time or may not be welcomed by all parties. The adoptee should be prepared and supported to navigate reunion relationships, which can be joyful and enriching but also challenging. | There can be a pervasive and ongoing loss throughout the life of the adoptee that can affect their ability to be vulnerable and trust others. They may date/marry outside their race to avoid the potential of dating/marriage to a possible birth sibling. | The adoptee may be able to relate well with others if they had successful relationships with former foster/kin siblings and benefited without being overcome by feelings of grief and loss. Obviously, ongoing contact helps the adoptee avoid that. Past successful positive relationships with foster/kin siblings can assist the adoptee with forming successful sibling relationships in the adoptive family as well as in school and later on in adulthood in personal and professional relationships. |
| Mastery/Control | The adoptee may struggle in knowing how to make contact, negotiate relationships, manage expectations and navigate ongoing contact; they may be vulnerable due to feared or actual rejection; siblings may not have knowledge of the adoptee. | The adoptee may deny any interest or desire to know or meet siblings or create a dramatic event; they may not know how to carry out a search or what to do if siblings are found. Lifelong unresolved longing may be sublimated elsewhere. | The adoptee may live for years with emotional siblings (kin or foster) who are not regarded as important relationships when the placement moves, and this can create a perception that all relationships are potentially in jeopardy. |

# Chapter 22

# The Search and Reunion Experience through the Lens of the Seven Core Issues in Adoption and Permanency

### Gina McKernon-Cindrich

The experiences of adoption and permanency impact millions of people throughout the world, and the sagas around those experiences are as diverse and unique as the individuals whose lives are forever transformed. So, too, are the numerous tales of those who seek to search and reunite with those they have been separated from through adoption and permanency; these search and reunion experiences are certain to connect the searcher with the strong feelings and issues. Those who do not seek to reconnect but are "found" will also experience a resurgence of their deepest emotions. These feelings, emotions and behaviors are represented in the Seven Core Issues in Adoption and Permanency and are dynamic, interwoven and multigenerational. They often intensify, wax and wane during the search and reunion experience. Awareness and understanding of these issues can be the gateway to healing and wholeness.

Everyone connected to adoption and permanency, all constellation members, are impacted by the experience. This is not an event, but rather a life-changing journey for those who are touched by it. Search and reunion is often a necessary part of making that journey complete. Some cope with their connection to adoption and permanency by avoiding, denying or minimizing the thoughts and feelings around their experience, while others cannot deny the impact that it has made on their lives. Many have awareness of the issues underlying the experience and process the issues in a wide variety of ways. Searching for and reuniting with loved ones separated from them is often a means by which constellation members seek to answer questions and make sense out of a life forever altered.

There are many cultural, religious and personal influences that may impact an individual's adoption and permanency experience. The need to search and reunite is most often associated with "closed" adoptions; however, the term "closed" is truly more on a continuum than a clear open versus closed situation. Constellation members may have accurate information, completely incorrect information or a mixture of facts, fantasy and partial truths about the circumstances of the adoption or the constellation members from whom they have been separated. There are many reasons, motivations and issues that may lead to a search and desire for reunion. Most search and reunion efforts are made to help fill in missing pieces of information, answer previously unanswered questions and complete what was left incomplete. Whether on a conscious or unconscious level, the desire to search and reunite is most often fueled by the desire to heal the wounds and unresolved injuries of the heart and soul.

While the term often used is "search and reunion," this consists of two distinct efforts. To search for someone separated through adoption/permanency may mean learning about their identity, where they live, what they do and other personal information. Reunion may include making contact through a variety of means, including letters, telephone contact, social media or meetings in person. For some, knowing their loved one is alive and safe is enough to satisfy their curiosity. For others, once the gate of interest has been opened, it is difficult to simply learn facts and information about a loved one, and the desire to meet and develop a relationship pushes them further into reunion. Each search and reunion journey is unique and varies from constellation member to constellation member but is certain to ignite the core issues.

So, who searches? Everyone touched by adoption/permanency is a constellation member and may choose to search for a loved one or may potentially be the loved one who is found. The most commonly thought-of search and reunion situation is between the adoptee and the birth mother. However, fathers, siblings, grandparents, aunts, uncles, cousins, second generations, third generations and any constellation member may seek to find and connect with kin who have been lost. It is important to acknowledge that each constellation member holds a unique perspective on how the core issues are experienced in search and reunion. These perspectives require respect and understanding.

Everyone loves a happy ending. Most of us believe that "all is well that ends well." We have all seen the emotionally charged, happy-ending reunion news stories that show loved ones previously separated shed tears of profound joy as they rush into each other's arms. But what happens after the cameras are gone and the often long-dormant feelings emerge and begin to influence the thoughts, words, behaviors and actions of those who have reconnected? Many hope and believe that the mere act of reconnecting will itself heal and restore all wounds and hurts. The process of searching for and potentially reuniting with loved ones can certainly bring healing and restoration. However, meaningful, restorative healing involves working through the core issues related to the original wounds of loss.

Constellation members may engage in search and reunion, but some believe that it is better to "let sleeping dogs lie" and question why anyone would seek to "stir the pot" and unearth the feelings and emotions long ago silenced and sealed away. These naysayers of search and reunion will liken the process to the proverbial opening of Pandora's Box. The metaphor of opening Pandora's Box recalls the unleashing of something unknowingly uncontrollable, resulting in problems that did not previously exist or were not known of before. The truth is that the contents of Pandora's Box have been present and influential all along. The desire to "know" for many constellation members is less of a choice and more of an insatiable desire. The anticipation around search and reunion can be both frightening and extremely exciting. Search and reunion can bring forth many unexpected and unknown situations. However, it can also help to provide opportunities to identify, clarify and better understand the mysteries contained in that box and by doing so move constellation members towards growth, healing and completion of what was previously incomplete.

So, with Pandora's Box now ajar through search and reunion, the issues long present, and possibly already within awareness, may emerge or re-emerge. When experienced through the lens of the Seven Core Issues of Adoption and Permanency, there is potential to avoid problems, conflicts and further exacerbation of the existing and emerging issues. Moreover, utilizing the framework of the core issues can provide insight, understanding, potential for greater restoration and guidance through the uncertainty of search and reunion. While it is not intended as a guide for search and reunion, by utilizing the core issues to thoughtfully approach and move through the process, searchers and those being found may avoid or reduce the deepening of wounds and allow search and reunion to be a healing and redeeming journey.

A person's expectations and perceptions greatly affect how the issues are experienced. It can be difficult to keep perspective once you enter the search and reunion vortex. In addition to having awareness of the core issues, it is important to have emotional support and objective perspectives to help balance the emotions that are most likely to occur. This is where having a supportive, objective friend, family member or mental health professional to help process thoughts, feelings and emotions can be invaluable. Since adoption and permanency changes the natural formation of the family structure, reconnecting with others from that altered family can present challenges. Search and reunion is much like exploring uncharted territory. Creating your own points of reference and landmarks can be invaluable in the exploration process. Having the core issues as points of reference can help clarify and provide grounding to what may be sensitive issues for the searcher as well as for those being found. Search and reunion being judged a "success" is on a continuum and much about opinion and perspective. Developing and keeping a healthy perspective can best be developed through understanding the core issues; each will be explored in the following sections.

## Loss

Loss is the price of admission to adoption and permanency. All constellation members have experienced at least one major loss. In considering loss within the context of search and reunion, it can be helpful to view loss experiences as events and grief, as the process we go through as we make sense of those losses and adjust to life without the person, place or thing we are missing. Arguably, the experience of adoption and permanency includes multiple losses that emerge over time for all constellation members involved. The losses are some of the deepest and most profound anyone can experience in life—the loss of a child, the loss of a parent and/or the loss of family members.

The multiple layers of losses can reveal themselves in both small and large ways, with many of those losses being ambiguous in nature. Whereas society acknowledges death as a "real" loss, the losses of adoption are more complex and do not receive the same level of recognition, acceptance or legitimacy. The secrecy often associated with adoption and permanency adds additional layers of complexity to the experience of loss for constellation members, which can make the path to healing more circuitous and challenging.

Since adoption often involves absent, partial or false information, being able to identify what has been lost can be difficult. However, acknowledging that a loss has occurred is necessary in the grieving process. This is where awareness of loss in adoption and permanency and search and reunion can be helpful to fill in the missing pieces and aid with the healing process. The desire to know more about what and who has been lost is most often the motivation for searching and reuniting.

Search and reunion seems a logical way to address the losses. If something is lost and is missed, then finding it will take away that sense of longing and sadness. This seems simple, but search and reunion can bring forth a flood of emotions, both old and new, and can re-ignite feelings from previous experiences of loss as well as potentially create additional losses. Since many of the losses associated are so deeply rooted, the process of search and reunion can bring them into focus and make them more of a reality. However, search and reunion can also bring the potential to help restore, at least partially, many of the losses. Understanding feelings and fears can be essential to searching with realistic expectations and entering reunion with understanding and awareness. Doing so provides the most opportunity for healing and wholeness.

It is the act of understanding that provides the most opportunity for healing, not simply the information found in search and reunion, although some may believe the information alone may provide such healing. One example of this comes to mind. While doing post-adoption services, I once received a call from an adoptive mother frantically requesting the identity of her son's birth mother. She went on to explain that she needed this information right away as her 42-year-old son had just learned he was adopted and she needed to "make it right for him." I could feel this mother's pain and concern for her son as she expressed her belief that if she got the name of his birth mother all would be well. Of course, the situation was more complex, and information alone does not "make it right," but understanding, acknowledging and processing loss can indeed provide a path towards healing.

## Rejection

For most constellation members, rejection is at the top of the list of greatest fears in search and reunion. This core issue can create "rejection hypervigilance," as many constellation members dance around relationships whenever potential rejection is sensed. It is understandable that constellation members are particularly sensitive to rejection. The logical mind may provide many explanations for separation, but the heart tells another story, one that is filled with fears of being flawed, unworthy of love and certainty of a fate of being abandoned and left alone. It also makes sense that those sensitive to rejection will do whatever is needed to avoid experiencing more rejection.

This often occurs by either avoiding true connection with their family member(s) or by rejecting others before they can be rejected themselves. Others may manage their fears of rejection through extreme people pleasing, working to be "good enough," or efforts to win back a family member through changing behaviors or yielding to the wishes of others. All of these behaviors can be considered proactive-reactive actions to rejection. Like the momentum involved with nuclear reaction, the dynamics of rejection can become a mighty and powerful force that gains in strength. This is where understanding the role of rejection in the adoption experience can help avoid or reduce the potentially uncontrollable dynamic to rejection in search and reunion.

A situation where the issue of rejection complicated a search and reunion occurred when Sara, an 18-year-old adoptee, sought information about her birth mother Karen. Karen had already been in contact with the agency she had relinquished her daughter to years earlier. Both Sara and Karen were extremely open to and excited about reconnecting, but both feared rejection from the other. Sara was convinced her birth mother would not like her, and Karen felt her daughter would be angry about her adoption and would be judgmental of her life choices. As it turned out, each anticipated rejection, and their fears came to fruition as the dynamic of rejection between them played out. With phone number in hand, Sara promptly called Karen and the two spoke for an hour before Sara hopped into her car and drove the three hours that separated them to meet Karen for the first time since her relinquishment.

Immediately on meeting, Sara told Karen of every imperfection and shortcoming she saw in herself. She later reflected this was a way of giving Karen the opportunity to send her away before Sara got attached to her. Once she felt Karen would not send her packing, she then began assimilating into Karen's world, listening to the same music, identifying similar likes and tastes in food, and even starting to smoke for the first time ever. Looking back on this time of her life, she recognized how much she wanted to convince her birth mother she was worthy of her love and acceptance. Karen too wanted Sara's acceptance and forgiveness. She told her how much she regretted her decision to place Sara for adoption but then went on to tell Sara she was "lucky" to have escaped a childhood with her for a mother. She told Sara she wouldn't blame her for hating her and even encouraged her to "not stick around." These conversations were interspersed with tales of family history and attempts to find ways to connect and "reclaim" Sara as her daughter. After Sara moved in with Karen, their issues around rejection intensified and Sara began to feel she was too different and not enough like Karen, and she sensed that Karen was going to kick her out of her home and her life. Karen felt Sara saw her for who she really was, and since Sara had been raised differently and grew up with more privilege and opportunity than Karen could offer her, she believed Sara would soon return to her "successful mom."

Eventually, the dynamics around rejection escalated in their relationship and both experienced hurt, disappointment and the feelings they had so wanted to avoid. After coming to understand the role of rejection in their reunion experience, they were able to do some specific healing around the issues that had once driven them apart. Sara and Karen both wished they had known of the role rejection played in their relationship as they ventured into their reunion. They believe that a better understanding of the core issue of rejection could have helped them avoid significant hurt and pain in their reunion.

## Shame and guilt

The issues of guilt and shame are emotions that are certain to arise in search and reunion. Guilt is best understood as being emotional discomfort/ distress related to an action that has been done. Shame is experienced as an intensely painful feeling of being fundamentally flawed or worthless. Both can be difficult, but not all guilt is "bad" if it is looked at with objectivity and reasonableness focused on identifying preferred behaviors and principles to work towards. Guilt can also impair decisions and choices. Being mindful of how guilt influences actions is essential to making good choices. Guilt can be unhealthy and detrimental when it is based on irrationally high expectations or judgment. Conversely, shame serves no real benefit and can be severely debilitating, influencing decisions in a negative way and impacting one's sense of self-worth. Being aware of the shame that can be so engrained and inhibit self-worth can be helpful in breaking the pattern of detrimental self-beliefs. When shame is experienced, considering a more objective perspective can be invaluable. To question whether the feelings are shame based or reality based can lead to reasonable clarity.

Staying focused on the goals of search and reunion can serve as a guiding light. Guilt and shame are major detractors to reaching those goals, with guilt stalling or preventing action and moving forwards, while shame interferes with one's sense of worthiness and confidence. Both can lead to sabotage of the goals in search and reunion. These issues can also greatly impact relationships as they develop through reunion. Being honest about areas of guilt can be difficult, but helpful in avoiding poor choices or inaction or in redirection of behaviors in a more healthy and productive direction. Shame is important to identify as well and may require specific work and attention to move towards healing and wholeness.

Examples of guilt and shame can be found in the story of Danny, Janice and Jenny. As Jenny's birth parents, Danny and Janice both felt a significant level of guilt for having yielded to the pressures of their family's disapproval of the pregnancy and the choice to place Jenny for adoption. While both felt guilt, they would not have made a different choice if given another chance. This led to great shame for Danny in questioning himself about the kind of man that did not want to take responsibility for his own child. Compounding his shame was Janice's "tape loop" of asking herself, "What kind of woman would give away her own child?" Together the young couple beat themselves up with their guilt and shame. They both coped with these feelings with the use of substances and "punished themselves" by making poor choices in life. While both were bright and had great aspirations, neither ever achieved most of their goals in life. Moreover, Janice's mother Mary, Jenny's birth grandmother, experienced many of the same issues with guilt around having judged her young daughter for becoming pregnant, and shame for allowing her to relinquish the only grandchild she would ever have.

When Jenny contacted her birth parents, these deeply felt emotions resurfaced and Danny plunged deeper into drug use and Janice into the throes of alcohol use. Jenny's grandmother too experienced long-buried feelings of guilt and shame that re-emerged with their reunion. Jenny had an understanding of the power of guilt and shame, and while working through her own feelings of guilt towards her adoptive parents for wanting to search for her birth parents and shame about "something being wrong with her" that had led to her adoption, she was able to share information about the issues of guilt and shame with Danny, Janice and Mary. While the many years of guilt and shame had left an indelible impact on them, the awareness of the power of these core issues led to partial healing for her birth family and provided deeper understanding and a greater level of healing for Jenny.

## Grief

Grief is the process of making sense and, potentially, peace with our losses in life. Grief is a naturally occurring result of loss, albeit a painful and often overwhelming part of loss. The grieving process is a unique experience for each person who grieves, may be different in each situation and can change over time. The healing process begins with identifying and acknowledging losses that are experienced. Because grief is often complicated by the many factors associated with adoption and permanency, it can be more chaotic, unidentifiable and more challenging than other loss and grief experiences. Moreover, grief often occurs in seasons and cycles and has been likened to the layers of an onion being peeled away. Search and reunion provides opportunity to grieve previously ungrieved or partially grieved losses. Grief is the gateway to healing from loss, and with awareness and acceptance that grief is a normal and healthy part of the search and reunion experience, it can be an amazingly powerful part of the process.

Delayed or complicated grief can influence relationships in many ways. This was evident as Janine reunited with her birth mother, Sue. Janine felt loved and accepted by her adoptive family and was not interested in searching for her birth mother, but when she was contacted by Sue she agreed to meet and get to know her. Sue, who had named her daughter Fiona at birth, after her grandmother, had difficulty calling her newly found daughter Janine. She would tell her, "I have thought of you as Fiona all these years and I can't stop now."

Janine acknowledged this was difficult for Sue but shared how awkward it made her feel when she called her Fiona. This angered Sue and created tension in their relationship, which ended in an argument and a break in contact.

With counseling, Sue was able to recognize that she had yet to grieve the child she had placed for adoption. It took her several months to work through her feelings of loss and recognition that the child she had loved for so many years as Fiona was now a beautiful young woman who identified herself as Janine. She had also struggled with seeing her as a baby, as this is how she last remembered her. Her delayed grief had kept her frozen in time. Once she was able to process some of her loss through grief, she was able to begin to develop a relationship with Janine for who she was, not the child named Fiona she had held on to for so many years. For her to love and accept Janine, she first needed to grieve the loss of her baby, Fiona.

## Identity

Identity is another issue sure to emerge during search and reunion. Identity occurs within the context in which we live. Since adoption and permanency changes the foundational context in which constellation members exist, developing a healthy and functional sense of identity may require thought and process. As many of the core issues are interwoven, grieving can often aid in building the foundation of healing around identity issues. Questions can arise for adoptees about who they are within their family and birth family and an uncertainty of what aspects of their being are simply unique to them. Adoptive and birth parents/family may question their legitimacy in connection to the adoptee and as parents/family. Concerns for how each constellation member will fit into the life of a loved one can be made especially challenging as each struggles to establish their identity in the others' lives. Grieving what may have been expected or anticipated can be quite helpful in finding a true sense of identity and fit within the context of their families.

As with most of the core issues, identity is multigenerational. An example of multigenerational identity issues can be seen with the birth of Amanda. Amanda's mother, Grace, had been adopted as an infant by Rosemary and her husband, Randy. Grace had reunited with her birth family a few years prior to her own pregnancy. The reunion had been difficult for Rosemary as she felt threatened by her daughter's relationship with her birth mother. During Grace's pregnancy, Rosemary experienced great anxiety about who would assume the role of grandmother in Amanda's life. After her birth, Amanda spent some time in the neonatal intensive care unit at the hospital. While Rosemary was visiting her granddaughter in the hospital, one of the nurses commented to the family how much of grandma (Rosemary) she could see in Amanda. She went into detail about how much they looked alike and even had similar expressions. While this comment was well intended, it provoked great sadness for Rosemary, as any similarities were not genetic, and this comment from the nurse only served to further her anxiety and distress about her legitimacy of being Amanda's grandmother.

Eventually, Rosemary came to see that there was room for Amanda to have more than one grandmother. The comment made by the nurse prompted Rosemary's grief around her identity as mother and grandmother. Once she was able to acknowledge the losses around her biological connection to her daughter and granddaughter, she was able to grieve. This allowed her the opportunity to establish an authentic identity as mother and grandmother. On doing this, her anxiety decreased and she felt far less threatened by involvement from Grace's birth mother and her birth family.

## Intimacy

Issues around intimacy can be challenging for most constellation members; establishing true intimacy requires a sense of comfort and confidence with one's own identity. The ability to connect with others requires vulnerability and a sense of "knowing thyself" within many contexts. As adoption can often disrupt the sense of self and confidence of identity, reunion has the potential to fill in missing pieces and help form the foundation needed to experience true intimacy. Identity is interwoven with the other core issues and can influence the constellation member's ability to experience intimacy in relationships. Because intimate connections can be frightening and new, and renewed relationships lack the familiarity of established ones, there can be an approach/avoidance dynamic that occurs in search and reunion. However, with understanding and awareness, there is potential for deeper connections with new and renewed relationships as well as existing ones.

There are many ways issues with intimacy can emerge in search and reunion. The intimacy between partners is an area for potential disruption when a child of one partner who was not known to the other partner emerges through reunion. Roman's adult daughter, Helen, from a relationship in his early twenties, contacted him, and he informed his wife of over 50 years of her existence and that she wanted to meet him. His daughter was previously unknown to his wife Brenda, who was shocked and very angry that he had not told her sooner. This created a significant rift in their otherwise stable union. Fears about other secrets sparked arguments between Brenda and Roman as well as concerns for how this might impact his relationship with their son, who was also unaware of the existence of his half-sister. The depth and intimacy of their relationship was significantly changed by the news of Roman's daughter, and in a state of deep despair, Roman sought therapy for the first time in his life.

After recognizing how his shame and guilt kept him from sharing with Brenda that he had a daughter from a previous relationship, he and Brenda engaged in couples' therapy. With the guilt and shame that had once resulted in the keeping of secrets now out in the open, they were able to work through their feelings and reported experiencing more intimacy and closeness than ever before. Moreover, Roman felt that he had likely been affected in his relationships because of his guilt and shame for much of his life. After working through some of the other issues around his connection to adoption, he felt more open and able to engage in a genuine relationship with Helen as well. At last contact, Roman was working up the courage to tell his son of his half-sister Helen.

## Intimacy and genetic sexual attraction

Many wonder if they might fall in love with a close relative by accident since they do not know all their lost relatives. This may hinder their openness to pursue romantic relationships. With inexpensive DNA testing readily available, this dilemma can easily be addressed; however, it does resolve issues of genetic sexual attraction (GSA). GSA is a phenomenon where constellation members who have been separated by adoption and permanency can experience intense physical and emotional connection on reuniting. Some may ask, how can this happen? While not without its critics, the Westermarck Effect may lend some insights as it hypothesizes that infants are desensitized to those who they live with in early life because the bonding process prevents sexual attraction with close relatives. It is thought to be a result of evolution, to prevent and lower the prevalence of disabilities or recessive traits. A less sophisticated explanation may be found in acknowledging that we share a close connection with our biological relatives. When the naturally occurring intimacy and identity roles in families is disrupted and/or delayed, that chemistry can be misinterpreted and experienced as a sexual connection during the highly emotional process of search and reunion. When these situations arise, it is necessary to seek professional help from those familiar and trained in this area. Again, this is an area in search and reunion where awareness and understanding can help to avoid serious problems and difficulties.

## Mastery and control

Mastery and control can present as a double-edged sword in search and reunion. The experience of adoption and permanency leaves many feeling a loss of control and sense of disempowerment. Search and reunion has the potential to bring clarification, forgiveness and redemption. There may be a sense of control for the constellation member choosing to be proactive by searching and possibly reunifying, as well as frustration and disempowerment around lack of access to information or vulnerability with the responses or actions of others. Those being found may experience feelings of powerlessness in not having had a say in being contacted and lack of control over how this will impact and change their life. Regardless of which end of search and reunion one may be on, every constellation member can experience mastery and control through education, awareness and understanding. Regardless of the circumstances in a constellation member's life, the ability to make sense of their experience and see the fullness of their connections can be the most empowering aspect of the adoption experience. Utilizing the Seven Core Issues in Adoption and Permanency as a framework for which to build that understanding can be amazingly powerful.

Ellen had lost her son through the courts and, following his adoption, she spiraled into substance use. She felt she had been successful in putting this experience behind her and years later got clean and sober and established a career for herself in bookkeeping. While she never had other children or a significant romantic relationship, she believed she had reached a place of peace in her life when she was contacted by her son. She had not wanted to re-open this painful chapter in her life and was annoyed that he had intruded on the solace she felt she had established in her life. After several years of negotiating the core issues that arose for her within the context of their reunion, she finally found herself acknowledging the importance of her son's presence in her life. It was about this same time that he stopped all communication with her. There was no significant event, no blow up and no explanation as to why, just a complete cut off in communication. This reignited her anger and feelings of powerlessness.

In coming to understand the big picture of her journey and gain a grounding in how all the core issues had affected her throughout the years, she was able to make sense of her experiences and for the first time truly establish a sense of peace. While she had not wanted to reunify with her son, did not want a relationship with him and felt out of control when she was found, she began to appreciate how she had had opportunities and choices all along. By understanding the issues that had once made her feel so out of control, she no longer felt victim to them. She was indeed in control for the first time since her story began. As of the time of this writing, she never did know what happened with her son and why he stopped communication with her. This is a sadness she still experiences, but she finds peace in knowing that without his having searched and reunited with her, she would still be living with the wounds and issues that had so greatly directed her life for so many years. She has since enjoyed a stable romantic relationship for several years and feels she is no longer controlled by the issues in adoption but rather embraces them and walks through them as she gains strength and understanding of them.

## When it doesn't go well

There is always the fear that search and reunion efforts will not go well. Preparation, support, realistic expectations and having a firm understanding of the core issues can all be essential in adjusting to a search and reunion that does not go as hoped for. Doing your homework and knowing what core issues are most relevant to you is essential to standing strong when search and reunion does not go well. It can be difficult to anticipate the emotional state of the constellation member who is being found or even know how the searcher may experience emotions during reunion. Entering the search and reunion process with support from family, friends, support groups or professionals can provide an emotional safety net in the event the outcome was less than fantasized or not exactly what was expected. Even the best-laid plans can turn out differently from what was anticipated, so adjusting expectations along the way may also be necessary. What is most important is to remember that each journey of search and reunion is unique and there is no right or wrong way to experience it. Make a solid plan, adjust the plan when necessary and ask for help and support as needed.

## Philosophical tidbits

When a life is altered by the experience of adoption and permanency, there are choices to be made along the way. As with most experiences in life, there are both positive and negative aspects and outcomes. The polarization of thoughts, feelings and beliefs around how loss has impacted one's life can range from one end of the spectrum to the other. Some proclaim it has not impacted their life in any meaningful way, while others profess it has ruined theirs. If we apply a philosophical perspective to the experience, it can help provide an opportunity to tell the story of individual experiences in a way that lends meaning to events we may not believe have meaning or purpose. Finding common ground with others who have lived with similar experiences can help provide grounding and perspective as any of the Seven Core Issues in Adoption and Permanency have the potential to become a vortex that can suck constellation members into polarized thoughts and beliefs.

Being philosophical about the impact of adoption and permanency and embracing the idea that there can be benefit from even the most challenging, hurtful and disappointing situations can be helpful to lessen the potential for imbalance of thoughts and feelings. For anyone considering a search and potential reunion with loved ones, it is wise to educate yourself about the issues, keep your sense of humor, learn to "roll with the punches" and look for ways to move through the difficult and focus on the positive. Keep in mind that nothing bad will last forever and neither will the good, so hang tight when times are tough and let in all that is good while you can.

Making sense of adoption and permanency can be done in many ways. Search and reunion can be an important part of fully embracing the experience, which can be painful and challenging at times and rewarding and joyful at others. While search and reunion can feel much like an emotional rollercoaster ride, embracing each of the core issues before, during and after search and reunion can bring about a depth of understanding, fullness of joy and true appreciation for how adoption and permanency can shape a life. Through this fullness of joy, an ultimate sense of mastery and empowerment can potentially be reached.

| | Child: opening a closed adoption | Adult adoptee | First/birth parents |
|---|---|---|---|
| Loss | The child may have rekindled feelings of abandonment and a renewed desire to grow up with the birth family. There is a fear of losing everyone again, both in the birth family and the adoptive family, and possible anticipation of other/additional losses. | The adoptee has a realization of the loss of biological mirrors, connections and history while growing up. They acknowledge the lost years together, and past/current relationships due to death. They may have no interest in reconnecting. | There is delayed acknowledgment of the years and milestones lost. The adoptee is lost to another family. There may be surprise that the child is older/different than they remembered or thought of. |
| Rejection | The child may have a fear of rejection from the birth family and engage in efforts to "be good" to earn love, or people-pleasing behaviors to avoid anticipated/feared rejections. Or they may reject others to avoid rejection from others. | There is anticipation of additional rejection. What if the birth family rejects me again? Societal judgment for search or reconnection with the birth family may be present. | A birth parent may feel undeserving of reconnection with the adoptee, or fear rejection from current partner/other children when they learn of the search/reunion. They may expect rejection or anger from the adoptee and set themselves up to be rejected. |

| | | | |
|---|---|---|---|
| Shame/Guilt | The child may feel that the blame/responsibility lies with them for "causing" the adoption. They may have guilt for desire to be with the birth family and/or adoptive family. | Adoptees can believe that an internal/innate flaw led to the adoption. There may be guilt for the desire to know the birth family, as it is seen as a betrayal of the adoptive family. Any secrecy during the search/reunion may compound existing inner conflict. | Some birth parents feel unworthy and experience extreme guilt for past actions. There may be deep shame for being a "bad" person—not keeping/trying hard enough and abandoning the child. They fear judgment from others when they learn of the adoptee's existence. |
| Grief | Reconnection may provoke intensified grieving. It may be the first time there is acknowledgment of what might have been as they realize their losses. They may have unfulfilled fantasies. | The search/reunion may rekindle losses and remind the adoptee of the years, experiences and relationships lost. The delayed acknowledgment of losses can cause a flood of sadness at what might have been, how life could have been different. The adoptee may realize the misfit with their adoptive family. | There may be a flood of grief from delayed/denied acknowledgment of loss. The lost years of relationship become real and are no longer avoidable. |
| Identity | The timing of search/reunion may influence developmental stages. There may be conflict between birth and adoptive families and identity components. The child experiences split loyalty between the two families and engages in extreme behaviors in an effort to fit in. They are in crisis, connected to a sense of belonging or not. | The adoptee may experience a crisis of self within the context of both families: who am I? This is possibly the first time they have knowledge of their biological connections. They may attempt to fit in with the birth family, integrating themselves within the family. | There may be undefined roles and complicated expectations, as well as awkwardness in establishing their place in the adoptee's life. The birth parents can be conflicted over entitlement versus unworthiness to search/reunite. |
| Intimacy | The child fears people leaving again as their anxious attachments influence their capacity for meaningful relationships and they have difficulty with trust. | The adoptee has fears of repeated loss or poor boundaries, tending to rush into intense relationships. They may have complicated and intense feelings towards biological relatives—genetic sexual attraction. | There may be an impact on their relationships with current partner/family/other children. Fear of anger/rejection from the adoptee may impact their ability to connect. They may have unrealistic expectations. |
| Mastery/Control | The child may display passive-aggressive behaviors, or act out due to feelings of frustration, anger, fear, disappointment and a generalized sense of helplessness. | Lack of control currently and in the past may make the adoptee feel vulnerable. They may struggle with self-responsibility and internalized self-control, and their inability to control circumstances and the actions of others. | Relived feelings of powerlessness/pain/frustration around the original event may be present. Struggles with the unknowns of the search and reunion experience are exacerbated by previous experiences. |

|  | Extended birth family | Adoptive parents | Extended adoptive family |
|---|---|---|---|
| Loss | There is realization of the loss of the family member and their involvement in family events, traditions, memories. The child belongs to another family. | Adoptive parents are reminded of the missing biological connection to the adoptee. They fear losing the adoptee to the birth family. Due to their infertility, the loss of their immortality is actualized. | Feelings of losing the child to the birth family create a renewed sense of loss of genetic heritage. |
| Rejection | As they did not step forward to raise the child, the extended family may experience societal rejection for allowing the child to be lost from the family. They may also suffer rejection from the child for not having "claimed" them within the family. | There may be ultimate fear of the birth family reclaiming the adoptee and/or the adoptee choosing the birth family over them. They may feel anger and hurt related to the adoptee's desire to connect with their birth family. | They may fear rejection from the adoptee and birth family as they are not the "real" family, and societal rejection for not being good enough. |
| Shame/Guilt | There may be stigma around losing a family member and regrets/blame for not maintaining naturally occurring familial roles/responsibilities. There is potential shame in not being able to show the same lifestyle as the adoptive family. | The search/reunion process serves as affirmation of the shame of infertility and their inability to procreate. Guilt may be present for having "taken" the adoptee from the birth family. | There are concerns for the judgment that the adoptee's need for a family was not met by the adoptive family. They may feel shame for not being "enough" for the adoptee. |
| Grief | There is sadness around lost relationships, shared experiences and continuation of family traditions—many "what ifs." | A desire for a "fantasy child" is rekindled and there is ongoing pain of not being the adoptee's biological connection to the world. | The family may grieve for the loss of genetic heritage, and the realization of the lack of biological continuity. |
| Identity | The family may question their role/relationship with the adoptee and there may be conflict around their rights and responsibilities to the adoptee. Will the adoptee claim the birth family as their own? | There may be confusion over their role in the adoptee's life. They may struggle with the right to "claim" themselves as parents, and question their legitimacy of being parents. | There are challenges around their role in the adoptee's life, and these affect their sense of worthiness. Will the adoptee no longer identify as belonging to the family? |
| Intimacy | There is an avoidance of closeness, connection and vulnerability in the reunion relationship. They fear getting attached to a child who no longer belongs to their family. | Fear of additional loss and rejection may inhibit closeness. Struggles with their partner around infertility issues may emerge again. | Relationships and depth of connections become complicated. Relationships with the partner, the adoptee and others may be impacted. |

| | | | |
|---|---|---|---|
| Mastery/Control | The family has no say in decisions that have been made. There is a lack of "rights" to advocate for relationships and they live with the impact of decisions made by others. | They fear losing the adoptee to the birth family and feel a sense of helplessness over their inability to protect the adoptee from disappointment. Overly controlling behaviors may emerge in an effort to overcome these feelings of helplessness. | The extended adoptive family members are observers of the search/reunion process but not active participants and have no real control over the situation. |

⊙ Chapter 23 ⊙

# The Seven Core Issues in International Adoptions

## Lynne Silver

In 1983, I gathered a trusted Board of Directors, built a portfolio of my credentials, and established a not for profit, tax exempt licensed adoption agency for international adoptions; there were only a few agencies that provided international adoptions at that time. In 1983, I became the Founder and Executive Director of Adopt International and Domestic Services. We were approved as a full-service adoption placement agency, international, domestic, and foster care. The focus of my agency was and continues to be on education, preparation and support of adoptive families.

My adoption work included placements from over thirty countries, opening programs in South and Central America, Africa, Asia, and Eastern Europe. I have participated in over 2500 adoptions, both international and domestic, with over 125 placements a year at the height of international adoption. My love for teaching encouraged me to conduct training programs with orphanage staff and government officials, including providing information on basic infant and child-care and the importance of early attachment.

Becoming a mother was also my dream. I was certain that adopting, as a single woman, was what I wanted, and I was fully supported by my family and friends. My first child's birth/first mother and I met and developed a close relationship; she came to stay with me during her last month of pregnancy. We both wanted an open adoption with a life -long relationship. My second child joined my family three years later and I had the flexibility to have the birth mother live with me again. My last child came into my life as a teen foster youth. Becoming a transracial family brought challenges about which I had taught but now lived with daily.

As an adoptive parent of three adults, an adoption professional, and an educator, the Seven Core Issues has guided my understanding of the ongoing process of adoption and foster care since the 1980s. Although retired as Executive Director, I still teach families as they prepare to adopt.

The history of international adoption is significant. Children from war torn areas were placed internationally as early as World War II and the Korean War. In 1980, I escorted three children from Korea to families who were unable to travel to pick up their children. Families had limited vacation time, or they hadn't traveled abroad and were fearful of the unknown. It was years before the attitudes became more understanding of the importance of adoptive families seeing the orphanage or foster homes of where their children had lived. Most international placements are both transracial and transcultural. Few families learned about their child's background because it was thought the faster you can "Americanize" the child the better for the whole family. Adoptive families were not educated about how to raise a child of color, leaving a void in the child's ability to understand and prepare for these differences within the family and community.

In the early 90's, our first families to adopt from China traveled there and went directly to an orphanage where they completed an adoption in the local province. Couples and single parents were able to visit an orphanage and identify a child that they felt was the right child for them, primarily based on age and appearance. In ensuing years, the practice became child- centered where families were matched to waiting children based on the needs of the child.

Romania's children needed adoptive homes after the fall of their dictator, Nicolai Ceausescu in 1989. Food and resources were extremely limited; children were starving. People turned to international adoptions as an "easier route" to adopting a child of the same race and to avoid a birth/first parent stopping or overturning an adoption. The fees were often higher than domestic agencies, but worth it for a process that only took a few months. With no regulations established, families adopted one, two, or three children who were usually not biologically related. Even when the home study approval was for one child, the prospective parents would be presented another child whom they also accepted. Having a family approved for one infant under a year was ignored and the family would return home with two newborns that became "artificial twins".

Many of these children suffered from the deprivation of food, touch, stimulation, and love, creating a population with developmental delays. The children had learning disabilities as well as physical awkwardness because of living in cribs or crowded conditions on the floor, with limited access to walking, playing, and running. Rocking in the cribs caused children to use side-to-side motions to entertain and calm themselves. Adoptive families were not prepared for the severe needs of the children they brought home.

Orphanages are quiet places, with no sounds of play or laughter; crying doesn't get attention or needs addressed. Many are sterile with few or no toys. More recent use of foster homes has made a tremendous change in the child's development.

Natural disasters, war, poverty, and political unrest led more and more children into orphanages. Countries opened to international adoption and then shut down because of corruption or child trafficking.

On April 1, 2008, the United States, along with over eighty other nations, became a signatory of the Hague Convention on Intercountry Adoption. A Central Authority in each sending country took years to establish individual policies and practices to meet the guidelines of the treaty. The primary purpose was to "prevent the abduction, sale, or trafficking of children in connection with international adoption." The implementation and management of the treaty in the United States became the responsibility of the Department of State, Office of Children's Issues in the Bureau of Consular Affairs.

The implementation was assigned to The Council on Accreditation. High fees have been charged causing small and medium sized agencies to close, leaving the larger and predominately religious based agencies. Singles, gay and lesbian couples, and older prospective adoptive parents have had a more difficult path in finding an agency to represent them even though state laws and some countries have more inclusive laws. Each sending country establishes their laws. Most countries now have post adoption requirements to assure that the children placed are in loving homes with medical and educational services. Individual states and agencies may also dictate the number of visits required in addition to meeting the country of origin requirements. The United States is primarily a receiving country with very few children born here leaving the country. Efforts to place children with family members is a priority, then placement in the child's birth country and, only if not possible, children may be considered for international placement.

In 2007, prior to the implementation of the Convention, Americans adopted more than 20,000 children annually which has declined to 9,000 annually. Children being placed are now generally over the age of four, have high needs and/or are in sibling groups. Legal adoptions are completed in many countries prior to the child leaving with his or her adoptive parents; other countries give legal permission or guardianship so that the adoption is approved in the United States following the post placement requirements. Post adoption reports may be filed in most states to allow a re-adoption, where the child is issued a new birth certificate from their state and meets all rights of inheritance.

The information that I have shared in this chapter comes from my personal and professional experiences of living in the world of adoption for thirty-six years.

| | Child | Adult adoptee | First/birth parents |
|---|---|---|---|
| Loss | The only thing that a child has in their early days is their name that is changed, possibly several times prior to a permanent placement. Birth names may have been changed in foster care or in the orphanage. The child may be pre-verbal, and the adoptive family may not know how to pronounce the child's original name.<br><br>The child's first culture may be a mystery. Adoptive families often buy one item from the country, such as a book, sculpture, Russian box or Chinese doll to maintain the child's identity. The adoptive family may not have a connection to the child's culture and therefore introduction to the culture may not be encouraged. Some families have stated that once their child becomes an American that becomes their primary identity rather than seeing that the family shares a variety of cultures. | The young adult may have had no access to speaking or hearing their first language. This lack of knowledge becomes more noticeable as the adopted person has more access to the larger world and recognizes this loss.<br><br>Developmental milestones are generally unknown from the family of origin and therefore are not able to be compared to other birth relatives.<br><br>Both accurate and inaccurate information provided at placement may come to light and the adopted young adult may now also recognize what is missing. The adult adoptees create explanations to make sense of the lack of information. Creative explanations about the birth/first family or country may take the place of having limited or no information. For instance, the original history forms may have reported that the birth mother was married with other children. During the search and possible reunion, this may not be the situation. This young adult is then expected to adapt again. | Services are not usually available after placement of the child. The child may have been dropped off at the door or gate. The birth/first mother returns to her village with no information on how to obtain updates about the child. In a state of grief, this mother generally travels home alone. This practice is changing slowly but only in some countries.<br><br>Orphanage directors are often medical doctors, but do not provide counseling services to the birth/first family. There is a lack of healthy adoption knowledge available to the staff. Our agency provided training to staff in many countries around the world, including steps on how to provide counseling and follow-up. The training was well received from staff providing social services, but on return trips, there were often new staff members who had not completed the training or no longer used those techniques and skills. Birth/first parents were encouraged to "let go." |

*cont.*

| | Child | Adult adoptee | First/birth parents |
|---|---|---|---|
| **Loss (cont.)** | There may likely be siblings, some of whom are in other orphanages or with other age groups in the same orphanage. They are often not placed together because one child would be placed with a family requesting "as young as possible," while the other sibling may be school age and not within the age boundaries requested by the family. Adopting families are encouraged to accept the placement of an older sibling as well as the child originally matched to them.<br><br>Birth father information is generally missing or extremely limited, leaving the child with a huge gap in their identity. Due to American regulations, even the child's actual status as an orphan may be questionable if the father is known. A birth father may be out of the home, may be the father of other children in the home, or possibly even may have left the home and area. Children may see themselves as orphans but they may have living birth mothers and fathers.<br><br>Currently, there are countries that are attempting to change their procedure to gather more information, but not many. | Racial identity may have been compromised and can have a profound effect on an adult. Adoptees may seek out classmates, college and work friends who may be from other cultures and ethnicities to feel more normal. | Very few adoptive families have the chance to meet the birth/first families; for those that do, the time allotted and translators are often limited. There is limited or no contact between the child and first/birth parents to say goodbye, take pictures or gather memories. |

| Loss (cont.) | The development of language is stunted at the age that the child leaves their birth country, and communication in the familiar language is halted. In many languages, one word may have multiple meanings, or one action may have multiple words to describe it. The child's language growth is stopped, so when the child becomes older, their language remains at the age when they stopped speaking it. Their vocabulary remains for some time at the age of placement, so a 4-year-old child would continue to use words that a young child would, even though they are now 7 or 12 years old. It limits their ability to even speak with others in the new community who may speak the language from their original country. Psychologists speak about the trauma that has already taken a toll on brain development. The separations of children adopted internationally are often abrupt, with no explanations. Children are often not allowed to say goodbye to their friends. | | |
|---|---|---|---|

*cont.*

| | Child | Adult adoptee | Birth/first parents |
|---|---|---|---|
| Rejection | The child feels rejection from their birth/first family, extended birth/first family, orphanage and country. The assumption is made that the child will feel grateful once they see the hotel, toys, new house and their bedroom, as well as feeling wanted with hugs and kisses. The child has generally come from a background of poverty with limited resources, including food and shelter. All the largesse can be overwhelming.<br><br>Their culture may look unfavorably on single parents, unmarried parents, parents of a different race, or LGBT parents wanting to raise a child. They may feel further rejection because they are placed with families their country would not accept as legitimate.<br><br>Limited food and nourishment, and a lack of touching and care, can cause brain changes that alter their ability to accurately understand their loss and feeling of rejection. Their reactions include defending their birth/first families by stating that they should stay in the orphanage because they have been told someone will be back for them. After years, they remain committed to the explanation, even though no family members can be located, or relinquishments obtained. | The young adult may have made previous assumptions that bad behaviors caused their rejection. A younger child may state that it was because of their behavior that their birth/first parent relinquished or didn't return to the orphanage. The assumptions become more complex for the young adult who is trying to make sense of the earlier separations.<br><br>The adult feels rejected because of their assumptions about family, country and culture. As they learn more of their history, they begin to balance truth and assumptions. However, coping with unknowns perpetuates some of the early feelings that future separations are a realistic expectation.<br><br>Adults can deal with rejection by finding out the truth and separating what are assumptions.<br><br>Understanding that poverty is the most likely explanation for placement is a challenging concept. Unmarried single women often are not able to provide for their children, especially when there are other birth children who are living at home. The adopted adult will ask why they were placed and not the older or younger birth sibling. They question if they were less attractive, more challenging, needier or talked back, and therefore the one rejected by the birth/first family or caretakers. | Birth/first parents felt rejection when there was a presumption made in the 1990s that they were rejecting the child by bringing them at an orphanage. However, orphanages were often homes where parents could bring a child while they tried to get work in order to be able to parent the child again in the "near" future. Unfortunately, due to the extreme poverty and lack of social services, these first/birth parents often were unable to have their children returned to them in a reasonable time. Each country determined what that timeframe would be, most likely 6, 12 or 18 months. After that time, the child could be matched to an adoptive family.<br><br>Children were told that their first/birth parents made the best decision possible. This creates a future sense of distrust when another person in their future is making decisions about them—does that mean that to love someone is to "let go" of them?<br><br>On my return to countries such as China and Russia, we would request any other information that was available on a specific child. On rare occasions, there would be a note from a birth/first parent that was pinned to the child's clothes so that, when they were found, the police knew that the child was not lost, but "abandoned." |

| Rejection (cont.) | Children need to know that their birth/first family, country of origin and their culture are valued by the family so that they feel valued. A child needs to understand that their history is not eliminated in becoming a member of the family.<br><br>Children are the first to notice when they are treated differently within their new family from their siblings or cousins. Receiving fewer birthday or holiday gifts is painful to understand and can be interpreted as rejection. Birth children may be invited on extended family member trips while adopted children are left behind. | | Abandonment is the terminology used when a child is left alone, but it does not truly describe when a child was left on the steps of the train station, with the intent of being found. China would issue an abandonment certificate, necessary to complete the international adoption. Years later, on homeland trips with the adoptees, we learned that some birth/first families had come forward to meet the children stating that they were relatives or foster parents but were turned away. The children were told that they would not be able to locate first/birth families during these return trips; many found that they could and did meet the extended family.<br><br>Birth/first families feel not only the loss of the children, but of the country and culture that they feel has let them down with no services to help with the care of the children.<br><br>Reclaiming generally did not happen, but when a grandparent or relative visited, even on an annual basis, the child was then not available for placement. |

*cont.*

| | Child | Adult adoptee | First/birth parents |
|---|---|---|---|
| **Shame/Guilt** | Institutionalized young children may have no idea how they came to live in an orphanage. Even explanations that their birth/first parent may return for them or may visit don't provide the hope that a child can understand, especially with the passing of time. Expecting to be reunited one day becomes a dream, not their reality.<br><br>Adoptive parents request young toddlers and infants, in part so that the child doesn't hold memories that cause them shame and sadness. Children recall or create stories that led to their institutionalization. Being ego centric, the child can express what they think that they did to cause the need for a care facility and eventually an adoptive home. Shame is carried into their new situation, knowing that they have been "naughty" or done something to cause this change in living situations.<br><br>Deserving a family becomes questionable, leading the child to wonder what they have done wrong and taking responsibility for actions that they did not cause. Seeing other children leaving contributes to their shame that they aren't worthy of a family. Low self-esteem may lead to the child becoming more withdrawn or challenging, with behaviors not welcomed in institutional care. | The adult adoptee may feel shame or guilt about asking questions, when they feel the need to protect their adoptive families. Early fears of being sent away or not accepted by the new family become an established pattern of behavior.<br><br>These adults are now able to ask questions for themselves: How come I survived and got out? Where are my siblings and family? Why did I get the chance for a better life? Maybe I would have been happier staying in my country? Should I be helping my birth/first family or country when I can?<br><br>The adopted adult may feel conflicted about the expectations of gratitude often considered necessary by others. In working with families, it is critical to help the child and young adult not assume the feelings that they hear from others: "Aren't you happy they adopted you?" "You must be grateful to your family."<br><br>As adults, they may now recognize their attitudes and feelings about countries that have orphanages; they may wonder what is wrong with this system of care that it cannot provide a family for every child. They ponder, "Why wasn't I kept in my family? Was there no other family member who could care for me? Was there no one in my country who wanted me?" | First/birth parents are very isolated and alone. They rarely came to meetings with family members. Through translators, they can explain that their mother was watching their other children, but this child needed another option. Perhaps the child was from another birth/first father, bringing shame to the husband or parents.<br><br>Birth/first mothers are often told to not discuss the situation with anyone because they are unmarried, married to another man or abandoned by their partner or parents. Single parenting is often a reason for placement.<br><br>They are isolated with their emotions, and not supported in meeting or speaking with other women in the same situation. Decisions are often made without understanding local resources. First/birth parents may not discuss the child's placement with others, so when the adoptive parents assist in searching for them, the shame and guilt felt is not relieved. |

**Shame/Guilt (cont.)**

There is no opportunity for a child to receive a positive response when they express feelings of grief in an orphanage. There aren't enough staff to care for the emotional needs of each child. They turn to friends or buddies with whom they share a bed or crib. Older children who may have had similar experiences provide comfort to younger children.

When the child meets and goes home with their new adoptive family, the child must learn to trust their parents before they can share any feelings that they had in their previous "homes" with their birth/first family or orphanage caretakers.

Other children in the new family and community ask questions about where the child was born and where their real parents are. Hearing these questions, the child wonders about the answers, and being told that they are now in a "forever family" doesn't address the shame felt when they were separated from others they cared about. Fear of another separation is realistic, and the child will likely act out to know if they can cause this to happen again.

Adoptive parents want to make every effort to comfort their new child and build attachment. Attention should be paid to building the child's self-esteem while reducing their fears of another move.

Adults are faced with answering questions from others, such as "How much did you cost?" Equating adoption placement with someone being paid large sums of money is shaming; people feel bought like an object. They wonder what would have happened to them if their family did not have the money to adopt them. Were they worth the money? The adoptive families, having spent significant sums of money, including expensive travel expenses, can create doubts for the young adult trying to understand that large sums of money were processed for them to have a family.

Shame may surface when, at a family member's death, the adopted person learns that their parents or grandparents have wills that leave their property, jewelry or art to non-adopted relatives so that they remain in the family. Is the fear that an adopted adult might leave that same family treasure to their birth/first family relatives?

Poverty separates birth/first families and makes having a relationship with a financially secure adoptive family challenging. Adoptive families are fearful that a birth/first family might want to reclaim their child, which is not legally possible internationally. These young women are expected to move forward with their lives, build new relationships and are likely to have more children, living the entire time with the guilt and shame that was experienced at the time of separation from the child.

*cont.*

| | Child | Adult adoptee | First/birth parents |
|---|---|---|---|
| Grief | Children act out their emotions because it is not safe to expose themselves to caretakers and other children. Often, children will ask visitors to the orphanage if the visitors have come for them. They don't understand where the other children who have left went to, but they understand that the caretakers prepare children with photos and stories. They are not introduced to the concept that they will feel sadness and grief.<br><br>An orphanage is one of the quietest places I have ever been. There are limited sounds of crying or distress. The children have no reason to cry. When a young child is raised in a family and cries, the child expects that they will then have comfort, which is generally not provided in orphanages where there is limited staff and funding. Scraped knees and cuts are not nurtured as they are in family homes. When we visit children in their new family, it is surprising to notice that after a child falls and has a scrape or bump, they do not even turn to the parents. The child must learn to feel the pain, both physical as well as emotional. This can only happen after the child begins to trust the parent and learns that they can receive comfort. New parents need to be encouraged to notice these events and teach the child that this bloody scrape must hurt and therefore needs attention. Newly placed children can be seen wearing six to eight band-aids on an arm when they want attention for bruises that previously went unnoticed. | Adult adoptees need to express a range of emotions about their placements, and have their own grief to address. This grief does not diminish what they feel or have received from the family that adopted them.<br><br>As a young professional, I had learned that the adoption process is lifelong. Having repeated that for most of my career, I don't think I truly understood what it meant until recent years. With each new piece of information gathered, young adult adoptees are continually readjusting their thoughts about their own life experience. With each new piece of the puzzle put into place, the puzzle becomes more complete. As adoptees reach adulthood, the decisions needed to complete the puzzle may or may not be within their reach. Each distinct piece carries a multitude of emotions beginning with loss that needed to be grieved.<br><br>Internationally, puzzle pieces are found over months and years. An adult adoptee can organize a trip abroad without the support of the adoptive family. Traveling to their birth country takes planning and coordination with people located in the country. The attorneys and agencies that assisted in their placement may no longer be available to help with the search. Professionals may no longer live in the same locations. Adoption records may have been destroyed accidentally in fires or relocated to boxes stored elsewhere. | Birth/first parents placing their children experience intense grief when they have to make the decision to leave them in an orphanage or place them for adoption. Fees paid by the adopting family may have included counseling, although it is rarely used for this. They receive little if any pre- and post-adoption counseling. Birth/first mothers are on their own to cope with unfamiliar emotions. Women are told that they may perhaps have a few pictures sent to the adoption authority in their country, and that they can go there to see the photos, along with reading follow-up reports.<br><br>Adoptive families are told that until the placement and/or court date occurs in the child's country of origin, the birth/first parent has the right to change their mind. This is almost impossible for the birth/first parent to achieve because of the expense of traveling to the central authority or orphanage, and the lack of family support.<br><br>Birth/first parents are not included in selection of the adoptive family for their child except for possibly seeing a small set of photos showing the adoptive family, their home and some activities that they enjoyed. Letters and more detailed information are limited and not translated. |

| | | | |
|---|---|---|---|
| Grief (cont.) | A child may express their grief in the new home through food. Excessive eating is expected, including hiding food and overeating. Children may hide food to take to their room to be assured that they won't be hungry. Leaving healthy foods and snacks in multiple places in the home can help the child be reminded that, in this family, they will not go hungry. Anger can come out at unlikely times. The parent's use of communication and support can help the child learn to understand how their grief could be ignited. | Finding resources abroad has become easier; however, it is essential to find reliable people who want to preserve the integrity and privacy of the birth/first family, while honoring the adoptee's rights as well. When my daughter first met her birth sister, the two young adult siblings designed a tattoo with a linked puzzle piece on one wrist of each sister. One heart divided in half was on each puzzle piece. Their separation and grief were expressed as well as their love and future commitment to one another with the permanence of a tattoo. | There is limited time to be with the child prior to separation—it was believed not to be good to extend "saying goodbye." The foster mothers in China bring the child to meet the adoptive family, and occasionally they stay for a day or two, sitting in the hotel lobby or outside in the event the family needed assistance. When a child continues to cry, the adoptive family is encouraged to let the child be with the familiar caretaker and make a more gradual separation. |
| Identity | Children raised in orphanages with caretakers have no genetic information or way to know how they might look like someone else. Occasionally, there are siblings placed, either at the same time or as each child becomes older and in need of placement. Siblings are rarely kept together but are divided by age groups. More progressive institutions are separating children into groups to model family life with "sibling-like" ages placed together. A 6-year-old would then become a big sister to the younger 2- and 4-year-old placed in the same group. The older children look after the younger ones, with caretakers taking the role of the parents. Community kitchens include the children in "family"-like tasks, setting the table, helping make food and serving the "family." | Adopted adults who are emancipated from the adoptive family have their first experience of claiming their identity in their life and community. Other people in the community don't look at them as an extension of a family, but as an individual with their own skin color, hair texture and shape of face. When my son turned 21, we had a bowling party and several of his friends who had never met me began to ask about the white woman sitting at a table at the bowling lane. They asked, "Who is she? How do you know her?" He answered casually, "She's my mom." "No, really, who is she…she is white!" We were vacationing with three adoptive families and our nine children, whose appearances, culture and race were all different. As people observed us and enquired, this group of older teens and young adults responded that they were all cousins in a family. The young adults took the responsibility to speak out about this. | A young birth/first mother is left with the grief of losing a child who now has a new identity. The crisis has changed her. She may wonder, "How could I have done this? How could I have placed my child? Who am I now in society/my family?" Stigmatizing terminology dictates how this person sees themselves in their community and country. The community labels her as a woman who "gave away," "gave up" or "put up for adoption" her child. None of these phrases speaks to a placement decision but creates doubts in the birth/first parent's mind about their ability to care for children, other siblings and future pregnancies. Many pregnancies are hidden out of shame. |

*cont.*

| | Child | Adult adoptee | First/birth parents |
|---|---|---|---|
| **Identity (cont.)** | Caucasian parents adopting from countries where children are from racial backgrounds different from the adoptive parents are required to become educated on those issues that could arise in their child's search for their identity. However, the actual parenting of children who look different from their family is regularly challenged by others wanting information about the family formation. The child and parents face questions from strangers, family, friends or supermarket clerks who notice the differences in appearance.<br><br>Developing a strong identity without having enough information from your past makes creating family and community a definite challenge.<br><br>Educating children about being in an adoptive family is critical so that they can gain competency in representing themselves. Being selective in their disclosure of personal information helps them gain a stronger personal identity.<br><br>Institutionalized children will have moderate-to-severe delays in meeting the tasks of each developmental stage. They need to complete certain missed skills and interpersonal issues to successfully move forward in the building of identity. | Children deal with their identity in every family photo. The children and young adults who were previously unable to put words to what they were feeling now begin to understand why they turned their heads or made a goofy face to mask the moment etched into their minds through these photos. They recognize that no one else in the photo is like them.<br><br>Part of identity is being able to select your own clothes, makeup and surroundings and to make choices based on individual preferences rather than what others choose for you.<br><br>Using a name that someone chooses for you may not keep you connected to the person you knew as yourself before your adoption and may disconnect you from your culture and language. A teen joined her new adoptive family in the United States and was given a new name by them. After conducting some of the post-adoption meetings, it was clear the family did not want to keep the child. They requested that a new family be found for her. When the child was asked what was important for the adults to know in selecting a new family, she responded that she wanted her original name back. She had been called four different names in her multiple placements. She was able to claim her identity, once again feeling empowered to be herself.<br><br>Rolihlahla Mandela was given his Christian name, Nelson, from his teacher at school. His teachers couldn't pronounce his name, so it was changed. He added his new name as his middle name and kept the identity of his birth, country and culture. | With international openness rising, birth/first parents are not left in the dark and are better able to define themselves in a more positive light. There are limited resources to create opportunities for visits, but this practice is increasing. Having the chance to see the child as they grow up can give the birth/first mother more confidence in the major decision she made. |

| Identity (cont.) | | |
|---|---|---|
| | Rituals can assist children in asking questions and learning more about their birth/first family and country. On designated dates, the child's story can be told and retold, focusing on the topics requested by the child. Questions may be revisited, or new ones addressed. Birth/first fathers are rarely part of the international adoption process. Their name may have been identified, but in most cases, the birth/first mother stated that she wasn't sure of his identity or was unaware of his whereabouts. Under the old adoption regulations, prior to 2008, a child was only eligible for international adoption if the mother was single and there was no father to support them. | Children entering adoptive families usually take on the religious practices of their parents. Older children who have grown up with specific religious beliefs may want to continue with their familiar practices. In some programs, maintaining the adoptee's religious identity is required. Adoptive families have expectations that their children will follow their religious paths but need to recognize that, as young adults, the adoptee needs to make their own choice, balancing the religions that they were born into and those in which they were raised.

Finding churches or synagogues where there are congregants who look like the child is ideal. Parents may choose to attend a local religious institution or go to one with attendees of similar backgrounds to their child's. Support can be significant as the adoptee may be the only one of or one of a few people of color in the parents' congregation.

Young adults want to explore their options and make their own choices. As they confront questions or comments, they may learn new ways to respond: "You don't look Jewish." "You don't seem to know the prayers!"

As they seek out congregations that meet their interests, they can attend alone, with family or friends.

Does the new religion conflict with the one in which the adoptee was raised? "Who am I in my spiritual beliefs?" "Am I free to develop my own spiritual practices without losing my adoptive family?" |

*cont.*

| | Child | Adult adoptee | First/birth parents |
|---|---|---|---|
| Intimacy | Children raised in institutional care learn at very young ages that those people closest to them disappear and may not be seen again. This begins with the separation from the birth/first parents and family who made the placement. The children are unable to remain with a caretaker for more than one or two years before they move to the next age group and another caretaker. Staff members are often called "mama." Children may have shared cribs, beds next to one another, or even sleep in a family-style bed with others, who disappear.<br><br>After adoptive placement, children are given the "benefit" of having their own bedroom, making it difficult for them to adjust. The child doesn't hear the familiar sounds of ten other children breathing and rolling over; the isolation creates fears. Parents are encouraged to have children sleep with other siblings or with them during this adjustment period, which will build trust.<br><br>An observant child will notice that their toys and clothes appear to be excessive until they identify those belonging to other children in the family. These new relationships may create conflict when the newcomer helps themselves to toys or pieces of games that belong to the siblings or family. Being identified as a "thief" causes delays in creating positive self-esteem and becoming a full and permanent member of the family. | This emerging adult may have been placed as a toddler but may have only been in the home for a few years. They may be fighting a daily battle to catch up on their developmental milestones.<br><br>They have many questions about building relationships. Are they expected to date people who look like their family or themselves? What is locked in their genetics that they don't know about? Could they pass something scary on to their children? Will anybody want them? "I am not white but not Chinese either." "How do I feel intimate when I don't understand my own body?"<br><br>When a child enters a new family, conversations about personal hygiene are important but difficult. There may be language differences as well as different values about personal care. How often one showers, shaves or even brushes their teeth varies based on previous life experiences. The new adoptive family assumes the parenting responsibility to discuss issues with their child. As the young adult emerges, these earlier lessons may need to be revisited to include purchasing products such as deodorant, foot sprays and hair products. | We are so limited on the information we have available about birth/first parents abroad. They, like birth/first mothers in America, are faced with the questions: "Can I be a good mother to my other child?" "Will I ever trust another man, parent or the authorities who took my child from me?" Depression can cause birth/first mothers to withdraw their emotions to protect themselves or even to understand the underlying cause of becoming more distant in relationships.<br><br>Birth/first families wish for reassurance that the child will meet them again. They fear that they won't connect with their child even when they meet again.<br><br>There is the fear of having relationships that create future pregnancies. Secrecy exists in their future relationships when they are afraid to disclose that they have had a child.<br><br>Avoiding closeness helps to eliminate scary connections, truth-telling, transparency and privacy.<br><br>Re-engaging with the child is a dream come true. Having an opportunity to know, feel and see the person you created but did not raise, and with whom you may not be able to communicate, can be bittersweet. |

| Intimacy (cont.) | When siblings are left behind in the orphanage, the newly placed child expects this behavior to happen again in their new adoptive home and may withhold becoming intimate for fear of future separation. These young people are expected to become attached to new siblings when they may have never had the opportunity to understand what a previous sibling relationship entailed.<br><br>Intimacy can only occur after the child begins to identify and understand who they have become in this new environment. In the orphanage, they had to behave for caretakers who were unable to meet individual children's needs; they were just one more child, not an individual. A child who lives in poverty is searching for food and shelter and focuses on survival, not on learning about their specific characteristics that make them unique. Unique is not a desired quality in an institution. | One young adult expressed her dissatisfaction with her hair and her inability to "tame" it and make it look like her friends. The parents understood but didn't think about taking her to a salon with people of the same background. They did the best they could and thought that as an adult she could cut or change her wild curls. After seeing a hairdresser as an adult, she kept saying aloud, "I am so beautiful!" As her self-esteem and identity became clearer, she was more available to enter more intimate relationships with confidence.<br><br>Single parents need to find ways to address these issues with their children by seeking help. With no racial or cultural role models, the parent may not even know what products are good for their child.<br><br>The child's own body becomes unfamiliar to them. They can't have an intimate feeling about others if their identity is compromised.<br><br>My son came into my life when he was 13. How could he understand what life was going to be like after being traumatized by being alone on a very frightening experience to get to the United States? He needed experiences of attachment, honesty and trust to build relationships. To develop new relationships after feeling rejected by his birth/first family and country, he created distance as he told his own version of his story as a way of gaining control over his life and existence. After being in multiple foster situations, he stated, "If I go to one more foster home, I won't be able to have relationships with anyone. I will shut down!" | |

*cont.*

| | Child | Adult adoptee | First/birth parents |
|---|---|---|---|
| Intimacy (cont.) | | The questions are many: "Will I be attractive to others? Is there something I need to do physically to be seen by others? Who do I deserve to be with? How do I care for myself when I don't even know how to purchase personal hygiene supplies? How do I learn to do my hair when there are no men/women to teach me? Is this too much gel or not enough? Will I look the same as my friends?" | |
| | | These types of questions are asked by young adults frequently. They also need help developing an "exit" plan when expectations in relationships exceed what they believe they are capable of meeting. | |
| | | As an adoptive mother, I realized that finding similarities that brought us closer was challenging, especially when there are no physical features we share. Although my blonde, blue-eyed daughter was a mystery to me with her fair skin that needed sunscreen every day, it was a greater mystery in becoming a mother to a dark-skinned young man with straight thick hair, speaking a language we could not share. | |
| | | When our young adults become sexually active, it is rarely attached to true intimacy. Reminding a young adult about the difference between sex and intimacy is important so that they can experience the pleasure of intimacy, not just meaningless and fleeting encounters, and will not fear true closeness. | |

**Mastery/Control**

The child is overwhelmed when meeting a new family and trying to understand the family's expectations. It is clearly different from those behaviors needed in a group or institutional setting. Children in orphanages are generally not allowed to chat during meals; the purpose is to eat and prepare for naptime or school. They have come from very gray, bland-looking rooms that had limited toys, books, puzzles or blocks. Stuffed animals were not hygienic and were usually given to the staff members to take home for their children.

Once children have a sense of belonging with a family, they can be encouraged to talk about their day during dinner or on returning from school, and they might have juice and snacks waiting for them. As children become more comfortable and trusting in their new environment, they request certain foods or toys. They sometimes help themselves, even if the toy or food belongs to someone else. They haven't yet learned the rules of good family behaviors; they push the limits, and even try being "naughty."

Older children may request posters or specific colors for their new rooms. Some families want to present the child with an already-decorated space, but the child has not had the opportunity in the past to use their own power, voice and preferences for such things. The child should be encouraged to join the parents in decorating and selecting things.

Becoming young adults brings independence and the ability to respond to questions on their own. Competency allows a variety of reactions and answers that were previously modeled by parents or extended family members. Young adults can make personal statements without having them scrutinized by loving adults standing nearby.

Attending college or working allows young adults to no longer stand out as different, because they can choose with whom they want to spend time. This much broader life experience helps them to explore how pieces of their story are accepted or questioned by others.

Young adults develop a strong need to understand themselves and seek out those who can help with this process. They may have wanted to protect their parents from misinterpreting this as rejection, when it is about gaining information to fill in the missing pieces.

College and university groups reach out to invite the young adult to specific clubs, often related to background and race, such as Latino or African American clubs. It may be one of the first experiences where others who look the same become prominent.

Providing guidance to these young adults while they gain mastery over the story of their lives is ultimately the goal— for the adult adoptee to take control over their future while being supported by family and friends. Making decisions about schools, careers and places to live allows the young adult to have a sense of pride, pulling together their variety of life experiences and addressing previous traumas to move forward.

Inexperienced translators use their own judgment as to what is important to translate. When the birth/first parent is included, and questions asked to her directly, she is more likely to have the feeling that she is in control over her child's placement.

More involvement with the birth/first mother, including recordings of her conversations with her child, helps the adult with a sense of being in her role as a mother. Sending something of hers along as a gift can be helpful for all parties.

Providing education to help to answer questions about what happened to their child gives the birth parents power and authority in facing others.

Some birth/first parents tell others that their child died to avoid having this conversation.

When birth/first families are told that they can have some degree of openness, they may not understand the concept. With explanation and some positive experiences, the process becomes more meaningful to the birth parents/mother.

Developmentally, this young woman may still be accomplishing tasks that will later define her, her personality and how she lives her life. The more she gains understanding of herself at the time of a crisis, the better able she will be to claim mastery in life.

*cont.*

| | Child | Adult adoptee | First/birth parents |
|---|---|---|---|
| Mastery/Control (*cont.*) | Clothes have been well used and passed down. Now the child has the chance to select the colors and styles that they want to reflect their personality. At first, young teens select clothes that they might find in their country, but it is best to limit the new purchases. Very quickly, they want to select what friends wear; those early purchases may be set aside as they are gaining a voice.<br><br>Testing continues for about six months before the child begins to trust that this is their new home; the child can continue to push back for about two more years until their security is internally recognized and attachments form. Attachment allows the child to feel some choice, power and mastery of their environment. | Making decisions about examining the beginning of their life, race, family and country can be painful, but the adoptee is resilient in their search to seek out answers.<br><br>As each of my adult children experienced more contact with their birth/first families, I wanted to be present so that I could help them process their emotions after the meetings. Each told me clearly, "This is my experience and I have to do it alone." I received multiple texts and calls for support; I received photos and questions to clarify past events. The clearest message was one of competency and mastery: "I can manage this myself."<br><br>Young adults are finally in the position to make decisions about wanting to travel to their birth countries. They can emotionally cope with the poverty, the unknown information and challenging journeys to small towns. They have a strong desire to immerse themselves in their language and culture.<br><br>My adult son has recently announced that he wants to return to his birth country for several months so that he can learn who he is. Blending values from birth/first and adoptive families may present conflicts, but at this age, the young adult now is able to make personal choices in defining their own values. Meeting the birth/first family and seeing where you spent those first years of your life can bring more meaning and value to achieving mastery in the future. | |

| | Extended birth family | Adoptive parents | Extended adoptive family |
|---|---|---|---|
| Loss | With international adoption, the extended birth/first family is generally not involved. It is a rare experience for the birth/first parent to involve their parents or first family in the process. They may not be told by the birth parent of the pregnancy or placement, they may choose to remain silent and don't want to be involved, or distance may keep them from being at any advisement or relinquishment meetings.<br><br>First/birth fathers and their extended families are generally not part of the international adoption process. The United States' orphan status needs to be met for international adoption, and, prior to 2008, if both a birth/first father and a birth/first mother were present to provide for the child, the child would not be eligible for the defined orphan status. Single birth/first parents qualified to make the relinquishment or abandonment decision for the child. Extended family could be considered as a potential permanent family in some countries but with no legal obligation to provide care.<br><br>Documentation of the relinquishment generally includes an address or location of the birth/first mother, but listing extended family members is not required. If the birth/first mother lived with her extended family, an address may be provided. Moving is expensive and it may not be culturally accepted for a single woman to leave her family home until she is married or attending school elsewhere. A birth/first mother was not obligated to disclose any additional information, making it even more challenging to reach family members in the future. | A loss for people adopting internationally is the expectation of adopting a child that they can choose with the closest similar appearance to them. It is rare to have a prospective adoptive parent who is satisfied with the few photos provided. They are commonly heard to ask, "When can we get more photos and more information?" There is a strong desire for more medical information when none exists, or very limited information is available. Even with adoption education requirements met, prospective adoptive parents are hopeful that their assigned child may have an abundance of history and documented information.<br><br>More information may become available with time or it may not ever be available. Their loss, if not addressed, can prevent them understanding the child's losses as well. | Extended family members have hoped for their grandchildren or relatives to have a family resemblance. They have lost the opportunity to share their genetics with another generation as well as the opportunity to see themselves reflected in the appearance of the adopted child. Grandparents may have wanted to see the genetic link, family history and appearance as a lifelong dream.<br><br>Any internationally adopted child has gaps in time that could have been spent with the extended family. They have missing stories of their family being at their birth, when they took their first steps and so on. This limits the stories that can later be shared, such as "I remember when…" There may be no childhood photos in the collections of extended family members; bragging about the great moments during the child's early years may be limited compared to other children in the family.<br><br>Creating attachments to the extended family is generally delayed until the child has made some progress with their new parents.<br><br>Support during important life changes and family growth is part of how family members envision their role. Being asked to wait to visit or having rules when being with the child changes the dynamics of this developing relationship. Family members need education and support to learn about adoption, attachment and trauma. |

*cont.*

| | Extended birth family | Adoptive parents | Extended adoptive family |
|---|---|---|---|
| *Loss (cont.)* | Extended family members may experience or suffer the loss of the birth/first mother as well as the child, possibly without disclosure or discussion.<br><br>Relationships with some family members may come to halt knowing that the birth/first mother has a secret to maintain. Fear of having her story identified keeps her distant from those who may have been a support system.<br><br>The extended family may have limited connection to the birth mother/first family, including other children who may have been placed by the family. The daughter whose child was placed may have left her home to live elsewhere to avoid having her secret become public where she may be judged or distanced from family members. The family may have supported one placement, but an additional child being placed may remain a secret to her family. When this secret is known, it is yet an additional loss.<br><br>The extended family experiences the loss of a family member, possibly a daughter who had to make this difficult decision.<br><br>Being unable to provide support and love becomes an additional loss.<br><br>Extended family residing in another town or city may not have access to updates and current information about the adopted person: Is the child alive and well? Does the child look like us? Do they have other grandparents, aunts and uncles? In what country does the child live? Does the child remember us? | | Due to the high cost of adoption, many extended family members contribute to the expenses of an international placement. They want to support their children in the adoption but run the risk of losing money or savings if things don't work out. Alongside this, with the privacy that the adoptive parents need during the process, the extended family may have no influence in contributing to decisions that their family members make.<br><br>When a child is born into a family, extended members visit, bring gifts, make food, give baby showers and enjoy the early days of the child's development. The series of events may change with an international adoption, so it is important to educate those around the new family so that they can share in the celebration, easing the loss of what was anticipated.<br><br>Relatives rarely travel to meet the child for the first time. Understanding of the child's early surroundings is absent, as is familiarity with the child's country and culture.<br><br>Extended family members recognize that the decision to be included is not theirs. Teaching about how to form attachment in a hotel room is generally focused on the adoptive parents, who need to hold, cuddle and give the new child all their attention. If extended family members travel with the adoptive family, their job may include caring for other children in the family rather than having time with the newest addition, thus adding to the loss of how they envision welcoming this child. |

| Rejection | Family members are often not told about the adoption decision. The option to care for the child may not have existed, contributing to feelings of rejection by their own family member. | Knowing that the oversight agency has the power to remove the child makes parents worry. The family hopes to parent in ways seen as acceptable by the approving agency.<br><br>Emotional fears can contribute to a longer attachment period. These may include concern for the child's health, adjustment and attachment issues or withholding of parental love until they see the child accepting them. Fear of rejection by the child during the first few months can cause a lack of confidence in parenting.<br><br>While meeting the post-adoption report requirements, the family may still hold fears that the country will remove the child; however, the reality is that, once the family returns to the United States, this is not a possibility. Home visits are designed to assist families, but a social worker's presence can cause fears that are unnecessary.<br><br>Good parenting requires establishing good boundaries even if dealing with fears of rejection. The horror stories of children who do not attach to their new families run rampant in the media and in support groups. Separating fears from reality can be helpful to families in making plans to overcome not only fears, but also behaviors that lead to feelings of rejection. | Extended family members may not feel as connected to this child as other children born into the family.<br><br>They may not respond to the child, and the child may reject them, because of their age, appearance, smell, discipline methods and expectations.<br><br>Family members may feel rejected by the adoptive parent for the decisions that were made that the extended family did not accept.<br><br>The extended family might reject the birth/first family, their country and their culture. Relatives may state that the child is now an American and encourage the adoptive parents to no longer share the child's previous culture. Negative stories about the child's country, food, clothing or housing are seen as rejection of the child's past. This can cause family separation due to lack of acceptance.<br><br>Current adoption practices may not be shared with extended family members. Books or articles can be beneficial in understanding the child's behaviors as they enter the family. Managing expectations can help to avoid rejection and move towards acceptance. |

*cont.*

| | Extended birth family | Adoptive parents | Extended adoptive family |
|---|---|---|---|
| Shame/Guilt | Extended birth family members may experience shame about holding a significant family secret. Holding someone else's secret from others may increase the guilt as they examine their own role in the past events.

Explanations and clarifying the story to others increase shame.

The extended family may wonder if they should have done more to help their relative raise the grandchild, niece or nephew. Could they have helped more, even if temporarily, until the birth mother was able to provide for her child without their help?

Just observing what was happening with a family member and not acting may cause guilt, which can contribute to distance and separation from the distress when support is most needed. | During the adoption home study (an assessment of prospective adoptive parents) process, couples may be embarrassed or reluctant to admit their desire for the "smarter" and "more beautiful" child that would remind them of their spouse or themselves.

Parents adopting internationally must be financially secure to meet the federal adoption requirements. These families are hesitant to disclose their financial history for fear of being taken advantage of, but the total costs, including travel and donations, are far greater than most domestic adoptions. A lack of understanding about the financial commitments of international travel by family and friends can lead to secrecy as the prospective adoptive parents withhold information from their support system. Keeping significant issues from those closest to them increases their guilt and continues to remind them of their difference from those who don't understand adoption issues.

Adoption may be inaccurately equated with buying children. Adoptive families can easily become resentful that foreign professionals charge such large fees for services. These fees can be mistaken for bribery or baby selling, even when they are thoroughly and accurately disclosed prior to the family beginning the process. Concerns include, but are not limited to, the following: "The cost of living is less." "What do they do with the money?" "Who benefits from the child's placement?" | Extended family members have shame, guilt and fear that they will not feel or do not feel the same for the child adopted internationally even though they want to support their adult children or relative's decision.

Coping with anger at the birth/first family for the pain that the child experienced may not be verbalized.

Shame and guilt may occur when family members cannot handle the medical issues of the child who joined the family. Adoptive parents may withhold or diminish the issues to avoid their own shame and their family's shame. In some countries, a medical diagnosis is required for an international placement to occur. The list of medical ailments may be used to cover the liability of the placement agencies. This can be hard for the extended family to accept.

Shame may be demonstrated when the extended family introduces the adopted child to others. How is the child introduced? Does the family see the adoption as the key issue rather than the child as a true part of the family? |

| | | | |
|---|---|---|---|
| **Shame/Guilt** *(cont.)* | | When donations are required in orphanages, some adoptive parents demonstrate their generosity and some withhold money because of their own resentments, shame and guilt.<br><br>Comparisons of an adopted child with an unknown "perfect" birth child whom they would have expected if pregnancy were possible are painful to admit. Adoptive parents want to protect their families from the pain that they themselves feel, especially after being "matched" with a child. The fear that this will yet be another dream that does not become a reality makes them keep emotions closely tethered.<br><br>Many families report concern about being judged by family and friends. They may be the first couple facing infertility or looking at an international adoption. Assumptions may be made that produce feelings of letting others down. All the above initiate issues of feeling guilt. | It is the adoptive parents' responsibility to prepare and protect the child from these uncomfortable encounters with extended family members. When the child visits the extended family and is treated differently, options may be painful, but the entire family benefits by standing together. The family could all leave the situation, empowering the child who witnesses this support. Holidays may bring turmoil as the adoptive parents see that their child receives fewer gifts than birth children; or family heirlooms bypass the adopted child to be presented to birth children. |
| **Grief** | Family members may have been raising another child from the birth/first parent but cannot raise this child. Resources, both financial and emotional, may be limited. The pregnancy and placement may only become known years later.<br><br>Homeland trips have become more popular in recent years. Grief may be triggered when the child returns and the family members learn of the child's existence for the first time.<br><br>A grief response may be expressed in anger, which may cause even more separation from other family members. | The adoptive parents' dream to become pregnant and have a perfect delivery and an easy attachment to their child is dead. Adding to their overwhelming grief is the high cost of international adoption. Their grief is diverted into talking about cost, inconvenience, making difficult last-minute travel arrangements, the inconvenience of the family assessment, and the inability to spend time away from work for an extensive stay in a distant country. Adoptive parents believe it is helpful to "choose" their child, that having control will resolve this deep sadness. In accepting that they can't choose their child, they gain understanding that a child is matched to the family who can meet the child's needs. | Family members express their sadness for their relative who must cope with infertility and then the process of adoption. International adoption can be a huge risk for their family members to undertake, having to face language and cultural differences. International fees and travel expenses sometimes mean that adoptive parents seek help from their families to make the adoption possible. When the extended family is unable to help at all or as much as they would have liked, this contributes to their feelings of grief. |

*cont.*

| | Extended birth family | Adoptive parents | Extended adoptive family |
|---|---|---|---|
| Grief (cont.) | | Many families haven't had travel experiences internationally, especially in developing countries. They have fears of being mugged, taken advantage of or getting lost. Demonstration of their grief and fears can then delay the attachment process needed to help their child through this difficult time of living in a small hotel room for weeks waiting for paperwork before they can return home. | Occasionally, extended family members do not accept the child as a "full" member of the family. They may not be accepting of a transracial or transcultural placement and do not treat this child the same as other children born into the family. Adoptees recognize the differences in how they were treated growing up. They identify those extended family members who treated them as equal family members. |
| | | Children show their grief by crying and expressing their feelings of rejection and sadness at their separation from the familiar orphanage or caretaker. This triggers the parents' grief as they believe they don't have the skills to comfort their new child. It is important that the grieving parents accept that their child must express their own grief, which is normal. Grieving together for the adoptive parents and child enhances attachment. When a child does not demonstrate grief, there is a suspicion of previous neglect and that the child has diminished attachment skills. | The extended family may have gratitude for having the adopted person as part of their family and may worry about losing them if the adoptee becomes connected with their birth/first family and country of origin. |
| | | At different stages of the child's development, we see adoptive parents revisiting their own grief. | |
| | | My dreams were altered with adoption, triggering grief even at times of incredible joy. Being present for the birth of one of my daughters brought elation and sadness at the same time. | |

| Identity | | | |
|---|---|---|

Family members believe that they have failed the birth/first parent by not being available to them when they needed help. They see themselves as the ones who couldn't provide a solution and as the person who could not keep a relative in the family.

Being a person who could maintain this secret becomes a slice of their identity, perhaps believing that they are unkind and can't protect their family.

If adoptive parents cannot see themselves as "real" parents, they may question if they are less than other parents. Having a child look like them and carry their cultural values and their belief system becomes important to adoptive parents' identity. Questioning the degree of the child's love for them is delicately intertwined with the adoptive parents' identity.

Family identity changes when the adoptive child brings a new culture. The responsibility of learning and sharing the information with the child belongs with the adoptive parents, who themselves may be strangers to the child's culture, language or race. It is not a reasonable assumption that I, as an adoptive parent, am qualified to teach my child how to be Hawaiian, Guatemalan or Irish. It is the responsibility of the parents to find opportunities for their family to learn and experience ways to build a new family identity.

Adoptive parent identity ranges from pride in being a family to hiding the adoption from others. The family must define itself in its changing environment. Our family and individual responses to others are in constant flux. We are perpetually evaluating our surroundings so that we can provide the guidance to our children.

Changing schools, neighborhoods or even towns are decisions perhaps not previously considered when planning a family. Having diversity surround your family includes the child's school mates and teachers, neighbors and spiritual centers, coaches and mentors, stores where families shop, and parks where children play.

How are we related to this new family member? The extended family may ask, "Are we 'real' grandparents/relatives?" "How can I identify with a child that looks and sounds foreign to me? What do we have in common?"

The family identity has been changed through a new family member's culture, race and background. Family culture is taught through influence: "Will I allow myself to be influenced with these new additions to the family?" "Can I embrace the identity the child's country of birth, holidays, foods and customs?" "Can I display and appreciate art from the country of the child's birth?" "Can I read books by authors from the child's birth country?"

When asked, family members respond to their understanding of cultural competency by stating that they enjoy the food of the child's birth country. But eating an occasional Thai or Chinese meal has limited value in gaining cultural competence.

How do we become attached to a child with whom we are not familiar? The family may be excited to welcome the new member and want to learn of the child's culture and background. Acceptance into the family includes having conversations about similarities and differences in cultures. Other backgrounds already exist in the family, and many see this addition as beneficial for all to celebrate.

*cont.*

| | Extended birth family | Adoptive parents | Extended adoptive family |
|---|---|---|---|
| Identity (cont.) | | Family boundaries change when adopting a child from another country. You are no longer the family you thought you were. Defining and modeling how you see yourselves as a family helps the children to be comfortable within the protections of the family. <br><br> Family identity changes over the years with the addition of other new members. Building and expanding your adoption community reinforces the choice of becoming a transracial and transcultural family. Making friends with other international adoptive families helps normalize how the family functions within the greater community. | Holidays, meals and travels related to the child's birth country could be shared with the extended family. Being invited to attend cultural events may be of interest to the larger family. <br><br> With older children, professionals often suggest a period of quietness when the family first returns. It is challenging to ask those closest to the immediate family— grandparents, aunts, uncles and cousins—to wait before meeting their newest family member. I have witnessed family celebrations with over 100 guests, all speaking a different language from the child, all wanting to hug and kiss this stranger. Honoring and respecting the child's privacy and space and allowing them time to adapt to the new home, food, toys, bed, sounds and smells is critical. |

| Intimacy | The inability to care for a missing family member is painful. | Adoptive parents may struggle building emotional intimacy with a child who is very different from them in culture, ethnicity, race, language, appearance and so on. | If the adult children were giving birth, the family would likely be present or come soon afterwards. With international adoption, most adoptive parents travel without familial support. It is incredibly helpful to have other family members available to watch over the other children in the family, leaving the parents to spend the individual time needed to help the newcomer adapt. |
|---|---|---|---|
| | Birth family members protect their emotions by avoiding intimacy which could lead to feelings of vulnerability, guilt and shame when discussing the loss of the family member. A strong desire to avoid feeling judged may propel them to keep secrets about the loss. Taking risks to become close to others requires sharing personal stories where experience may be limited around adoption information. | The new demands of parenting a child with traumatic losses and significant developmental needs can put stress on the marital relationship. Emotional resources of the couple are now diverted to the child. | The extended family can be politely educated and asked to hold back with welcoming the newest child until the parents and siblings have had the opportunity to begin their attachment. Feeling excluded diminishes opportunities to become attached and therefore intimacy with a new family member can be delayed. Grandparents may have cared for birth grandchildren from very young ages, but international children are not placed as newborn or young infants. |
| | | | When an older child is adopted, life in their new family does not involve changing diapers and feeding—both tasks that foster attachment. Becoming intimate with a stranger may be uncomfortable and an unrealistic expectation. Learning how to become intimate with this child takes time. As the connection develops, grandparents may be a good outlet for the child's expression of fears or upsets, being slightly more removed from the immediate family. |

*cont.*

| | Extended birth family | Adoptive parents | Extended adoptive family |
|---|---|---|---|
| Intimacy (*cont.*) | | | Grandparents have had the opportunity not only to raise their children, but also to have experienced and survived the terrible twos, independent thinking at 7, and the tumultuous adolescent years. However, they may not know how to relate to an older child with an extensive medical or psychosocial history. They may have incredible sadness for the grandchild, niece or nephew as well as concern for their son or daughter who has adopted a child that they don't know much about. Knowing that the child had been hungry or cried going to sleep contributes to a feeling of making up for what was missed. Wanting to spoil the child is a normal reaction.<br><br>Where can I touch this child? Can the child sit on my lap and can I cuddle them as with other grandkids that I have known since birth? What does their culture teach about touch, eye contact, touching their head? What am I allowed to know? Where are this child's scars? What birthmarks does the child have?<br><br>Grandparents can play games, read and give breaks to exhausted but excited parents. The extended family can help with laundry and food preparation to allow more dedicated time for parents and child. Bringing food to allow the parents to have more time playing with and adapting to the family changes is most beneficial. |

| Mastery/Control | The extended birth/first family has lost control of this important issue within the family. Gaining mastery over this situation is very difficult, limited or impossible.<br><br>Pray, think, hope and plan when the opportunity arises. | To learn mastery means the adoptive parents can create balance to meet the needs of the birth/first family, themselves and the child. Providing information for search and reunion possibilities is part of that journey. Reunions are becoming more available with international adoption. A geneticist and adoptive father recently commented that the future will include easier DNA testing to locate more birth/first family members abroad.<br><br>Adoptive parents may have deep feelings about losing control over this journey but must master their fears and be supportive of the child that they adopted.<br><br>Although adoptive parents may occasionally question their decision to adopt internationally, seeing their child become an adult, attached to them, claiming their own identity and honoring the identity of the adoptive family becomes mastery for the adoptive parents.<br><br>Creating opportunities for trips to the child's land of birth can answer many questions for the adoptive parent and child. By confronting the truth, such as who the child looks like, creates a deeper attachment between the adoptive parents and child.<br><br>Witnessing a reunion between the child and the family of origin and experiencing love, understanding, compassion and joy for the child and their extended birth/first family is mastery. | Family members feel proud to identify with the adopted child/adult in the same way as any other family members. Past fears become manageable through helpful conversations as the secrecy decreases. The ability to be open about the family composition becomes selective and comfortable, balancing privacy and secrecy.<br><br>Extended family members often know more than the child has been told. They may have been helpful in reviewing past medical or psychosocial information on the child. This information is then no longer fully "private" and can be used against the child in future years. The child acts out, and family members may be quick to chime in: "You knew that her birth mother had challenges, what did you expect?" When birth children act out in a similar manner, their response may come with laughter: "Just like you did as a child!"<br><br>Adoption education continues throughout our lives. Our children are continually changing and learning, as are their personal stories. Allow the children to help guide these future steps. The extended family can be instrumental in being available to answer questions, listen and comfort, guide and create a fun place to "hang out" in when things are tense. |

*cont.*

| | Extended birth family | Adoptive parents | Extended adoptive family |
|---|---|---|---|
| Mastery/Control *(cont.)* | | Emotions become mastery for the parents as they exhibit their ability to deal with their own emotions as well as the child's. | |
| | | The reunion is a moment of truth and mastery for the whole adoptive family, answering questions such as "Who does the adoptee look like?" and "How tall will they grow?" | |
| | | When the adoptive parents begin to relax and deeply understand that this meeting may or may not end in the ways anticipated, it becomes critical that they focus on their child's needs and adjustment; they must acknowledge their own fears as parents that the child may feel connected in appearance and personality to their birth family. This is not a rejection but offers another opportunity for mastery. As the young adult adoptee matures and makes their own decisions about contact with the birth family and country, the adoptive parents have even greater faith in the permanence of their family. | |

# Chapter 24

# Openness and the Seven Core Issues in Adoption and Permanency

### Sharon Kaplan Roszia

Open adoption and permanency is defined as direct contact and relationship building between the birth/first family and parenting family over time. It is an attitude of the heart. It preserves linkages and heritage; role models; builds bridges; keeps information up to date; and shifts the "work" of adoption/permanence on to the shoulders of the adults to save the child from having to decide to search and then integrate new information into their identity. It transforms the child from being placed as "a gift" or an object to a link between families that all have a purpose in the child's life. The connection may not be between the birth/first parents who are unavailable or not presently safe due to addiction, mental illness or lifestyle choices, but may be with other family members or former resource parents who hold part of the child's story. Cast a wide net of inclusivity as you keep safety issues and availability in mind. It should include reaching out to *both* the birth/first mother and birth/first father's sides of the family. There may be individuals who do not join these relationships from the beginning but become available later in the child's life.

Openness acknowledges that adoptive and permanent parents are the present and maybe legal parents but will never be the genetic parents and that the child needs that genetic information, as do the parents, to adequately parent the child that they are parenting. This shift makes the placement about addition and not subtraction. It cuts losses for children. It concedes that these relationships are more like a marriage than a biological birth into a family. When we marry, we don't ask the spouse to flip a coin to decide which family we will continue to keep in our lives. We may not like or trust some of our spouse's family, but we honor that they are a part of our spouse's background and connections.

Openness is not about co-parenting or "ownership" of the child, not about open doors or lack of privacy, but it does include setting boundaries that can be moved as needed rather than building walls that people cannot easily go over or see through.

One relationship that is important to all children is the one they have sustained or lost with siblings. These include full siblings, half-siblings, foster siblings, siblings claimed in orphanages and group homes, siblings who existed before they were born and those who came after they were born. Openness allows for sibling relationships to grow and flourish.

Attachment to the parenting family is deepened when there are no secrets, lies or severing of connections; disconnects can result in confusion, betrayal, anger and fear that it could happen again. The ongoing contact can diminish adoption trauma. For the adopted person, adoption will always create questions like "Why did this happen?" and "Why did this happen to me?" Their ability to have their questions answered by the people who hold that part of their story allows for the full understanding and integration of that part of their story. In addition, being able to know maternal and paternal birth/first family members allows for a deeper knowing of oneself through the genetic mirroring and reflecting we can only get from family members with whom we share genetics.

Openness is not a new concept; it is referenced in the Hebrew bible. The concept has been researched for several years and there are now many people who have grown up never losing contact with their birth/first family.

Extensive long-term research by Dr. Ruth McRoy and Dr. Harold Grotevant (1998) has shown that children do better in placements that do not sever their previous relationships. This allows the child to understand what has occurred and not blame themselves. It allows them to ask questions and have mirror images of themselves as well as necessary racial, ethnic and cultural role models that the parenting parents may not be able to provide. As they age, parents and children can directly ask questions as they arise of all members of the family of origin. The same research indicates that children are not confused by the roles that different people play in their life. They do attach to their parenting parents, who are meeting their daily needs for safety, permanence, connection and love. Adults can love more than one child, so why can't children love more than one parent or type of parent? Children know who is in charge! We don't limit the number of grandparents, aunts, uncles or cousins they have because we think there are too many to love. Each relationship is distinct and may change over time.

For the birth/first parents, it allows them to validate their decision over time or understand any benefits from their loss by knowing that their child is alive, healthy, safe and loved. The child is not frozen in time and can be seen as a growing, living, breathing separate person in the world. It gives some birth/first parents the incentive to tackle their life challenges and get healthy, so they can stand with pride with their children over time; it offers siblings, past or future, the opportunity to know each other; and the original family's rituals, heirlooms and belief system can be shared with the parenting family, expanding their knowledge of the child they are raising. It lifts what could be a shaming and guilt-producing experience that leads to secrecy into the realm of truth. It can become an empowering choice and offer additional family links and relationships.

For the new parents, it offers ongoing access to information that allows them a better parenting strategy for the children they are raising—updated medical information, additional family and less fear of "what or who is out there." The parents can feel more entitled to parent when they have been chosen to do so by the family of origin. The parenting parents are the gatekeepers to all relationships when children are young but also the preservers of the child's connections to others.

As seen in the accompanying grid, openness is not problem free. Whenever we move a child from one or two family trees to another, it is complicated. The Seven Core Issues of Adoption and Permanency are still at play, and are typically expressed differently by different constellation members. We are addressing the needs of several individuals who also change over time, as do their lives—people marry, divorce, get educated, mature, age, die, relocate and so on. As the child grows and matures, they also add more dimensions to the relationships. They can more clearly see what they inherited from the family of origin and what they have received from their family and what makes them uniquely themselves. Because all the parents and extended family have preserved these links, the child may also choose to include or exclude certain individuals or may strengthen or minimize specific familial relationships due to their personal preferences.

Openness is more difficult when families are in crisis or are thrown together at the last minute or when they do not understand the roles and boundaries and desires of each party or do not share common values. It is also difficult when some professionals advise the adoptive parents to say "yes" to an openness request of the birth/first parents but have no real understanding of the concept or the long-term commitments involved, or how difficult the first years can be as parties grieve the loss of a child and their counterparts are experiencing joy and working on attachments and integration of the child into the family system. Some families can do well until the child begins to understand who the birth/first family really is to them and becomes anxious or scared.

All parties must learn to:

- define their own needs and realistic limits

- speak up about their needs

- negotiate and share

- communicate and problem solve

- confront disappointment

- take more risk

- allow for mistakes to be made

- recover, adjust and move forward

- live with uncertainty and some fear

- practice living in the present

- nurture themselves and have faith in themselves and others

- love, which includes forgiveness (of self and others)

- accept difference

- witness people changing and growing

- stand in their own truth and value themselves and their beliefs

- take others' needs into consideration

- keep their eyes on the long-term reason for expanding their family kinship—*the child!*

Openness works best when clear roles and boundaries are in place, people can share their fears and expectations with each other, clear and respectful communication is used, and everyone is focused on coming together to meet the needs of a child. Discussion of other family members must be honest and respectful. People don't have to be the best of friends to be in a relationship. Allowing for differences of opinion, life choices, religion, preferences in hobbies, style, neighborhood, vocations, manner of speech and educational and monetary differences is crucial. This models important life skills for a child.

Reading, support groups and counseling can move the parties in openness onto more solid ground. An open adoption support group can be a wonderful place to connect to peers who have lived experience and can support all members of the constellation in building and sustaining meaningful and healing relationships.

The adage "the truth will set you free" is the best avenue to healthy permanency, but nowhere is it written that this comes easily, is without risk, problem free, always endorsed by others or comes with any guarantees.

## Children's rights and open adoption

- Self-determination is a fundamental principle under which all discussion of rights is built. The goal of children's rights is to:

    - improve family life, not destroy it

    - empower children, not make them helpless

    - enhance the adult world, not diminish it

    - make all forms of family building about addition, not subtraction.

- Children are to have access to both maternal and fraternal birth/first and adoptive family members.

- Children are active participants in the decisions that affect their life and relationships. Until children can exercise those rights, a parent's duty is to preserve their heritage and linkages.

- Children are to be seen as people, not possessions, and treated as adults in training.

- Children's rights should be seen exclusively as their own, not a reflection of the rights of the adults in their lives.

- Children have a right to know their genetic and medical history and to have access to the information about their origins and the circumstances that separated them from the birth/first family. This information should not be limited, changed, given away to others before the child knows this information, or kept as a secret from the child. Information about a child's origins is private (but not secret) information that should not be shared outside the family without the child's permission. The information needs to be updated so it is always current and accurate. The beauty in an open adoption is the ability to go "to the source" to clarify and update.

- Children have a right to this information as they are able to understand it developmentally, able to deal with it emotionally and not given as a one-time revelation. Therefore, parents need to take advantage of

396 ⦿ Seven Core Issues in Adoption and Permanency

books, classes, conferences and mentors to help them understand this very important task.

- Children should not be knowingly deceived, either by what is said or left unsaid. Even potentially disturbing information needs to be shared at an appropriate age and always before a child leaves home.

- People should not wait for a child to ask questions but should anticipate the child's needs and look for appropriate opportunities to share information.

- Children have a right to express their feelings about the information they are given and should be encouraged and supported as they do.

- Children have a right to ask questions and express feelings without worrying that doing so might threaten their relationships with any of their parents.

- Children are not responsible for other people's feelings about each other or other people's feelings about events that led to placement, foster care or adoption.

- These rights should be applied to children of every age, even when the children are infants and toddlers and cannot exercise their rights. There is no magic age when people suddenly acquire rights. If rights are not acknowledged as a natural part of a person's life, it is difficult to grow up understanding and expecting them. Losing a family is a major loss of power and control, and having rights protected becomes a way to empower children through this major life loss.

| | Adopted child/adult | Birth/first parent | Adoptive/permanent parent |
|---|---|---|---|
| Loss | The child may feel loss as they know they were not kept.<br><br>There is the loss of growing up in the household of the birth/first family—waking up, brushing their teeth, experiencing bedtime rituals, birthdays and holidays, and spending time with birth siblings on a daily basis.<br><br>Time is lost with the birth/first family after the birth while the adoptive parents attach. The birth/first family may disappear from the child's life, causing further loss.<br><br>The adoptee may feel a loss of control about the choices made, and a loss of privacy and anonymity which a closed adoption might offer.<br><br>They feel loss at not being the same as most other adoptees, having to explain who those "other people" are to friends and community at shared functions.<br><br>They have lost the role models of those who have grown up in an open adoption.<br><br>There is a need to deal with adoption much more frequently, and they lose the ability to use denial as a defense mechanism when appropriate at certain stages of development. | The birth/first parents are not recognized by the extended family as the mother or father and lose daily contact with the placed child; they are replaced.<br><br>They lose the role as "Mommy" or "Daddy" and miss all the "firsts": first word, first step and so on.<br><br>They don't have the opportunity to provide guidance to the child daily or to assume the role of the everyday parent and legal parent.<br><br>There is a loss of the ability to separate from the other birth/first parent as one might in a closed adoption.<br><br>As the adoptive clan are an ongoing part of the birth/first parents' life, the birth/first parents lose the opportunity to be private about the placement.<br><br>They may lose the opportunity to focus on their own needs if they see the child's needs and want these to supersede their own.<br><br>There is potential loss of the open adoption connections, and a change of the relationship if the adoptive family or the child states that is what they want.<br><br>Future relationships are lost because of the open adoption, and community or family support is lacking because of the choices they made.<br><br>They miss out on important milestones as the child grows, and lose the joy of Mother's Day and Father's Day. | Adoptive parents feel a loss of the exclusivity of the role as parents. They have to share the title of mother or father.<br><br>There is a loss of privacy, and possible loss of the extended family who may not support the open adoption.<br><br>They may feel the loss of the birth/first family, and/or of being a part of the traditional adoption community; needing role models and guidance from others who know how this works over time.<br><br>Clear, definable boundaries may also be lost. |

*cont.*

| | Adopted child/adult | Birth/first parent | Adoptive/permanent parent |
|---|---|---|---|
| Rejection | The adoptee may still feel rejection, although not abandonment. This is heightened when some children are kept in the birth/first family and they were not.<br><br>They may experience rejection from other adoptees who were raised in closed adoptions.<br><br>Rejection is also felt when the birth/first family exits the open adoption; becomes involved with drugs or alcohol; or is mentally ill.<br><br>If the birth/first parent marries someone who does want them to be involved with an open adoption and the birth/first parent chooses the new relationship over the open adoption, the adoptee may feel rejected.<br><br>They may feel rejection by siblings or if the birth/first parents do not share their existence and they have a child that remained a secret.<br><br>The adoptive family may not like or may reject the child's family of origin, causing the child to feel rejected also. | There is more exposure and potential for rejection as they must discuss their status more publicly and face possible rejection from family, friends, the spiritual community and other birth/first parents.<br><br>They may feel a sense of rejection of their lifestyle.<br><br>They face possible rejection from the child they placed, from the adoptive parents, extended adoptive family and/or from the other birth parent.<br><br>If they have regrets about the adoption choice or the family they chose to parent their offspring, they may feel they are to blame and reject themselves.<br><br>Feelings of rejection can arise when they observe the child calling someone else "Mom" or "Dad" and going to those people for comfort.<br><br>There may be rejection by a future spouse and even from their future children. | Rejection when one spouse supports the open adoption relationship and the other does not.<br><br>Rejection by family and friends who do not support the open adoption.<br><br>Rejection by a birth/first parent for the parenting style or decisions that are made that the birth/first parent does not support.<br><br>Rejection from the child.<br><br>Rejection from the birth/first family when they chose to withdraw from the open adoption.<br><br>Rejection from the external culture who questions or judges your parenting and decisions regarding openness. |

| Shame/Guilt | The adoptee may feel shame that they were not kept in the birth/first family, and at having to explain their family system over and over, often to outsiders.<br><br>Possible shame or guilt arises if they are embarrassed by, are afraid of or don't like members of the family of origin.<br><br>They may feel shame or guilt that they would rather be with their family of origin or that they did something that caused them to be separated from their family of origin.<br><br>Guilt may be connected to feeling relief and "lucky" to have the adoptive family and perhaps an easier lifestyle. They don't want to visit or be with their birth/first family: "I just wanna be a 'normal kid.'" | They feel guilt about what led them to have to place their child, and shame when they meet new members of the adoptive family.<br><br>There may be guilt about a difference in lifestyle, which may relate to education, language or financial considerations. They cannot arrange to see the child more often or offer more "things" to the child.<br><br>Guilty feelings arise when they do not respond to the adoptive family to get together because of their shame, or when they have to talk to their child about why they were adopted and the "poor choices" they made. | Adoptive parents have guilt about how they feel towards members of the family of origin.<br><br>Maybe one child has a certain level of openness that another does not, or they have added family members to their family system who bring problems and tension.<br><br>They may want to minimize the contact because of the child's reactions before, during or after visits and feel guilty because of this.<br><br>The adoptive parents may not know if they are confusing the child by allowing open relationships; outside people are advising them that it's not necessary and this may confuse the child.<br><br>Guilt can arise when the birth/first parents offer "advice" and suggestions that the adoptive parents don't want to implement or consider. |
|---|---|---|---|

*cont.*

| | Adopted child/adult | Birth/first parent | Adoptive/permanent parent |
|---|---|---|---|
| Grief | The adoptee may feel grief about being separated from their family of origin in the first place, or as they watch the unfolding life of their family of origin, with the successes and failures, and marriages and new children.<br><br>As their developmental understanding of adoption unfolds, they may experience grief.<br><br>There is grief if people disappear from the open adoption.<br><br>There may be grief as they imagine what they lost not growing up with their birth/first parents, especially as they get to know more extended birth/first family members.<br><br>Meeting new siblings from the birth/first parents may cause them to wonder why the birth/first parents couldn't keep them and what it would be like to be raised by them. | The child's relationship with them keeps changing over time. Grief may arise as the child asks them questions about why they made the decision to place them or why they didn't work harder to keep them (addressing addictions, mental illness or the need for help).<br><br>There is grief if they are unable to stay on track to meet their own life goals, or if the adoption plans of openness change.<br><br>Grief arises when they see the child being unhappy or angry or ill, and each time the child leaves them.<br><br>*Grief may always be present and the birth/first parent may struggle with a range of issues:*<br><br>Can I show my grief or talk about it without being told I am not moving on with my life or being ungrateful for the openness and my chance to see my child? Can I still be sad and glad?<br><br>When the child has been longer with the new family than with mine, does that mean the child is now more theirs?<br><br>Where does my grief live in my body? | The birth/first family may be suffering, making poor life choices or pulling away from them. As the adoptive parents see the sadness and grief process unfold for the family of origin, they may not know how to process their own grief issues because they are supposed to be happy about parenting this child.<br><br>As there are different levels of openness with different children in the family and one child has pain because they don't have what the other does have, this may be a source of grief for the adoptive parents.<br><br>Grief is present when they see the child struggling with the adoption issues, as they watch their child yearn for and miss their birth/first parents.<br><br>When the child they love looks and acts more like the birth/first family, there is sadness for the adoptive parents as they must acknowledge they will never be the genetic parents. |

| *Questions around identity arise for the adoptee:* | *Questions around identity arise for the birth/first parents:* | *Questions around identity arise for the adoptive parents:* |
|---|---|---|
| Can I clearly see, as I grow into adulthood, the nature and nurture that contribute to my identity and claim what is uniquely me as well? | Am I good person or a bad person? A martyr? | Do I feel validated as my child's parent or do I feel competition with the family of origin? |
| Do I feel free to ask for the missing pieces of information from all my relatives to fulfill my identity formation or do I hold back for fear of hurting someone? | Am I still a mother/father? How does one measure motherhood and/or fatherhood? | Am I fully entitled to parent my child? |
| I may still have a piece of "mystery history" if a family tree is missing. | What are my roles, rights and obligations? | Do I need to ask permission for anything, such as religious beliefs, values, culture and traditions? |
| Are all my siblings' relationships valid or only the ones I grew up with on a daily basis? | Can I claim this child publicly by putting pictures up at home, in my office, saying I have a child even if I am not raising them? | Does being an "adoptive parent" mean I'm less than other parents? |
| Who are my role models who have grown up in open adoptions? | Do I sign my cards as "Love Mom" or "Dad" or "sister"? | Will I still be my child's parent when they are grown and leave home? |
| With whom do I identify the most? | How am I introduced or spoken about, to others? | If we don't look alike, are we still parent and child, and how does society see us? |
| Am I going to have the same struggles as my birth/first parents had or have? | Can I attend important events in my child's life and share who I am with others? | Who am I to the birth/first family and their other children? |
| What's locked in my gene code—from whom did I inherit what? | *The birth/first family may feel restrained even if the parenting parents don't ask them to be:* | When introducing the birth/first parents to my family or friends, I'm not sure what to call them or how to explain our relationship. Will people question my parenting or my role as my child's parent? |
| If one birth/first parent tree is missing and I don't relate to or look like the birth/first family I am involved with, where are my mirror images? | Who are my future children, in-laws and others to this adoptive family? | |
| | Who am I in relation to other children who join the adoptive family by birth or adoption? | |
| | Who am I to the other birth/first parents connected to this adoptive family? | |
| | The child looks like me but calls someone else mother. | |

*(Identity)*

*cont.*

|  | Adopted child/adult | Birth/first parent | Adoptive/permanent parent |
|---|---|---|---|
| Intimacy | *Questions around intimacy arise for the adoptee:*<br><br>What is the story of my conception?<br><br>Who do I get my body characteristics from?<br><br>Am I normal?<br><br>It is hard to get close to these different families at the same time. Is it safe to get close?<br><br>Will I have to move again? If I don't act right, they might leave forever.<br><br>I long to be close, but at the same time, I'm scared to be too close.<br><br>I am different from my adoptive family but feel deeply attached to them and sometimes need information about my changing body from my birth/first family and that can feel embarrassing.<br><br>What will people I date think about this open adoption and all the "extra" relatives?<br><br>With whom do I share all of my thoughts, feelings, fears, concerns and questions? Do I share them with anyone? | *Questions around intimacy arise for the birth/first parents:*<br><br>What is the story of my child's conception? Is that something I share and when? Do I need permission from the adoptive family to discuss these parts of my life?<br><br>What was my pregnancy and delivery like?<br><br>Who was in the delivery room and did that feel deeply intimate if the adoptive parents were there?<br><br>How do I feel about my body?<br><br>Do I share personal aspects of my history like when I first menstruated, saw my body develop or first had facial hair or a wet dream?<br><br>Will I ever see the child I brought into the world naked again?<br><br>Could feelings develop between my children, some of whom are with me and the other in another family? Do the normal rules and boundaries hold between siblings who do not grow up in the same home?<br><br>How do I feel about the other birth/first parent and the adoptive parents?<br><br>When gaps of time go by, I must adapt to a new person as they have grown and we must reaffirm our relationship. I see myself reflected in my child or the other birth/first parent in the child. | *Questions around intimacy arise for the adoptive parents:*<br><br>If I adopted because of infertility, has the intimacy in my marriage healed after all the treatments?<br><br>Is my relationship with the genetic parents of my child comfortable? Can we discuss issues of sexuality and developing bodies?<br><br>Do we have similar values and beliefs about appropriate behavior?<br><br>How close should we get to the birth/first parents and family?<br><br>How much closeness and contact do we allow our child to have with the birth/first family?<br><br>How much information do we want the birth/first parents to be sharing with our child? A lot of the information and details may be intense, painful and scary for our child. How do we want our child to hear these parts of their story? Should it come from us or their birth/first parents? |

| Mastery/Control | *Questions around mastery and control arise for the adoptee:* | *Questions around mastery and control arise for the birth/first parents:* | *Questions around mastery and control arise for the adoptive parents:* |
|---|---|---|---|
| | I was not in charge of this life event that changed who I am forever. (The child lost everything because of a person's youth, economic status, unmarried status, addiction, mental illness, abuse/trauma and/or lack of support, but hopefully sees that his/her birth/first family is alive, maybe thriving, and still values them. Love can be experienced from both the birth/first family and the adoptive/permanent family.) | Did I feel I had a real choice in how this all came about? Did I receive all the information I needed; get the choice of family and get to know them before placement; get the support and counseling both before and after placement that I wished? | I did not see myself doing this kind of parenting; it was often hard and confusing. |
| | | | My honor is intact as I kept my contract with the birth/first family. |
| | | Did I learn about open adoption, both its benefits and its challenges? | Even though it was challenging, I know I did what was best for my child. I kept their needs front and center. |
| | I can see more clearly who I am because I did not have to lose a family to gain permanency at a time when I was young and vulnerable. | Do I feel treasured for my role in my child's life? Do I have good status in both the adoptive and my family systems? Does my child value my role in their life? | I can see that my child loves me and is attached and will always be a part of the family. I feel as if I have more family and children because we did this form of adoption. |
| | I have my mirror images through the open adoption and have not lost my culture, ethnicity or racial connections. I did not have to decide whether to search for people or do the work to locate them and then build relationships; they have been there all the time. | Were all the agreements that we made at the time of placement honored? | I could be a better parent to this child because the birth/first family was so open, honest and helpful with ongoing information. |
| | | Are there any secrets I have held? Have I always been honest in this relationship? | I gained many new skills, became more flexible and open hearted and learned I could really care about people who may be very different from myself. |
| | I understand why this decision was made at that time in the lives of my birth/first family. | Did the benefits outweigh the losses? What did I gain from this adoption and open relationship with others who may be very different from me? | I know I helped the birth/first family with their grief and loss process as they were able to avoid losing their child forever. The connections between all of us have allowed us all to learn, grow and heal. |
| | I did not lose my siblings. | I did not have to wait for my child to become an adult before knowing the outcome to the story/decision. | |
| | Because I grew up with openness I am able to see clearly what I received from the parents that raised me, the family whose genetics I share and my own unique characteristics, interests and qualities. | | |
| | I feel whole and know that I have access to the ongoing relationships that I need to continue to grow and thrive. | | |

# Chapter 25

# Single Parenting and the Seven Core Issues in Adoption and Permanency

## Mary McGowan

I never thought I would be on this journey alone 30 years ago when I became a foster parent. My intention was to help protect children from abuse and neglect, if even for a short time. I wanted them to experience safety and calm, what it's like to have a routine.

I thought I was fully prepared as a woman in my twenties; after all, I was a psychology major and studied emergency medicine. I was equipped for any child they would place with me—or so I thought.

Being single has had an impact from day one. During the licensing process, I looked like the "dream" foster home, with my background in handling medical issues and emotionally unstable children. Yet after I was licensed, when they found out I was single, the placements didn't materialize. They even sent me to a therapist, who quizzed me on developmental stages and parenting skills, which I passed with flying colors. Still, nothing changed until I went to a supervisor and shared my concerns. Not long afterwards, I got a call, presenting a sibling group of three. They stated that one was a pyromaniac, one a kleptomaniac and the third had been sexually abused. Now as eager as I was to get my first placement, I knew this was a set-up. I declined. Finally, after many hurdles, I received my first placement. After I proved myself with this first child, they continued coming for 26 years.

Since I was young, I'd thought often about how much I wanted a family. I had always dreamed of having a little "Mary," but as I cared for the children and youth who were passing through my home in these years, I found what I was really looking for. When one of my placement's rights were terminated, I was asked if I wanted to adopt her. I thought long and hard: What would happen to me, to my personal life, my work life? Would anyone want to date and settle down with a woman who had an adopted child with special needs? Could I even handle this as a single caregiver? I had started seeing someone who was supportive of the adoption. Then, as I was going through the adoption process, my foster daughter's adoption worker had a baby who needed an immediate permanent home. After much thought, I decided to take the new baby as well, adopting both girls at the same time.

This was the start of my life as a parent, making a home for children with special needs, and for a time I had a partner living with me, sharing the responsibilities. After a while, however, with the stress of working, the seemingly impossible tasks of parenting the children, and trying to find time to put into the relationship with my partner when it never felt as if there was any to give, I became single again.

I wound up taking in more children and eventually adopted a total of five— three girls and two boys—from foster care. After 26 years of fostering, I let my license lapse, so I could care for my family of five in a meaningful way.

As I ponder the Seven Core Issues of Adoption and Permanency, I see areas that many of us who foster and adopt share, but also many unique struggles and benefits that come from being a single parent.

There isn't a single person involved in foster care and adoption who doesn't experience loss. The children seem to lose most everything—their first home, family, neighbors, school, belongings and, for many, their very identity. How could they be expected to just pick up and adjust to a new home in a strange place with a new mom or dad? I think about my own girls: What was it like for them to be with one parent? How would it affect them over their lifetime?

From an adoptive parent's perspective, I had to let go of the dream of having my own baby, the little Mary that looks like me.

As a parent of children with special needs, the loss of neurotypical and developmental milestones was hard and exhausting. I had to adjust my expectations to look at their development and abilities. Once I was able to do this, the joy was there as I watched them achieve small important steps towards healing.

As a single parent, there was no one for me to pass the baton to for a break. So many times over the years I've felt alone and isolated. I've lost friends and even family members over my choice to create a family from different ethnic backgrounds and special needs. Some of my biological family members and close friends questioned my decisions, pointing out everything that could go wrong as a single working caregiver. Every time this happened, I felt my support was weakened. I needed to make my own family and find ways to build my own village of help and support.

The biological family's loss is also heartbreaking, no matter what the reason was that their child entered the system. I can't imagine losing one of my children and/or how shamed I would feel. Nothing could fill that void or shield me from the judgments made by family and friends. Extended family members may feel loss as well—the dream of a "real" grandchild to carry on the family line that can't be realized.

Shame, guilt and rejection often go together with loss. I haven't had the experience of a licensed parent getting my biological child—that person being deemed a "good" parent—but I can imagine feeling abandoned and replaced. I was instructed with my first placement not to befriend her birth parent, to keep a distance. This only triangulated the child, making her feel as though she had to choose between her birth family and me. But as I talked with them to learn more about what their child liked, I began to see the good in them. I offered once to give the mom of one of my foster children a ride to parenting class. I will never forget that day; it was September 11, 2001. The radio was on in my car and we speculated together about what was happening. The experience drew us close, creating a bond that helped until this child was able to return home.

Many children blame themselves, thinking they were taken out of their home because they were bad and their parents didn't want them. Many will act out in placement, thinking they will be sent home, only to find out they must start again in yet another foster home. They question why their birth family had to go, and imagine their parents were good and ideal; some develop magical thinking around how they were parented.

Young adult adoptees often are still in search of their identities, and question where they belong. Can they find their biological families and build a relationship to help fill the void that they carry? If they do, it's not always a positive experience, however; one of my adult daughters found her family but was quickly crushed by the reality of who they were. The feelings of rejection can start all over again. Another of my daughters found a sense of freedom during this time, only to start using drugs and making poor decisions for a time as a young adult.

While the greatest effects of being a single foster and adoptive parent have been constant exhaustion and sometimes burnout, there have been many delights and positives to balance out the challenges.

As a single parent, I've also been able to devote more time and energy to my children. I've loved the intimate bonds we've been able to create. I love being able to decide on parenting routines and bedtimes, and deciding with my kids all the fun things we want to do together. And I've learned more about my own identity through these years. My life may not have followed a "traditional" line, but my experience as a single foster and adoptive mom has forced me to reflect on my own family of origin, my expectations and ideas about what family means, as well as how critical these bonds are to healthy development.

You could say that my choices to foster and adopt children with special needs opened a door to my position as director of a non-profit organization devoted to helping other families and professionals dedicated to serving kids like my own. Of course, I didn't know when I started on this path 30 years ago that I would wind up here, but my professional and personal life have blended and complemented one another in significant ways.

I know I've given my kids everything I can: love, warmth, fun and an open mind about what families look and feel like. They've grown up to know there are many types of families and all are truly wonderful in their uniqueness.

# Chapter 26

# The Seven Core Issues and Third-Party Reproduction and Surrogacy

## Kris Probasco

The history of donor conception dates back to 1884 when the first case of donor insemination was documented in Philadelphia, Pennsylvania. At that time, physicians were using their own sperm for conceptions (Snowden 1983). The first documented case of egg donation was in 1983 (Buster *et al.* 1983) and started with known donors, but changed quickly to anonymous donors. Embryo placement as an adoption began in 1997 (2009). Surrogacy has been with us since biblical times. Commercial surrogacy started in the 1980s, and now gestational surrogacies, where the surrogate carries non-genetic embryos to hopeful birth, are common. The genetics are from both the intended parents or a donor egg or sperm. There needs to be more emphasis on the psychological needs of the child born to a surrogate. They are born to the surrogate mother and placed with the intended parents, but the baby did not expect to have these parents. The baby's sensory system is already attuned to the surrogate mother and experiences a major disruption which requires adaptation. Donor conceptions are typically leveraged by couples with male or female infertility, women who cannot carry a child, individuals who have genetic disorders they do not want passed on, marriages where there has been a vasectomy, single women, and homosexual families. The number of births from a donor conception is not tracked; however, estimates show that there are thousands of children born by donor conception each year in the United States—many more than there are traditional adoptions. Most of the embryos transferred have a frozen history.

It has been over 130 years since our first documentation of a donor conception and, sadly, not much has changed. A recent article by BioNews dated November 2016 (Ross 2016) showcased a Canadian fertility doctor accused of using his own sperm to impregnate patients. The well-being and rights of children were completely ignored, not even considered. This Canadian fertility doctor is facing a class action lawsuit by families of some of his former patients who allege he used his own sperm in donor conception procedures without their knowledge or consent.

A recent list from the mental health group of the American Society for Reproductive Medicine indicated that a single egg donor had donated eggs to 43 families. She would go to many clinics to donate, but not indicate she had been a prior egg donor. She has been diagnosed as bi-polar, with schizophrenia and borderline personality disorder. Children born from this donor are at an extreme risk of inheriting these very serious disease factors. There is also at least one facility in California that is providing manmade embryos for embryo donation. At this facility, individuals or couples are able to request specific donor qualities and work with the facility to recruit these individuals to meet those qualifications. How many generations of people separated from their genetics will it take before there is acceptance of children's rights by the medical field? It should be best practice to acknowledge the genetic and identity needs of offspring that are being produced by anonymous donors. These lives are planned and have been forever changed by not having a full understanding of their genetics and family history. Without acknowledging children's rights, such practices are contributing to the consequences.

Nightlight Christian Adoptions in California started their Embryo Adoption program in 1997. This was the first in the country to treat embryo adoption as an adoption. Full assessment of the adoptive parents was provided as well as counseling for the genetic family. The genetic family was involved in selecting the adoptive family for their embryos. Therefore, all social, emotional, legal and psychotic factors were discussed with the genetic family as well as the adoptive family. Openness is typically involved in these arrangements where both families know of each other through the agency or direct contact.

The Donor Sibling Registry was created in 2000 by Wendy Kramer and her son Ryan. Ryan was conceived through sperm donation and has known of his donor birth for many years but grew curious of others like him. They initially started a Yahoo group that quickly turned into a full registry. They have close to 60,000 members registered at this time and have been successful in connecting half-donor siblings with each other as well as donors with their offspring. This registry is similar to those provided in other countries. It is my hope that a national registry will be developed in the United States. One of their registered sperm donors had 150 families genetically connected to him. Of course, there is a growing concern among the donor constellation for the potential negative consequences of having so many children fathered by the same donor, including the possibility that genes for rare diseases could spread throughout the population. Some experts are calling attention to the increased odds of accidental incest of half-siblings, who can often live in close proximity to one another. These are the consequences offspring will suffer as long as secrecy, anonymity and the lack of regulation are imposed on alternative forms of reproduction. In order to make educated medical and life decisions, donor-conceived individuals should have the knowledge of the medical history of their donor conceptions and the availability of current medical factors.

Wendy Kramer has proposed a citizen petition to the Food and Drug Administration (FDA) for it to look into the state of affairs surrounding all donor conceptions, creating hope among the community of developing an appropriate regulatory oversight and national registry. In doing this, she received comments from donor-conceived people, parents and donors.

The consequences of the lack of regulation of donor conception have been reviewed in the grid that follows at the end of this chapter. The core issues defined by the donor population are very similar to the concerns expressed by the adoption community.

Here are some quotes from the donor constellation that were included in Wendy Kramer's FDA petition.[1]

## Donor parent

We discovered many years later that psychological screening was not provided to the donor. Meeting him twenty years later we discovered he suffers from bipolar. He was hospitalized as a teenager. My daughter also suffers from bipolar, a highly genetic disorder. Another offspring has committed suicide; another was in residential treatment as a teenager and prison as an adult. I consider this unspeakable harm to the offsprings.

A recent case involved a former sperm donor who misrepresented himself as having a genius IQ and advanced degrees and was later found to have schizophrenia and a criminal record. There is currently no independent verification of personal and family medical history.

There is no standard identification system, therefore one donor can donate at multiple banks without disclosing this information.

Knowing our biological roots and medical and current history is not a commodity to be bought and sold, but a basic civil right. Without regulations, a family will never know how many offspring are connected to their child, and what type of health information is not being shared.

---

1   Researcher & Donor Parent—Post on Donor Sibling Registry (www.donorsiblingregistry.com) to submit to FDA citizen petition, January 19, 2017.

> Known donor or donor identity release should be made a requirement for all egg, sperm and embryo donation; it is proven to be best for those people born of these situations.

A professional researcher and donor parent based in the UK states:

> It is the human right of every person to know their genetic, gestational, and legal parents and this applies just as much to donor-conceived and surrogate born individuals as anyone. Should the US acknowledge these rights in this way, it would send a powerful message around the world.

> DNA testing was able to locate the donor and found out the information that was provided from their cryobank was not corrected.

> The industry needs to be regulated so that donor information is factually correct and that the cryobanks are being forthright and honest in their dealings with clients.

> A parent of a donor-conceived child states that it is shocking to see that there are no regulations regarding record collection or keeping, medical updates, medical information sharing, tracking of offsprings or limits on offsprings.

## Donor

> I was a sperm donor during graduate school and medical school and joined the Donor Sibling Registry. I have had the privilege to become acquainted with some genetic children who are very much loved by their families and are happy with their lives. The children want to understand more about their genetics and other medical information as well about their origin of their personality traits. I support regulation of the industry to ensure that children who result from donations can access information related to their genetics and heritage.

A group of eight individuals brought a complaint against a retired US fertility doctor accused of using his own sperm to inseminate patients of his clinic in 2014. They believe they are all biological siblings. Initially the physician claimed his innocence; however, DNA tells the truth. The physician has now pleaded guilty to misleading investigators and has admitted to "donating his own sperm to women around 50 times."

Another donor stated that "he did not realize that his sperm samples would be used for so many children. For that he is very sorry, and that was not his intentions."

## Donor conceived

At age 31, after randomly taking an Ancestry DNA test to gain greater clarity of my ancestors, I quickly realized through my results that my father was not my biological father. It took my parents several months before they would reveal that they used a sperm donor to conceive triplets. This has been the shock of my life and an incredible blow to my identity. I returned to the physician's office that provided the sperm donor as I needed to process my biological identity. Her office maintains that all records, even non-identifying information about the procedure and donor, had been destroyed. (It was very common in the early years of adoption that records were destroyed. Kansas City Missouri was a hub of Maternity Homes at one time having at least thirteen homes. The common response regarding records was that they were destroyed by a fire.) Her parents were informed that the clinic destroyed the records immediately after the procedure, thus never even maintaining relevant records for the required ten years. My brothers and I each have inheritable medical conditions and zero access to our paternal medical records. I have always thought that physicians took the oath of causing no harm, this definitely is harmful. It has become increasingly apparent that open adoption and likewise open donor conceptions are best practice, resulting in healthier, better adapted offsprings. It is the fertility industry's responsibility to right this wrong and hopefully find them on the right side of history in recognizing the best interests of children that they assist in medically creating.

I was born in Canada in 1986 through anonymous sperm donation. Years later, my mother tried to get copies of her records but they were destroyed. It is horrifying to me that the fertility industry was permitted to disavow any medical responsibility to the offspring they helped produce. A paid donor's rights to complete privacy is viewed as all-important whereas the rights to vital information about my health are viewed as irrelevant. It is clear that these priorities are not motivated by any reasonable standard of ethics but by a desire to avoid liability of harm.

I have been diagnosed with a genetic connective tissue disorder that is a result of disease cluster among people with autosomal dominant genetic connective tissue. For the treatment, a complete family history is necessary which I do not have with my paternal genetics. It is alarming that I have been at risk of so many medical complications my entire life with no indication of that because of a deliberate decision of medical practice to keep this information from me.

A donor offspring states that allowing a donor to be anonymous is unethical. In the world of adoption, society has acknowledged benefits of open records including their psychological and emotional health. Sperm, egg and embryo donation is no different. The onset of DNA testing has shown very clearly that anonymity can no longer be guaranteed. Extensive records are required for animal breeding, but when it comes to humans there is nothing substantial.

"As a donor conceived person who discovered the facts of his donor conception in his adulthood, I am horrified in the lack of regulation in the infertility donation industry." The donor conceived person states that "the basic rights for donor conceived people are highly neglected in a continuously growing population." Late discovery adoptees tell us the same story of being horrified of finding out about their adoption. Identity crisis for all of these adults.

A change would recognize that the inherently complex needs of children born from reproductive technology must be addressed first and foremost. This includes removing several layers of secrecy and recognizing biological identity as a fundamental human right.

"Did you think about me and what I would need?" Donor conceptions for the most part are adult focused—what is best for the adult and their image—and little is thought of the child's needs.

. . . . . . . . .

The practice in the fertility industry has been constructed over decades to accommodate the preferences of the industry professionals, the donors and the recipient parents. The best interests and medical needs of the people they produced have been undeniably ignored. The children ultimately are the ones who can be most negatively affected with their health and well-being. Their needs should be the driving force over any donor conception. In many parts of the world, laws require donor identities be made available to donor-conceived offspring when they reach a certain age, usually 18. Sweden was the first country to pass such law in 1985. Other jurisdictions have followed suit, including Australia, Germany, Switzerland, the Netherlands, Norway, New Zealand and the UK.

The UK's Human Fertilisation and Embryology Authority provides a good model of legally required identification systems. UK law requires donors to enter personal information into a federal registry, including non-identifying information: the donor's physical description, year and country of birth, and marital status. Identifying information, including the donor's name, birthdate and last-known address, is also provided. A donor-conceived offspring can apply for the donor's non-identifying information and identifying information at 18 years of age. The UK limits the number of children from a single donor to ten, screens for genetic disorders and provides donors with only modest compensation to cover expenses.

The US is one of the last-developed countries to address the need for oversight in the fertility process. Regulation of this field of medicine is important and necessary. Having a registry where all members of the donor constellation can contact and exchange information is crucial to the health and well-being of future generations.

Since this practice began, the infertility banks have been making progress in maintaining the medical and social history of their donors. However, the medical information is frozen in time. Without a system in place to exchange information, the parents of a donor-conceived offspring will not be aware of ongoing and unexpected medical difficulties. For example, a sperm donor may complete his current medical history to the best of his knowledge, but family medical history does change over time. If a registry was in place, vital new information such as his mother's death from breast cancer following his donation could be shared.

The fertility industry has often been referred to as high-tech reproduction since the first in vitro fertilization (IVF) birth of Louise Brown in 1978. The industry has proceeded with high-tech medical advances such as providing pre-genetic screenings of embryos to ensure the transformation of healthy embryos. However, the industry has been severely lacking in the forward thinking of the needs of the children that it is helping to create with this advanced medical practice. As the offspring take charge of their own medical decisions, the lack of ongoing medical information regarding their genetics can put them at risk for many possible genetic difficulties. If they are aware of their medical history and genetic diseases, measures can be set in place to either prevent or delay the onset of the disease.

The Donaldson Adoption Institute in New York created a policy and practice perspective for applying adoption research to assisted reproductive technology (ART). The institute reports that the problematic effects of secrecy and withholding information for adoptive people, birth families and adoptive families offer insight for ART policies and practices related to the circumstances of a donor offspring's conceptions, disclosure of medical and other background information and the identity of those involved. The child-centered focus of adoption provides a perspective for children conceived through ART.

One of the recommendations from the findings is that children should be able to learn the circumstances of their births as well as their biological family and medical backgrounds. To ensure that this happens, the US should join the UK and other countries to mandate that donor-conceived offspring be given access to this information. Practice models should be implemented for ART practitioners to provide such disclosure. The US should also establish a national database to collect, maintain and facilitate such information to enable gamete providers to routinely update the medical, historical and other information they provided at the time of donation. The establishment of enforced regulations for sperm, egg and embryo placement and a registry where communication can be maintained for all parties should be made mandatory. Other countries have been forward thinking in establishing donor registries.

With so many donor offspring coming forth and talking about their physical and mental health issues, it should be clear to the fertility industry that the model of "do no harm" is not being practiced. The Seven Core Issues of Adoption and Permanency provide a foundation for looking at all the factors that affect the donor constellation, including all members of the donor family and extended family. These losses are similar to those of adoption. The adoption community should embrace donor families. When the best interests of the child are first and foremost, decisions and procedures will be more restrictive and regulated. This will bring more security to future generations.

In closing, I would like to recognize the further needs of children born by donor conception. Birth psychology tells us that people have cellular memories and continue these memories through their lifetime. The conscious baby (Chamberlain 2013) tells us that baby senses start early. At five weeks' gestation, touch is able to be felt and emotion and relationship are beginning; the relationship with carrying mother starts after seven weeks. When a pregnancy is created by donor conceptions and surrogacy, we need to be mindful of the baby's emotional and psychological development. In these pregnancies, the prenate's needs can be assisted by touch, calm and relaxing sounds, and verbalizing that they are safe, loved and wanted. What babies need to know from the very start is that they are wanted, welcome, seen, felt, safe and protected, that they belong to a family and that they are lovable.

All these messages can be transferred to the baby throughout the pregnancy. It is obvious that these donor programs would look quite different if the focus was on what is best for the baby. In the donor world, the focus is on the adults who are involved with the process, including the donor, the intended parents and the pregnant person, as well as the medical practitioners. As a culture, we often come at babies from the outside in, meeting the needs of the adults. The opposite is from the inside out—what is best for the baby. No one would be involved in any of this process if it wasn't for the baby. We, as clinicians, have a responsibility to prepare parents for the needs of their baby from the embryo onward.

*Note from the author: It was Annette Baran and Rueben Pannor who poked the fertility bear by their book* Lethal Secrets: The Psychology of Donor Insemination *(1993). I had the pleasure to be introduced to Annette by Sharon Kaplan Roszia in 1989. I was fortunate to have Sharon and Annette as my mentors. Annette and I presented at many conferences regarding donor conceptions. It was an exciting adventure. I am so happy to have this journey with Sharon.*

**The Seven Core Issues and Third-Party Reproduction: Surrogacy**

| | Child born of surrogacy | Adult born of surrogacy | Gestational surrogate |
|---|---|---|---|
| Loss | The child may be confused as the intended parent isn't who their brain was prepared to bond to. They may feel a loss of safety about relationships, and have physiological confusion. | The adult may feel a disconnect, if there was an egg/sperm/embryo donation—most are anonymous. Pieces of the puzzle are not available. | The surrogate does not experience time with the family, or day-to-day events with the child. There is a lack of surrogacy pregnancy support, and ideal relationships with the intended parents. |
| Rejection | The child experiences physical separation from the surrogate and surrogate family. | The adult may question why the surrogate did that and if money was involved. They may wonder if she thinks of them. | People may ask her, "How can you give 'your' baby away?" Or they may think she is heartless or a baby-making machine. Surrogacy may be against her family's beliefs/morals. |
| Shame/Guilt | If there are two male intended parents, the child may be concerned about where their mother is, or even if they have a mother. They may feel shame if money is brought up in personal conversations when discussing surrogacy. | A lot of money was paid to have them: "My parents made sacrifices to have me. Am I living up to their expectation?" | The "how much are they paying you?" question brings up shame. It may be inferred that she just wants to "get rich quick." |

| | | | |
|---|---|---|---|
| Grief | Separation trauma will likely occur if the child is not prepared for the letting go—they won't always remember but will have emotional recall. | Grief may create relationship difficulties, and parenting issues for the adult. | The surrogate may find that it is harder than she thought. Grief is felt at the end of the surrogacy journey. |
| Identity | If the child was conceived by a donor, they may never meet or know about them. Hopefully the surrogate is available for contact. | If donation was involved, the adult may find it hard to feel whole. They may search for who they are over and over, with a sense of an incomplete story or a history of self. | The surrogate may struggle with being a pregnant person and then suddenly not being that person. She may lose her sense of self in conforming to the needs of the intended parents. She may wonder who she is to the (surrogate) child now. |
| Intimacy | Direct contact between the surrogate and the receiving parents, including transferring a blanket, clothing or stuffed animal that carries the surrogate's smell, assists with minimizing separation trauma and supporting attachment to the new parents. In addition, a recording of the surrogate's voice singing or talking to the baby can be played to comfort and soothe the newborn. | There may be a hunger to attach to people, but without knowing if it is safe. They may question relationships. There may be a feeling of genetic disconnect. | The surrogate enjoys carrying another family's child and providing a home for them, but when it is over, the intimacy of the plan is gone. |
| Mastery/Control | The child was prepared for this as a conscious baby—they were given a story and plan. They can know their identity, know their people. | The adult can decide to do DNA testing, or register with the Donor Sibling Registry to make possible connections with the surrogate family and others like them. It shows mastery to be open about the outcome of this. | There is mastery/control in knowing that she can do this for a family and can give back the baby to the intended parents. |

| | Surrogate | Intended parents/genetic parents | Intended parent family |
|---|---|---|---|
| Loss | She may feel the loss of time with a husband and children, and will feel the loss of the surrogate child. | They have a lack of control over what the surrogate does. They will miss giving birth and there may be a loss of genetics. | They may be unable to watch the pregnancy progress and may worry that the surrogate will let go of the baby. They may feel the loss of a genetic connection. |
| Rejection | She may not understand the meaning of surrogacy. The children in her family may reject the idea of a possible sibling, even though it isn't going to be with them. | They may feel rejection in the surrogate relationship. There may be a language barrier for international intended parents. | They may worry that they did something to cause the intended parents' infertility and that their story is different. |

*cont.*

|  | Surrogate | Intended parents/genetic parents | Intended parent family |
|---|---|---|---|
| Shame/Guilt | Her own mother may be upset that she was not able to help her: did she need money that badly to sacrifice her life? The surrogate may feel guilt because her pregnancy has caused friction between family members. | They may feel shame and grief that they weren't able to create a family without help, and that they paid a lot for this baby, maybe even going into financial debt. There may be shame that they "custom built their baby in a lab." | There may be guilt or shame that it has cost so much money, that they had no control over events, and that they could not offer advice during the pregnancy. |
| Grief | She may want to know about the child. Will the relationship continue? The surrogate's own children may wonder if they will also be placed in a different family. | They may feel sadness about the pregnancy and birth experience, and in telling the story. Will the baby be attached to the surrogate family? | There may be a sense that this is not normal, as families usually carry their own babies. Will they be able to attach to the child? |
| Identity | She and her family may feel that they are a family of x— and how does the surrogate baby count? | Confusion over whether they are really parents and how they bond may arise. The intended parents may try to control the pregnancy and lifestyle of the surrogate. During the pregnancy, everyone's life is impacted while awaiting the birth and transfer of the baby from the surrogate to the intended parents. | Their story is different from other grandparents: "Are we really grandparents?" |
| Intimacy | The pregnancy may make it more difficult for marital relationships. Sleeping arrangements may be interrupted; hugging is more difficult; she may not be able to lift her other children as she did before. | There are attachment concerns for the baby and parents. The lifestyle change is abrupt—one day they are not parents, the next day they are. | The family may lack the closeness of the pregnancy experience and may not have a connection to the surrogate and baby. |
| Mastery/Control | She can experience mastery by being open with the family about caring for a child until they are ready to go to the intended parents, and educating others of the many ways a family can be created. She may use the surrogacy as a teaching moment to show compassion to her own children. | They can educate each other about surrogacy, learn to understand their own loss of a genetic child and educate the child about their experience. | Mastery and control can be felt by helping the intended parents prepare for parenting and the baby, and educating others about the experience of surrogacy. They look forward to celebrating and to taking on the role as grandparent/family member. |

|  | Donor-conceived child | Donor-conceived adult | Sperm, egg, embryo donor |
|---|---|---|---|
| **Loss** | They lack a genetic connection—information about the past and future. There is no knowledge of the donor as human, only as a donor.<br><br>The child may ask, "Why would they give up their genetics?" | There may be a sense of intergenerational misinformation and bewilderment.<br><br>They lack a story to give to the next generation. | With whom are their genetics placed? How many offspring do they have and where are they located?<br><br>There is a loss of comfort about the decisions made and an inability to update genetic information. |
| **Rejection** | They may feel that they are not the child their parents truly wanted. They are a substitute for their parents' fantasy child. | They may feel that their children are not truly theirs, but a part of the ghost of their donor.<br><br>Their true self has been rejected—how can they accept themselves? | They fear rejection that the child might direct at them in the future—rejection of themselves for what and how they did it or by society for creating children for money. |
| **Shame/Guilt** | In representing the fantasy child, they take on the guilt of the parents.<br><br>Their life brought shame to their infertile parents. They are a reminder of what the parents couldn't make themselves. | There are times they may wish they weren't born. Their parents only thought of themselves, not them.<br><br>Stuck in shame and secrecy, they don't know how much joy they can expect to receive. | Having given away a piece of themselves, they have no control over where their genetics go. Is their biological child alive, dead, ill or well?<br><br>They didn't think of the consequences of their donation for themselves or their family. Pieces of them are out there, but where? |
| **Grief** | The child may grieve because they were made by technology—they are all alone and there is no one like them.<br><br>They may wonder how to grieve for something they don't understand. | Until they know their complete story, they will be incomplete.<br><br>There is acknowledgment of the great emotional struggle of having many siblings, and the mystery of it all. | There is concern for the child—do they have good parents? Are they happy?<br><br>How does this affect the children the donor raised and didn't raise?<br><br>How do the children feel about being donor conceived?<br><br>The grief process feels intangible because of the lack of ongoing connection to several different offspring. |
| **Identity** | There may be a sense of false identity: "I am okay only if I fake who I am. Didn't my parents think it was important to me to have a full identity?"<br><br>They may wonder if there is a way to get the information they need. | Their current medical history is unknown. How can they make good decisions?<br><br>They have to explain to medical personnel that their paternal, maternal (or both) medical history is unknown.<br><br>They may not feel normal or loved.<br><br>Knowledge of the donor(s) is critical to the identity of donor-conceived people. | The donor may wonder if the child/ren know about them.<br><br>They have to question how having donor offspring affects them and their family. The donor's decision is creating families for many generations to come. |

*cont.*

|   | Donor-conceived child | Donor-conceived adult | Sperm, egg, embryo donor |
|---|---|---|---|
| **Intimacy** | Secrecy impacts attachment and bonding. Humans seek honest connections. There may be a fear of incest or the pull of genetic sexual attraction to unknown genetic relatives. | Being a donor offspring can restrict relationships—who would want an incomplete person? For instance, "I need your DNA test results before we become intimate. I want to make sure we are not genetically related." | The donor may question whether their role and worth are based on the selling of sperm/eggs. Will their offspring meet each other? Will their children connect with an offspring? Will their choices impact their ability to create emotional, authentic intimacy? How do they feel about their genetic kin? They may not know with whom to share that they are the donor, as the child was not conceived through a loving act. |
| **Mastery/Control** | Secrecy and untruth diminish the child's sense of self, control and identity; honesty and truth give the child a sense of mastery and ownership of all parts of their history and narrative. | Mastery can come from searching out DNA and joining the Donor Sibling Registry. Finding genetic kin will assist in the formation of self and sense of mastery. | There was no control about how many offspring were created. Did sperm and egg banks set limitations on numbers of offspring created? Large numbers of offspring could create genetic problems. Mastery includes finding genetic kin through DNA and the Donor Sibling Registry. |

|   | Extended donor family | Adoptive/donor parents | Extended adoptive family |
|---|---|---|---|
| **Loss** | They may not have known about the grown adult giving their genetics—what were they thinking? There is a loss of potential relatives—the donor gave away a piece of the family. | They will not have a genetic child. The pregnancy gave them a child but not their genetic child; the child reminds them of the loss. Self-esteem is greatly impacted by infertility, and the marital relationship may be stressed. Full and complete ongoing information needed to effectively meet the needs of their child may be lacking. They are not the only mother or father and have to share the role. | They may feel loss for their adult children who have to make this difficult decision, and may not know how to support them. Family members may not be genetic kin. |

| | | | |
|---|---|---|---|
| **Rejection** | They may feel rejection by the relative who made a decision that impacts the family without considering them.<br><br>There may be rejection from the offspring or the family who raised the child.<br><br>If the facts surface about the donation/s, the extended family may fear rejection from this. | Is a donor conception second best? If they share the truth, will the family reject the parents or the child?<br><br>They may fear that the child will reject them if they know the truth.<br><br>To avoid the truth/rejection, they may engage in fantasy—thinking that they are selecting a donor that is identical to the non-genetic partner. | There is concern that they may reject the child who is not genetically connected to them.<br><br>If divorce occurs, the genetically connected parent could reject the non-genetic part of the family.<br><br>They fear that the child may not see them as kin since they're not genetically connected. |
| **Shame/Guilt** | Shame and guilt create anger and resentment within the family system.<br><br>Shame that a family member would do this for money creates guilt because the extended family could have stopped them if they had known. | One parent may feel as if they let their spouse down, and that they should divorce so the other parent can find a fertile partner.<br><br>Or they can only proceed if they can pretend this is their genetic child: "DNA doesn't lie, people do, when they are ashamed."<br><br>One parent may be ashamed because they are jealous of the spouse who is genetically connected to their child. They feel guilty when they don't tell the truth about their child's beginning. | They may wonder if they did something that created the infertility. There is guilt at jealously of friends with genetic grandchildren, nieces/nephews and so on: "My friends have their 'own' grandchildren."<br><br>Angry or negative feelings towards either the fertile or infertile member of the couple may exist.<br><br>There is guilt that they don't feel the same way towards non-genetic kin. |
| **Grief** | Other family members are brought into the family by celebration and acknowledgment of marriage, birth and adoption. Family members are grieved for when they die or disappear. Ongoing feelings of loss and grief are connected to where the relatives are and whether they are alive or dead. | Grief continues to be felt for the loss of the genetic child. Each failed fertility treatment is grieved for. They grieve that they cannot produce, create or carry a child.<br><br>Alternatively, they may feel that they don't know how to grieve for an unborn child.<br><br>They may feel as if they are not normal. | The family grieve the fact that the child won't experience the same kind of connection or closeness the extended family has in their relationships.<br><br>There is sadness over the loss of genetic mirroring—they won't see themselves in the child.<br><br>If the birth of the child is couched in secrecy, the family will grieve the loss of honest, open relationships with family members. |

*cont.*

|  | Extended donor family | Adoptive/donor parents | Extended adoptive family |
|---|---|---|---|
| Identity | They may not know who to claim as a relative, and what role they play in their life. Who is their true family?<br><br>Are these donor offspring "really" family? | They may question if they are truly a parent if they are not genetically connected to the child.<br><br>Their body let them down: "Any fool can reproduce, but not me; am I 'really' the mother or father?"<br><br>"I am not fully man or woman."<br><br>Is it okay to ask the child to assume a fake identity to preserve their identity as a fertile person?<br><br>That one spouse can reproduce via egg/sperm donation gives the parents uneven connections to their child. | The parents have brought another family's genetics into the family lineage with the possibility of little or no accurate information.<br><br>The donor decision is intergenerational—it impacts generations to come.<br><br>The unknowns surrounding donor conception impact how the family feels about the relative and what each member calls themselves in relation to them; for instance, "Am I 'really' the grandparent?" |
| Intimacy | These people are genetically connected to them but the family is unsure how they feel. Do they have a right to find them and build a relationship?<br><br>Emotional intimacy with other family members can be diminished by a lack of honesty concerning the donor offspring; for example, do the grandchildren know they have siblings with whom they do not have a relationship? | The parents may question if they can really attach/bond to a non-genetic child by pretending that they are genetically connected.<br><br>Has the marital dyad remained intimate through the infertility and birth by donor? | If not genetically connected, can the family become emotionally intimate with the donor child?<br><br>Family secrets negatively impact familial relationships.<br><br>If there is anger and jealousy between fertile siblings and non-fertile siblings, can they be a close family? |
| Mastery/Control | Control is lost when relatives made decisions without input from others.<br><br>Mastery includes encouraging donor relatives to seek DNA and Donor Sibling Registry information. | The parents are not in control of the infertility journey.<br><br>The partner who is genetically connected to the child can use that as an element of control over the non-genetic parent, particularly when the child is not told the truth.<br><br>There should be acknowledgment that they can make other choices to become parents.<br><br>Mastery includes the sharing of information about donor conception as a means to family building; both for the child and other family members. | They lost control over how the extended family came to be; other people made the decisions.<br><br>Other people control what information is shared and known.<br><br>Mastery includes acceptance of another person's genetic history; there must be emotional acceptance of the child, the parents' decision in family building and another family's genetics being incorporated into the family.<br><br>Creating honest truth-sharing dialogue within the family system can lead to mastery. |

# Chapter 27

# The Seven Core Issues and Step-Parent Adoptions

## Michael Grand

In full adoption, two adults who do not share a genetic relationship with a child become the legal parents. In blended families, one parent has both a genetic and a legal relationship with the child, while the other parent has neither a genetic nor a legal connection. In step-adoption, one of the parents has a genetic, historical and affective relationship to the child prior to the adoptive parent joining the family as a legal parent. Almost all step-adoptions involve a birth mother and a step-father. While there are estimated to be four times as many step-adoptions as full adoptions (Sobol and Daly 1994), little research has shed light on this family form and the challenges that children and parents face in daily living. What follows is a brief summary of the highlights of step-adoptive family life. Observations are drawn from an unpublished study by Grand (2008) of adult step adoptees recalling their experiences in this family constellation.

## What motivates the decision to adopt the child of the spouse?

Two motives are usually in play: utilitarian ones that serve a purpose such as having everyone use the same name, granting the adopting father the legal status as a parent, and seeking greater commitment to the child and the spouse through adoption; and emotive ones such as believing that adoption is the natural reflection of who they already are as a family. These two motives clearly differentiate adult, step-adoptee-rated outcomes: utilitarian motives are typically offered in those adoptions that the adoptee evaluated as unsuccessful; emotive ones predict successful adoptions, even in the case where the parents subsequently divorced.

## Was consent given freely and with what subsequent result?

In most unsuccessful adoptions, consent is perceived to have been imposed on the child. There was little or no prior discussion. The child was simply told to sign the papers. This results in the adoptee feeling resentment for having been forced to give consent and not having been asked about their desire to be adopted. In all of the adoptions rated as successful, consent is freely given, thus supporting the adoptee's sense of mastery and control.

## Awareness of a shift in status

Typically, in positive adoptions, the child is excited to become an "official" member of the new family. The name is seen to give legitimacy to membership status. For those who experience a negative adoption, the name change is considered a betrayal of past relationships and represents a loss of a part of self.

## Identity of self as an adoptee

When considering a sense of self, the concept of "adoptee" rarely enters into the picture. The legal status does not contribute to a sense of self. If the adoption is construed as successful, step-adoptees see themselves as the son or daughter of the adoptive father but never the "adopted" child, at least in terms of the language that is used within the family. No one uses the designation of "step-adoptee." Some step-adoptees feel regret about who they might have become if circumstances had been different, and the birth mother and father had stayed together. It is the loss of this alternative self that they regret.

## Discussion of adoption

Rarely, in either successful or unsuccessful adoption, is there much talk about adoption. However, in successful adoptions, the fact that the birth mother and adoptive father are *willing to talk* is seen by the step-adoptee as a sign of their caring and trustworthiness. These step-adoptees view the tone of the conversations as open, available and calm, thus fostering a sense of closeness. In unsuccessful adoptions, if the circumstances that led to the adoption are ever discussed, the tone is perceived as angry. Birth fathers may be disparaged by the adoptive parent. This is considered a direct attack on the adoptee's DNA. Therefore, step-adoptees in unsuccessful adoptions typically avoid talking about the circumstance that led to the adoption.

## Feelings about the adoption

For most adoptees, the adoption per se is a non-event. In unsuccessful adoptions, adoptees feel cheated out of a relationship with their birth father and his family. They are angry about this. For many, they do not think beyond the functional utility of the adoption. In most successful adoptions, there is excitement and joy at the time of the legalization of the family through adoption. They continued to value the emotional importance of this symbolic event.

## Family dynamics

In the early life of successful step-adoptions, the adoptee thinks of the family as (adoptee + birth mother) + adoptive father. It takes some time to loosen the strong dyadic bond between the adoptee and the birth mother. However, in all positive cases, this does occur, often during periods when the birth mother is absented from the family, thus giving the adoptive father more opportunity to engage with the child. Eventually, adoptees see themselves as the child of both the birth mother and the adoptive father. In unsuccessful adoptions, the family dynamic is either (adoptee + birth mother) versus adoptive father or adoptee versus (birth mother + adoptive father). In the latter case, the adoptee feels anger towards the birth mother for allowing the adoption to have occurred in the first place. Furthermore, the adoption is construed as a betrayal. In these families, adoptees see themselves as being the child of either the birth mother or the birth mother and father. If the relationship with the birth mother is extremely problematic, there is a strong psychological connection to the mythic birth father who is seen as one who could "make the adoptee whole again."

## Factors affecting a positive connection between adoptee and adoptive father

- *Timing.* The adoptive father must show slow and steady involvement when developing a relationship with the adoptee. This is particularly important the older the adoptee is at the time of the adoption. The appearance of the adoptive father should not be seen by the adoptee as an attack on the (adoptee + birth mother) relationship, which is usually quite strong during the early days of the family.

- *Interest and involvement in the life of the adoptee.* The adoptive father must blend with the interests and style of the adoptee. It is less important whether the adoptive father is able to get the adoptee interested in the things the adoptive father likes to do. What is most important is interest in the ongoing life of the child at school, with friends, doing hobbies and during holidays.

- *Discipline.* The adoptive father should not impose discipline too early in the life of the adoptive family. First, he has to establish a relationship of trust and respect with the adoptee. That being said, until the adoptive father is comfortable imposing appropriate, although not extreme, discipline on the adoptee, he will not be seen to be occupying an authentic role as father. It is clearly a balancing act. However, in all unsuccessful adoptions, since the first step of establishing trust and respect is never accomplished, all disciplinary attempts are construed as coercive and extremely intrusive.

- *Quality of the birth mother–adoptive father relationship.* In the full adoption literature, the marital relationship is never mentioned as a variable that affects the quality of the adoptive experience. In step-adoption, it is eminently clear that the chances of a successful adoption are highly dependent on the quality of the marital relationship. If the marriage is seen by the adoptee to be a good one, then the adoption is seen in parallel terms.

- *Goodness of fit.* In successful adoptions, adoptees believe there is much similarity between themselves and the adoptive father. Sometimes it is appearance. However, more often it is either interest or personality style. In unsuccessful adoptions, there is almost universal rejection of the idea that the adoptee and the adoptive father share any features at all.

## Relationship to the birth father

If the birth father died prior to the adoption, there may be two forms of loss: there is the loss of the parent per se; and the loss of the relationship that could have been if the parent had lived. If the birth father abandoned the family, failed to support them financially, was an alcoholic or was physically or emotionally abusive, then the adoptee does not hold out positive feelings for him. Generally, the adoptee is angry about the birth parents' failed relationship and the loss of the family of origin constellation. However, if the birth father was a victim of circumstances, such as the birth mother having had an affair that ended the marriage, then there is more potential for the adoptee and the birth father to establish a future relationship. At the very least, the adoptee, typically, holds out hope for such an experience.

## Relationship with the extended family of the birth father

In most successful adoptions, there is a strong and continuing relationship with the birth father's family. This is encouraged by the birth mother and sometimes by the adoptive father as well. The adoptive father does not express defensiveness around the relationship, nor is it seen as a threat to the well-being of the adoptive family. In unsuccessful adoptions, the opposite is found. There is usually little access to the birth father's family. This is seen by many adoptees to be a significant loss, particularly when the adoptee entertains a fantasy that the birth father's family would provide a refuge for the adoptee, caught in an unhappy family situation and a poor adoption.

## Relationship with the extended family of the adoptive father

This is a key ingredient in a successful adoption. When the extended family treats the adoptee as one of their own, the adoption was always rated as positive. Grandparents do not refer to the adoptee as the birth mother's child, but as their grandchild. They give gifts at celebratory times of equal value to all of the grandchildren, including the adoptee, and make provisions in their wills for equal portions for all grandchildren, regardless of adoptive status. In unsuccessful adoptions, the adoptee rejects the adoptive father's extended family and the family rejects the adoptee.

## Search and reunion

The desire to search for birth kin is directly related to the circumstances that led to the adoptee being available for adoption in the first place. If the birth father was an aversive person, then there is less desire to make a reconnection. However, if the original separation from the family was the result of a divorce without fault on the part of the birth father, then there is more of a desire to search. Also, when the adoptee feels little comfort in the relationship with the birth mother and adoptive father, there is a strong desire to search as a means of grounding oneself in a family. Finally, life-changing experiences such as going to university, an emotional breakup or an illness often motivate the search. In some successful adoptions, there is a fear of hurting the adoptive father. However, in most successful adoptions, the adoptee is encouraged by the adoptive father and sometimes the birth mother, who might be somewhat hesitant about reunion given her past history with the birth father. Reunion experiences are mixed. Some feel a strong, positive and immediate connection to the birth father and his family. For others, the experiences are marked by stilted politeness, formality and difficulty in making affective contact.

| | Child | Adult adoptee | First/birth parents |
|---|---|---|---|
| Loss | The degree of loss is mitigated by the quality of the pre-adoption experience with the relinquishing parent. With greater negativity, less loss is experienced. Loss of a relationship with the relinquishing parent's family is also a possibility. The adoptee also may feel the loss of a close relationship with the mother as she directs her attention to the adopting father. | If the adoptive relationship is viewed negatively, and there is little openness, there is a sense of the loss of the birth parent and his family. In positive adoptions, there is less loss experienced. When the adoption is the result of the death of a parent, loss of the parent typically continues into adulthood. | Some birth parents experience strong feelings of loss but cannot negotiate conditions of divorce unless they give up their parental rights. Other non-custodial parents have their rights terminated through deception or fraud. A third group seem to show no remorse in giving up their rights to parent. Many of them have built new families by the time of the adoption. |
| Rejection | If step-adoption is the result of a parent's death, there is no sense of rejection. If it is a result of a hostile marital breakup, rejection may be felt prior to the divorce. | When step adoption is the result of a coercive divorce, the adoptee actively rejects the relinquishing parent into adulthood. | For those birth fathers who wish for contact after the adoption, rejection is often experienced if they are denied access to the child or if the child refuses to see them. |
| Shame/Guilt | Shame is rarely experienced except when the extended adoptive family treats the step-adoptee as a non-legitimate outsider to their family. Guilt may result if the child has a misplaced sense of responsibility for the divorce. | Neither shame nor guilt play a major role in the lives of adult step-adoptees in terms of the circumstances that led to the adoption. | Shame and guilt are usually only present when the birth father acknowledges that the divorce and loss of parental rights are the result of his drug or alcohol usage and he subsequently desires contact with his child. |
| Grief | In step-adoptions as a result of parental death, disenfranchised grief can occur when parents choose to bury the past. When the adoption is a result of previous parental discord, the child usually connects to the custodial parent and feels not grief but relief to be away from the non-custodial parent. | When the step-adoption is considered to be a failure, there is often grief for the loss of a self that might have been had the child been raised with the relinquishing parent. | Some birth fathers feel grief if they believe that they are responsible for the breakup of the family. |

| | | | |
|---|---|---|---|
| **Identity** | Step-adoptees view themselves at the beginning of the adoption as the child of the custodial parent and her extended family. | If the step-adoption is viewed as a success, step-adoptees see themselves as the child of the custodial parent and the adoptive parent and their respective extended families. If the adoption is viewed as a failure, they see themselves as the child of the custodial parent and her extended family. In either case, they do not have "adoptee" identities but identities as "people who have been adopted." Thus, for them, "adoptee" is a legal fact and not an identity descriptor. | Birth fathers think of themselves as divorced and as fathers with varying degrees of commitment to that role. |
| **Intimacy** | Interpersonal closeness with the adoptive parent is positively related to: the adoptive parent not pushing too hard and letting the relationship evolve; the custodial parent giving space for the child and adoptive parent to grow together; and the adoptive parent learning to independently discipline the child when necessary. Acceptance of such administration of discipline is a strong sign of a close relationship. | Adult relationship closeness with the adoptive parent is in part a function of the warmth of the marital relationship and willingness of the adoptive parent to be open and supportive of any attempts to connect with the family of the relinquishing parent. Emotional lessons learned in the step-family will influence the degree of emotional attachment to others in adulthood. | Intimacy, if it is to occur, is only directed towards the step-adoptee. This requires respecting the step-adoptee's feeling about the circumstances that led to the adoption and not disparaging the adoptive father–step-adoptee relationship in successful adoptions. |
| **Mastery/Control** | Mastery and control are fundamental to the experience of step-adoptees. Consent for the adoption that is forced on the child will often lead to resentment about the adoption. Forced change of surname represents a loss of identity and a feeling of being used to serve others' needs. | Adult tasks motivated by a need to regain mastery and control include searching for lost kin, changing back to one's original surname and building family relationships that reflect the opposite of the negative aspects of one's step-adoption. | For some birth fathers, there is a diminished sense of control when they are forced to agree to the adoption, even when they do not want it to occur. |

|  | Extended birth family | Adoptive parents | Extended adoptive family |
|---|---|---|---|
| Loss | In step-adoptions occasioned by the death of a parent, birth grandparents will feel deeply the loss of the child when the new family constellation is closed. | Some adoptive fathers feel both the loss of a genetic link with the child and an early relationship with the step-child. | In successful step-adoptions, the extended adoptive family sees the child as a positive addition to their family. In unsuccessful adoptions, the child is considered an illegitimate addition to the family and, potentially, a lost opportunity to gain genetically related kin. |
| Rejection | Connection to grandparents, when it is blocked by the step-adoptive family, is experienced as a profound rejection of their legitimate role as grandparents. | Particularly in the early days of the step-adoption, the custodial parent and child may be very close, to the exclusion of the adoptive parent. Adoptive parents who do not understand the importance of openness and connection to birth kin may experience the adoptee's interest in reconnection with kin as a rejection. | Adoptive grandparents play an important role in the determination of legitimate membership in the family. Referring to the child as their "adoptive" grandchild or the "child of the custodial parent" is a clear act of rejection. Adoptees who do not accept the adoptive family as kin contribute to the adoptive family's sense of rejection. |
| Shame/Guilt | Birth grandparents may feel guilty for not doing enough to keep the child as a legal member of the family. | Shame and guilt are rarely a part of the experience of the adoptive parent. | Shame and guilt are rarely experienced by the extended adoptive family. |
| Grief | Grandparents may feel deep grief for the loss of their grandchild in closed step-adoptions. | When the step-adoption is the end result of the death of one of the parents, the custodial parent may feel grief that colors the relationship with the adoptive parent. | Grief is not a typical experience of the extended adoptive family. |
| Identity | If a relationship with the child is closed off to the birth family, they may feel that the child has been stolen from them. If the relationship is maintained, there is a sense of wholeness within the family. | Identity as a family is dependent on the quality of the marital relationship, the comfort that the adoptive parent feels in being a participatory influence in the life of the child and whether the step-adoptee confers legitimacy on the adoptive parent as parent. | In successful step-adoptions, the extended adoptive family has an inclusive definition of family and sees the adoptee as their own. In unsuccessful step-adoptions, the family identity requires a genetic connection. |

| | | | |
|---|---|---|---|
| Intimacy | When the birth grandparents desire a relationship with the child and this is blocked, the result is often intense anger directed at the custodial parent. When the child has a relationship with the grandparents, there is gratitude for the continuing relationship, even though there has been a change of legal status. | Step-parent intimacy is dependent on factors that affect all marital relationships, the success of the adoptive parent to take on a comfortable parenting role and the support of extended adoptive kin, particularly grandparents. | If the step-adoption is seen by extended adoptive kin as positive, the result is a closer attachment relationship between grandparents and the adoptee. |
| Mastery/Control | Their sense of mastery and control is challenged by the fact that they have no role in the determination of whom the child is legally related to. Also, connection with the child is determined by the step-adoption family, hence decreasing their feelings of control over future contact. | The adoptive step-father's sense of control is in part determined by opportunities to parent without the custodial parent present to interfere or guide the relationship. The ability to impose non-coercive punishment is a milestone in the journey towards legitimacy as a parent. | The extended step-adoptive kin's sense of mastery and control is reflected in their ability to shape relationships within the nuclear step-adoptive family. |

# Chapter 28

# Adopted Children with Special Health Care Needs

## Carol Biddle

*The Federal Developmental Disabilities Act of 1984 describes chronic and severe forms of disability attributable to physical or mental impairment or a combination of both that will most likely continue indefinitely and result in considerable functional limitations such as mobility, self-direction, learning ability, care of oneself, economic self-sufficiency, capacity for independent living and expressive and receptive language.*

## Introduction

There is no one definition today that encompasses the many forms of disability, but rather acknowledgment of a broad spectrum of children with special health care needs that include developmental, intellectual, emotional (often trauma or neglect causation) and physical disabilities. The term "disability" may include functional deficits or diagnosis of a particular condition. For clarity in this chapter I will use the term "developmental disabilities" on which federal policy was originally developed. Modern usage typically will also include temporary, permanent or acquired disability and exceeds the original group whose physical or neurological conditions were accompanied by cognitive impairment. The descriptive terminology continues to evolve.

In 2005, there were an estimated 470,000 already-adopted children with special health care needs in the United States, representing 4.6 percent of all children with special health care needs. It is estimated that between 35 and 50 percent in the US child welfare system (presumably pre-adoption) experience at least one form of developmental disability from mild to severe. More current studies are desirable.

Institutional care for at least part of their lives was once typical but no longer the default plan for a child with significant developmental disabilities. Until the early 1980s, most foster children with developmental disability labels were considered "unadoptable," were court ordered into "long-term care," or may not have been referred to the child welfare system for consideration of family care. Gradually, the stigma and resistance to family care and permanence diminished. Beginning in the 1960s, American public institutions downsized in favor of local care. At the same time, western European nations began to focus on "normalization" of life experiences for developmentally disabled citizens. In developing countries, not much changed during this time to improve the life circumstances for the disabled.

After World War II and again at the end of the Korean War, American families began to adopt from other countries and responded to significant numbers of children with disabilities. US domestic adoption of the developmentally disabled was very rare at the time because most of the children were not served as part of the child welfare system and families had never been recruited for their care. Thus, in the US, the children were invisible and families did not recognize the need. In 1980, the Adoption Assistance and Child Welfare Act declared that states were to help reunite children with their biological parents or place them with adoptive families. The Act was broadly interpreted and became inclusive of youth previously destined to be in institutional care. While the intent is clear, difficulty remains in finding and supporting the number of permanent families needed for the waiting population of domestic foster children, especially those with diagnosed disabling conditions. The recruitment problem is even greater for children of color.

When the child entering the family has a host of medical and developmental challenges, the usual adoption issues differ in some ways from those of adoptive families of children with typical development. Usually, fostering parents will adopt their child when they know that they can continue to receive the support and services required. There are also no competencies identified for social workers in child welfare to assess and support children with special health care needs and their families. The field is learning from the resilient families who are forging ahead without a roadmap.

## The adoptive family

Infertility and replacement of *loss* may not be the primary motivation of families that adopt children with developmental disabilities. They may perceive themselves to have life experiences and unique skills required to parent a child with a disability. They commonly have prior experience such as working with school systems or health care providers. Their experience brings a level of awareness concerning how to advocate for a child with a form of disability. Some may have grown up in a family with a sibling or have a child who has special health care needs already in their home. They do not have fear of the care needs of the child and have interest and awareness in the child's inherent adaptive abilities to achieve a somewhat better life with special care and education. Their *identity* as adoptive parents starts on a firmer foundation. They do not have or respond to the stigma associated with being a parent by birth to a child with developmental disabilities. Adoptive parents usually have some level of personal experience that prepares them to know that each child is unique and will likely present with life skill difficulties, some more pronounced than others. Parents who have adopted children with a form of developmental disability speak of the levels of enrichment that come from helping a child to gain comfort, safety, satisfaction and appropriate accomplishments.

Adoptive parents must lead highly structured lives that require careful planning for the most normal range of family and community activities. They may experience *rejection* of their family and the child from others who have fear or resistance to the levels of disability. It is often difficult to find child care so that parents may have normal life activities or keep appointments. Such families do well to seek the support of other families with special health care needs children. Some churches and special education school settings are resources for developing social activities that accept the special child. For many families, the need for respite and in-home caregiving by others is a necessary support for the survival of the family unit and a sense of well-being of its members.

Planning for any level of independent life for the adult child is a constant goal and challenge for parents. Some, but not all, will be capable of semi-independent living and employment. Many will require supervised or custodial care for their lifetime. Additionally, a percentage of profoundly impacted children will experience a short life that is normal for their condition but brings *grief* to the families.

To achieve *mastery and control* of their untypical parenting path, most families will need and benefit from supportive policies and programs and public education, financial, health and social services support, throughout the parenting experience. Adoption assistance, Social Security Disability, Medicaid medical insurance, free special education programs and access to medical specialists are among the supports required. Mastery of parenting is so much more complicated when the child (or adult child) with special health care needs is considered.

## The birth/first family

Open adoption practice has given anecdotal stories about the experience and life path of the birth parents of the developmentally disabled child. There are no studies found for this particular group. In adoption, there may be more contact with a single birth mother or father and limited contact with other family members except in the case of permanency in a related family member's home. In intercountry adoption, often not much is known and contact is rare.

The dynamics of all parents who give birth to a child with special health care needs applies to the birth parents in adoption. Societal stigma contributes to *guilt*, *shame* and *grief* that may be pronounced. In some cases, the poverty, life traumas or substance abuse behaviors may be contributory to the child's conditions and the decision to place the child into care. It is not the intent of the parent to harm the unborn, and her sense of *loss* is profound. Occasionally, a child becomes severely disabled by parental neglect or abuse after birth, which negates ongoing relationship possibilities and court determination of the child's future.

When it is possible for the adoptive or relative family to share some degree of openness or regular communication with the birth/first parent(s), it is more likely that they will feel a positive role in the child's life, to make positive strides in their own lives and achieve a healthier adult *identity* development. Often respect and gratitude exist between birth and adoptive parents of children with special health care needs—respect for the birth parent's difficult decision that she could not provide for a child with such high-end needs, and gratitude on the part of the birth parent that her child is safe, nurtured and loved in a family. There is so much more that would be good to learn about the birth family's lifelong experience that has not been studied.

## The adopted person

It is obvious that there is wide variance in the intellectual understanding of their life situation and issues of adoption among adoptees. A child with a profound intellectual disability may experience only primary relief, comfort, nutrition, safety and love of his primary caregiver. At the other end of the spectrum, a child with physical or behavioral/attachment disabilities may have his intellect intact and will have similar issues to other adoptees without disabilities. Autism, on the pervasive developmental delay spectrum, is an example of a condition that can be quite mild to profound in how it impacts intelligence, communication and behaviors. A child with cerebral palsy may have associated intellectual disability or may be within the range of normal intelligence. Almost any major physical disability can have associated neurological, behavioral or intellectual impacts but should not be considered a profoundly disabling condition unless there is more than one interacting disability. Fortunately, society has moved towards embracing disabilities and promoting inclusiveness in the past few decades, informed partially by war injuries and veterans' needs.

It is critical to remember the principles of *normalization* and to not impose limitations that do not exist on a child who has higher-level intellectual and adaptive abilities. We all have adaptive behaviors that are a collection of conceptual, social and practical skills that we learn in order to function in our everyday lives. When adaptive abilities are limited, it changes one's ability to respond to life changes, environmental demands and the degree to which an individual may be able to be independent.

The child who understands that their particular disabilities contributed to why they are in an adoptive family will have the same range of questioning, and feelings of *rejection* and *loss*, as other children in adoption. Children may tell themselves life stories that include being responsible for losing their parent and will carry feelings of *shame* and *guilt*.

In the home, the school and the community, the adopted person benefits when their primary relationships have specialized knowledge and invest in supporting and normalizing the child's life experience and accomplishments. For this population in adoption, the social work community needs more education and growth to help to maximize success for family permanence.

## The social work community

Child welfare is overwhelmed with the safety, stability, placement and permanency needs of all children. There is no conclusive definition or description of developmental disabilities; child welfare has children with special medical needs over-represented in the population and there are no set of competencies identified for social workers to learn. In large public agencies, it is not untypical for children with pronounced or profound special health care needs to languish prior to achieving permanency, to never achieve permanency, or to remain in institutional or nursing care. These children often are bunched onto the caseloads of a few workers who have concern for them or who have had specialized training. Often, they are so relieved to find a safe institutional placement for a child with special health care needs that they stop looking for a family. Social workers will admit fear that a family might not be successful with a severely impacted child, that the child will end up requiring another safe institutional placement that will be harder to achieve. In my career, when I offered to take on permanency planning in public agencies for such children, administration was interested but referrals never came. Detective work finds the kids at the bottom of the case file stack, hidden from view. Empathy is high from social workers for the children with developmental disabilities. Fear of losing control over the child's safety and well-being is also a high-level concern should families fail. Lack of social work training and disbelief that such youngsters can do well in a family continue to contribute to way too many of these children never finding a family.

In addition to the Seven Core Issues in Adoption and Permanency that impact the child and family constellation, there is a need for considerable attention, training and coaching to help our social work professionals believe in themselves and gain the knowledge to arrange placements and supervise families who will receive and love children with special health care needs.

## In summary

In the child welfare field, we have traditionally looked at adoption as an *outcome*. It has in recent years been recognized as a *lifelong and intergenerational* process (Silverstein and Kaplan 1988).

For children with continued or emerging special health care needs, we must underscore that families need to adapt to meet the child's ongoing needs, and that while we celebrate permanency it is not a finite event as much as a lifetime and intergenerational set of relationships.[1]

---

1    There is an excellent reading resource that is currently accessible on the internet: *CW 360: The Intersection of Child Welfare and Disability: Focus on Children. Spring 2013*, School of Social Work, University of Michigan. Edited by Traci LaLiberte, PhD and Tracy Crudo, MSW. Available at http://cascw.umn.edu/wp-content/uploads/2013/12/Spring2013_360_web-FINAL.pdf.

| | Child | Adult adoptee | Birth/first parents |
|---|---|---|---|
| Loss | Understandable expression of loss may be related to the degree of intellectual ability or impairment of the child.<br><br>Various forms of expressing loss may be different and children may need more assistance identifying, labeling and expressing feelings connected to loss. Loss of a relationship with parents and also extended family is not uncommon.<br><br>Most children with special health care needs come to adoption via the child welfare system and not voluntary relinquishment. Loss and prior trauma may be profound. | Adoptees may require supervised living in the family or specialized settings. When the adult leaves the safety of the family there is loss of control, and fear to overcome.<br><br>Adoptees who remain in the adoptive family home may eventually experience the loss or disability of their parent due to aging.<br><br>Those adults who have learning and support to live independently and work or attend education programs will need support and assistance from the family and disability services and financial entitlements to avoid huge adult losses. | Birth parents (often mothers) experience loss if their life situation precludes raising the child with disabilities alone. It was not their intent for the child to be disabled, and the loss is profound.<br><br>Open adoption in the case of children with special health care needs may not be threatening to the adoptive parents and can be healing enough to lessen loss to the birth/first family. |
| Rejection | Stigma in community and school settings adds extra pain for adopted children with special health care needs. While normalization is growing and acceptance is becoming the norm, stigma exists in behavior, public settings and policies. | People with disabilities experience rejection throughout life because of stigma associated with people who are different from the norm. Adoptees raised in a family where normalization is the experience may have higher coping skills and can be helped to avoid stigma-loaded situations. | Birth parents may feel rejection from their own families, community and social services when they are not prepared to take on the care of a disabled child. |
| Shame/Guilt | Children who have the ability may create stories that their special health care needs are responsible for the rejection and loss of the birth parents. Shame and guilt may result.<br><br>Staring, teasing, labeling, name calling, ignoring or expressions of disgust (fear) from others may cause shame and guilt.<br><br>The child may experience guilt feelings from needing assistance from family members and others in the community. | The stories a child created about loss of birth family can cause shame and guilt to continue in adulthood.<br><br>Both shame and guilt are less likely to be emotionally disabling when the adult has been and remains in an environment where normalization is a natural part of relationships with others. | Shame and guilt are normal with all parents who give birth to a child with disabling conditions. It may be more hurtful when inability to care for the child is a part of the adoption decision, and they may have increased guilt when others are doing what they could not for their child.<br><br>When a respected foster parent later commits to adopt, that can be a source of relief to the birth parent, especially when there is respect between the birth and adoptive parents. |

| | | | |
|---|---|---|---|
| Grief | Grief is likely to be present in most adopted children. It is expressed in behaviors that may not be recognized by the adults. If grief and loss are acknowledged and normalized, the child is less likely to be made more disabled by the normal human condition of grieving and sadness. | Grief changes over time but may never become absent from an adult's experience. Closeness to the adoptive family, good relationships with others and a normalized daily life will modify or ameliorate grief rather than extend it. | Grief is a normal experience following the loss of a child for any reason. Failing to express and explore the grief may lead to dysfunctional decisions in life. An ability to be in relationship with the adoptive family can be healing. |
| Identity | Normalization by inclusion of the child in family and community activities helps form a healthy identity. Parent and professional attention and training for maximizing adaptive abilities (regardless of level of disability) increases positive identity in the child. (Pride in accomplishment is universal.) | Normalization of activities and interaction with people of many abilities helps identity formation and acceptance of differences.<br><br>Association with others who have special health care needs in activities of all sorts assists positive identity formation. | When the birth parent is able to accept the child's disability, respects the decision made regarding the placement and can have a continuing relationship, then identity is not corrupted by being frozen in a state of sadness, loss, guilt and shame about the birth. |
| Intimacy | Interpersonal closeness with the adoptive parents is required, regardless of the child's verbal or intellectual abilities.<br><br>Relationship development with teachers, extended family members and siblings is achieved by normalizing the child's interest and ability to be with others and enjoy their interaction (at whatever level possible). | Adult relationship intimacy includes a continuation of the model of intimacy achieved in the adoptive family. Modeling and teaching relationship skills is critical with children with special health care needs. | Intimacy may be a challenge as the birth parent tries to move into other adult relationships and parent other children. Understanding and support from the extended family helps. Counseling and support are desirable. |
| Mastery/Control | Mastery and control require the maximum development of adaptive abilities. The primary issues for the child with special health care needs are related to being as independent and interactive as is possible for their situation in life.<br><br>On the continuum of need, the child with higher needs will have fewer mastery needs related to the adoption. | Adulthood is a continuation of what begins in childhood regarding mastery and control. The adult needs the maximum development of adaptive abilities. The primary issues for the adult with special health care needs are related to being as independent and interactive as is possible for their situation in life. | Mastery and control for a birth parent include the ability to accept the child and their condition, respect the decision to place the child, have continuing respect and relationship with the adoptive family, and be open with future partners and children. |

| | Extended birth family | Adoptive parents | Extended adoptive family |
|---|---|---|---|
| **Loss** | The extended birth family may feel loss when they are unable to consider being the primary family to the child with special health care needs.<br><br>When relatives become the permanent parents for the child they may feel loss of closeness to their relative, who is the parent of the child, especially if the placement is through social services because of neglect, abuse or mental illness. | The adoptive parents' motivation is unique in the case of a child with special health care needs. They may have a personal mission and a familiarity and ease with people with differences that transcends personal loss. It is sometimes true that adoptive parents have siblings or other children with disabling conditions, so those relationships may have their own loss issues that are part of their motivation.<br><br>Loss is profound for adoptive parents who chose to parent a child whom they believed had no special needs and then over time discover their child to be developmentally disabled. | The extended family is more likely to worry about their kin making such a difficult decision in parenting than feeling a sense of loss about the child not being "normal." More than likely, the extended family is aware of the special qualities of their adult kin who takes on children with special health care needs. |
| **Rejection** | Rejection may be a factor if grandparents or other relatives offered to be custodial to the child or to adopt them and they were not chosen.<br><br>Rejection can come from the child's parent or in some cases from social services not positively assessing the ability of the relative to provide full care. | Adoptive parents' familiarity with rejection is usually in navigating the many demands of daily care and education of a child with special health care needs. They typically learn to overcome those feelings with advocacy and nerves of steel to navigate the various systems and get what their child requires. | Extended adoptive family members are likely to be engaged as advocates for the child as well. Those who don't engage might feel some rejection from their family members for not being team players. |
| **Shame/Guilt** | Birth grandparents may feel guilty for not doing enough to keep the child as a legal member of the family. | Shame and guilt are rarely a part of the experience of the adoptive parent in parenting a child with special health care needs because they did not give birth to them.<br><br>Parents may feel guilt over the constant demands of the child, which can sometimes lead to frustration for the inability to meet their own needs or those of other family members. | Shame and guilt are rarely experienced by the extended adoptive family. |

| | | | |
|---|---|---|---|
| Grief | Grandparents may feel deep grief for the loss of their grandchild in closed adoptions. | It is necessary to explore with all prospective adoptive parents their ability to address grief. Grief may be part of the developmental stages of raising a child with special health care needs. Some become more disabled, some plateau with adaptive ability training, and some die very young. It is necessary to explore preparation for grief with the adoptive parents before the adoption of a child with developmental disabilities. | Grief is not a typical experience of the extended adoptive family except when there is a loss of a child through death or necessary nursing placement. |
| Identity | If a relationship with the child is closed off to the birth family, they may feel that the child has been stolen from them. If the relationship is maintained, there is a sense of wholeness within the family. When there is openness in adoption, healthy identity is maintained. | Identity as a family is dependent on the quality of the relationships within the family unit and the comfort that the adoptive parent feels in their impact on the life of a child with profound special needs. | Positive identity as an extended adoptive family that values having members with special health care needs is likely if the relatives made the commitment to support the child entering the family and have participated in some way. |
| Intimacy | When the child has a relationship with the grandparents or other family members, there is mutual gratitude for the continuing relationship through openness and respect. | The additional tasks of parenting a child with special health care needs can create ongoing emotional stress in a marriage. Adoptive parents are likely to be most satisfied in their relationships when there is harmony in the care for the child and respect and contact with birth parents and other family members who are available. | If the extended family supported the adoption and remain part of the advocacy and support system, they don't have intimacy issues. |
| Mastery/Control | Their sense of mastery and control may not be as challenged when the child has profound health care needs. They most likely feel relief and respect that the child is safe in a family that also accepts them. | Adoptive parents expect to have ongoing mastery and control challenges as parents of a child with profound needs. Everywhere they turn, someone is either not understanding them or not wanting or able to help with critical needs. They do well when they accept challenges as normal and ramp up their advocacy efforts, not being personally bothered by the misunderstanding of others. | The extended adoptive family is just fine, usually. They are likely to be high on the empathy or frustration scale on behalf of the adoptive parent for their bravery and challenges. |

# Chapter 29

# Schools, Learning and the Seven Core Issues of Adoption and Permanency

## Blaze Newman

The Seven Core Issues of Adoption and Permanency, as described in this book, also impact children's learning and school experiences. Maslow's Hierarchy of Needs teaches that, in order to learn, students must have all the lower levels operating at a reasonably strong level. For many children who were separated from their family of origin, completion of this task may not be the case, especially the second most basic level: "Safety and Security." Many educators merrily assume students are ready to learn when they walk through the classroom door. Of course, the lack of safety (sometimes physical as well as emotional) is not limited to students who were adopted, or are in foster care or kinship care, but it is more likely to be a factor for adoptees and children in foster care.

After many years of often-painful school experiences, adoptees and children in foster care may be anxious about school and may, in fact, have grown rather diminished as a result of their years of struggle in classrooms. Many children experience multiple changes in schools as they are moved from one foster home to another. Each of these moves includes changes in parents/caregivers, which is always quite stressful for children as they must adapt to a whole new living environment. On top of this monumental change, the child must also adapt to a new school environment. As the school year approaches, many children and their families cringe, wondering what assignment (e.g. the dreaded family tree), insensitive use of language (e.g. "adopt-a-family" programs at the holidays), or cruel comment (e.g. "those aren't your real parents") awaits them.

Years ago, a student in one of my twelfth-grade English classes, after perusing the list of novels students could choose from for independent reading, asked if I had selected the books because many of them dealt with orphans (the dramatic term often used in book blurbs) and a surprising number of students in the class were adoptees. I was flabbergasted because I'd not seen that pattern; I'd selected books I thought students might enjoy and that met the school district's requirement that the course cover British literature. But there they were: *Jane Eyre, Wuthering Heights, Oliver Twist, Innocent Blood, Never Let Me Go* and *The Death of the Heart.* This experience, while seemingly small, helped raise my awareness of the ways students' adoption experiences can color all their other experiences and heighten their sensitivity to things many of their teachers and classmates don't ever consider.

Exploring the school experience via the lens of the seven core issues will, ideally, allow everyone involved to help students succeed in school, both academically and personally.

## Loss

Many adopted children experience mixed emotions of anxiety and excitement when they begin school in kindergarten or first grade. They hope to have fun and learn interesting things they have seen adults and other children do—such as read. However, many children who were adopted or in foster care, due to factors including in utero drug exposure, early abuse and trauma, disruptions in their previous schooling and past emotional instability, may not be able to succeed in school as easily as many of their classmates. Some children may also have a genetic predisposition to learning challenges or issues. Thus, these children experience additional losses—of their vision of school as a good place to be, of the learning they had anticipated, of their hopes to succeed at school and of seeing themselves as "smart."

## Strategies for helping children deal with this issue

- Adults involved in the child's education—parents, counselors and teachers—need to *accept the reality of the child's loss* and avoid ignoring or minimizing it. If the child can verbalize their pain related to school, adults need to listen carefully and acknowledge that pain (e.g. "Sounds like it's really hard to still be in that reading group when the other kids have moved on"). We must be careful not to encourage the child's negative feelings about school but also not to try to convince the child that they are wrong to have those feelings or that they are misperceiving the situation.

- We must look for ways to *help the child feel successful.* At school, the child can feel valued and successful by helping to hand out materials, running an errand for the teacher or organizing playground materials. Outside school, opportunities to feel successful include taking care of a pet, being a good friend, playing music or a sport, or serving as a role model. We need to communicate to all students that *school and learning are about much more than academics.*

- Children need to receive *regular, sincere and specific positive input* about their schoolwork, no matter how small the achievement. The scale of praise needs to match the scale of the achievement; great celebrations need to be saved for truly momentous achievements.

## Rejection

For many children who were adopted or are in foster care, school can seem to be mostly about rejection. Because they may not have had access to some of the input necessary to develop effective interpersonal skills, they may be rejected by their peers. They may be bullied because they are of a different race/ethnicity from the majority of the school's population, because they speak English with an accent, because they have not been schooled in the local community's norms, or because their family is "non-traditional"—the parents are older than other parents, are the same sex or are of a different race/ethnicity than the child.

Even teachers may reject children (or appear to do so) out of frustration about not being able to help them succeed. Since some adopted children may behave in odd or inappropriate ways in the classroom, teachers may exhibit anger or rejection. Often, teachers will send "naughty" children outside the classroom or to the office to be dealt with—which surely feels like rejection to the child.

## Strategies for helping children deal with this issue

- Children need to know that regardless of what is revealed about their struggles and shortcomings, *their parents won't reject them.*

- Teachers need to participate in *professional development* that addresses the challenges faced by many adoptees and that offers strategies for helping children cope with those challenges.

- Teachers and school professionals need to *be aware of their implicit bias* regarding children in foster care and children who were adopted. Remember that they are always children first and deserve the same dignity and respect that all other children are afforded.

- Schools need *strong anti-bullying programs* and, ideally, *ongoing education* for all students about human diversity and the need to show respect for everyone.

- Children may need instruction on how to behave in various social situations and how to interact with a variety of people. This support can come directly or, possibly more effectively, via books and movies. Whenever possible, adults need to *model and discuss appropriate interpersonal behaviors.*

- Teachers and parents need to collaborate to *find alternate ways of responding to the child's inappropriate behavior*, so the child isn't banished from the classroom.

- Schools and districts need to *provide family recognition and validation.* Even if only individual teachers, teaching aides, principals or counselors do so, that can be helpful.

## Shame and guilt

Because children may not understand the complex issues (e.g. lack of appropriate instruction at critical stages of their development, possible exposure to drugs or alcohol in utero or interruptions in their education due to repeated moves) that cause their difficulties with school work, many of them assume that the problems stem from intrinsic personal defects, such as their intelligence, their likeability, their work ethic, their concentration. Such assumptions can cause the child to feel guilty and ashamed—"If I just tried harder, I could do it, but I don't and so it's all my fault." A boy receiving special education services told me that for years he thought "RSP" (Resource Specialist Program, a category of special education) meant "Really Stupid People." Clearly, no child could *not* feel ashamed of being in a program they believed was for really stupid people.

## Strategies for helping children deal with this issue

- Parents and teachers need to help the children *identify their strengths,* based on clear evidence. Do not lie to the child or provide praise that cannot be backed up with specific accomplishments, because that false praise might be perceived as provoked by pity and thus lead to even more shame.

- Based on the child's age and maturity, adults should provide the appropriate level and amount of *information about some of the factors that may be causing the child to have difficulties* with schoolwork.

- Adults need to *show the child they are loved and also a source of pride* (again, for specific traits or actions).

- While not minimizing the value of school, children need to be helped to understand that *academic success is only part of being a success as a person* and that success in school goes beyond academics and includes being responsible, being creative, thinking for oneself and caring about others.

## Grief

Due to the losses, rejection and feelings of shame often associated with school, adoptees may connect school with pain. Children can experience grief that their school-related hopes and plans appear to have died. Grief can also lead to unrecognized depression that can further impede learning. To avoid feeling the pain of this grief, children may actively avoid (as much as they can) everything related to school. A valuable essay about school avoidance is Herbert Kohl's (1994) "I Won't Learn from You." Children who have been adopted or are in foster care have suffered through significant and traumatic losses. It is important to note that children don't leave their emotional pain and triggers at home when they come to school. Many of these children may be more "emotionally reactive" as they have experienced overwhelming amounts of distress, loss, trauma, abuse and neglect. Please note that children grieve differently from adults and can often appear impulsive, agitated, angry and disoriented.

## Strategies for helping children deal with this issue

- As with loss, children need to be *allowed to grieve* and not have their sadness ignored, minimized or disputed.

- Children need *clear, strong and consistent emotional support* to help them find the courage to face their grief. Just having a parent sit in the same room as the child while they do homework can be very reassuring for the child.

- Having *non-verbal ways to express their grief* can help children cope with the grief. One effective strategy is to have them draw pictures of school-related topics, for example how they feel at school, what the classroom looks like to them, how they think their classmates or teacher see them, and what their ideal classroom would look like.

- Schools might provide opportunities for children who were adopted or in foster care to *get together*, being careful to not brand the children. Such get-togethers might help children just by connecting with each other; they might also help children find coping mechanisms.

## Identity

Many children who were adopted or in foster care may have developed, as part of their identity, the vision that they are "losers" in terms of school. This vision may be reinforced by awareness that their birth/first parents may not have been successful students. They have formed an image of themselves that, while it is painful, is what they know and are used to. Actions that challenge this identity can, themselves, be frightening because they challenge the child's existing identity, which may already be fragile because the child was adopted.

Many school forms require information about race/ethnicity, which may be difficult or painful for children who were adopted transracially. Children who live in an area where their race/ethnicity is a minority may find that their classmates and even teachers ask them to "speak for" their race.

## Strategies for helping children deal with this issue

- Time in a *stable, nurturing and supportive environment* is necessary for children to feel safe enough to let go of painful beliefs about themselves.

- As children see the *option of having positive views of themselves* (because people they respect and care about hold such views of them), they begin to let go of negative parts of their identities.

- Children need support to *reframe their ideas of what "success" means in school*, that it includes more than just academic achievement.

- Children should be helped to *develop an ongoing list of positive words or phrases about themselves as learners*, such as determined, a good listener, helpful, curious.

- Children should never be asked to "speak for" their race; like all of us, they deserve the right to *speak for themselves*, to be seen as individuals.

## Intimacy

Letting others know about our weaknesses, confusions and inabilities is a form of intimacy and vulnerability. Children who fear intimacy, therefore, may strive mightily to hide this information, often by blustering that the work itself is stupid and worthless or by directly refusing to even try to complete it—since that effort might well reveal their weaknesses. By avoiding the work, they avoid the feared intimacy that is an integral part of the relationship between the learner and anyone helping them. It is also common for children in foster care who have experienced multiple placement disruptions—which includes a new school with every move—to be weary of getting too close to their teachers. It is difficult for children to get emotionally close and then lose those important and meaningful relationships.

### Strategies for helping children deal with this issue

- As children feel increasingly safe, they will (possibly very slowly) become more able to *risk the intimacy of revealing their fears and struggles*. So, step one is for adults to focus on building that sense of safety for the child.

- As a way for a family to strengthen their family bond while also supporting the child's academic needs, they can *learn something together*. Good topics are those the child wants to know about and the parent(s) don't know much about, such as Amazon snakes or the history of animation. Exploring the topic together lets the child see that even adults can be confused and lack knowledge, thus modeling being okay about such feelings. When possible, parents should find ways to involve the academic skills the child needs to work on (e.g. understanding charts and graphs or identifying main ideas in a text) but not push to make that happen. Mostly, families should enjoy being learners together and discovering cool stuff.

- Parents may have to accept—at least for the time being—that the child and the parent–child relationship may be better off if the parent does *not* try to act as a tutor for the child. However, this does not mean that parents stop communicating the importance of doing homework and providing a structure in which it is expected to be done (or, at least, attempted).

## Mastery and control

In the same way that people with anorexia starve themselves as a means of exerting control over *some* aspect of their lives, so some children (who often feel little control over their lives as a result of repeated moves) may refuse to do school work as a way to assert their control over this aspect of their lives. Also, because they may believe themselves incapable of doing the work (and thus being denied a feeling of mastery that way), they may give themselves an alternative sense of control by battling their teachers and parents over the assigned work. Herbert Kohl's essay "I Won't Learn from You" provides valuable insights for parents, despite being written for teachers.

### Strategies for helping children deal with this issue

- The more the parent fights with the child about doing the homework, the stronger is the child's commitment to *not give in*, because to do so would be to relinquish control.

- Rather than argue about the homework, *parents might choose to agree with the child that the homework is hard* (and agree with their other negative comments about it). Parents should make themselves and the child *a team against the homework* (but not against the teacher who assigned it!).

- If the child complains, commiserate with them about the homework, being clear that *whether or not to do it is completely their decision*. Parents should let the consequences of not doing the homework lie with the teacher, rather than with them.

- Before school begins each year, parents should *collaborate with the child to decide how they will do homework*: a good location, the best time period, how many breaks (and for how long) the child may take while working, acceptable activities during breaks, how to decide the order in which to do assignments, and how to ask for guidance on assignments. Make it clear that this time period is for doing *academic work*, so if there is no homework assigned, the child will still spend the agreed-on amount of time in the "homework" location, doing other activities that support their learning. Possible activities include reading, writing letters to friends or relatives, reviewing old schoolwork to strengthen skills, or creating and then maintaining a budget for saving and spending their allowance. Lots of ideas and enrichment activities are available online and in stores that sell materials for teachers.

- Parents must always behave and speak based on the knowledge that *their relationship with the child is much more important than any schoolwork.* Unlike poor grades and gaps in learning that can be compensated for fairly easily later, damage to the bond between parent and child will undermine growth in all areas.

## Further reading

- www.nacac.org/resource/adoption-and-the-schools
- www.childwelfare.gov/topics/adoption/adopt-parenting/school
- www.tolerance.org/magazine/fall-2003/out-of-the-shadows

# Chapter 30

# The Lifecycle of the Adoptive and Permanency Family– Stages and Tasks

### Sharon Kaplan Roszia

Just as individuals grow through a series of developmental stages with specific tasks and challenges, all families have normative stages with subsequent tasks and challenges. This lifecycle of the adoptive and permanency family has been adapted from an article authored by Sonya Rhodes and published in 1977 (Rhodes 1977). Families built through adoption and permanency might find themselves out of sync or at several stages simultaneously. Certainly, this is true for grandparents parenting again through kinship parenting and many foster parents who have been committed to that job for several years.

## Intimacy versus idealization/disillusionment

- This is the first phase of forming the couple relationship: achieve intimacy based on a realistic versus idealized perception of each other; learn to negotiate conflict and find mutually satisfying ways to nurture and support each other.

- When the couple decide to start a family and must confront the emotional, physical and financial impact of infertility, their marital dyad is stressed. Many decisions have to be made and they are usually made in unfamiliar territory. The couple may not be in agreement about what to do going forward and when to proceed.

- Their friends are experiencing success and joy while they are grieving their fantasy child. Each failed fertility treatment and each adoption that does not reach fulfillment retriggers this grief.

- The couple's support system may not know how to support them. There may also be cultural and religious considerations that need to be addressed.

- The prospective single parent, LGBTQ parent, kinship parent or foster parent may run into prejudicial comments, concerns and a lack of necessary and specialized supports.

- How these crises are addressed sets the tone for the building of the family unit. For kinship parents who get a "crisis call" to come and pick up one, two or three relative children, this stage can abruptly shift from intimacy to disillusionment and crisis.

## Replenishment versus turning inward

- These are the childbearing years: they begin with the first child entering the family, and end when the last child enters school. The tasks are development of nurturing patterns between family members and learning how to replenish resources while letting the child into the marital dyad.

- For the adoptive and permanency family, the stress of going to "strangers" to meet their goal of parenthood (i.e. the foster care system, an attorney or social worker), and having to share private information, feels intrusive. Loss may become a dominant theme for the family.

- The transition to adoptive, foster or kin parenthood can be complex as people learn new skills, including attachment to a "stranger."

- Parenting children who enter the family with a history of trauma and attachment impairments may add significant parenting challenges that require learning new parenting techniques and the opening of the home to therapists, wrap-around supports and advice from caring friends and relatives that may or may not be helpful.

- Vicarious trauma can drain the emotional resources of the parents and can limit the parents' emotional availability to each other and to the children.

- The adding of more than one child at a time, who are of different ages, complicates this stage.

- The integration of children into the family by birth, foster and adoption is another challenge.

## Individuation of family members versus pseudo-mutual organization

- In the preschool years, family members progressively achieve independence and freedom. The stress of letting go and trusting others with your child versus overprotection as a response to parenthood is a skill to be learned.

- The adoptive and permanency family is achieving an identity as an adoptive family, foster family or kinship family and may have to contend with intrusive questions from outsiders. They have to address the issues of wanting to overprotect their children from the child's own background history; explaining open adoption relationships; defending their decisions; and learning how and when to share private information about adoption and permanency with their children and outsiders. They must address issues of privacy versus secrecy. They have to create a family environment that supports the child's exploration of their own adoption and permanency information. This may also lead to helping the child cope with loss.

## Companionship versus isolation

- These are the teen years, and therefore the need to address sexual issues, separation and the development of companionship outside the family while staying close to those inside the family system are the tasks.

- Adoptive and permanency families must help the teens develop a positive self-image and identity where information needed may or may not be available. For some teens, the issues of search and reunion may surface. Fear of emancipation may keep the child setting up failure in order to stay at home or finding an excuse to leave the family too soon. The family's fears about whether the child feels attached enough to come back to the family when they leave may keep the children bound too long to the parents.

- Parents must address their lives outside the nuclear family system.

## Regrouping versus binding together

- The task is to allow the departure of the children and redefine the self and the marriage. Teens and young adults may search for their birth family, launch prematurely or not feel secure enough to launch successfully.

- The family must develop adult relationships with grown children, allowing for individuation which shifts parenting roles from dependency to support and guidance.

- Families may wonder if they should adopt or foster again in order to avoid experiencing the next stage of lifecycle development.

## Rediscovery versus despair

- For couples, a return to the marriage/relationship is the most important developmental task.

- In addition, the development of intergenerational connections and the incorporation of new family members is important.

- Learning to share relatives and seeing that grandchildren still do not resemble the genetics of the family can retrigger infertility losses.

## Mutual aid versus uselessness

- This is the time that starts when parents retire and ends at their deaths; the task is to develop a mutual aid system and to avoid feelings of uselessness.

# References

Baran, A. and Pannor, R. (1993) *Lethal Secrets: The Psychology of Donor Insemination*. New York, NY: Triadoption Publications.

Blau, E. (1993) *Stories of Adoption: Loss and Reunion*. Portland, OR: New Sage Press.

Bohl, D. (2018) *Parallel Universes: The Story of Rebirth*. Milwaukee, WI: HenschelHAUS Publishing.

Bonanno, G. (2009) *The Other Side of Sadness: What the New Science of Bereavement Tells Us About Life and Loss*. New York, NY: Basic Books.

Bowlby, J. (1988) *A Secure Base: Parent–Child Attachment and Health Human Development*. New York, NY: Basic Books.

Breggin, P. (2014) *Guilt, Shame and Anxiety: Understanding and Overcoming Negative Emotions*. Amherst, NY: Prometheus Books.

Brodzinsky, D., Schechter, M. and Henig, R. (1992) *Being Adopted: The Lifelong Search for Self*. New York, NY: Doubleday.

Burton, N. (2008) *Swimming Up the Sun*. Riverdale Park, MD: Apippa Publishing Company.

Buster, J.E., Bustillo, M., Thorneycroft, I.H., Simon, J.A., Boyers, S.P., Marshall, J.R. et al. (1983) 'Non-surgical transfer of an in-vivo fertilized donated ovum to an infertility patient.' *The Lancet 1*, 8328, 816–817.

Cajete, G. (2000) *Native Science: Natural Laws of Interdependence*. Santa Fe, NM: Clear Light Publishers.

Campbell, J. (1988) *The Power of Myth*. New York, NY: Doubleday.

Campbell, J. (1990) *The Hero's Journey*. Novato, CA: New World Library.

Campbell, J. (1991), *Reflections on the Art of Living: A Joseph Campbell Companion*. Selected and edited by Diane K. Osbon, Quote Page 8 and 24, HarperCollins, New York, New York.

Campbell, J. (2008) *Hero with a Thousand Faces*. Novato, CA: New World Library.

Campbell, L. (1977) *Understanding the Birth Parent*. Sherman Oaks, CA: Concerned United Birthparents.

Chamberlain, D.B. (2013) *Windows to the Womb: Revealing the Conscious Baby from Conception to Birth*. Berkeley, CA: North Atlantic Books.

Charlton, L., Crank, M., Kansara, K. and Oliver, C. (1988) *Still Screaming: Birth Parents Compulsorily Separated from Their Children*. Manchester: After Adoption.

Chronicle of Social Change (2018) Fostering Media Connections (publisher). Available at: https://chronicleofsocialchange.org.

Eck Menning, B. (1988) *Infertility: A Guide for the Childless Couple*. New York, NY: Prentice Hall Press.

FAIR (Families Adopting in Response), "A Healing Ritual." Summer 2005 Newsletter.

Farrow, T.F.D., Zheng, Y., Wilkinson, I.D., Spence, S.A. *et al.* (2001) "Investigating the functional anatomy of empathy and forgiveness." *NeuroReport 12*, 11, 2433–2438.

Felitti, V. and Anda, R. (1998) "Relationship of childhood abuse and household dysfunction to many of the leading causes of death of adults: Childhood Experiences Study." *American Journal of Preventive Medicine 14*, 4, 245–258.

Firestone, R. and Catlett, J. (1999) *Fear of Intimacy*. Washington, DC: American Psychological Association.

Frankel V. (1946) *Man's Search for Meaning*. Boston, MA: Beacon Press.

Goldberg, A.E. (2010) *Lesbian and Gay Parents and Their Children: Research on the Family Life Cycle.* Washington, DC: American Psychological Association.

Goleman, D. (1995) *Emotional Intelligence.* New York, NY: Bantam Books.

Grand, M. (2008) Adult step adoptees, recollections of their step adoptive experiences. Unpublished manuscript.

Grand, M. (2010) *The Adoption Constellation: New Ways of Thinking About and Practicing Adoption.* Self-published.

Grotevant, H.D. (1997) "Coming to terms with adoption: The construction of identity from adolescence into adulthood." *Adoption Quarterly 1,* 1, 3–27.

Grotevant, H.D. (2009) *Building an Adoptive Identity: It's Not Just About Adolescence Anymore.* Emoryville, CA: PACT's Point of View.

Grotevant, H.D. and McRoy, R.G. (1998) *Openness in Adoption: Exploring Family Connections.* Thousand Oaks, CA: Sage Publications.

Heffron, A. (2016) *You Don't Look Adopted: A Memoir.* Self-published.

Heller, L. and LaPierre, A. (2012) *Healing Developmental Trauma: How Early Trauma Affects Self-Regulation, Self-Image, and the Capacity for Relationship.* Berkeley, CA: North Atlantic Books.

James, S.E., Herman, J.L., Rankin, S., Keisling, M., Mottet, L. and Anafi, M. (2016) *The Report of the 2015 US Transgender Survey.* Washington, DC: National Center for Transgender Equality.

Klass, D., Silverman, P. and Nickman, S. (eds) (2014) *Continuing Bonds: New Understanding of Grief.* New York, NY: Routledge.

Knost, L.R. (2016) Available at: www.littleheartsbooks.com.

Kohl, H. (1994) "I Won't Learn from You." In H. Kohl, *"I Won't Learn from You" and Other Thoughts on Creative Maladjustment.* New York, NY: The New Press.

Kübler-Ross, E. and Kessler, D. (2005) *On Grief and Grieving: Finding the Meaning of Grief Through the Five Stages of Loss.* New York, NY: Scribner.

Lechner, A., Cavanaugh, M. and Blyler, C. (2016) *Addressing Trauma in American Indian and Alaska Native Youth.* Mathmatica Policy Research, submitted to the US Department of Health and Human Services.

Lester, N. (2009) 'Embryo adoption becoming the rage.' *The Washington Times.*

Lev, A.I. and Sennott, S. (2013) "Clinical Work with LGBT Parents and Prospective Parents." In A. Goldberg and K.R. Allen (eds) *LGBT-Parent Families: Possibilities for New Research and Implications for Practice.* New York, NY: Springer Press.

Lifton, B. (2009) *Lost and Found: The Adoption Experience.* Ann Arbor, MI: University of Michigan Press (original work published 1979, Dial Press).

Mayer, J. (2017) "In the Blood." From the album *The Search for Everything.* Columbia Records.

McKernon-Cindrich, G. (2009) *Construct Validation for Assessment Approach to Seven Core Issues in Adoption.* Oakland, CA: Saybrook Graduate School.

National Institute for Clinical Application of Behavioral Medicine (2017) *How to Work with Shame that Developed in Childhood: The Generational Effect of Shame on Loved Ones,* video 5, part 1 by Sue Johnson. www.nicabm.com online course.

O'Neill, B. (2018) *Dear Adoption.* Dearadoption.com, 8/16/2018. Available at: https://dearadoption.com.

Partridge, P.C. (1999) *New Legs: Seven Core Issues Poems.* Self-published.

Pertman, A. (2011) *Adoption Nation.* Boston, MA: Harvard Common Press.

Peterson, D. (2017) *Indians in the Family: Adoption and the Politics of Antebellum Expansion.* Cambridge, MA: Harvard University Press.

Pindar (no date) *Victory Odes,* Pythian 2, line 72.

Politi, D. (2018) "Oklahoma Governor Signs Law Allowing Adoption Agencies to Discriminate Against Same-Sex Couples." *Slate.* Available at: https://slate.com/news-and-politics/2018/05/oklahoma-governor-signs-law-allowing-adoption-agencies-to-discriminate-against-same-sex-couples.html.

Pratt, Capt. R.H. (1892) *The Advantages of Mingling Indians with Whites*. Reprinted in Pratt, R.H. (1973) *Americanizing the American Indians: Writings by the "Friends of the Indian" 1880–1900*. Cambridge, MA: Harvard University Press.

Rhodes, S.L. (1977) "A developmental approach to the life cycle of the family." *Social Casework 58*, 5, 301–311.

Romm, C. (2014) "Understanding How Grief Weakens the Body." *The Atlantic Daily*, 9/11/14.

Ross, R. (2016) "Canadian Fertility Doctor Accused of Using His Own Sperm to Impregnate Patients." *BioNews*. Available at: www.bionews.org.uk.

Satir, V. (1988) *The New Peoplemaking*. Mountain View, CA: Science and Behavior Books.

Schore, A.N. (1994) *Affect Regulation and the Origin of the Self: The Neurobiology of Emotional Development*. Hillsdale, NJ: Lawrence Erlbaum Associates.

Schweibert, P. and Deklyen, C. (1999) *Tear Soup: A Recipe for Healing After Loss*. Portland, OR: Grief Watch.

Siegel, D. (1999) *The Developing Mind: How Relationships and the Brain Interact to Shape Who We Are*. New York, NY: Guilford Press.

Silverstein, D.N. and Kaplan, S. (1988) "Lifelong Issues in Adoption." In L. Coleman, K. Tilber, H. Hornby and C. Boggs (eds) *Working with Older Adoptees*. Portland, ME: University of Southern Maine, Human Services Development Institute.

Snowden, R., Mitchell, G.D. and Snowden, E.M. (1983) *Elm Artificial Reproduction: A Social Investigation*. London: George Allen & Unwin.

Sobol, M. and Daly, K. (1994) "Canadian adoption statistics: 1981–1990." *Journal of Marriage and the Family 56*, 493–499.

Solomon, A. (2012) *Far from the Tree: Parents, Children and the Search for Identity*. New York, NY: Scribner.

Telingator, C.J. (2013) "Clinical Work with Children and Adolescents Growing Up with Lesbian, Gay, and Bisexual Parents." In A.E. Goldberg and K.R. Allen (eds) *LGBT Parent-Families: Innovations in Research and Implications for Practice*. New York, NY: Springer.

van der Kolk, B. (2014) *The Body Keeps the Score: Brain, Mind, and Body in the Healing of Trauma*. New York, NY: Penguin Books.

Westermarck, E. (1891) *The History of Human Marriage*. New York, NY: Allerton Book Company.

Wildcat, D. (2001) "Preface." In V. Deloria Jr. and D. Wildcat, *Power and Place: Indian Education in America*. Golden, CO: Fulcrum Resources.

Woititz, J. (1985) *Struggle for Intimacy (Adult Children of Alcoholics Series)*. Deerfield Beach, FL: Health Communications.

Wood, S. (2011) "Native Americans Expose the Adoption Era and Repair its Devastation." *Indian Country Today*. Available at: https://newsmaven.io/indiancountrytoday/archive/native-americans-expose-the-adoption-era-and-repair-its-devastation-Uinpv-VkFka0KeFfoMD4eQ.

# Further Reading

Brown, B. (2010) *The Gifts of Imperfection*. Center City, MN: Hazelden Publishing.

Brown, B. (2017) *Braving the Wilderness: The Quest for True Belonging and the Courage to Stand Alone*. New York, NY: Penguin Random House.

Child Wise Institute (2016) *Be Child Wise*. Helena, MT: Developed by Intermountain and presented by Child Wise Institute.

Cooper, A. (2017) *Adoption at the Movies: A Year of Adoption-Friendly Movie Nghts to Get Your Family Talking*. London: Jessica Kingsley Publishers.

Crumbley, J. (1999) *Transracial Adoption and Foster Care: Practical Issues for Professionals*. Washington, DC: Child Welfare League of America Press.

Crumbley, J. and Little, R. (eds) (1997) *Relatives Raising Children: An Overview of Kinship Care*. Washington, DC: Child Welfare League of America Press.

Eldridge, S. (1999) *Twenty Things Adopted Kids Wish Their Adoptive Parents Knew*. New York, NY: Dell Publishing.

Eldridge, S. (2003) *Twenty Life Transforming Choices Adoptees Need to Make*. Colorado Springs, CO: Pinon Press.

Fahlberg, V. (1991) *A Child's Journey Through Placement*. London: Jessica Kingsley Publishers (originally published by Perspectives Press).

Farrow, T.F.D. and Woodruff, P.W.R. (2005) "Neuroimaging of forgivability." In E.L. Worthington, Jr. (ed) *Handbook of Forgiveness*. New York, NY: Brunner-Routledge.

Foli, K. and Thompson, J. (2004) *Post Adoption Blues*. Emmaus, PA: Rodale Press.

Four Arrows (D. Jacobs), England-Aytes, K., Cajete, G., Fisher, R.M. *et al.* (2013) *Teaching Truly: A Curriculum to Indigenize Mainstream Education*. New York, NY: Peter Lang.

Franklin, L. and Ferber, E. (1998) *May the Circle Be Unbroken*. New York, NY: Harmony Books.

Gabb, J. (2008) *Researching Intimacy in Families*. London: Palgrave Macmillan UK.

Green, R. (ed.) (2003) *Kinship Care: Making the Most of a Valuable Resource*. Washington, DC: The Urban Institute Press.

Green, R. (2012) *Mastery*. New York, NY: Viking.

Griffith, K. (1992) *The Right to Know Who You Are: Reform of Adoption Law with Honesty, Openness and Integrity*. Ottawa, Canada: Katherine W. Kimbell.

Gritter, J. (2000) *Lifegivers: Framing the Birthparent Experience in Open Adoption*. Washington DC: Child Welfare League of America Press.

Harris, N.B. (2018) *The Deepest Well: Healing the Long-Term Effects of Childhood Adversity*. New York, NY: Houghton Mifflin Harcourt House Publishing.

Hemingway, E. (1929) *A Farewell to Arms*. New York, NY: Scribner.

James, A. (2009) *Brothers and Sisters in Adoption*. Indianapolis, IN: Perspective Press (now published by Jessica Kingsley Publishers).

Jay, M. (2017) *Supernormal: The Untold Story of Adversity and Resilience*. New York, NY: Hachette Book Group.

Johnston, P.I. (1983) *Perspectives on a Grafted Tree: Thoughts for Those Touched by Adoption*. Indianapolis, IN: Perspectives Press.

Johnston, P.I. (2008) *Adopting: Sound Choices, Strong Families*. Indianapolis, IN: Perspectives Press.

Karen, R. (1998) *Becoming Attached*. Oxford: Oxford University Press (original work published 1994, by Warner Books).

Keck, G. and Kupecky, R. (2009) *Adopting the Hurt Child: Hope for Families with Special-Needs Kids.* Colorado Springs, CO: Nav Press.

Keefer, B. and Schooler, J. (2000) *Telling the Truth to Your Adopted or Foster Child: Making Sense of the Past.* Westport, CT: Bergin & Garvey.

Kirk, H.D. (1985) *Adoptive Kinship: A Modern Institution in Need of Reform.* Brentwood Bay, BC: Ben Simon Publications.

Leonard, G. (1991) *Mastery: The Keys to Success and Long-Term Fulfillment.* New York, NY: Dutton Books.

Lerner, H. (1989) *The Dance of Intimacy: A Woman's Guide to Courageous Acts of Change in Key Relationships.* New York: Harper & Row.

Lifton, B. (1975) *Twice Born: Memoirs of an Adopted Daughter.* New York, NY: McGraw Hill.

Lifton, B. (1994) *Journey of the Adopted Self.* New York, NY: Basic Books.

Melina, L.R. and Roszia, S.K. (1993) *The Open Adoption Experience: A Complete Guide to Adoptive and Birth Families—from Making the Decision Through the Child's Growing Years.* New York, NY: HarperCollins.

Nickman, S. (1985) *The Adoption Experience.* New York, NY: Julian Messner Press.

Oppenheim, D. and Goldsmith, D. (eds) (2007) *Attachment Theory in Clinical Work with Children: Bridging the Gap Between Research and Practice.* New York, NY: Guilford Press.

Robinson, N. (ed.) (1999) *Touched by Adoption: Stories, Letters and Poems.* Santa Barbara, CA: Green River Press.

Rockman, A. (2016) *Social Confidence Mastery.* Self-published.

Rosenberg, E. (1992) *The Adoption Life Cycle: Children and Their Families Through the Years.* New York, NY: Free Press.

Schooler, J., Smalley, B.K. and Callahan, T. (2010) *Wounded Children, Healing Homes.* Colorado Springs, CO: Nav Press.

Seek, A. (2015) *God and Jetfire: Confessions of a Birth Mother.* New York, NY: Farrar, Straus and Giroux.

Silverstein, D. and Smith, S. (eds) (2009) *Siblings in Adoption and Foster Care.* Westport, CT: Praeger Press.

# Contributor Biographies

**Carol Biddle**, MSW, is founder and retired Chief Executive Officer of the Kinship Center in California. Her career in developing landmark programs in child welfare and child/family mental health includes having been a pioneer advocate for the intellectually and developmentally challenged child. Her early work in Nevada and then Los Angeles County resulted in a "systems changing model" for successful family recruitment and placement of the children who were at that time labeled "not adoptable." Carol lives in Athens, Georgia, and continues to coach and consult.

**Joseph Crumbley**, PhD, is a kinship caregiver and received his MA and PhD in Social Work from the University of Pennsylvania. He is in private practice as a family therapist, trainer and consultant. His most recent areas of specialization have been kinship care and transracial adoption. Dr. Crumbley has co-authored a book with Robert Little entitled *Relatives Raising Children: An Overview of Kinship Care*. His second book is entitled *Transracial Adoptions and Foster Care*. Both books were published by the Child Welfare League of America.

**Kathryn England-Aytes** teaches psychology at California State University, Monterey Bay, and is a board member and master trainer in the areas of historical trauma, resiliency and cultural awareness for the Native American Children's Alliance, an inter-tribal membership organization that promotes excellence in child abuse prevention in Native communities. Dr. England-Aytes is a Fellow for the National Center on Adoption and Permanency, and a 2017–18 Fellow of the American Psychological Association, Division 45, Council of National Psychological Association for the Advancement of Ethnic Minority Interests, Leadership Development Institute.

**Huyen Friedlander**, LMFT, is an adoptee who was adopted from Vietnam. She received her BA in Theater from the University of California, Los Angeles (UCLA) in 1993. When she first thought of becoming a psychotherapist, she wanted to combine the transformative power of performance with therapy. Huyen has been practicing psychotherapy for the past 20 years, with an emphasis on healing trauma, grief and loss. She currently works for a major health care company, providing critical incident response, management consultations, communication training and counseling to employees. Huyen is happiest when she is exploring the world with her son, daughter and husband.

**Abbie Goldberg**, PhD, is an adoptive mother and Professor of Psychology at Clark University in Worcester, Massachusetts. She studies diverse families, including adoptive and LGBT parent families. She is the author of over 100 peer-reviewed publications, including the books *Lesbian and Gay Parents: Research on the Family Life Cycle* (2010) and *Gay Dads: Transitions to Adoptive Fatherhood* (2012). She is the editor of three books, including the *SAGE Encyclopedia of LGBTQ Studies*.

**Michael Grand**, PhD, C.Psych, is Professor Emeritus in the Clinical Child and Adolescent Psychology Graduate Training Program at the University of Guelph. He has published on adoptive identity, search and reunion, demographics, family structure, legislation and first parent adaptation to placement. He co-founded the Coalition for Open Adoption Records, a Canada-wide initiative to open adoption records. He is the author of *The National Adoption Study of Canada* and *The Adoption Constellation: New Ways of Thinking About and Practicing Adoption*. He has a psychotherapy practice for adoptees, and their first and adoptive parents.

**Dee Dee Mascareñas**, LMFT, is an adoptee and has been working in the mental health field with individuals and families for 30 years. She is a Latina, fluent in both English and Spanish. She has worked with a multi-cultural population addressing such topics as adoption, attachment, parenting, abuse recovery, self-esteem and bi-culturation. Dee Dee is a Certified Trainer in Adoptions. She serves as a consultant for several non-profit and for-profit entities as well as teaching on a University level on numerous topics.

**Mary McGowan** is a foster and adoptive mother. She is the Executive Director of the Association for Training on Trauma and Attachment in Children (ATTACh). She has years of personal and professional experience and has worked with the North American Council on Adoptable Children (NACAC) doing successful grass-roots recruitment for foster and adoptive families and as a post-adoption specialist. She has earned accolades as the National Education Manager for the Professional Association of Treatment Homes (PATH) and is an experienced trainer who teaches and consults locally and nationally. Mary has fostered many children over 26 years and is a single adoptive parent of five young people ranging from 11 to 20 years old.

**Gina McKernon-Cindrich**, PhD, is an adoptee, social worker, therapist and "lifelong student of adoption." Working in the field of adoption and permanency for over 25 years, she has a special interest in understanding reunions and ongoing relationships. Having reunited with her birth family, she is passionate about helping others understand, navigate and embrace their own connections to adoption and permanency. She lives and works in San Luis Obispo, California.

**Blaze Newman** has a Master's in Leadership and Education Administration. She taught in a high school in the San Diego area for over 30 years, focusing on helping students improve as communicators, collaborators and thinkers. She also was a frequent presenter at local, state and national conferences for educators, sharing her commitment to focusing on skills rather than content and instructional strategies to achieve that goal. Also, she trained and supervised hundreds of high school and college students to be academic tutors for students needing extra support to achieve their potential.

**Kris Probasco**, LCSW, is a licensed clinical social worker practicing in Kansas City. Since 1972, she has specialized in adoption, reproduction and infertility. She consults with fertility programs providing services for donor conceptions and embryo adoptions. Her focus has always been preparing families for the best interests of the child in knowing their donor story. Her current interest is in birth psychology.

**Cynthia Roe**, LCSW, is a former foster youth and adoptive parent. She has worked in the field of mental health and child welfare for 26 years as a social worker, as a clinician in the public and private sectors and as a trainer. Her work has been focused on adults, children and families impacted by abuse and neglect, foster care and adoption. Additionally, she is a graduate survivor of the Colorado foster care system. Cynthia and her partner of 26 years are the proud adoptive parents of two young men who were in foster care in Los Angeles. They are now enjoying being grandparents and spoiling their 8-year-old grandson.

**Lynne Silver**, MA, is a foster and adoptive mother. She has taught child and adolescent psychology at the University of Hawaii. Lynne is the founder and Executive Director of Adopt International and Domestic Services in San Francisco and has over 32 years of providing services to institutionalized children as well as working with domestic infant adoptions.

**Heidi Staples**, MSW, an adoptee herself, has worked in the field of adoptions and child welfare for 40 years, as a social worker, supervisor, manager, consultant and trainer. She served as Director of Child Welfare for the UCLA Department of Social Welfare, as well as the National Adoption Specialist for the Children's Bureau of the Administration for Children and Families, where she oversaw the national adoption recruitment campaign, federal grants to states to improve adoption outcomes for foster youth, and two national adoption centers.

**Lynne White Dixon**, LCSW, graduated with her BA in Psychology and MA in Social Work from the University of Chicago. For over 40 years, Lynne has provided services to children, adolescents and their families in the areas of community mental health, child welfare and adoptions, private practice and higher education. She has expertise in adoptions and trauma and is a lead trainer for the Kinship Center's ACT Training, a nationally recognized adoption and permanency curriculum for child welfare and mental health professionals. In addition to her private practice, she teaches trauma-informed practice with children and adolescents for the MSW program at CSU Monterey Bay.

# Subject Index

# Author Index